UNDERSTANDING
PRIMARY SCIENCE

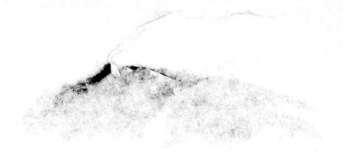

MARTIN WENHAM originally trained in plant biology and forestry, becoming a teacher in 1967, after four years in full-time research. His teaching experience has included work in secondary, primary and special schools, with pupils of all ages from 5 to 18. Between 1989 and 1998 he was a Lecturer in Primary Education at the University of Leicester, specializing in science and art.

Lynn D. Newton is Professor of Primary Education and Director of Initial Teacher Training in the School of Education, University of Durham. Previously a primary teacher and advisory teacher for primary science, she has extensive experience of researching and writing on science issues for primary teachers. She is the author of *Co-ordinating Science Across the Primary School* (1998) and *Meeting the Standards in Primary Science* (2000), both published by Routledge Falmer, and has edited *Teaching for Understanding Across the Primary Curriculum* (Multilingual Matters, 2003).

UNDERSTANDING PRIMARY SCIENCE

Ideas, Concepts and Explanations

Second Edition

Martin Wenham

P·C·P
Paul Chapman
Publishing

First published 1995
Second edition published 2005
Reprinted 2005, 2006, 2007

Paul Chapman Publishing
A SAGE Publications Company
1 Oliver's Yard
55 City Road
London EC1Y 1SP

SAGE Publications Inc
2455 Teller Road
Thousand Oaks, California 91320

SAGE Publications India Pvt Ltd
B1/I 1 Mohan Cooperative Industrial Area
Mathura Road, New Delhi 110 044
India

SAGE Publications Asia-Pacific Pte Ltd
33 Pekin Street #02-01
Far East Square
Singapore 048763

Library of Congress Control Number available

A catalogue record for this book is available from the
British Library

ISBN-13: 978-1-4129-0162-8 (hbk)
ISBN-13: 978-1-4129-0163-5 (pbk)

Typeset by Dorwyn Ltd, Wells, Somerset.
Printed in Great Britain by Athenaeum Press, Gateshead

Contents

For Freddy, Podzo and Mamu
with love

Preface to the First Edition

This book has been written to help teachers develop the background knowledge and understanding needed to teach science effectively at primary level. It is intended principally as a resource, and should not in any way be viewed as a summary of what it is felt teachers ought to know, still less of what they should teach or their pupils should learn. What it does attempt to do is to set out facts, develop concepts and explain theories which primary teachers may find it useful to know and understand in order to plan their own programmes of work effectively and answer children's questions with confidence. It is not primarily concerned with ways of teaching science, but with helping to provide the information and ideas needed to make children's learning in science more effective.

Two basic assumptions have guided the selection and presentation of material. The first is that children are most likely to develop an in-depth understanding of any object, change or event if they have experienced it at first hand. The second is that first-hand experience alone is not enough to develop scientific knowledge and understanding. If the scientific knowledge and understanding of children is to develop, teachers must help them to interpret their experiences and observations in terms of the facts, concepts and theories of science. To adapt a well-known proverb: without scientific knowledge, activity and investigation are blind; but without first-hand experience of finding out, scientific knowledge is empty.

The introduction of the National Curriculum in England and Wales has stimulated production of a large volume of activity-related primary science programmes, but these have not been accompanied by comparable development in the kind of knowledge-base for primary science which is needed to make them fully effective. The result, as one infant teacher ruefully remarked to me, is that 'We know what to do, but we don't really know why we're doing it'.

The aim of this book is to establish a knowledge-base for primary teachers which will enable them to exploit more fully the learning potential of the activities they and their pupils undertake. To do this, it has in some areas of science been necessary to develop approaches which are rather different from, though never in conflict with, those employed in secondary science. In most instances this has been necessary because the secondary approach relies on concepts, constructs and theories which are too abstract or too remote from children's experience to be usable at primary level. A principal concern throughout this book has been to ensure that the scientific concepts, theories and explanations are linked to objects, systems, events and changes which teachers and children are likely to have experienced at first hand. Numerous practical examples are given in the text as illustrations of the concepts or theories under discussion, and it is hoped that teachers will, wherever possible, try these out for themselves as an integral part of using this book as a resource.

The content and layout have been guided by the provisions of the National Curriculum for England and Wales. In addition to helping all primary teachers develop the understanding they need, the depth to which topics are discussed is aimed at enabling teachers to meet the Attainment Targets for pupils working at Levels 4 and 5, as set out in the Statutory Orders issued in January 1995. The range of topics has not, however, been restricted by the National Curriculum requirements. As a result of this wider range of topics, concepts and theories discussed, it is hoped that the ideas and explanations set out here will help to maintain and develop links between science and related areas of the curriculum, such as geography, technology, art and music.

Illustrations have been used only where they are indispensable. The main reason for this is that, while they are often a very efficient way of conveying factual information, drawings and diagrams cannot be a substitute for explanations in clear language, which teachers can then adapt to meet the particular needs and interests of their pupils.

Throughout the text, cross-references are given by referring to the relevant sections by numbers in brackets, thus: (5.2). It is hoped that this will promote a more integrated view of science, and encourage both teachers and their pupils to regard it as a living and growing net of ideas and information, as varied and exciting as the world which it seeks to understand.

Acknowledgements

No one can write a book of this kind without a great deal of support from colleagues, friends and family. It is a pleasure to record my thanks to Marian Barker and the staff of King Richard Infant School, Leicester, who first suggested the project to me; to Professor Maurice Galton who encouraged its development, and to Marianne Lagrange of Paul Chapman Publishing, who persuaded and cajoled me, with unfailing charm and good humour, into getting it finished.

Almost all the ideas, approaches and examples used have formed part of my own teaching in Leicestershire schools and in work with teachers, both on PGCE and GEST-funded in-service courses. To all my pupils and students, who have taught me far more than I can ever have taught them, I owe a debt which I hope this book may do something to repay. Tina Jarvis and Janet Moyles, my colleagues in the School of Education at the University of Leicester, have also been a constant source of positive motivation, always ready to share their knowledge and experience and to help me clarify ideas. Special thanks are due to Laurence Rogers, Clive Sutton and Sarah Wenham, who read and commented on parts of the book in draft form and, in spite of their own heavy commitments, gave unstintingly of their time and expertise to save me from many errors and misconceptions.

Lastly, my greatest thanks must be given to my wife Christine, without whose support, tolerance, forbearance and good humour this project would long ago have foundered without trace.

Martin Wenham
Leicester, 1994

Preface to the Second Edition

Since the publication of the first edition nearly ten years ago there have been numerous changes both in the primary classroom and in teacher education. In the UK the content of science education at Key Stages 1 and 2 has been reduced, but at the same time the requirements for science knowledge among student teachers have become much more extensive and detailed. These changes have taken place against a background of increasing public awareness and debate about advances in science and technology generally, and about medicine, the environment and biotechnology in particular. I have therefore made no reduction in the scope of this book for the new edition, in the belief that a wide background knowledge among teachers is now, more that ever, necessary for effective primary education.

Preparing a second edition has given me the opportunity not only to amplify and rearrange parts of the text (especially Chapter 14), but also to correct some minor errors and ambiguities and to incorporate new material. Some of this is aimed at bringing the text up to date and helping student teachers to meet the increased demands on their knowledge and understanding of science, but most has been included in response to questions and requests for information from children and teachers.

Acknowledgements

I would like to thank all the teachers and children who have sent queries to me, on topics ranging from looking through small holes to why midsummer day is not in the middle of summer! I am also grateful to Sarah Wenham, Dan Thomas and Jenny Edwards for information on particular topics. Special thanks are due to Anwen and Martin Williams, who not only lent me a computer to complete the work, but also, with great patience, taught me how to work with it. As always, my greatest thanks must be reserved for my wife Christine, without whose help and support no project could be completed.

Martin Wenham
Bangor, Gwynedd
February 2004

Introduction: Improving Primary Science Teaching

by Lynn D. Newton

The wide-ranging Education Reform Act of 1988 prepared the way for massive curriculum change in primary schools. The Act required science to be taught as a core curriculum subject for all pupils between five and sixteen years of age. It was to be on equal terms with English and mathematics in the National Curriculum.

Today, although science is meant to be a core subject in schools, it is rarely afforded an equal status with English and mathematics. As the Department for Education and Skills (DfES) focused on the quality of English and mathematics teaching to the exclusion of all else, science has languished. After a time of promise when the National Curriculum for Science was introduced, the amount of time given to it in primary schools has often declined. In the time given to science, teachers tend to teach scientific vocabulary and facts, and avoid causal explanations and teaching for understanding. For instance, teachers may ask which fabric is best for keeping the water warm in a cup but not ask why. They often acknowledge the value of 'investigation' but use it only to check facts, not explore ideas or develop explanations. For example, primary children often test different kinds of threads to find out which thread is the strongest but they are not encouraged to think about why one is stronger than another. I accept that scientific explanations can be hard to grasp, but I am not talking about teaching thermal conduction to seven-year-olds or tensile strength to ten-year-olds. But seven-year-olds are able to grasp the generalization that thick fabrics are more likely than thin fabrics to keep a cup warm and ten-year-olds can grasp the idea that some materials have more strength than others, that thicker thread is generally stronger than thinner thread and, in combination, this can explain their results.

Science lessons are the main source of children's experience of causal explanation (the water in the cup stays warm longer *because* the wrapping is thick; thread X takes more weight before it snaps *because* it is thicker than the other threads of the same material; at the same time, thread X takes more weight *because* it must be made of a stronger material than the other threads of the same thickness). Most of the rest of the week, they talk about purpose and intention, why people do things and what things are for. Vocabulary and facts are important in any subject, but in science the opportunity to work with causal explanation should not be missed.

Why does causal explanation not receive the attention I believe it should? One reason could be that some teachers do not feel confident enough in science to explain or draw out explanations from the children. They may play safe in their lessons, filling them with facts and avoiding reasons. Practical work is given to the children but it lacks a press for understanding procedures and conclusions. Certainly, such teachers talk much less with the children about the science. Another reason could be that teachers see science as being about facts. For these teachers, understanding in science will amount to grasping the words and descriptions. Others may know that science is about *explaining the world* but see such explanations as being beyond the comprehension of younger children. Children are, however, capable of understanding physical causation from a very early age. When adults think of scientific explanations, they tend to think of them as they are generally expressed by scientists. But there is a lot of science out there that can be taught for understanding to young children, with meaningful causal explanations, as was illustrated above.

One approach to improving primary science teaching is to accept that this is the way the teaching world is. To make it better, teachers should be given the 'right' materials and trained to open them at relevant pages. According to this model, what teachers know or do not know does not matter. Point them at the class, turn them on and watch the learning build up. This factory model of teaching, of course, ignores the human element, both in the teacher and the children. A teacher with particular conceptions of science and science education will consciously or unconsciously shape his or her teaching in line with these conceptions. For example, if teachers believe that science is about facts and descriptions, that is what they will emphasize and give marks for. The danger is that this, in turn, will shape the children's conceptions. Even the most perfect teaching materials can be bent into other shapes, even by well-intentioned users. Then there are the children. No 'right' materials can allow for their infinite variety. What if one of them asks that unanticipated question? And what if it is the dreaded 'Why?' question? And, of course, what is 'right' for one teacher and one child at one time may not be right for others at that time or for anyone at another time. Very quickly, the situation dissolves into the real world where the teacher has to draw on his or her own resources. The point is, that you cannot beat knowing the subject. This is the view taken in an alternative approach.

The alternative approach is to help teachers construct worthwhile lessons that suit the needs of particular children. This means you would expect to see one lesson on, say, simple circuits in one school and a different lesson on that same topic in another. While the lessons would probably have things in common, the teachers would have tuned them to the needs of the particular children in each school. But teachers need to know enough science to produce and tune lessons to the needs of their children. Not the least part of this is being able to answer questions and help the children construct scientific explanations.

However well intentioned, there is an inherent danger in 'official' schemes and lesson plans, like those of the government-endorsed Qualifications and Curriculum Authority (QCA) Scheme of Work for Science. Although it may not have been the intention, their origin induces teachers to adopt them and follow them closely, perhaps believing that Office for Standards in Education (OFSTED) inspectors will approve their office's products. The danger is that hard-pressed teachers use them without due thought, that science lessons become the same everywhere, and that development and creativity in primary science teaching is stifled. From the point of view of the classroom teacher, the last point stands repetition. A joy of teaching is in the creative opportunities it presents. A lesson, personally crafted for the occasion, taught with interest and enthusiasm, can make the day worthwhile. The ability to craft that lesson needs a teacher who does not follow blindly the plans of others. It needs one who knows what the subject is about, who understands the science that he or she is teaching. Teachers need to grasp three important things about science, namely, that it involves:

- products (the body of scientific knowledge, facts, descriptions and *explanations* of the world);
- processes (ways of thinking and working scientifically, explorations, investigations and experiments); and,
- people (science is a human enterprise that has bearing upon both those who engage in it and those who live with it).

Although preparation to teach science is compulsory on initial teacher training courses, such courses are generally too short. The breadth of science (biology, chemistry, physics, geology and astronomy) is such that there is not the time to cover everything. How to teach primary science is exemplified but the teaching of every aspect of each subject is impossible – everything cannot be covered. New teachers must inevitably meet topics that they must plan for themselves. At the same time, even the model lessons they have seen in schools or tried for themselves are limited and need to be adapted for different occasions. Experienced teachers may also be keen to further develop their expertise. Yet the current focus on literacy, numeracy and information and communications technology has resulted in very little opportunity for continuing professional development support in science.

Evidence from educational research and school inspections indicates that effective primary science teaching involves:

- a security that comes from having a sound understanding of science;
- control of the science material being taught;
- careful planning that tunes lessons to the needs of particular children;
- well organized and managed activities (mental as well as physical);
- a high level of oral interaction (teacher and children talking about the science);
- clear responses to questions and provision of high-quality scientific explanations; and
- the use of the assessment of progress to set clear targets.

Training courses tend to focus on subject application. This means that teachers are expected to draw upon and develop their own subject knowledge to a significant extent. But, of course, their own prior knowledge of science can lack breadth as well as depth. Many current trainees' experiences of science teaching may have been adequate to pass elementary examinations but itself has failed to give them an adequate conception of the breadth of science, science as products, processes and people, and of science as explanation. This makes it difficult at times for trainees to develop the above attributes.

This book is intended to help you teach science successfully, whether you are a trainee teacher acquiring the basic skills and knowledge or an experienced teacher who wants to become more effective. It offers you the knowledge of science to enable you to plan good lessons with confidence. If successful, it may halt the marginalization of science and return it to its proper place among the core subjects in the primary school.

Lynn D. Newton
Professor of Primary Education
University of Durham, 2004

1

Science: Investigation, Invention and Experiment

1.1: Approaching scientific knowledge and investigation

Science is a way of exploring and investigating the world around us, both natural and manufactured, with the aim of learning more about it and understanding it better. One way to increase the ability to investigate and understand is to increase knowledge, but scientific knowledge on its own is not science, any more than a collection of paintings and sculpture is art. Science is not only a way of knowing: it is also a way of doing, and each shapes the other.

Re-thinking the nature of science. During the past forty years, scientists and philosophers have carried out what amounts to a complete rethink on the nature of scientific knowledge and investigation. Many of their ideas are relevant only to full-scale scientific research, but the basic view of scientific knowledge and activity which has emerged can help teachers understand children's investigations much better than older and more rigid views of science could.

The facts, concepts and theories which make up scientific knowledge are neither permanent nor beyond dispute. They are much more like a report on progress so far, which future investigators will modify and even, maybe, contradict. Any scientific theory is, to put it simply, the best agreed explanation which scientists have produced up to the present. Theories are not final, and certainly not true with a capital T: they are provisional, and are used until something is observed which contradicts them or which they cannot explain. When that happens to an important and influential theory, something rather like a scientific revolution occurs: old theories are discarded and new ones are invented, tested, discussed, negotiated, refined and eventually accepted, or rejected, by the scientific community.

Perhaps the most fundamental change brought about by the rethink of the nature of science is the realization that large-scale scientific theories such as the theory of evolution can never be proved true beyond doubt. Older views of science held that the strength and reliability of scientific knowledge and its claim to be highly regarded were based on its certainty; on the way it had been tested and proved true.

Newer ideas take almost exactly the reverse view. Today, the strength of science is thought to lie in its openness to criticism and correction. Science is regarded as a powerful and influential activity precisely because the truth of scientific knowledge cannot be taken for granted and because it is always open to question. This does not mean that science is simply guesswork or that 'anything goes'. On the contrary: whether in the research laboratory or the primary school, no observation, idea or theory should be accepted until it has been tested in as fair and as thorough a way as possible (1.7), while remembering that testing ideas and theories cannot prove that they are true. Testing may be essential, but it can do no more than help us to decide whether our answers and explanations are good enough to accept for the time being, until they obviously need correction or a better idea emerges. How then can there be any measure of the reliability of scientific knowledge? Because when it is used in research, technology or everyday affairs it is constantly being tested against experience and what can be observed in the world.

Three kinds of knowledge. Science education aims at developing three kinds of knowledge, which have been called knowledge 'that', knowledge 'why' and knowledge 'how to'.

Knowledge 'that' is factual knowledge, concerned with facts, events and changes. It is the kind of knowledge which grows out of, and enables us to answer, factual questions beginning with what, where, when and how. Examples of knowledge 'that' are that muscles only pull and do not push (3.5), that if steam is cooled it condenses into liquid water (6.3) and that steel is a magnetic material, but brass is not (15.3). Knowledge 'that' is important because it gives us an account of how the world is thought to be, and helps to frame our expectations about what we may see or what may happen in the future. For example, if a child knows that when sugar dissolves in water it does not disappear but mixes with the water, she is likely to expect the solution to taste sweet, whereas if she does not have that knowledge the sweetness is likely to come as a surprise. Surprises are particularly important in both scientific research and education. We feel surprise when things do not happen as we expect, but what we expect grows out of what we know and understand. This means that surprises always call for investigation, which usually leads to a growth both in what we know (knowledge 'that') and in our understanding of it (knowledge 'why').

Knowledge 'why' is concerned with identifying causes for what has been observed (1.3) and with seeking explanations; with understanding rather than factual knowledge. It is the kind of knowledge which grows out of, and enables us to answer, questions beginning with 'Why ... ?', and which can be summed up in statements beginning with 'Because ...'. Knowledge 'why' is usually more complex than knowledge 'that', because it starts with the facts and seeks to explain them. Most established scientific theories are highly developed and tested examples of knowledge 'why'. For example, why does the Sun seem to move across the sky during the day? It seems to move because the Earth is spinning and we are carried round with it, so the angle from which we see the Sun changes through the day; an explanation which grows out of the theory that the Sun is at the centre of the Solar System and the Earth is in orbit round it (18.1). The nature of knowledge 'why' is explored further in section 1.4, in relation to the making of hypotheses.

What is commonly thought of as scientific knowledge is made up of knowledge 'that' and knowledge 'why', but the third kind of knowledge, knowledge 'how to', is no less important. Science is not only concerned with knowing and understanding: it is also concerned with investigating, and the ability to investigate effectively is particularly important in primary science, where children's learning is likely to depend as much on personal, first-hand experience as on being told about things or reading about them. Knowledge 'how to' is often undervalued in science education, but it is an essential part of any activity. There are two main kinds. One is concerned with procedures, particularly with devising 'fair' tests for ideas and theories (1.7). How, for example, can it be shown that a parachute with a small hole in the centre is better than one with no hole? Without the ability to set up and carry out fair and thorough testing, no clear answer can be given to questions like this and scientific ideas remain mere guesswork.

The other kind of knowledge 'how to' is more practical, concerned with making things work in a controlled and predictable way, and so is often on the borders of science and technology. Most testing of scientific ideas and theories involves knowledge 'how to' of both kinds. For example, if children want to find out which of a collection of play-balls is the bounciest, they have to carry out a fair test. This will involve not only a knowledge of how to conduct a fair test by identifying and controlling variables (1.7), but also the practical ability to devise and use a method for measuring accurately how high each ball bounces. Without this kind of knowledge and practical ability, the most ingenious ideas can never be tested and evaluated.

The relevance of scientific investigation. In the primary school, scientific knowledge and understanding are not only, nor even principally, about other people's discoveries. An important and integral part of primary education is to help children develop the ability to investigate things for themselves: to perceive problems, think up possible answers, find out whether their ideas stand up to testing and communicate their findings clearly. Scientific investigation has an important and direct contribution to make to this process, but it also has a wider relevance in helping to develop a critical awareness of science and its influence within the community.

As far as anyone can predict, the lives of children who are in primary schools today will be affected even more by science than the lives of their teachers and parents are at present. There is an obvious need for as many people as possible not only to understand something of the scientific knowledge and theory which affects their lives, but also to be critical of scientists' claims. Critical evaluation of any kind of knowledge or discovery is impossible unless one knows how the results were arrived at. This is because, in any kind of investigation, results and ways of working depend on and shape each other. What is discovered depends not only on what is investigated, but also on the methods used (1.2) and the ideas, knowledge and experience of the investigator. This means that first-hand investigations are relevant and valuable not only because they develop knowledge, understanding and the ability to investigate competently, but also because they help to give children a more realistic insight into how science works, its achievements and (equally importantly) its limitations.

The case-study approach. Primary science is largely concerned with investigating through first-hand experience and helping children to understand the world around them. This presents the teacher with great opportunities, but can also raise problems. One major problem when trying to develop a science education based on first-hand experience is that it is impossible for children to investigate everything in their lives, so choices have to be made. Another is that real-life situations are usually much more complex than the artificially simplified world of the science laboratory. A third is that the experience which children bring to school, and the learning opportunities offered by each school's locality, are as varied as the localities and life itself. The case-study approach used in several parts of this book offers one way to overcome such problems: to exploit local conditions and resources effectively and to help ensure the relevance of science investigations to children's lives and experience.

There are two main ways of using the case-study approach. The first is in essence no more than a topic-based approach to science, focused on particular resources and opportunities. For example, if there is a building-site near the school it could, with good liaison, act as a focus for work on the properties of materials, physical and chemical change, as well as related work in most other areas of the curriculum. The second use of the case-study approach is perhaps more far-reaching. A major problem for teachers, particularly when working with living things, the environment and Earth sciences, is the great variety of animals, plants, environmental conditions, soils, rocks and climate which they might encounter. The case-study approach offers a means of reducing such complexity to manageable proportions. For example, instead of trying to investigate a range of ecosystems (5.7), a case-study could be made of one or two (preferably small and simple) habitats. Using expert help where necessary, the animals and plants can be identified, conditions measured and an understanding of each ecosystem built up, which can be related to general theories and principles. Using this approach, children are likely to gain a greater insight into, and respect for, areas which they might previously have ignored as trivial. It has the added advantage that information, understanding and expertise can be accumulated over a period of time, so that the burden of preparatory work becomes less as the quality of experience for the children increases.

The case-study approach is also recommended when children are learning and investigating in the context of large-scale scientific theories such as adaptation (5.5, 5.6) or chemical change (9.2–9.5). The productive approach here is likely to be for the teacher to choose one or two examples as case-studies, research these in detail and help the children to see, through their own investigations, how these relate to the broader scientific ideas.

1.2: Patterns in scientific investigation

One important result of the rethink of the nature of science (1.1) is that science has, to some extent at least, been demystified. Scientific investigation and research are still seen as very complex, but it is possible to see how they are rooted in, and grow out of, the commonsense sort of investigations which people use in everyday life. Although scientists have agreed ways of working and testing ideas, and use special materials, equipment and methods, there is no 'scientific method' which is right for all kinds of enquiry and which always leads to the discovery of the truth if it is properly applied. This more open and flexible view of scientific investigation is particularly important for primary education because it makes it possible for teachers to see a clear relationship and progression between investigative, exploratory play in the early years, and increasingly thorough investigations of a more obviously 'scientific' kind in which children engage as they grow older.

Scientific investigation grows out of exploratory behaviour as a whole. What makes it scientific is not a special method, but the fact that it is carried out in an agreed and thorough way, into questions and problems which scientists find interesting and significant, using existing scientific concepts and theories which are tested by being used in this way. Very similar kinds of investigation are carried out by many people – historians and archaeologists, for example – but their work is not science because their concerns are different.

Variety and style in learning and investigation. The rejection of the idea that scientific investigation is governed by rigid formulas and precisely defined methods does not mean that there are no patterns and sequences in learning and problem-solving. One of the most fundamental patterns in any investigative activity is the synthesis between two apparently opposing qualities: creative imagination and strict criticism. In science, the ability to come up with bright ideas has to be allied to the logical thinking, thoroughness and practical ability as an investigator needed to test both one's own ideas and those suggested by others.

The concept of strict standards and fairness is useful in developing an understanding of how scientific ideas are tested (i.e. criticized), but the process by which the ideas themselves are created cannot be described in this way. It is not that there are no patterns in the ways that ideas, knowledge and possible solutions to problems (hypotheses, 1.4) are arrived at. Quite the reverse: there are so many patterns that it is impossible even to attempt to describe them. As much as anything else, it is a matter of personal style. Different children and adults trying to learn and solve problems are likely to look for knowledge and possible solutions in quite different ways. The two extremes of learning-style can be represented by the 'knowledge first' and 'experience first' models:

Knowledge first: facts, concepts and theories are learned and integrated with remembered experience and existing knowledge. They are then made meaningful, extended and modified by being applied to observation, interpretation and prediction of real-life situations.

Experience first: hands-on experience, coupled with existing knowledge, is used to develop a new idea. This is then verbalized, communicated and made meaningful by modifying or extending existing knowledge.

In practice, no one seems to rely solely on either of these models. Any person's learning is likely to be a complex, interactive activity within which elements of both can be identified, but individuals may show a marked preference for one of these styles of learning and avoid the other.

Some topics in science may also lend themselves more readily to one style of learning rather than the other. For example, when learning about basic plant structure (4.2), the 'knowledge first' approach is likely to be helpful. Basic and partly familiar concepts such as stem, leaf and bud can be introduced and related using a diagrammatic plan (Fig. 4.1) as an 'advance organizer' before children try to identify and interpret the varied forms of real plants. In contrast, children can arrive at concepts of magnetic and non-magnetic materials and magnetic poles (15.3, 15.4), through exploratory play. Their ideas can then be verbalized and shared in discussion, brought into line with accepted scientific terminology and consolidated by being used in further investigations.

Creativity and criticism. In working with children, it can be observed that generally the most effective ideas come, like science itself, from a combination of imagination and criticism. Children who seek safety in plodding through all the possibilities methodically can usefully be encouraged to guess more boldly and take a bit of a risk. Those who simply guess can be shown that it saves a lot of time and effort if, instead of announcing a bright idea as 'the right answer' and sticking to it come what may, one really thinks about it to see if it makes sense and fits all the observations before going through the work of testing it. Through guessing, criticizing and trying things out, everyone can learn that ideas can be changed and improved. A really useful and testable idea is often arrived at in several stages, each one getting nearer to the final idea by eliminating what can be shown not to fit the facts, or adding some new information. Once a testable solution (hypothesis, 1.4) has been arrived at, much stricter rules and patterns of activity have to be followed in order to test it properly, particularly those concerned with the identification and manipulation of variables (1.7).

Even though the idea of a precisely defined scientific method cannot be upheld, it is possible to identify and observe a range of skills and processes used in scientific investigation. By doing this and talking to children about their activities, teachers can gain a much greater insight than is possible otherwise into how children learn through investigation. The skills and processes involved can usefully be thought of as falling into five groups, discussed in sections 1.3–1.7: observing, hypothesizing, predicting, experimenting and fair testing.

1.3: Observing

Observation can and does take place through any of the senses, but for the sake of simplicity, and because vision is for most people by far the most important of the senses in scientific investigation, attention will be focused here on observing through sight. Vision is not simply a matter of opening our eyes and allowing light into them. It is a complex process, involving the eyes and the brain, by which we carry out an exploration or investigation of the world around us (3.10). The brain directs the scanning of the eyes in response both to the information reaching it, and what is known or remembered. The result is that what is seen usually depends very much on the knowledge, understanding and experience of the observer. A rare or unusual plant, for example, is likely to attract the attention of a knowledgeable person, whereas someone who knows little about plants may not even be aware of it, even though both are looking in the same place. As scientists use the term, however, observation implies something rather more than simple recognition: it can usefully be thought of as seeing-with-understanding.

A person can be said to have observed something in the scientific sense when they have both perceived it and realized something of its importance or significance. For example, most trees have green microscopic plants (algae) growing on their trunks and branches, but only a small proportion of the people who see the trees are likely to be aware of the algae, or to observe that on most trees they grow in a definite pattern. To say that the pattern has been observed does not necessarily mean that the observer can explain it, but it does imply that he or she has realized that there is something to be explained. Once a pattern of this kind has been investigated and understood, it is much more likely that similar patterns will be observed elsewhere, on walls and buildings, for example. In science, observation and understanding reinforce one another: the more we know and understand, the more we can observe, and the more we observe, the more we will learn.

It is important to realize that observation rarely if ever takes place on its own, but only as part of a directed and purposeful activity. If I wish to observe how woodlice behave when given a choice between damp and dry conditions, for example, I will concentrate on the pattern of their movement and activity rather than on the details of their structure, even though those details are there to be observed and, in other circumstances, might be the focus of attention. What this means is that observation is a very disciplined activity: adult scientists may have to postpone their interest in some fascinating aspect of what they are observing in order to carry out the investigation in hand. Learning to concentrate and observe in this directed and purposeful way is for most children a very gradual and long-term process, and one which requires a great deal of patience and skill from the teacher if it is to be successful.

In many scientific investigations, observation has to be accompanied by measurement to be effective. This requires the development of a complementary range of observational skills related to numeracy and computational ability on the one hand, and manipulative skill on the other. Here again, the experience and judgement of the teacher are likely to be fully exercised to ensure that the kind of measurement, the scales used and the accuracy required match both the nature of the investigation and the understanding and skill of the pupils.

1.4: Hypothesizing

The question 'What is a hypothesis?' has probably caused more confusion in primary science than any other. To avoid this is a simple matter: rather than asking what a hypothesis is, begin by asking what part it plays in a scientific investigation. Scientists carry out investigations in order to answer questions or solve puzzles and problems. Hypotheses are simply the tentative answers or untried solutions to these questions or problems. The first aim of investigations in science is to increase the knowledge and understanding of those who carry them out, whether they be research scientists or children in primary school. It has already been pointed out (1.1) that scientific knowledge can be regarded as being of three different kinds: knowledge 'that', knowledge 'why' and knowledge 'how to'. Much of the confusion over scientific hypotheses has arisen because they are very varied in character, but they can be seen as being of three basic kinds, corresponding to the kind of knowledge or understanding which the investigation aims to develop.

Descriptive and predictive hypotheses. Hypotheses which relate to knowledge 'that' are either statements about matters of fact (descriptive hypotheses) or simple predictions about what is expected to happen (predictive hypotheses), and there is often very little difference between them. For example, if children are investigating rolling cars down a ramp, they may make a descriptive hypothesis such as 'The steeper the ramp, the further the car goes across the floor'. The hypothesis could also be stated as a prediction, such as 'If we raise the end of the ramp, the car will go further', but this is simply a different form of the same idea.

Descriptive-predictive hypotheses are particularly important in primary science because, in the form of simple statements or predictive guesses, they are a very common starting-point for children's hypothesizing. Examples could include 'The red car will go further than the green one', 'The ball bounces better on the floor than on the carpet' and 'The paper towel absorbs the most water'. All these are quite straightforward descriptive or predictive hypotheses. They claim to say something about a part of the world which the child has experienced and is investigating, but they are untried. Like all hypotheses, they need testing to see whether or not they are true, but unlike the more complex causal-explanatory hypotheses (see below), they usually indicate in a simple way how this might be done.

The importance of descriptive-predictive hypotheses does not diminish as children's ability as investigators develops, because they can often lead directly on to more complex testing and learning. Do all balls bounce better on hard surfaces than on soft ones, for example, and is there a way in which we might be able to explain this? Simply finding out for oneself that something is the case can lead not only to significant learning or reinforcement of scientific concepts, but also to a deeper understanding through the attempt to arrive at scientific explanations for what has been observed.

Causal and explanatory hypotheses. Scientists investigate to find out about the world, both natural and manufactured, but they are rarely if ever content with factual knowledge (knowledge 'that'): they also seek understanding (knowledge 'why'). There are often, if not always, two aspects to scientific understanding. The first is to identify the cause for what has been observed; the second is to seek an explanation of it. For example, if I run fast my pulse rate increases. The cause of this is that my heart is beating faster, but identifying the cause does not explain why it happens (see 3.9). This is usually more difficult, involving scientific knowledge, understanding and previous experience, and much of this book is devoted to providing scientific explanations for commonly observed objects, events and changes.

Seeking causes and explanations, attempting to develop knowledge 'why', calls for a kind of hypothesis different from the descriptive-predictive hypotheses discussed earlier. For example, when a candle is lit it often burns with a small flame, which becomes much bigger after a few minutes. Why does this happen? Children observing the change might hypothesize that 'The flame gets bigger because the wick gets longer'. This is a causal hypothesis: it identifies the cause of the change but does not explain it. To do that, an explanatory hypothesis is needed, which might be, 'Because the wick is longer, melted wax is vaporized and burnt at a greater rate, so the flame is bigger' (9.4).

If children make a statement, whether a guess or something more considered, which could be rephrased to begin 'It happens because ... ', they are almost certainly making a causal or explanatory hypothesis. Once this kind of statement is recognized, it will be realized that such hypotheses, far from being rare or obscure, are something that most children are generating all the time. Most of their intuitive theories about the world and themselves, which have been the subject of much research, are ideas of this kind; for example, the idea that seeing consists of sending out a ray from the eye to the object which is seen (17.1). The teacher's role is to help children identify causes and think up possible explanations using their observations, scientific knowledge, understanding and experience; and this is likely to be a long, gradual process.

Sometimes explanatory hypotheses can be generated easily. For example, children watching woodlice disappear into damp leaves are likely (among other, less testable ideas) to hypothesize that they do it 'Because they don't like light' and 'Because they like damp places'. Often, however, causal and explanatory hypotheses have to be arrived at by longer and less direct paths. When trying to find out why some seedlings grow more than others, for example, or why an electric lamp is dimly lit, it may be necessary to identify causes by eliminating possibilities: 'It can't be the water because we watered them all the same', or 'It's not the battery because we tested it with another lamp'.

Identifying causes and seeking explanations grows, like much of scientific exploration, from children's spontaneous activities. Causal and explanatory hypotheses which lead to learning in science are generated when children develop and modify their own intuitive explanations through reason, observation, knowledge and understanding. Perhaps the greatest challenge facing science teachers is to develop the knowledge and understanding without stifling the spontaneity and creativity.

Procedural and technological hypotheses. The third kind of scientific knowledge is knowledge 'how to', concerned with the procedures and practicalities of experimenting and fair testing. The hypotheses called for in order to develop this kind of knowledge are again simply science-related versions of solutions to everyday problems. Procedural hypotheses are concerned with setting up fair tests (1.7). For example, in order to test the (descriptive) hypothesis that the weight of a person affects how easily a shoe slips on the floor, a procedure has to be arrived at which satisfies the requirements of fair testing. In this part of an investigation, it is the untried method of testing which is the hypothesis: a possible solution to the problem which may have to be modified if it is found to be unfair, for example if there is a factor which has not been properly controlled.

Technological hypotheses are concerned with the practical problems of carrying out fair tests, reliable measurements or controlled observations. Traditionally, such activities have been regarded as 'merely' technical; but in science education at least this view is unhelpful. Imaginative ideas and logical thinking are no use if the investigator has not the practical know-how and ingenuity to make things work and take reliable measurements. For example, if children are testing the 'strength' of magnets by repulsion, or comparing the tearing strengths of different papers, they have to invent some device to carry out the test. It is most unlikely that they will achieve this without a process of testing and modifying, but creating hypotheses in the form of verbal statements or design drawings is of very limited use, because words and pictures can convey only a small part of what actually needs to be done. During the development process the children are likely to go far beyond what they have expressed or could express in words or drawings, through what they actually make and test. It is the devices themselves which are the trial solutions to the problem; the technological hypotheses. Like other hypotheses they have to be tested, and again they are testable in the most direct way possible: do they satisfy the requirements of fair testing and do they work reliably?

1.5: Predicting

Predictions are statements about what is expected to happen in the future. They are used in scientific investigation in two rather different ways. The first form of prediction is the predictive hypothesis (1.4), which young children especially are likely to make in the form of a simple guess, such as 'If you load the trolley with plasticine it will go further'. The ability and willingness to predict in this way (and so risk being wrong) is of great importance in developing an awareness and understanding of the links between causes and effects.

This awareness can be further developed and refined in many situations into a related and very useful skill: the ability to perceive a pattern emerging and predict accurately how it will continue. For example, if children are investigating changes of shape in rubber bands or flexible sticks when weights are added, they can usefully be encouraged to look for the pattern in their results, which could be recorded by drawing or measuring, and predict what each succeeding result will be. The ability to predict in this way can be used to sharpen observation and help in the search for explanations wherever predictable patterns are to be found.

The second form of prediction is more complex. It becomes important when a causal or explanatory hypothesis is being tested. In theory at least this cannot be done directly: it is necessary to make a prediction based on the hypothesis and find out, by observation or experiment, whether it is true or false. For example, if children hypothesize that the bending of plants towards a window is caused by light coming from one side, it could be predicted that if the plants are turned through 180° they will straighten up, then bend towards the light again, and this prediction could be tested.

Although strict logic requires that a prediction be made when a causal or explanatory hypothesis is being tested, children and adults often dispense with it and go straight from hypothesis to testing by observation or experiment. Children who hypothesize that woodlice do not like light, for example, will usually set about devising some kind of choice-chamber to test their idea. This does not mean that they have no clear idea of what they expect to happen, simply that they have not made their prediction explicit. If things go as the children expect and their hypothesis is upheld this does not matter, but if their implicit prediction is wrong and the unexpected happens, it may be necessary to backtrack and tease it out with some questions such as, 'What did you expect to happen?' and 'Why did you think that would happen?'

1.6: Experimenting

'Experiment' is a much misunderstood and misused word in popular science and science education. Most of the suggested practical examples in this book consist of carrying out a procedure in order to demonstrate a scientific principle. This is a valuable way of developing knowledge, understanding and practical skill, but it is demonstration, not experiment. The term 'experiment' is also used quite often when what is really meant is investigation by trial and error. For example, children making, testing and modifying parachutes to find out which designs and materials work best would be described by many people as 'experimenting', whereas they are doing something much wider and more varied. Experimentation, where it occurs, is only one part of an investigation. To confuse the two is to run the risk of failing to notice all the other skills and processes (such as hypothesizing and predicting) which are being used as part of the overall activity.

Experiments are special situations which are devised and set up to test hypotheses. Many hypotheses cannot be tested in this way. For example, if I hypothesize that the pattern of green micro-plants on a tree is related to water supply, I have to test that idea by controlled observation, interfering with the natural situation as little as possible. If, on the other hand, my hypothesis is that the amount of water used to mix concrete has an effect on its strength when set, observation is not going to help much. I have to set up a special test situation, under strictly controlled conditions (1.7) in order to find out whether the idea is true or false. It is this special test situation which is the experiment.

Quite often in the course of an activity, children switch from a broad investigation (How to make the best parachute) to a much more focused enquiry involving systematic experiments (How does a hole in the middle change how a parachute works?). It is useful to be able to identify this switch, because children may begin experimenting without being entirely clear as to what idea it is they are testing; in other words, with an unstated hypothesis. As with unstated predictions (1.5), this may raise no problems, but if the experimental procedure becomes too complex to manage or the children find it difficult to communicate their findings, it may be necessary to go back and help them make clear to themselves exactly what idea it was they were testing, and what they expected to happen.

Effective experiments rely on a wide range of knowledge, understanding and skill. Most fundamental, perhaps, is the ability to decide what evidence is needed to uphold or reject a hypothesis: can the experiment really be a good test of the idea? Then the experimenter needs the ability to identify all the variables which need to be controlled (1.7) and the ingenuity to invent ways of controlling them, as well as the practical skill to think up a valid, workable experimental procedure and carry it out. This apparently complex process is possible at primary level only because, like other science skills, experimentation in a well-managed science programme is an extension of children's exploratory and investigative play: a more refined, reasoned and disciplined version of what they do spontaneously.

1.7: 'Fair testing' and the control of variables

Although the idea of a single scientific method cannot be upheld, the scientific community expects that hypotheses will be tested thoroughly and fairly before they are published in research papers or books. Children can and should begin at primary level to develop both an understanding of the principles behind this kind of testing and the practical ability to carry it out.

Identifying variables. The first stage in scientific testing is to identify clearly what the focus of interest is, and this may not be simple. For example, if children are investigating how far a trolley will move when pushed by a rubber band, there are many factors which could be changed and which would affect the outcome if they were. Each one is called a variable. In the trolley investigation, the variables include: the kind or number of elastic bands used, how far they are stretched, how the trolley is released, how large a load it carries and the surface it runs on.

The independent variable. Once the variables have been identified, it is necessary to decide which of them is relevant to the hypothesis under test, and this in turn may require children to state their hypothesis and predictions in a much more precise way than they had done up to that time. For example, if the hypothesis were that 'Using two elastic bands makes the trolley go further than one', then the focus of interest is the number of bands used. This is the variable which the tester is going to change in order to see what happens, and it is known as the independent variable.

The dependent variable. The second stage of the testing procedure is to identify what outcome is to be observed or measured in order to find out the effect of changing the independent variable. This is called the dependent variable, and in our example it would be the distance travelled by the trolley.

Control variables. Once the independent and dependent variables have been identified, the next stage of the testing procedure is to identify all other variables which could affect the outcome. For the test to be fair, these must be controlled, which means that they must be kept the same throughout the test procedure. These are known as control variables and in our example these include all those listed, except the number of bands used. If these variables are not controlled, the test cannot produce a valid result. For example, if the number of bands was varied, but the amount by which they were stretched was not kept exactly the same each time, it would be impossible to say which of the two factors had produced any differences observed, so the hypothesis would not have been fairly tested.

Devising a test procedure. Working out a test procedure can be made easier by adopting a simple sequence of questions:

What should be changed in the test? (Identify the independent variable.)
What should be observed to see the effect of changing the independent variable? (Identify the dependent variable.)
What should be kept the same to make sure the test is fair? (Identify the control variables.)
How will the results be used to decide if the hypothesis can be upheld? (Work out what conclusions different outcomes would lead to.)

Although children often like to rush into carrying out tests, it is good scientific practice to adopt a more disciplined approach and make sure that these questions have been clearly understood and answered before the practical work begins. If not, a great deal of time and ingenuity may be wasted on what turns out to be an invalid or badly devised test procedure.

1.8: The role of scientific concepts and language in science education

In science, as in any other human activity, the need to communicate clearly and efficiently has led to the development of a specialized language, which can become a jargon if it is used insensitively or out of context. When scientific language is used correctly, a term such as 'gravity' is like the tip of the proverbial iceberg: a convenient verbal shorthand for a complex set of concepts which the speaker shares with the remainder of the group, and which contribute both to understanding and the ability to use scientific ideas to investigate further.

The problem of using specialized language in primary science becomes acute when mere use of a technical term is taken, either by the teacher or by the children, as evidence of understanding. When trying to describe or explain what has been observed, both children and adults often assume that the correct use of a word in an appropriate context is all that is required. Instead of being the tip of an iceberg of shared understanding, the word has become a thin layer of cat-ice over a void of ignorance. For example, if I hold up a ball, then release it so that it falls, and ask what happened, even quite young children are likely to answer 'Gravity pulled it down!' and sit back, convinced that this answers all possible questions about what they have just seen. This raises two problems for me as a teacher. The first is that I am sure the child does not understand the full implications of what has happened; the second is that the reply, if accepted, will short-circuit all the observation, reasoning, discussion and growth of understanding to which even so simple an event can give rise.

The 'describe-explain' strategy. The premature use of scientific language is unproductive, even when it is appropriate to the context, because it leads away from the experience which children need in order to develop their knowledge and understanding. There is, however, a very simple strategy which can overcome this problem. Basically it consists of making as sharp a separation as possible between a description of what has been observed and an explanation of why it happened or came to be that way: first describe, then explain.

In the example of the dropped ball, description might be: 'While it was being held, the ball was not moving. When it was released, it started to fall. It fell straight down and seemed to get faster as it fell, until it hit the floor. It bounced four times, getting lower each time, then rolled across the floor and stopped. After that it didn't move any more.' What is noticeable about this quite detailed description is that it does not involve any specialized scientific language or concepts, and this is true of the overwhelming majority of events, situations and changes that children at primary level will observe and investigate.

In most if not all situations, it is premature to attempt an explanation of what has been observed until it has been thoroughly described, with all relevant details noted. Until this has been done, it is often not possible to see exactly what needs to be explained. In the case of the falling ball, there are clearly two separate sets of events to consider and explain: what happened before the ball hit the floor, and what happened afterwards. Before the ball hit the floor, it began by not moving and then moved when it was released. This means that the way it was moving changed, which in turn means that forces which were out of balance were acting on it (14.3, 14.6, Fig. 14.7d). Since the ball seemed to carry on moving faster, the force making it fall must have been acting on it all the time it was falling. At this point, the nature and identity of the force can be explored through a directed sequence of questions, such as: 'In what direction did the force act?' (Straight downwards, i.e. vertically.) 'Does the force always seem to act that way?' (Yes.) 'Is it acting all the time?' (Yes.) 'Do you know a name for this force which tends to make things fall, always acts straight down and acts all the time?' (Gravity!) Unlike description, scientific explanation does require the use of special concepts and language (in this case, forces out of balance), but technical terms should be used only after the explanation has been developed, to communicate what has been found out. Technical terms are important, because as scientists we need to communicate effectively, but their use can be deceptive if the user does not fully understand what they signify.

The role of scientific concepts. The 'describe-explain' strategy is useful because it not only helps to prevent short-circuiting of investigation by premature use of scientific language, but also shows clearly the role of concepts in science and science education. At primary level and indeed in most everyday situations, scientific concepts are not needed to describe the world. Their role is in identifying causes and developing scientific explanations for what has been observed, in helping people to make sense of their experience in scientific terms and to make accurate predictions. Separating description and explanation can make it much easier for teachers and children to understand both the nature of scientific concepts and the proper use of the specialized language to which they have given rise.

The 'describe-explain' strategy is to some extent an artificial one. Particularly as children grow older, descriptions may require specialized language if they are not to become over-long and wordy, and explanations often lead back to fresh observations and the attempt to make a better description. If the children reach this stage, however, it is unlikely that the premature use of scientific language will be a problem: it is far more likely that the investigation itself will have assumed its proper role as the driving force behind the children's activity.

2
Life and Living Processes

2.1: The concept of 'living'

Whether at the beginning of their learning or later, there is a need for children to develop, as part of their understanding of living things, a concept of what it means to be alive. This is often introduced by way of a classification exercise, aimed at distinguishing things which are alive from those which are dead (i.e. were once alive but are no longer), and those which are non-living (i.e. never were alive). The problem with this approach, especially in the early years, is that many living things such as plants are not obviously doing anything, as one looks at them, which gives a reason for saying that they are alive. Indeed many children (and not a few adults) do not regard plants as being alive, or think that they are somehow less alive than animals.

In secondary science, living things are usually characterized by a set of common life processes: nutrition (feeding), respiration (breathing and energy transfer), response to changes in the environment, movement, excretion (removal of waste), growth and reproduction. This is a very useful check-list, but here again there are problems with using it as a set of criteria to distinguish living from non-living things. Not all living things do all the activities (worker bees, for example, do not reproduce), while some living things, such as dormant trees, bulbs and seeds, do not seem to be active at all. For primary age children, especially, a different approach is needed to the development of a concept of being alive.

2.2: An alternative concept of 'living'

Imagine a motor car in a field with a ring fence round it, left for a hundred years. How would it have changed by the end of that time? The steel bodywork would probably have rusted away completely, with the rust washed away into the soil, and little would be left of the remainder apart from lead from the battery, any other metals resistant to corrosion, plastics and glass. Now imagine a young oak tree, fenced round and left in the same way. In a hundred years it would be fully grown, the habitat for hundreds if not thousands of animals, and probably surrounded by young oak trees.

16

This simple thought-experiment sums up what is distinctive about living things: the way they change over time. If left to themselves, non-living things sooner or later break down and become simpler, the materials which make them up spreading out and becoming dispersed in the environment. Living things, on the other hand, if not interfered with, eaten or afflicted with disease, change on their own (spontaneously) in almost exactly the opposite way. They grow larger, more complex and usually make more living things like themselves. They do this by taking in material from their environment and incorporating it into their own bodies. Non-living materials can of course be built into complex things such as motor cars, but these changes are not spontaneous: they are brought about by humans working on the materials, not by the things on their own. It is their power of spontaneously growing larger, more complex and more numerous which makes living things so distinctive. The fact that once they are dead they decay, often very quickly, shows that the only special property they have is that of being alive. Very few non-living things can grow or reproduce, and those which can (crystals, for example, 8.6), do so only in very special conditions, and even then neither grow more complex nor carry out any of the other activities we associate with living things.

Most animals are obviously alive. To show that seeds, dormant bulbs and other plants are alive, it is necessary to give them the conditions they need for growth (4.3), to observe them over a period of time and keep careful records of their appearance by drawing or photography, to see whether and in what ways they change. If they are growing bigger and more complex, and especially if they are reproducing more individuals like themselves, they must be alive. Having established the basic concept that living things are distinguished by the ways in which they change without interference from outside, the concept of life processes can be used to direct enquiry and develop children's knowledge in more depth and detail.

2.3: An overview of living processes

Nutrition is the process by which living things obtain and, if necessary, modify the materials they need to sustain life, grow and reproduce. There are two fundamentally different patterns of nutrition. Plants (and some microbes) can take in simple chemicals from the environment and use light energy from the Sun to build up complex, high-energy food chemicals (photosynthesis, 4.4). All other living things, such as animals and decomposers (5.8), have to obtain their food chemicals ready-made by feeding on plants or other living things (5.7). This usually involves digesting the food (3.3) into simpler chemicals which the body can absorb. Food chemicals are used both as a source of energy (respiration, see below and 3.6) and as the raw material for building up and replacing tissues in growth, reproduction and maintenance of the body (3.11).

Respiration is the process by which living things break down some kinds of food chemicals in their bodies and use them as a source of energy. To do this, most (though not all) living things need a supply of oxygen and a means of removing the waste gas carbon dioxide. The process of gas exchange, by which oxygen is made to enter the body and carbon dioxide to leave it, is called breathing. Larger animals have special organs to make this process very rapid and efficient: examples are the lungs of humans and other mammals (3.6) and the gills of fish. Respiration, of which breathing is a necessary part, is a complex chemical breakdown process in which energy from food (chemical-potential energy, 12.4) is made available for all life-processes, including the movement of muscle (3.5) and the building up of new and replacement tissues (3.11, 3.12).

Respiration is sometimes said to be rather like a process of burning, with food as the fuel. This is fundamentally misleading. Burning (9.4) is a high-temperature process in which fuel and oxygen are combined chemically very rapidly, so that the burning material and the environment are strongly heated. In contrast to this, respiration is a low-temperature process in which food is broken down and energy transferred in a series of controlled steps, so there is much less heating and the energy can be transferred in ways which the body can use.

Response is necessary because living things exist in an environment which is constantly changing and often threatens their survival. They are much more likely to survive if they can detect and respond to changes which could affect them. The overall response of an animal or plant is called its behaviour (5.6). Larger animals have specialized sense organs to detect changes (3.10) and many of their responses are very fast: for example, a frog catches a fly in less than a hundredth of a second. Most plants do not have specialized sense organs and most of their responses are slower, made by growing in different ways (4.3).

Movement is often the most obvious response made by both animals and plants to changes in their environment. Because animals need to find food, most are able to move about actively. This also makes it possible for them to avoid other animals which could kill and eat them and to seek out favourable conditions, such as shelter, refuge or a social group. Some animals do not move around in this way, but remain fixed and capture their food as it passes: sea anemones and barnacles are examples. Plants, because they make their own food, do not move around as animals do, and (apart from some floating waterplants) need a fixed root system for anchorage and taking in water (4.2). With the exception of 'exploding' seed-pods, fast plant movement is very rare. Most examples of plant movement which children can observe result from patterns of growth, such as seedlings bending towards light, the opening of flowers and the twining of tendrils.

Excretion. All chemical processes in living things produce waste materials which must be removed. The process by which this is done is called excretion. Both plants and animals produce carbon dioxide as a waste product of respiration (see above) and release it into the atmosphere. Plants in light produce oxygen as a waste product of photosynthesis (4.4) which maintains the gas balance in the atmosphere

(5.8). Because animals eat other living things, they usually have a surplus of some food chemicals which cannot be stored and must be broken down and excreted from the body (3.3). Plants, on the other hand, produce only the food chemicals they need and so have much less of a waste-disposal problem.

Growth is the name for overall increase in size of a living thing. Growth of living things, viewed over their whole life-span, doesn't mean simply becoming bigger (as a growing crystal does), but becoming more complex, able to do more and behave in a greater variety of ways: compare a newly hatched tadpole with an adult frog, or a seedling with a mature tree, for example. Growth involves building up new living material and requires both food chemicals obtained through nutrition and energy from respiration. Most large animals are organisms of definite growth. They have a normal size range and a growth period when young, after which their size does not increase. After this growth period, animals do in fact keep growing, but in another way: their body tissues 'wear out' and have to be replaced. Plants, in contrast, usually keep growing for most of their lives, either continuing to get bigger, as grass and trees do (4.3), or multiplying by non-sexual reproduction, as bluebells and other bulbs do (4.5).

Reproduction can be viewed as a special kind of growth, which tends to increase the size of the population rather than the size of the individual. Living things are vulnerable. Most of them have a limited life-span and there is always the possibility that they will be eaten, or killed in some other way. Without reproduction, there would be no younger animals or plants in the habitat to replace those which die, so it is the process which perpetuates life on Earth. If it fails, as sooner or later it does for most kinds of animal and plant, the result is extinction (5.5).

In many plants, some kinds of (asexual) reproduction are simply an extension of the way they grow (4.5), but both plants and animals have developed a more specialized, sexual mode of reproduction. Sexual reproduction essentially involves the formation of special sex cells, often but not always in different parents, and their joining in the process of fertilization. In the main examples about which children will learn (mammals and flowering plants) a female cell which does not move (the egg-cell) is fertilized by a much smaller male cell (sperm or pollen-grain) which moves towards and eventually joins with it. From the fertilized egg-cell, the new individual (foetus in animals, seed in flowering plants) develops.

Both kinds of sex cells contain information in the form of DNA (2.4), which controls much of the new individual's growth and development. Variation in inherited DNA, however, (5.5) ensures that although sexually-reproduced offspring resemble their parents, they are never exactly like them.

2.4: Organisms, cells and DNA

Organisms and cells. Individual living things are known as organisms. Most organisms we see, such as humans and familiar animals and plants, are made up of very large numbers of units called cells. In most cases these cells are so small that they can be seen only with a microscope, and though each cell is separated from those around it, cells can communicate in a variety of ways and chemicals can pass in and out of them.

Some very small organisms are made up of only one cell. Many of these inhabit almost every part of our environment, including our own bodies, in enormous numbers. Single-celled organisms children may know about, observe or investigate include bacteria and yeast (5.3, 9.2), and the alga *Pleurococcus* which forms a green crust on walls and tree-bark (5.2).

Specialization: tissues and organs. A single-celled organism carries out all its living processes (2.3) in its one cell, but larger organisms such as humans, domestic animals, garden plants and trees have a range of specialized parts, each of which carries out a smaller range of activities. Much of Chapters 3 and 4 is taken up with discussing these in more detail. In order to carry out their functions more efficiently, cells in different parts of animals and plants become highly specialized and very different from each other, both in appearance and in what they can do.

Specialized groups of cells are known as tissues, for example muscle and bone. In both animals and plants, different tissues develop together to form organs, and work together to perform particular functions. Familiar examples include the skeleton, which supports the body of many animals (3.5), the heart, which pumps blood around the body (3.8), and the leaves of plants, which make food and activate water transport (4.2, 4.4).

Control and information: the cell nucleus and DNA. Living processes do not occur haphazardly or at random: they are highly organized and ordered, just as many human activities are. The order and organization of activities such as designing and making something or communicating with other people depends on information, and the same is true of the living processes in cells and whole organisms. The activities of almost all cells are controlled by information in the form of a complex chemical known as DNA (deoxyribose nucleic acid). In animal and plant cells most DNA is concentrated in a special part of each cell, known as the nucleus. The DNA in the nucleus can communicate with all parts of the cell by way of special 'messenger' chemicals.

Genes. Each activity of the cell is controlled by a different part of the DNA, known as a gene. Because complex organisms such as humans and large plants carry out a very wide range of activities, their development and living processes are controlled by many thousands of genes. In most cases, the way an animal or plant appears and behaves depends on very complex interactions between the information in its genes and the environment in which it develops and lives. Sometimes, however, the results are simpler and we can see them more easily. In humans and some other mammals, for example, small groups of genes control the colour of hair and eyes, and we can even see a few characteristics in ourselves which seem to be controlled by just one gene each. Examples include the ability to roll the tongue lengthways into a U-shape and the ability to twist the tip of the tongue over.

The human genome and 'genetic fingerprinting'. The overall order and arrangement of genes in an organism is known as its genome. In human beings the arrangement of genes (the human genome) is the same for most people, but because we have many thousands of genes, many of which exist in slightly different forms, and because these are recombined in reproduction (5.5), every one of us is unique and has DNA which is unique. An international project has now mapped the whole of the human genome. This is potentially of great importance to medicine because there are many diseases caused by defective genes (mutations, 5.5). Knowledge of exactly which genes are affected, where they are located in the genome and how they change the working of the body opens up the possibility of helping sufferers through new medicines or gene therapy (5.5).

The ability to map and detect patterns in DNA has also been exploited to investigate human differences and similarities. Differences in our DNA make it possible to link individual people to human material with a high degree of accuracy; a technique known, rather misleadingly, as 'genetic fingerprinting' and now much used in criminal investigation. Patterns in parts of the DNA in a sample are compared with DNA from other samples or from known individuals. The results indicate with a very high degree of probability (though not with complete certainty) that samples and individuals are, or are not, linked. A different but related technique looks for similarities in the DNA of populations to find out if the people taking part are related, not only within families but also throughout whole countries and continents. Among other achievements, this second technique is enabling archaeologists to trace human migrations in historical and even prehistoric times.

DNA and heredity. Because DNA controls the ways in which organisms develop and function, the passing on of this information from parents to their offspring is an essential part of reproduction. The patterns on which characteristics are inherited by each generation from the previous one are known as heredity, and genetics is the science which investigates it. Knowledge of how DNA operates within living cells and is inherited has led to scientific and technological advances on many fronts; for example, our understanding of the diversity of life on Earth and modern biotechnology (5.5). Although a detailed understanding of genetics is well beyond the scope of primary science, children are likely to become increasingly aware of its effects and implications, both scientific and social, as the development of biotechnologies gathers pace. Older children may already be aware of debates on (for example) cloning, gene therapy and genetically modified crops (5.5). In future it is likely that we as teachers will be increasingly called on to answer their questions on these difficult, controversial and rapidly changing issues.

3

Humans and Other Animals

3.1: Basic human anatomy

Learning about how the body functions and how it may be cared for is difficult unless one has at least an outline knowledge of its structure and the activities of its main parts. A logical way to learn about human anatomy is to begin with the skeleton as the framework of the body and then to build on this by learning about the muscles and other organs which are attached to it and both supported and protected by it. Some of this knowledge can be gained only from information resources such as books, charts and CD-ROMs, but to be effective at primary level this approach needs to be linked closely to children's experience and knowledge of their own bodies. One effective way to begin is by learning or revising the names of the main external body parts, which can usefully be linked to work in English and physical education. Learning about internal anatomy can then begin with an investigation of body 'landmarks'. These are points at which the skeleton can be felt beneath the skin. Children should link the landmarks they can feel on their own bodies with drawings or, preferably, models of the human skeleton. This should enable them to gain a much more accurate sense of body structure than is possible otherwise.

The main body landmarks are:

Head: the top of the head or cranium (young children must feel this gently); eyebrow ridges, cheek-bone and eye socket; lower jaw, its joint and the angle below the ear.

Arm and hand: shoulder and elbow joints (feel movement); lower arm (twist and feel that there are two parallel bones); wrist, knuckle joints.

Neck: collar bones between the hollow at the base of the neck and the shoulder on either side.

Chest: ribs; breast-bone; base of breast-bone and bottom of rib-cage.

Spine: bend forward, feel bones (vertebrae) below neck and in the small of the back.

Hip region: the upper edges of the hip-bone (pelvis) from the side of the body round towards the back.

Leg: top of thigh-bone and joint with hip; knee-cap; shin-bone; ankle and heel bones; joints of toes.

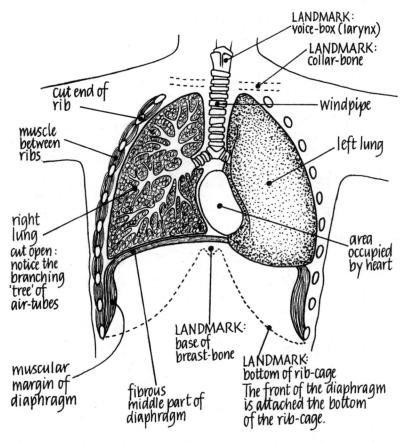

Figure 3.1 *The position of the diaphragm in relation to body landmarks and the main organs of the chest region, seen from the front*

Major internal organs of the body. The central organs of response and control in the body are the brain, which fills the upper part of the skull (cranium) completely, and the spinal cord. This runs from the brain, down through a tube formed by a large hole in each of the bones of the spine (vertebrae). The remaining major organs (apart from muscles, see 3.5) are all in the main part of the body, or trunk. To understand their basic layout it is useful to think of the trunk as being divided into two regions, the chest region (thorax) and the belly region (abdomen). The organ which separates the two regions is the diaphragm, a dome-shaped sheet of fibre-tissue (tendon) and muscle, which is attached to the lower edge of the rib-cage (Fig. 3.1). Once the shape and position of the diaphragm are understood in relation to the skeleton, learning about the other major organs is much easier.

The top of the diaphragm is about level with the bottom of the breast-bone.

Above this is the chest or thorax, which is filled with the two lungs, together with the main air-pipes which serve them (3.6), and the heart (3.8), with its large blood-carrying tubes. The heart lies slightly to the left of centre at the level of the fifth rib, counting downwards. To gain an idea of where and how big it is, clench the left fist and place it on the chest so that the inside of the wrist is over the left nipple. The fist itself then shows, approximately, the size, shape and position of the heart.

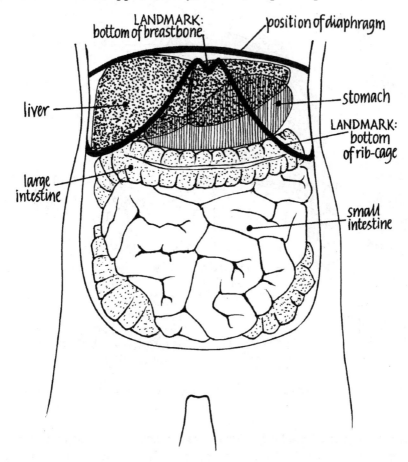

Figure 3.2 *Position of main abdominal organs in relation to the diaphragm and rib-cage, seen from the front. The liver is directly under the diaphragm and partly protected by the front of the rib-cage. It lies partly over and in front of the stomach*

Below the diaphragm is the abdomen. The position and size of the main abdominal organs (stomach, liver, small and large intestines) is shown in Fig. 3.2. The stomach and liver lie just below the diaphragm and are partly protected by the lower part of the rib-cage. The stomach is much higher in the body than is commonly imagined. Its size and position can be shown approximately by placing the left hand flat over the front of the body, with the thumb folded into the notch at the bottom of the breast-bone. The kidneys (3.7) are just inside the body-wall at the back, on either side of the spine. Their position can be felt by finding the gap on either side of the spine between the upper edge of the hip-bone and the bottom of the rib-cage.

3.2: Nutrition: teeth and dental care

Apart from water and salt, our food consists of complex, high-energy chemicals (3.4). Very little of the food we eat is in a form which can be used by the body. Nearly all of it has to be broken down into simpler chemicals, a process known as digestion. To carry out this process we have a long tube through our bodies called the gut (alimentary canal). Food is taken into the gut through the mouth, and waste (faeces) is expelled from the anus (3.3).

Digestion begins with chewing, which is carried out by the teeth and jaws. This breaks up the food, mixes it with saliva and softens it so that it is easier both to swallow and to digest (3.3). Teeth grow from, and are anchored in the bones of, the upper and lower jaws. Each tooth is a bony structure, with a nerve and blood supply at its centre and a covering of smooth, white dental enamel, the hardest material in the body. The main bony part of the tooth, the dentine, is fairly hard and very tough (ivory is dentine), and it supports the enamel, which is much harder (7.3) but also more brittle (7.8).

Humans have two sets of teeth in their lifetime. The first set (milk or deciduous teeth) are formed in early childhood and shed as the second, permanent, set grow under them and push them out. Care of permanent teeth is particularly important because, unlike bones and most other body parts, tooth enamel cannot be repaired or renewed if it is chipped, cracked or damaged chemically. Damage to the enamel makes it possible for microbes to attack and decay the softer dentine underneath. If the decay reaches the nerve and blood supply in the centre of the tooth, pain (toothache) will be felt, which if untreated may lead to a serious infection (abscess) in the root of the tooth and the bone of the jaw.

There are two main causes of damage to enamel and subsequent decay: abuse of the teeth and poor dental hygiene. Teeth are for chewing food and should never be used for holding, pulling or breaking things, any of which is likely to crack or chip the enamel. Even when food is chewed safely and thoroughly, teeth will still be at risk if they are not cleaned. Chewed food of any kind is usually more or less sticky and often fibrous. Even thorough brushing may fail to remove particles of food which lodge between the teeth. Unless the remains of food are removed by careful use of dental floss or special interdental brushes, the teeth will be very quickly colonized and decayed by microbes already living in the mouth, which is one cause of bad breath and sore gums.

One by-product of food decay is acid which attacks tooth enamel chemically, roughening and pitting its surface, so making it easier for bacteria to form a layer (plaque) and attack it still further. Acid production is encouraged by consuming too much sugar, particularly in the form of sweets, some soft drinks and ice lollies, which in effect coat the teeth with a thin film of sticky syrup. This quickly becomes acidic as microbes feed on it.

The main way of preventing tooth decay and gum disease is regular, thorough brushing with toothpaste, which contains a very fine abrasive capable of removing bacterial films and so preventing the buildup of plaque. Coupled with the use of floss or interdental brushes, it greatly reduces the frequency of tooth decay in most children and adults. More controversial is the use of fluoride in drinking water or tablets, though it is now added to most toothpastes. Very small amounts of fluoride absorbed in childhood make tooth enamel harder and more resistant to decay, but some people fear that there may be long-term side-effects, even though some areas have naturally fluoridated water which seems harmless.

The number and form of the teeth which an animal has can give a lot of information about the kinds of food it eats and therefore about its relationship with other living things. Because humans have a varied diet, our teeth are not very specialized. The front ones (incisors and canines) are good for chewing or pulling pieces from a larger lump of food, while the broad back teeth (premolars and molars) are well-adapted for crushing and macerating food to a pulp. Many other animals have much more specialized teeth related to their diet (5.6).

3.3: Nutrition: digestion

Swallowing. Food, softened and moistened by chewing and saliva, is formed into a ball by the tongue and moved to the back of the mouth. There it triggers a reflex action (3.10) which results in swallowing. There are two tubes running down through the neck. In front is the windpipe (trachea) leading to the lungs (3.6), and behind it the gullet (oesophagus), leading to the stomach. To feel where the gullet runs, swallow a mouthful of warm (not hot) water. In swallowing, a flap (epiglottis) closes over the top of the windpipe so that food or liquid does not normally enter it, but goes further back and down the gullet. If liquid or solid material does enter the windpipe accidentally, it triggers a choking reflex, consisting of violent coughing which continues until the material has been ejected. The gullet is a muscular tube, which moves the food pellet down to the stomach. As the food reaches the lower end of the gullet, the upper end of the stomach opens to let it in.

The stomach. The stomach is a muscular bag, closed at both ends by a ring of muscle, whose function is to collect food and begin its digestion. It does this by adding water with chemicals in solution and churning the mixture into a semi-liquid pulp. The liquid added to the food contains quite strong hydrochloric acid, which kills nearly all the microbes eaten with the food. It creates highly acidic conditions favourable for the working of the digesting chemicals, also present in the stomach juice (enzymes, see below). When the food has been broken down sufficiently, the ring of muscle at the lower end of the stomach opens to allow it, a little at a time, into the next part of the gut.

Peristalsis. The whole of the gut is a muscular tube, which mixes the semi-liquid food inside it and moves it along by waves of squeezing action, rather like squeezing toothpaste to one end of the tube. This mixing and moving activity is called peristalsis. Although the churning action of the stomach is quite a violent example of peristalsis, we do not normally feel it at all. If some bad, poisonous or indigestible food is swallowed, however, the normal action of the stomach goes into reverse, we feel the churning of its muscles and are sick. Vomiting is a very important defence by the body against poisons (excess alcohol, for example, 3.13) and infection by microbes.

Digestive enzymes. Chewing and pulping of food in the mouth and stomach is only the preliminary phase of digestion. The actual breakdown of foods into a form the body can use is a chemical process, carried out, like all chemical changes (9.1) in the body, by special chemicals called enzymes. Enzymes similar to the ones we use to digest food are used in 'biological' washing powders, to digest food and stains so that they dissolve in the water and are washed away. This is exactly what happens in the digestion of food. Enzymes made by the body are mixed with the liquid food, so that the complex food chemicals are broken down into simpler ones which will dissolve in water. In this form they can be taken into the body and transported by the blood (3.7).

Absorption and transport. When the partly digested food leaves the stomach, it enters the first part of the intestine (the duodenum), then the small intestine, where digestion is continued and completed. The small intestine has a remarkable structure. Its lining has millions of small projections which look like the pile of a carpet, with tiny blood-vessels (capillaries, see 3.8) running through them. All together these have a very large surface through which digested food from the gut contents can be absorbed, so that the blood can transport it. All the digested food is transported by the blood to the liver, which is like a complex chemical factory. It receives the digested food, processes some of it further and distributes it to the rest of the body as it is needed for growth or respiration (2.3).

Defaecation. When all the useful digested food has been taken out of the gut contents, what remains is passed to the large intestine. Before the waste is removed from the body, most of the water added to the food in the stomach is absorbed by the intestine and so made available for re-use by the body. Normal reabsorption of water makes the waste food in the gut into a solid mass (faeces) which is moved through the large intestine by peristalsis and finally ejected through the ring of muscle (anus) at the lower end of the gut, a process known as defaecation. One reason why fibre is an important part of a healthy diet (3.4) is that it helps peristalsis to work efficiently, so food and faeces are moved through the gut quickly and we don't become constipated. In contrast to this, harmful microbes in the intestine may mean that the body needs to get rid of the waste food very quickly, which results in diarrhoea. Very severe diarrhoea, caused by diseases such as dysentery and cholera, results in uncontrolled dehydration of the body, which may be fatal. Such diseases, caused by contamination of drinking water, were very common in Britain before the middle of the nineteenth century and are still a major problem in the developing world today.

3.4: Nutrition: food and diet

The overall range of food which an animal eats is its diet. A correctly balanced diet for any animal is the range of foods which will enable it to stay healthy in the long term. For humans, a balanced diet includes a variety of foods, together with the vitamins they contain, water and minerals.

The main foods of animals are complex, high-energy chemicals obtained by feeding on other living things, whether plants, animals, or both. There are three main groups of foods: carbohydrates, fats and proteins.

Carbohydrates are chemicals which the body uses as a source of energy, or converts to fat for storage. The two main carbohydrates eaten and digested by humans are sugars and starch. The sugar glucose is the only common ingredient of our food which can be absorbed directly and very quickly by the stomach without digestion. Other sugars, and starch, are changed to glucose by digestion and then absorbed. Glucose is also the main material used as an energy source in respiration (3.6) and the body is constantly supplied with it by the blood (3.7). The only carbohydrate stored by the body is a small amount in the liver. If more sugar and starch are eaten than the body needs, the surplus is stored as fat. In times of food shortage this may be life-saving, but when food is plentiful it can lead to obesity. There is no way that the body can dispose of an excess of carbohydrate other than by respiring it (during exercise, for example) or storing it.

Obesity. Obesity is becoming a major problem among children and adults in both Britain and the USA. Discussion of the complex social and biological factors which have contributed to this situation are beyond the scope of this book, but most children are likely to benefit from being helped and encouraged to eat a balanced diet (see below), eat in moderation and take more physical exercise (3.9). Science education can play a significant part in this process by promoting children's understanding of their own bodies and their response to food and exercise.

Fats, which may be in a solid or liquid, oily form, are a very efficient way of storing high-energy food, both for animals and plants. Fat taken in as food can, after digestion, be used as an energy source in respiration (3.6), and fat stored in a person's own body is used in the same way if other energy sources such as carbohydrate are insufficient for their needs. As with carbohydrate, excess fat in the diet cannot be removed from the body and has either to be respired or stored in fatty tissue.

Proteins. Carbohydrates and fats are, as far as animals are concerned, useful only as sources of energy. Proteins have a more varied role. When digested, they produce a range of up to twenty chemicals called amino-acids. These are used by the body as the raw material for making or replacing living tissue. This means that adequate supplies of protein are essential, not only for growth in childhood, but for continued health throughout life. The protein supply also has to be fairly constant, because surplus amino-acids cannot be stored and they have to be removed from the body. This is done by the liver, and produces chemicals which can be respired or stored as fat, and a waste product (urea) which is removed from the blood by the kidneys (3.7) and expelled from the body in the urine.

Vitamins are complex chemicals which the body needs in small quantities but cannot make for itself. They are not foods in the ordinary sense of the term, but are more like a chemical tool-kit which enables the body to carry out complex chemical changes. Detailed information on vitamins and foods which contain them can be obtained from health promotion agencies. If a particular vitamin is missing from a person's diet, they will suffer from a distinctive illness called a deficiency disease because one or more essential body processes cannot be carried out. For example, sailors on long voyages in historic times often had no fresh fruit or vegetables for long periods, so there was no vitamin C in their diet and they suffered from the deficiency disease known as scurvy. To overcome this, the British Navy issued rations of lemon or lime juice to its sailors, which led to the American nickname for the British: 'limeys'. A balanced and varied diet (see below) usually supplies all the vitamins a person needs, but people on restricted diets may need to take vitamin supplements to remain healthy.

Water. Humans share with all land-dwelling animals the problem of water conservation. Living tissue is made up largely of water, and to humans and most living things even a moderate loss of water is fatal, so unless water supplies are plentiful, dehydration is a constant danger. Humans are fairly efficient at conserving water: we have an almost waterproof skin, quite good water recovery from waste food in the gut, and kidneys which can concentrate chemical wastes in the urine. But in spite of this, each of us wakes up in the morning about 1kg lighter than we went to bed, because of water loss from the lungs during breathing and slow evaporation (6.3) from the skin.

Even without vigorous exercise and sweating, humans need to drink water daily if they are to remain healthy and active. Twenty-four hours without water usually results in acute thirst, and more than a few days can be fatal. The water in lakes, ponds and rivers contains many kinds of microbe, a few of which can cause serious or fatal diseases in humans, such as cholera and dysentery (3.3). This danger is greatly increased if water is contaminated, for example by inadequate sewage disposal. Water also dissolves many chemicals, some of which are poisonous. Examples include fertilizers and industrial chemicals, which are serious pollutants if allowed to contaminate natural water supplies (5.9). Water purification is therefore one of our most important technologies, since our whole lifestyle and civilization depends on an abundant supply of purified drinking-water. Indeed, an abundant supply of clean water is likely to be the biggest single contributory factor in the improvement of health in any society, far outweighing the whole of medicine in its overall beneficial effects.

Minerals in the diet are rather different from minerals in the earth (11.7). As part of our food, 'mineral' means a simple chemical we need to stay healthy. The main examples children may need to know about are salt, iron and calcium. Salt (sodium chloride) is found in solution in the blood and all other body fluids. If salt is lacking in the diet the body can conserve it to some extent, but some is always lost in sweat and urine, so at least a small intake is necessary. During vigorous exercise, salt loss in sweat increases and there may be a need to take salt in order to prevent cramp (severe, uncontrolled muscle contraction). Excess salt in the diet is removed from the body by the kidneys, but in the long term can cause medical problems such as high blood pressure.

Two other very important minerals are chemicals containing iron, needed for making the haemoglobin in red blood cells (3.7), and others containing calcium, which is essential for the hardening and strengthening of bones and teeth (3.5). Normally both are obtained in sufficient quantities as part of food, but if they are lacking in a particular diet, or if large quantities are needed (calcium in pregnant women, for example), mineral supplements may be needed to maintain health.

Dietary fibre. Although not a food for humans since they cannot digest it, dietary fibre or roughage is an essential part of a balanced diet. Dietary fibre is made of cellulose, the main structural material of plants (4.4), and the main sources of it in the human diet are vegetables, fruit, whole-grain cereals and bread. Without it, the gut cannot move food and undigested waste efficiently (3.3) so waste stays longer in the large intestine and constipation sets in. This is not merely uncomfortable: it has been shown to contribute, in the long term, to cancer of the large intestine. Animals which feed mainly on plants (herbivores, 5.7) can digest cellulose, which is for them the main source of carbohydrate.

Balanced diet. Detailed advice on diet and healthy eating related to local conditions and foods is readily available from health promotion agencies. Humans, like other mixed-diet animals (omnivores, 5.7), can digest, use and stay healthy on the basis of eating a very wide variety of foods. Some modern methods of processing, however, make foods which taste good but which are lacking in some ingredients necessary for health, such as vitamins or dietary fibre, or which have too much of otherwise good things, such as sugar, fat and salt. In Britain, prepared foods should now have an analysis of their food and fibre content on their labels, which are informative when learning about diet and healthy eating. Unless they and their families are already diet-conscious, children can usefully be encouraged to eat less sugar, fat (especially animal fat), salt and highly processed foods generally, and more high-fibre and raw, unprocessed foods. Sugar, fat and salt need special attention because they are often concealed in the diet. Sugar is used in a very wide variety of processed foods (look at a can of baked beans, for example) and even lean beef (red muscle) is 40 per cent fat, whereas chicken meat and white fish are very low in fat.

3.5: Skeleton, joints, muscles and movement

Movement in animals is brought about by a specialized type of tissue called muscle (see below). On its own, muscle would not enable an animal to move about: the force exerted by the muscle has to be applied in some way. Animals have a wide variety of methods of applying muscles for movement, but the one with which children will be most familiar is the jointed skeleton. Two great groups of animals have developed jointed skeletons: the arthropods, including crabs, woodlice and all the insects, whose skeletons are on the outside; and the vertebrates or backboned animals, whose skeletons are inside their bodies (see 5.1).

Bone. Humans are mammals and, like birds, reptiles, amphibians and fish (except sharks and rays), they have skeletons made of bone. As a material, bone is very strong in relation to its size, fairly hard, and tough (7.3–7.8). Thinner bones such as ribs are slightly flexible; thicker ones such as the long bones of the arm and leg are more or less rigid. Bone is a living tissue. It is formed when a soft, tough tissue, rather like the gristle in meat, is hardened by the addition of minerals, mainly calcium phosphate, which are taken in as part of the diet (3.4). Bone forms in the foetus during pregnancy (3.12), and the skeleton continues to grow until adulthood. At birth, the top of the skull has not hardened because the brain inside is not fully grown, so there is a soft area on a baby's head (the fontanelle) which must be treated gently and with great care.

The skeleton is the complete system of bones joined together. It has four main functions:

- protection of some vulnerable organs (brain, spinal cord, lungs, heart and liver);
- forming a framework which supports the main organs of the body;
- making a lever system on which muscles pull to enable the body to move about;
- making red blood cells in the soft tissue (marrow) inside ribs and pelvis.

The skeleton is made of bones which are either rigid or only slightly flexible, but it allows movement because most of the joints which connect the bones can be moved. There are three main kinds of joint in the skeleton. The joints between the bones which make up the main part of the skull (cranium) and between the spine and the pelvis normally allow no movement at all. The second kind of joint is found in the spine, whose bones (vertebrae) are joined by thick discs of tough, flexible tissue. Each joint allows only a small amount of movement, but together they allow the whole spine to be flexible and at the same time very strong. Most of the other joints in the skeleton are of the third kind, which allows fast movement: examples are the joints of the shoulder, elbow, wrist, fingers, hip, knee and ankle, and the joint between the jaw and the main part of the skull. The bones are held together, so that the joints are prevented from falling apart, by very strong elastic strips of tissue called ligaments.

The skeleton as a whole forms a complex set of lever systems, with the bones as the levers and the joints as the pivots (14.9). The forces required to move the levers are exerted by muscles which are attached to the bones and pull on them.

Muscle and tendon. All movement in the body is brought about by muscles. Our muscles are very like the lean red meat we see in butchers' shops, which is the muscle of cattle or other animals. Muscle has a very distinctive property. If a nerve message reaches it from the brain or spinal cord, it will contract, becoming shorter, wider and more firm to the touch, and exerting a pulling force on whatever it is attached to. It is important to realize that muscles can move in only one way: they can only pull; they cannot push.

In order to make the bones of the skeleton move, the muscles must be firmly attached to them. The attachment is by way of very tough, strong cords called tendons. Tendons are easily felt and seen, for example by sitting on a chair, putting one hand under the seat beside you and pulling upwards with the elbow bent. A tendon can then be felt, like a hard, rigid cord, on the inside of the elbow. When the arm is resting on the table the tendon can still be felt, but it feels softer and is more flexible because it is not under tension. Tendons at the back of the knee (hamstrings) and ankle (Achilles' tendon) can be felt and seen when half squatting.

The action of muscles on the skeleton can be understood by remembering that they can only pull, not push. This means that any to-and-fro movement of a joint, such as bending the elbow and straightening it again, must involve at least two muscles. In fact, muscles operate joints in pairs. This can be shown by investigating the muscles of the upper arm.

Let one arm hang loosely. Feel the muscle (biceps) in the front of the upper arm: it is relaxed and quite soft. Now sit in front of a heavy table or desk, put your hand, palm up, under the edge and pull up as if to lift it. Feel the biceps muscle again: it is tense and much firmer because it is 'working' and pulling on the bones of the lower arm. To feel how the muscle changes shape when it contracts, let the arm hang loosely again and, holding the biceps muscle with the other hand, pull up your forearm as far as it will go, until your hand nearly touches your shoulder. When the elbow is fully bent, the muscle is much wider (and shorter) than when the arm is straight.

The muscle which moves the lower arm the other way and straightens the elbow (called the triceps) is at the back of the upper arm. It can be felt by standing near a wall and pushing against it with the flat of your hand and the elbow half bent. The triceps is hard and tense, but the biceps is soft and relaxed because it isn't pulling. Although the triceps muscle cannot push, it enables the hand and arm to exert a pushing force because it pulls on the outside of the elbow joint. This action can be felt by holding the back of the elbow while straightening the arm.

Muscle pairs can also be felt when bending and straightening the knee (muscles in the thigh) and ankle (muscles in the calf of the leg). Pairs of muscles which move a joint are called antagonistic pairs, not because they work against each other, but because they make the joint move in opposite directions.

3.6: Breathing and respiration

Humans and other animals require a constant supply of oxygen in order to remain alive. The oxygen is used in respiration, the process by which energy in food is transferred for activities such as growth and movement. Breathing is the part of the respiration process in which oxygen is taken into the body. At the same time as oxygen is taken from the air, the waste gas carbon dioxide has to be removed from the body, so breathing is not just an intake of one gas, but an exchange of two. Some animals such as earthworms can breathe through their skins, which are permanently damp and slimy, but most land animals have dry, waterproof skins and rely for gas exchange on specialized internal organs called lungs. A few animals use both skin and lungs for breathing: frogs are an example.

Lungs. Humans and other mammals have two lungs, which are complex air-sacs in the chest (3.1). In the living animal the lungs are always filled with air and so have a spongy structure. They are supplied with air by the windpipe (trachea), which runs down in front of the neck from the throat. The windpipe is reinforced by rings of tough, flexible tissue so that it remains open even when we are asleep. In the chest, the windpipe divides into two tubes, one serving each lung. Inside the lungs, the main air-tubes branch repeatedly, forming a tree-like structure with thousands of branches. At the end of each branch is a cluster of tiny air-sacs, from which oxygen is absorbed into the blood (3.7).

Breathing. In order to maintain the oxygen supply to the body, the air in the lungs must be constantly replaced. This is done by pumping stale air out and sucking fresh air in; the set of actions we call breathing. The lungs cannot fill and empty themselves because they are unable to move or change shape. The pumping action is achieved by changing the shape of the chest, which is done in two ways, both of which can be investigated by children and result in air being sucked into the lungs and pushed out.

The first method can be experienced by sitting upright and using the muscles between the ribs to pull the rib-cage upwards and outwards. This makes the chest and lungs larger, so air is sucked in down the windpipe. When the muscles are allowed to relax, the rib-cage falls again and air is pushed out. The second type of breathing can be experienced by lying on your back on the floor. The weight of the body then pushes the rib-cage up, so it is difficult to pull it up further in order to breathe. In this situation, breathing is carried out by using the diaphragm (3.1). When breathing in, the diaphragm pulls down and flattens, making the chest larger and sucking air into the lungs. At the same time, the liver, stomach and intestines are pushed further down, so the abdomen is pushed out and becomes rounder. When breathing out, the diaphragm relaxes and muscles at the front of the abdomen pull in and flatten, making the organs inside push the diaphragm up again so that the chest becomes smaller and air is pushed out of the lungs.

Normal breathing, when a person is at rest, uses both of these breathing actions, but diaphragm breathing is the more important of the two. Because rib-cage breathing can take in and pump out large quantities of air very quickly, it is particularly important during vigorous exercise such as running (3.9). Diaphragm breathing is more important when the rib-cage cannot be lifted easily, for example when a person is lying down or asleep, and for singers who need a lot of breath control.

Gas exchange. The lungs of an adult human contain about 5 litres of air. In normal breathing when the person is at rest, only about a tenth of this is changed with each breath, but this so-called tidal volume increases during exercise (3.9). Each of the thousands of tiny air-sacs in each lung is supplied with a network of very small blood-vessels (capillaries, 3.7), through which the blood is constantly circulating. Oxygen from the air passes through the thin lining of the lung, is taken up by the red blood cells (3.7) and transported to the heart to be pumped round the rest of the body. In normal breathing, about a quarter of the oxygen in the air is taken into the blood. At the same time, carbon dioxide produced by respiration (see below) is released from the blood into the air within the lung, water evaporates from the moist lung lining and the air is heated by the blood. As a result of all these changes, air breathed out is warmer, more humid (11.4), has less oxygen and more carbon dioxide than air breathed in.

Respiration is the process of chemical changes which uses oxygen to break down food (in humans, usually the sugar glucose) in order to transfer energy (12.2) for movement, growth and other living processes. Respiration is carried out in every part of the body, so every part needs a blood supply to deliver oxygen and remove carbon dioxide. It is a complex, low-temperature process, quite different from burning, which can be summarized:

$$\text{glucose} + \text{oxygen} \rightarrow \text{carbon dioxide} + \text{water}$$

3.7: Blood

Blood is the red fluid which is circulated to all parts of the body and which acts as its main means of transport. Blood consists of a pale yellow watery fluid, the plasma, in which are suspended a variety of living cells, each of which has special-ized functions. The main functions of the blood are the transport of oxygen by the red blood cells, response to injury and infection by the white blood cells, and trans-port of digested food and waste products by the plasma. By becoming heated in some parts of the body and cooled in others, the blood also plays an important part in maintaining body temperature (3.9).

Red cells, which give the blood its characteristic colour, are formed in the soft tissue (marrow) of the ribs and hip-bone. Each red cell in humans is active for only about four months, so very large numbers of new ones are formed, and old ones destroyed, each day. The cells are red because they are filled with the iron-containing pigment haemoglobin. If not enough iron is present in the diet (3.4), insufficient red cells will be formed and the person will suffer from a form of anaemia. Haemoglobin has the property that it takes up and carries large amounts of oxygen from the lungs, but can release it again in the tissues of the body where it is needed for respiration (3.6). The red cells are also partly responsible for carrying carbon dioxide produced by respira-tion from the body tissues to the lungs so that it can be breathed out.

White blood cells. Like red cells, white blood cells are formed in bone marrow, but they are much less numerous. There are many different kinds, which together form a very important part of the body's defences against microbes and viruses (the immune system). Some can chemically recognize and attack microbes; others make special chemicals capable of killing microbes or rendering them harmless. Another kind congregate in an injured area and clean up dead or damaged tissue so that healing can take place more easily.

Blood plasma. Plasma is the liquid part of the blood, which contains a very large variety of chemicals in solution. It transports digested foods, which are controlled by the liver, to all parts of the body. They are extracted from the blood by the vari-ous body parts which need them for life processes such as respiration and growth. Plasma also carries waste products in solution, including some of the carbon diox-ide produced by respiration and urea, the waste product from breakdown of excess protein (3.4) in the liver. The urea is carried to the kidneys, where it is removed from the blood before being excreted from the body in urine.

Blood plasma, together with tiny bodies in it called platelets, is also responsible for clotting, which is the main defence against bleeding from wounds to the skin. When blood is exposed to air, a complex series of chemical changes occurs, which results in the plasma becoming solid and sticky. The platelets stick to the solid mass, so that bleeding is stopped and a protective layer is formed, beneath which healing and repair can proceed.

3.8: The heart and circulation of the blood

In order for the blood to act as a transport system, it has to be moved round the body. This is done by the heart, which is a muscular pump situated in the chest just above the diaphragm, to which it is attached, and slightly to the left of centre (Fig. 3.1). The heart is in fact a double pump, whose two halves work together. One half receives blood from the body and pumps it to the lungs; the other receives blood returning from the lungs and pumps it round the body. This ensures that all the blood regularly goes to the lungs to have its oxygen supply renewed and carbon dioxide removed.

The action of the heart. Each half of the heart consists of two chambers which pump blood (Fig. 3.3). The upper chamber (atrium) on each side is thin-walled and acts mainly as a blood reservoir. The lower chambers (ventricles) have thick, muscular walls with a unique spiral structure. Each ventricle has an inlet and an outlet valve which prevent blood flowing backwards, i.e. in the wrong direction. At the start of a heartbeat the muscles of the ventricle relax and blood flows through the inlet valve from the atrium into the ventricle on each side. Then the muscles of the ventricles contract, so that blood is pumped out of both ventricles at once. The spiral structure of the muscles means that blood is not simply squeezed out of the ventricles but is almost wrung out of them, giving a very efficient pumping action. This action closes the inlet valve between the atrium and the ventricle on each side, so that blood cannot flow back into the atria, but opens the outlet valves leading to the large blood-vessels (arteries, see below) which carry blood from the right side of the heart to the lungs and from the left side to the body.

Arteries. Blood circulates round the body in a strictly one-way system, through living pipes or blood-vessels. Every time the heart pumps there is a surge of blood through the system, and the large blood-vessels carrying blood from the heart have thick, elastic walls to withstand them. These blood-vessels are called arteries, and most of them lie deep inside the body where they are protected from injury. This is important because blood flow in a large artery is so fast that if the wall is cut or punctured it is very difficult to stop the bleeding and this may be fatal.

Capillaries. As they reach different parts of the body, arteries branch many times, each time leading to smaller and thinner-walled blood-vessels. These lead, in all parts of the body, to fine networks of tiny, very thin-walled blood-vessels called capillaries. Looking carefully at the white of the eye with a magnifying glass, it is possible to see some of the small arteries and the way they branch in the transparent outer layer, but capillaries are much smaller still and visible only with a microscope.

Arteries and capillaries are rather like a road transport system. The big arteries are like motorways: they allow very fast passage of traffic, but there are only a few places where one can get onto or off them, so delivery and collection of goods is impossible while travelling on them. Capillaries are like small roads in a city or the country: traffic moves much more slowly, but it is possible to collect and deliver goods easily. The blood in capillaries flows slowly. In most parts of the body it delivers oxygen and digested food and collects waste for disposal. The lungs also have a very dense network of capillaries, but there the exchange works the other way: the blood delivers waste in the form of carbon dioxide and collects oxygen.

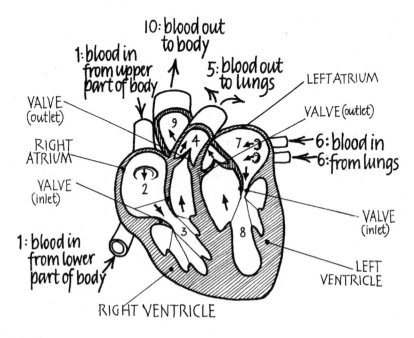

Figure 3.3 *The heart cut open to show its chambers and valves. Cut surfaces are shaded. The sequence of numbers and arrows show the path of blood from the body to the heart (right side) and out to the lungs (1–5); then back to the heart (left side) and out again to the body (6–10)*

Veins. After passing through capillary networks and exchanging material with tissues of the body, the blood flows back to the heart through blood-vessels called veins. Veins have a slower blood flow than arteries, with little or no pressure surge, so they have thinner walls and valves to prevent blood flowing backwards. Many of them run close under the skin and can be seen through it, for example on hands and arms. Because their walls are thin, the deep red blood inside veins makes them appear as bluish lines, darker than the skin on either side.

Pulse. Each heartbeat produces a surge of blood in the arteries. At a few points on the body, arteries run close enough to the skin for these surges to be felt. This is the pulse, which can be used to find out how many times the heart is beating each minute (3.9). There are two places at which children should be able to feel their pulse.

To find the pulse in the wrist (radial pulse), hold out one hand, palm upwards. Stretch the fingers and feel the two tendons running up the wrist to the hand. Let the hand relax and feel for the pulse with index and middle fingers, in the hollow just to the outside of the tendons, below the base of the thumb. Once the radial pulse has been found, a good way of showing it to children is to mount a drinking-straw upright on a drawing pin (thumbtack) using a blob of Blu-tac and place the head of the pin on the pulse-point, keeping the hand very still. The pulse will move the skin and make the straw rock to and fro in time with it.

The neck or carotid pulse is found by lifting the chin and finding the angle in the lower edge of the jaw-bone. The pulse is found in a hollow about 3 cm below and slightly forward of the jaw angle, and only a very gentle pressure is needed to feel it. Once it can be found reliably, the carotid pulse is usually easier to feel and count in children than the radial.

3.9: Exercise and its effects

Exercising and observing the effects of this on the body is one of the most useful ways in which children can begin to investigate the ways in which their bodies work and respond to changing conditions. It is useful to have a range of exercises. A good basic one is the step-up. This is done by stepping up with both feet onto a platform at about the height of a chair on which the child would normally sit. A chair can be used for step-ups, but should always be held firmly by an adult. A complete step-up is four movements (each foot up, then down) and should be done in a measured time: four seconds is convenient, giving 15 step-ups a minute. Step-ups give a standard unit of exercise which can act as a control (1.7) with which other forms can be compared.

Measurements and observations of the changes brought about by exercise should include: pulse rate (3.8); breathing rate (breaths per minute) and observations on the use of ribs and diaphragm (3.6); observations on skin condition (flushing, sweating, see below). The effects of a standard exercise, say 30 step-ups in 2 minutes, can then be compared with other exercises, such as 60 step-ups, sprinting 50 m and playing a fast-moving game for 5 minutes.

Safety note: at no time should children or adults attempt to measure the volume of air breathed, either in total or with each breath. Measurements of this kind, especially with young children, should be made only under medical supervision. If any children participating in an investigation show signs of distress, they should stop exercising immediately and rest under observation by a responsible adult.

The main short-term changes likely to be observed after exercise are: increase in the pulse rate; increase in the breathing rate; change in breathing action with more use of the rib-cage; flushing of the skin; sweating. To explain such observations requires three related chains of reasoning, but can be used as a very effective example of the way in which scientific understanding is built up using observations, existing knowledge and information obtained from elsewhere.

Exercise and heart rate. During exercise the body is moved much more in each minute than when at rest, so the work-rate of the muscles which move the body increases, which requires them to transfer energy at a faster rate (12.1). Energy transfer in living tissue is brought about by respiration, which requires oxygen, so the demand for oxygen also increases. Oxygen is delivered to the muscles by the blood. Increased oxygen demand requires the heart to increase the blood supply to the muscles, which it does by beating faster.

Exercise and breathing. An increased rate of respiration in muscles increases not only the demand for oxygen, but also the rate at which the waste gas carbon dioxide is produced. Increased carbon dioxide in the blood is detected by the brain, which stimulates the muscles responsible for breathing (3.6) to work more rapidly and vigorously, so increasing the breathing rate and volume of air taken in with each breath.

Exercise, heating and cooling. The increased activity of the muscles causes them to become heated by work (12.3) so their temperature rises. This causes them to heat the blood flowing through them, which if not controlled would lead to over-heating of the body and possibly to brain damage. The increase in blood temperature is detected by the brain, which controls the blood flow to different parts of the body. More blood is diverted to flow through the skin, which becomes hot and flushed as a result. The hot skin heats the air around it, so both it and the blood are cooled. At the same time, the sweat glands in the skin produce a thin film of perspiration on the skin, which evaporates (6.3), so cooling the skin and the blood still further.

Longer-term effects of exercise. In the longer term, consistent moderate exercise has many beneficial effects on both children and adults. The ability to continue exerting oneself (stamina) and levels of performance increase, while the action of the heart, breathing and circulation all become more efficient. Moderate exercise, coupled with a balanced diet, can also make a major contribution to reducing obesity or preventing it altogether (3.4).

3.10: Senses, response and control

One of the most distinctive features of living things is the way they respond to changes so that their chances of survival are usually increased. Many responses of animals are to changes in their own bodies. One important set of these, which children can investigate, are the changes in breathing, pulse rate and the body's cooling system brought about by exercise (3.9). Other responses are to changes in the environment. Humans, like other animals, use specialized sense organs to detect changes and to gather information about their surroundings. There are five sense modes:

Vision: the eye forms images from light entering it.

Hearing: the ear responds to sound.

Smell: the lining inside the top of the nose detects chemical vapours and gases breathed in.

Taste: the tongue (usually together with the sense of smell) detects substances in solution in the mouth.

Touch: a range of sensory organs, both in the skin and in most parts of the body, respond to touch, pressure and temperature change.

In all cases, what the sense organs do is generate a very complex set of messages in the form of nerve impulses (see below). These travel through nerves to the brain. Through investigation and learning, much of which is carried on through play in early childhood, humans learn to recognize and remember thousands of items of information about things as diverse as the faces of familiar people, the sound of different musical instruments, the scent of roses, the taste of strawberries and the difference in the textures of silk and sandpaper.

At primary level, children's learning about their senses is likely to focus less on the sense organs themselves than on a wide range of experience, learning to identify and distinguish in all the sense modes, and the vocabulary associated with these activities. Examples could include colour matching, discrimination and naming; identifying the sources of different sounds, musical and other; matching smells and flavours (eyes shut) with their sources (eyes open); identifying and describing the forms and textures of objects felt but not seen. Of all human senses, sight is for most people the most important, and for children it is the sense which they can investigate, and with which they investigate, more than any other, so attention is focused on it here, with some additional notes on the other senses.

Vision. The eye focuses light entering it (17.1) into an image on the sensitive lining at the back of the eyeball (Fig. 3.4). The image is upside-down, and seeing the right way up (i.e. so that sight and touch match up) is learned in very early childhood. Focusing the light and forming an image means bending the light rays by refraction (17.6). Most of this is done by the curved front of the eye. The lens, whose shape can be changed, is only for fine adjustment. This is why people whose eye lens has become opaque (cataract) and been removed can still see with very thick-lensed spectacles or a plastic replacement lens in the eye.

The coloured part of the eye (iris) surrounds a black hole (pupil), through which light enters the eyeball behind. Our ability to see clearly in a wide range of light conditions depends partly on the response of the iris. In bright light the iris expands, making the pupil smaller and preventing too much light entering the eye. In dim light the iris contracts outwards, enlarging the pupil and allowing more light in. Children can easily see these changes by observing each others' eyes, but they should never shine a light into an eye, either their own or anyone else's. It is thought that the detailed pattern of colour in each person's iris is unique to them,

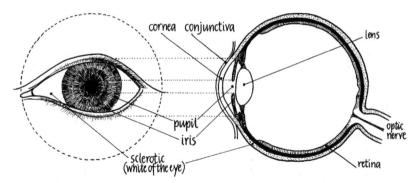

Figure 3.4 *The eye as we see it, related to a section of the eyeball. The cornea and conjunctiva together form the clear, curved front of the eyeball. Notice how little of the eye is normally exposed: this helps to protect it*

and in the future this may be widely used as a means of identification.

The layer at the back of the eye (retina) contains two kinds of light-sensitive cells: rods, which respond to light and dark; and cones, which respond to colour (17.8). When light falls on these cells it causes a complex series of energy transfers (12.2), which result in electrical signals to the brain. Cones do not respond strongly unless the light is quite bright, so in poor light conditions we see mainly in shades of grey with very little colour. Colour-blindness, which often runs in families (i.e. is hereditary, 2.4), occurs when some or all of the cone-cells do not respond normally to particular colours of light.

We see clearly only a very small part of the scene in front of us, on which our gaze is fixed. This can be shown by enlarging some text on a photocopier and trying to read a line without moving the eyes at all: only a few letters can be seen clearly enough to read them. The picture we have of our whole field of vision is built up by the brain, which directs very rapid scanning movements of the eyes. These can be seen by giving a person a large and interesting picture to look at, then watching their eyes move as they explore it visually and learn about it.

Mammals and birds which feed by hunting (predators, 5.7) have eyes at the front of the head. This enables them, by looking at the same object with both eyes at once, to judge how far away it is; an obvious advantage when chasing or pouncing on prey. This is binocular vision, which can easily be investigated by trying to decide whether similar objects are the same distance away, or which is slightly nearer, with both eyes open and then with one eye shut. Comparing success rates usually shows clearly the dependence of judging distance on binocular vision.

Hearing. Apart from the external ear or pinna, the ear is wholly internal and so cannot be observed, but there are nevertheless some simple observations which children can carry out which will help them understand their hearing better. The pinna acts as a funnel, directing sound waves (16.1) into the tunnel leading to the eardrum, but normally humans can hear sounds from all round them. In contrast, many animals use and move their external ears much more than humans do, in order to increase sensitivity and locate the source of a sound. This can be experienced by making an ear-trumpet from a cone of thin card with a small opening at the narrow end. Placed carefully in the ear, this makes it possible to hear sounds further away than normal, but hearing then becomes much more directional so the area from which sounds can be heard is smaller.

The sensitivity of different people's hearing can be compared by holding the source of a soft sound, such as a ticking watch, at differing distances from the ear in a very quiet room and finding how far away it can be heard. Judging where a sound is coming from can also be investigated, first with both ears open and then with one muffled. As with vision, both ears have to receive sound (binaural hearing) for the direction of the source to be judged accurately. Both investigations offer excellent opportunities for devising 'fair testing' procedures (1.7) and for finding how widely different people's perceptions vary.

Smell and taste are linked. Apart from four basic tastes (sweet, sour, salt and bitter), the detection of flavour requires the nose membranes to be active as well as the tongue. This can easily be shown by sucking a peppermint. With the nostrils pinched it merely tastes sweet, and the peppermint flavour is detected only when air can flow up from the mouth and out through the nose. Mapping the areas on the tongue which respond to the four basic tastes is often described as a simple investigation, but without quite elaborate experimental design and precautions (for example, blind trials and washing the mouth after every tasting) the results are almost certainly bogus.

Touch is in fact three senses, each with its sensory organs in the skin and tongue. Near the skin surface are the nerve-endings which respond to temperature change and register pain if the skin is injured. The skin is temperature-sensitive, but not in the way that a thermometer is: it is change in temperature, rather than degrees of hot and cold, which is felt. This can be shown by the classic demonstration of dipping one hand (not just one finger) into hot water and the other in cold for two minutes, then moving both to tepid water and observing the sensation registered by each.

Contact sensors are near the surface of the skin, but their distribution over the body is very uneven. There are far more in each square centimetre of the skin on the fingertips than any other part of the body except the tongue and lips, so the skin there is correspondingly more sensitive, an adaptation (5.5) to the extensive use of the hands for manipulation of tools and materials. This can be shown by pushing pins into either end of a bottle cork: one at one end and three, about 5 mm apart in a triangle, at the other. Touching the skin on different parts of the body with the single pin or three at once, and finding whether the subject can tell the difference, demonstrates variations in sensitivity. It is also useful to compare the lower lip with the cheek and the tongue, and to extend the investigation by using different numbers and patterns of pins.

The third kind of touch is sensitivity to pressure. The sensors which register this are much deeper in the skin, and provide information on how hard the skin is pressed against a solid object. This in turn is very useful when using the hands to manipulate tools and materials by squeezing, pulling, bending and twisting them (7.1).

Our sense of touch is linked in everyday actions with our awareness of exactly where our body parts are in relation to each other. For example, even with their eyes shut, most children know very accurately where their hands are in relation to their heads. This awareness is made possible by stretch receptors in muscles which tell us not only how far limbs are extended and in what direction, but also how hard our muscles are pulling (3.5). Gymnasts and dancers, in particular, develop this kinaesthetic awareness to a very high degree.

The brain and nervous system. The main way the various parts of the body have of communicating is by way of the nervous system. The central parts of the nervous system are the brain in the skull and the spinal cord in the backbone, from which nerves branch out to every part of the body. They carry information both to and from the brain, in the form of tiny electric currents, which are conducted chemically, in quite a different way from metallic conductors (13.2). The brain receives and co-ordinates a very large amount of information from all parts of the body and sends nerve impulses back which control all the main body activities.

The activities of which we are usually most aware are those which we can control consciously, such as walking, picking up a pen or catching a ball. This kind of activity is called voluntary action, because we can choose when and whether we do it. In contrast, a great many activities on which our lives depend go on without our having any control over them or, in many cases, even being aware of them. These are called involuntary actions and examples include peristalsis in the gut (3.3) and the pumping of blood by the heart (3.8). The regulation of breathing involves both kinds of activity: although we have some voluntary control over it (holding the breath, for example) an involuntary control takes over when we are asleep or under stress from severe exertion.

A third kind of control is most often associated with emergencies, when very fast response is needed to prevent or minimize injury. When the hand is accidentally put onto a sharp or very hot object, for example, it is jerked away before pain is felt. This is a reflex action, and is so fast because an 'emergency' message goes to the central nervous system and a return signal is sent back immediately, in this case to the arm muscles. Only later, when signals reach the main part of the brain, is pain felt. Other examples of reflex actions include the coughing reflex when solid or liquid enter the windpipe (3.3), and blinking when something moves very fast near the eye. Because the whole point of most reflexes is to prevent damage, this kind of action is something to know about rather than experiment with.

3.11: Growth

Apart from their bony skeletons, the bodies of animals with backbones, unlike those of plants (4.3), tend to grow all over rather than at particular places. The more obvious kind of growth is growth in size, which involves the building up of new living

tissue from materials provided by digested food (3.3) and delivered by the blood
(3.7). Because more complex structures are being built up from simple chemicals,
energy transfer from respiration (3.6) is also needed. The main food needed for
growth is protein, so if the diet of children is deficient in protein their growth is
likely to be retarded. They are also likely to have other health problems because
their resistance to disease is low.

As children grow in size they are also carrying on a less obvious kind of growth: tissue replacement, which continues throughout life. Most living tissues, especially if
they are very active, need constant replacement and repair if they are to continue
working properly, and this goes on all the time in most parts of the body, even in children. Once adulthood has been reached, growth by replacement and repair continues,
even though increase in size slows down and stops. This explains why adults as well as
children continue to need protein in their diet. If adequate supplies of protein are not
available, tissue replacement is either reduced or stopped altogether, so tissues such as
muscle waste away, and the undernourished adult becomes weak and emaciated.

Growth is controlled by a range of chemicals (hormones) made by the body
under control from the brain. From birth to adulthood the balance of hormones
changes, so that there is not only overall growth but also specialized development
such as the changes at puberty which lead to sexual maturity.

3.12: Reproduction

Reproduction can be viewed as a specialized kind of growth which leads to the formation of new individuals. In mammals, birds and other animals with backbones
(5.1) reproduction is exclusively sexual (2.3), an egg-cell produced by the female being
fertilized by a sperm from the male. In most fish and other backboned animals which
breed in water (apart from mammals such as seals and whales), the male releases a
fluid containing sperm into the water as the female lays the eggs, so fertilization
occurs outside the female's body. This is not possible for animals which breed on land,
because the egg-cells and sperm must be protected from drying up. As a result, land-
breeding animals have developed a variety of ways by which sperm can be introduced
into the female's body during mating, so that the egg-cells can be fertilized internally.
In birds, for example, fertilization takes place some time before egg laying. The fertilized egg-cell is then supplied with a large amount of food (white and yolk) and covered in a protective shell before being laid and then incubated. In nearly all mammals,
the fertilized egg develops inside the body of the female until birth.

Development and maintenance of the human foetus. In humans, the fertilized
egg becomes embedded in the lining of the womb (uterus). There it develops into
two main parts: the baby (foetus) and a special structure (placenta) to maintain it,
which grows into the wall of the uterus. The foetus and placenta are joined by the
umbilical cord. Blood from the foetus circulates through the cord to the placenta

and back again; blood from the mother through the lining of the uterus. A two-way exchange is set up, by which the foetus is supplied with digested food and oxygen from the mother's blood, while its waste products, including carbon dioxide, are transferred to the mother's blood for removal. The foetus, surrounded by a sac of watery fluid which helps to protect it, is totally dependent on the mother.

Birth. The wall of the uterus is mostly muscle, which as the foetus develops becomes thicker and stronger as well as larger. The baby is born by being pushed out of the uterus as the very powerful muscles contract and force it down the birth canal (vagina). As the baby is born, a lot of changes happen very quickly. Blood supply to the placenta is cut off and the circulation of blood to the baby's lungs takes over. The baby takes a first, very large, breath to fill its lungs with air, and cries loudly. This is a reflex action which helps to expand its lungs fully and get its breathing muscles working. The umbilical cord is cut and tied to prevent infection and any leakage of blood. The cord has no nerve supply, so neither the mother nor the baby is hurt by this. Later, the placenta detaches itself from the lining of the uterus and is expelled from the birth canal as the afterbirth. Some days later, the end of the cord left on the baby withers and drops off, forming the scar tissue called the umbilicus or tummy-button.

Parental care. Baby mammals vary very much at birth in how far they have developed and what they can do. The young of plant-eating herd animals such as cattle, deer, sheep and horses can stand and move with the herd within a very short time. In complete contrast, the young of flesh-eaters and other animals which have secure refuges (dogs, cats and rabbits, for example) are blind and completely helpless at birth and for some weeks afterwards. All mammals, however, care for their young to a very high degree. Mammals are the only animals which feed their young with milk, an emulsion (6.4) of fats in water which also contains proteins and other foods in solution. Its mother's milk is under normal circumstances the best food for any young mammal because it is not only a perfectly balanced diet, but also helps to complete development of the baby's resistance to disease (immune system).

Most mammals and birds do not merely feed their young, but also teach them skills they need for survival, such as how to find food and how to fit into a social group. It is interesting and revealing to compare patterns of reproduction and parental care in different animals. A frog, for example, lays several hundred small eggs but does not care for them at all. A blackbird lays between three and six much larger eggs and not only incubates them, but feeds the chicks after hatching, teaches them to fly and helps them to begin looking for their own food. A human mother usually has one baby at a time, which is very large in comparison with her own size, and which in favourable circumstances is cared for within a social group (typically, the family) for many years. This pattern can be reinforced by looking at other examples, but is clear: at one end of the scale, animals have many small young with no parental care, relying on big numbers and chance for some to survive. At the other extreme, only one large offspring is produced at a time, is fed, cared for and taught for many years in order to give it the best possible chance of survival. Humans are right at one extreme of this pattern of reproduction, and understanding this can contribute to personal and social education.

Human babies, though not blind at birth, are helpless, and their development in all cultures is longer and more complex than that of any other animal. It is most likely to be successful when the baby is born into a social group whose members care for and help each other. This is why, even at the biological level, families or other stable social groups within which children grow up are not a luxury or an optional extra: they are an essential part of our survival strategy as a species.

3.13: Tobacco, alcohol, drugs and their abuse

The following notes are intended only as a guide to the main concepts which are needed for a basic understanding of how these harmful substances affect the body and behaviour. Education in this area is complex and sensitive and, with the exception of tobacco and the effects of smoking, which can usefully be discussed in connection with work on breathing (3.6) and blood circulation (3.8), should not be undertaken without special training or guidance. It is essential for non-specialist teachers to obtain up-to-date information on substance abuse from health promotion agencies and the police, who may also be able to offer advice and help on appropriate teaching.

Tobacco, alcohol and other drugs are substances which all have marked effects on the way the body works, a person's behaviour, or both. Tobacco and alcohol are exceptional in that their consumption by adults is still legal, whereas that of other 'soft' and 'hard' drugs is illegal unless they are used, as some are, under medical supervision. All these substances are potentially harmful, but vary very much in their effects. A minority, of which alcohol is one, do not seem harmful in small quantities unless taken under the wrong circumstances, for example before driving a car. They are, however, harmful in excess. The majority are always dangerous, either because they can have unpredictable and lethal side-effects or because, like tobacco, they damage the body and impair health when taken in any quantity. The main reasons why these substances are grouped together, and regarded as potentially or actually dangerous, is that anyone taking them regularly will develop a tolerance of them and may become dependent on them, with consequences for their health and personal life which may range from the unpleasant to the disastrous.

Tolerance. When tobacco smoke, alcohol or a drug is taken for the first time, it produces an effect on the way the body works, on behaviour, or both. This may be pleasant, but more often is unpleasant: first doses of most of these substances produce nausea and quite often induce vomiting. If the substance is taken repeatedly, however, the body adjusts to it and a tolerance to it is built up. One effect of tolerance is that the effects of the substance are reduced: a greater dose has to be taken in order to produce the same effect as before. This is easily observable in people who drink alcohol or smoke tobacco in an attempt to relieve tension or anxiety: if not consciously checked, their consumption increases. This property of inducing tolerance by the body and the need to increase consumption as a result is one reason why tobacco, alcohol and drugs are regarded as being dangerous.

Dependence develops as a result of tolerance, when a person cannot work or behave in what they regard as a normal way without repeated doses of the substance. Dependence is shown by a person's behaviour or physical state when the substance is not taken at all, or is taken in smaller quantities than their habitual dose. If their behaviour is affected, for example by anxiety, bad temper or depression, they are said to have an emotional or psychological dependence. If their physical state is affected so they have withdrawal symptoms such as pain, vomiting, or uncontrolled shaking, they have a physical dependence, which is also called addiction.

Although there are differences between emotional and physical dependence, they are closely related. Experimenting with any potentially harmful substances is very dangerous (and illegal), but individuals most at risk are those who are vulnerable in other ways. Severe physical and emotional dependences, and substance abuse generally, are closely linked to social and psychological factors such as boredom, anxiety, despair, lack of a feeling of personal worth and the desire to become or be seen as one of a high-status social group.

Tobacco and smoking. Because smoking is not illegal and still (though decreasingly) socially acceptable, smoking is often not regarded as an example of substance abuse, but it should be. Tobacco smoke, whether inhaled directly or from someone else's cigarette, is harmful in any quantity.

Tobacco smoke is a complex mixture, but the substance in it which has the most effect on the body is nicotine. The nicotine content of smoke is variable, and is measured by collecting the sticky residue (tar) from smoke, so cigarettes are classified in health warnings according to their tar content: the higher the tar, the more harmful the cigarette. In the short term, cigarette smoke causes the air passages of the lung to pull inwards and become smaller, so breathing becomes more difficult. At the same time it reduces the amount of oxygen the blood can carry. It also prevents the lining of the lung from clearing itself naturally of dust and other irritants, and causes it to make more of the liquid (mucus) on its lining.

The long-term effects of smoking may take years to develop, but are usually severe and very often fatal. A large-scale survey published in 1994 estimated that half of all adult smokers die as a direct result of smoking, and that the others are likely to be disabled by it. The main effects are lung cancer, which results from chemicals in tobacco smoke causing genetic mutation of normal cells into cancerous ones (5.5), emphysema, chronic bronchitis and coronary heart disease. Pregnant women who smoke also risk damaging their babies.

Emphysema is the breakdown of the fine air-sacs in the lungs which are responsible for the absorption of oxygen. These are weakened by the smoke, then further damaged and burst by violent coughing brought about by bronchitis (see below). The result is that the lung can take in only a small fraction of the oxygen it normally does, so the sufferer becomes out of breath after only the smallest exertion.

Bronchitis. Because the air-tubes (bronchi) in the lung are irritated by smoke, they make more of the slimy fluid (mucus) which normally covers them. At the same time they are prevented from working to clear themselves as they normally do. The result is that the smoker has to try to clear the lungs by coughing. This irritates the air-tubes still further, causing bronchitis and greatly increasing the likelihood of infection (pneumonia). It may also contribute to the development of emphysema (see above). Over 95 per cent of people suffering from chronic (i.e. constant) bronchitis are smokers.

Coronary heart disease. Smoking increases the tendency for arteries (3.8) to become blocked with fatty deposits. This can lead to obstruction of blood flow in any part of the body and 95 per cent of people with diseases of their leg arteries are smokers. If the heart's own blood supply is blocked, the result is a heart attack. About 25 per cent of all deaths from heart attacks are thought to be as a result of smoking.

Lung cancer. Cancer is caused when cells mutate (5.5) and the normal control over the rate of growth of a tissue is destroyed. If this is untreated the tissue grows uncontrollably, usually forming lumps of cancerous tissue (tumours) which make it impossible for that part of the body to work properly. Some kinds of cancer can be caused by chemicals (carcinogens), and tobacco smoke contains at least 17 different ones. Tumours develop in the air-passages of the lung, so making part of the lung useless. Ninety per cent of lung cancer is caused by smoking, and even inhaling other people's smoke (passive smoking) is harmful. A person who smokes any cigarettes is 8 times more likely to die of lung cancer than a non-smoker; if 20 cigarettes are smoked every day the risk is 13 times greater.

Smoking and pregnancy. Smoking reduces the capacity of the blood to carry oxygen. Probably as a result of this, babies born to women who smoke during pregnancy are on average smaller than those of non-smoking mothers, and more of them die in the first year of life. Smoking during pregnancy also carries a higher risk of stillbirth or miscarriage.

Advice on smoking. For both children and adults, basic advice on smoking is simple: if you haven't started smoking, don't; if you have, give up now. If you can't stop on your own, seek help. The idea that smoking when young damages a person for life and that they might as well carry on is entirely false. If a person who smokes twenty cigarettes a day stops smoking entirely, after ten years the risk of disease will have reduced to the same level as a non-smoker of the same age.

4
Plants

4.1: Plants as living things: observing and recording change

Many children and some adults have difficulty in believing that plants are alive because they show no obvious activity: they don't appear to 'do anything'. This belief is unlikely to be refuted or replaced quickly, and it is important not to assume that children have a scientific concept of plants as alive, but rather to investigate plants, wherever possible, in such a way that their ability to grow, respond and reproduce (2.3) is emphasized. This always means observing how plants change over time (2.2), but even when this principle is familiar and accepted, the belief may still persist that although plants are alive, they are somehow less alive than animals are.

Plant activity can usually be observed only by recording change, but this is compensated for by the ease with which many plants can be cultivated, even in the rather inhospitable environment of the classroom. Work in this area provides excellent opportunities for recording in a variety of modes. When growing and responding, plants change in size and shape. This can be recorded by drawing, photography and measurement, which are made much more reliable if a leaf or stem is marked harmlessly, for example with a small dot of white correcting fluid, to provide a reference-point.

Height, number of leaves and length of stem between leaves can all be simply recorded in tables. Changes in the shape of growing leaves can be recorded and, if necessary, their area measured, by drawing round them carefully on squared paper. A decorative alternative is to spray a water-soluble dye such as 'Brusho' onto paper with a leaf pressed gently to it. Dye can then be washed off the leaf, which should continue to grow normally, while the 'shadow' of the leaf on the paper provides a permanent record of its shape.

From their active growing points (4.3), many plants produce sequences of very similar leaves or flowers, arranged at intervals down the stem. Because the youngest parts are nearest the tip, shoots and flower-spikes of this kind form what is in effect a time-sequence, showing the way in which the parts develop. Once the principle of growth and change with time is well established, these can be used very effectively to observe development, particularly that of flowers and fruits (4.5).

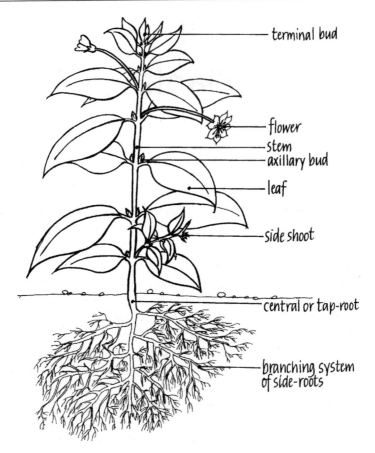

terminal bud

flower
stem
axillary bud

leaf

side shoot

central or tap-root

branching system
of side-roots

Figure 4.1 *The main parts of a flowering plant. The part of the plant above ground is the shoot system; the part below ground is the root system. The side-shoot and flowers have developed from axillary buds.*

4.2: Basic structure and function in flowering plants

The basic structure of flowering plants (other kinds of plant are briefly discussed in 5.2) can be understood in terms of a central axis, with specialized parts growing from it. Fig. 4.1 is a diagram of a generalized flowering plant. No actual plant is exactly like this, but the diagram can usefully be thought of as a basic construction plan on which many variations are possible. It is then a useful reference-point when trying to understand the forms of particular plants and identify their parts. In most plants that children will observe, but not all, the part above ground is the shoot system; the part below ground, the root system.

Stem. In a shoot system the central axis is the stem. This supports the leaves so that they can exchange gases with the air and absorb light energy in order to make food (4.4), and the flowers in positions where they are likely to be pollinated (4.5). Stems also transport water and mineral nutrients (4.3) from the root system (see below) to the leaves and flowers. In many plants the stems are upright or branching, but in others they creep along the ground and may take root, so allowing the plant to colonize and reproduce itself (4.5).

Support, water supply and transport. In order to support leaves and flowers effectively, upright or branching stems need a remarkable combination of mechanical properties (Chapter 7). They must be stiff enough to support the weight of the shoot system as a whole, but flexible enough to bend and so avoid damage when the wind blows or animals push past them. They need to be elastic so that they will spring up again after they have been bent over, and very tough, so that if they are damaged they do not break off short and there is a possibility that they could repair themselves and carry on growing. In woody plants, the stems live for many years and grow in thickness, becoming harder, increasingly strong and very tough, as the trunks and branches of trees.

All stems gain strength and toughness from their fibre-tissues, which also lend the same qualities to materials made from them, such as paper, card and some kinds of string. However, in both leaves and younger stems, water has a very important part to play in supporting the plant. Soft plant tissues are full of watery sap, which makes them quite stiff but also springy and elastic in bending (7.4–7.6). This stiffness not only keeps the plant upright but also keeps leaves held out so that they can intercept sunlight for photosynthesis (4.4). The importance of water can be seen if the plant loses too much by evaporation. Leaves and young stems wilt and droop down, and if the plant cannot obtain water within a short time, it may die.

As well as being partly supported by it, stems transport water upwards from the root system to the leaves and flowers, together with nutrient chemicals (4.3). Water evaporates from the shoot system and more, with nutrients in solution, is pulled up through a specialized tissue (xylem) to replace it. In trees and other woody plants, the xylem of older stems is the wood. Transport of food is more complex. It is carried out by a specialized tissue (phloem), which in trees forms part of the bark. In a tree during the growing season, food is transported down from the leaves for use or storage, but also upwards to growing shoots, flowers and developing fruits. In trees in spring, large amounts of stored food are moved up through the bark again, to provide materials and energy for the growth of new leaves (see also 4.4).

Leaf. The leaf is part of the shoot system. Leaves develop on the sides of stems, by which they are supported and supplied with water. Leaves can usually be distinguished because each has a bud (axillary bud) in the angle between its base and the stem (Fig. 4.1). The overall flat, thin form of most leaves is an adaptation (5.5) for their main function of making food by photosynthesis (4.4). Their form allows them to take in light energy and exchange gases with the air very efficiently. At the same time, all parts of the leaf have to be supplied with water and need a transport system to carry away the foods they have made to other parts of the plant. Both are provided by the midrib and veins of the leaf which form a branching network system, easily seen with a hand-lens in a leaf held up to the light. The midrib and veins, like the stem, also have tough fibre tissues which help them to support and strengthen the thin leafblade without making it too stiff. As a result, leaves are flexible: they can bend and move easily in air currents and remain undamaged unless the wind is very severe.

Deciduous and evergreen trees. In many parts of the world plants have a problem in obtaining enough water during part of the year, usually in the dry or cold season. Large plants such as trees solve this problem in two ways. Deciduous trees and shrubs shed all their leaves for part of the year, so that each leaf lives only for six to nine months. Evergreens, in contrast, have leaves which live for longer than a year but which are protected from drying up in a variety of ways. Some (for example holly, ivy and rhododendron) have a thick, glossy wax coating, while others are needle-like (pine and other conifers) or tiny scales (heather). A common misconception is that the leaves of evergreens are not shed because large amounts of food are stored in them, but this is not so: evergreens store food in their stems and roots just as deciduous trees do (4.4). They do shed leaves every year, but because each one lives for longer than a year, they are not usually shed all at once.

Flower. Flowers are special shoots whose function is sexual reproduction (4.5). Their various parts can be seen most easily in simple, open flowers such as the buttercup and tulip (Fig. 4.2 a, b). In the buttercup flower, the outermost parts (sepals) form a protective jacket round the flower-bud as it develops. The tulip has no sepals, but its petals are thicker and tougher, so they protect the inner parts of the flower in a similar way. Flowers pollinated by insects (4.5) need to attract them. To do this their petals may have bright colour, scent and make a sugary liquid (nectar).

Inside the petals are the reproductive parts of the flower. The male parts (stamens) each consist of a stalk (filament) carrying a small sac (anther) which makes the male sex-cells (pollen). The filament holds the anther in such a way that an insect visiting the flower is likely to brush against and carry pollen away to another flower. The central part of the flower is the female part (ovary) in which the seeds will develop if pollination is successful (4.5). The ovary may be made up of many small, separate parts (carpels), as in the buttercup, or the carpels may be joined together to form a single structure, as in the tulip. The ovary, or each separate part of it, has a special receptive area (stigma) which receives pollen and so is often sticky. The sticky stigma of a tulip flower is particularly large and easy to see. In many flowers the stigma is held on a stalk (style) in such a position that an insect visiting the flower is likely to brush against it, before it reaches the stamens, and leave pollen from another flower on it. The bluebell is one flower which shows this clearly.

Buds and bulbs. A bud is a shoot whose stem has not grown in length and whose leaves have not expanded, so they are tightly packed together. A Brussels sprout is

a : buttercup : cut in half

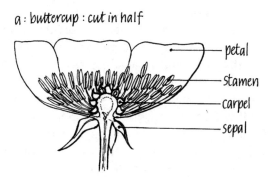

petal

stamen

carpel

sepal

b : tulip : 3 petals and stamens removed

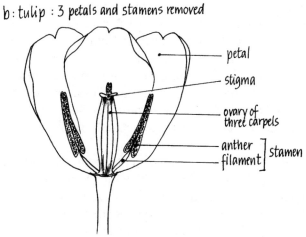

petal

stigma

ovary of three carpels

anther ⎤
filament ⎦ stamen

Figure 4.2 *Parts of flowers*

an example of a large bud which is also edible. Most buds found at the bases of leaves are much smaller than this, but once they start to grow they will form shoot systems. A good way to see buds develop is to take cuttings and root them in water or compost. Suitable plants include willow twigs in late winter, pelargoniums ('geraniums') in late summer, and varieties of Tradescantia at almost any time.

In some plants, buds grow large and make specialized kinds of shoots. One kind, which children can easily plant and see growing, are the bulbs of hyacinths, daffodils, tulips and onions. These are specialized underground shoots which are greatly enlarged buds. The fleshy scales are the leaves, which store food and water. They are joined to the stem, which is the 'plate' at the base of the bulb, from the bottom edge of which the roots also grow. Each year, new leaves grow from the centre. Their tops are the green leaves we usually see; their bases are the juicy storage leaves which make up the bulk of the bulb. When these grow old and die they form the brown papery 'skin' which helps to protect the bulb. The corms of crocuses are rather similar, except that the bulk of the corm is a short, stout stem.

Root system. The root system of plants is usually underground, because its main functions are to exploit the soil in order to meet the plant's needs. In most plants, the root system anchors the plant in the soil, providing the shoot system with stability and support; absorbs water and mineral nutrients from the soil (4.3); and transports these to the base of the shoot system. Some roots also store large amounts of food, transported to them from the leaves by the stem.

Roots have as many different forms as shoots have. Some plants have a large central tap-root in which food is stored: carrot and parsnip are examples. Others have a central root when young, which branches out as the plant develops to exploit increasingly large volumes of soil, in order to meet the needs of the expanding shoot system. On a small scale, this kind of root system can be seen in bean plants, which are easily grown in the classroom (4.3), while on a larger scale it is developed by most trees. Some other plants such as grasses never have a central root at all, but develop a highly branched system of slender, fibrous roots.

In many plants, roots can develop directly from stems. This is what gardeners hope will happen when they take cuttings, but it also happens naturally when plants such as strawberries and creeping buttercup send out runners to colonize new areas (4.5). Ivy is a plant which climbs by means of roots, which grow out of its stem into cracks in walls or tree-bark. These aerial roots do not absorb any water: their only function is support. Roots also grow directly from stems when a bulb (see above) grows roots from its base.

Some plants have 'roots' which are not roots at all. Iris and Solomon's seal, for example, have a stout, slowly creeping stock which looks like a root, but is actually a stem (rhizome) because it has buds from which green shoots and flowers develop. It also has roots growing from it which anchor the whole plant and take up water in the usual way. Ginger is a rhizome used in cooking.

Roots as anchorage. In order to anchor plants effectively in windy conditions roots, like stems, have to be tough and flexible, but their main strength needs to be in withstanding pulling rather than bending forces (7.4). When plants such as trees grow for many years and develop large shoot systems, their root systems are usually about equal in size. In an oak tree, for example, the roots do not usually go as deep as the shoots are high, but spread a good deal further, giving the tree a broad, stable base. Like the trunk and branches, the roots of trees grow in thickness, becoming woody, strong and extremely tough to support the great weight of the plant above ground.

Absorption: root-hairs. Apart from support, the main function of roots is the taking up of water and mineral nutrients (4.3) from the soil. To do this effectively, the outer layer of a growing root develops, just behind its tip, what looks like a covering of white fur. This is made up of root-hairs: very slender outgrowths which can push between soil particles as they grow, providing a huge area through which water can be absorbed. Root-hairs can easily be seen by cutting small slits in a thin sheet of plastic foam, putting a cress seed in each, soaking the foam in water and hanging it inside a jar with the lid on. As the seeds germinate and their roots grow out, they will form root-hairs in the humid air, so children can see them easily. In most plants, root-hairs are short-lived. They grow only on new, extending roots and last only a few weeks. The advantage of this for the plant is that the soil it is exploiting for water and nutrients is continually changing, so a good supply can be maintained.

4.3: Plant growth

A major difference between the growth of plants and that of animals, which children can easily observe, is that whereas animals grow all over, the roots and shoots of plants grow in particular places. The most obvious growth is at shoot tips, where new leaves or flowers are forming, expanding and being moved apart as the stem grows longer, but observation of seedlings (see below) will show that roots grow at their tips in a similar way.

In long-lived woody plants (trees and shrubs), stems and roots become thicker all over, but here again all the growth comes from a special layer (cambium), just inside the bark. This produces wood to the inside and bark to the outside. Because wood is not produced in winter it grows in layers (annual rings) with a more or less distinct line between one season's growth and the next. Bark can easily be stripped from most woody twigs in spring and summer, because the cambium is active, soft and easily pulled apart. As tree trunks grow in thickness, the expanding wood stretches the outer layers of the bark so that they split, forming furrows or peeling off in pieces.

Seeds and germination. Seeds are the product of sexual reproduction in flowering plants and conifers (4.5). The seed is an undeveloped plant (embryo), with a store of food, in a protective coat. Many plants are grown for their edible seeds. In a cereal grain, for example, the food store is mostly carbohydrate (starch), the embryo is a source of protein and the protective seed-coat provides us with dietary fibre (3.4). Most seeds are fairly hard, dry and apparently inactive: they are alive, but dormant (2.2). In order to become active, the seed has to be in conditions which are favourable for growth. Some seeds need special conditions to break their dormancy, but for most the three conditions needed are: a supply of water, a supply of air and a suitable temperature.

The early phase of a seed's growth is known as germination. The best seeds for children to observe are large ones, such as broad beans. These can be grown in jars lined with absorbent paper and then filled with sand. Seeds pushed down between the paper and jar are held firmly, and watering can be carried out easily by keeping the sand damp. Root and shoot growth will proceed in a more natural way if the jar is shaded with black paper.

It is difficult to show that air is needed for germination, but showing that water is needed is simple: if the seeds remain dry, they never germinate. The importance of temperature can be shown by placing soaked seeds in a refrigerator, with a control batch in the classroom. The seeds in the cold will not germinate until they are brought into warmer conditions. It should also be noted that, although light is needed for healthy plant growth, it is not needed for germination of most seeds, which will readily begin their growth in the dark.

The first phase of germination is water uptake. Beans can be measured, weighed and drawn before and after having been soaked in water for 24 hours, to show the large quantity of water they absorb. Water enables the embryo to become active and start digesting the food reserves of the seed so that these can be used for growth and respiration. The first sign of growth is usually the splitting of the seed-coat as the root (radicle) begins to emerge. In most seeds the root grows out before the shoot, to provide anchorage and absorb water. When the root emerges from a bean, children will be able to see whether they have planted the seed the right way up, i.e. so that its root points down as it emerges. If not, the root will respond by turning as it grows until it points down; an example of plants' response (see below).

The shoot, which usually emerges some days after the root, responds in the opposite way: if upside-down, it will turn as it grows to point up. The emerging shoot is bent over, so that as it pushes up through the soil the delicate leaves in the bud at its tip will not be damaged. As it emerges into the light the shoot-tip unbends and the leaves start to expand. As the shoot of the seedling grows, the root system will also be expanding, branching out so that it can absorb more water and nutrients to support the rapid growth of the whole plant.

Many seeds have their food-store in two very thick structures which are actually leaves. In some, such as the broad bean, these seed-leaves (cotyledons) stay in the ground during germination, but in others such as the sunflower they emerge as the first green leaves of the shoot: thick, rounded and quite unlike the leaves which develop later.

Conditions for healthy plant growth. The conditions under which plants will continue to grow well are similar to those needed for germination, but with two additional requirements. Because seeds have a food-store they can germinate and begin to grow with no more than a supply of water and air. To sustain growth in the long term the plant has to be able to make food by photosynthesis, and for this light is needed as an energy source (4.4). In addition, a supply of mineral nutrients is needed for the plant to use the food it makes for growth, in particular for making proteins. Mineral nutrients are simple chemicals which plants normally take in with water, through their roots from the soil.

The need for nutrients can be shown by growing plants in sand culture, in which silver sand, which supplies no nutrients, takes the place of soil. Suitable plants are seedlings of cereals such as wheat or oats, all planted in similar pots. Some, given pure water only, have no nutrient supply. Others are watered with liquid houseplant fertilizer, used in accordance with the maker's instructions. After a few weeks the difference in growth and appearance shows clearly the role which nutrients play in healthy growth.

Light is also necessary for healthy plant growth. If seedlings are germinated in the dark they grow more rapidly than normal but become thin, spindly and have only a yellow colour in their leaves rather than the normal green. A more successful way to show this, however, is to start bulbs into growth in the dark, then bring some into the light as they begin to sprout. Daffodils can be used in winter; onions during the rest of the year. Those left in darkness show the same rapid growth and yellow colour as the seedlings, but when brought into the light they recover better, developing the normal green colour of chlorophyll (4.4).

Some plants which live in dry regions of the world can survive for a long time without water, but in order to remain alive and grow, most plants need a constant supply. If they are deprived of water their shoots wilt and become floppy. If water is supplied at once, wilted plants will usually recover, but eventually a point is reached where they cannot recover and they die.

Growth and response. Observing plants germinate and develop shows clearly that they are just as active as animals are, but live at a slower pace: the changes take longer. The same is true of their responses. Plants respond in many ways to changes in their environment, and some of their responses are easier to observe than those of animals, but because they take hours or days rather than seconds or minutes, they are often overlooked. The responses children can observe most easily are those to light and gravity, which can clearly be related to the plants' survival.

Shoots need to be in light to make food (4.4) by photosynthesis, and they have the best chance of doing this if they grow both upwards and towards any light source. A potted plant placed on its side will respond to gravity by growing more on its lower side so that in a few days it turns upwards, even in the dark. Seedlings make a similar response, but even more quickly. If put in light from one side, almost any plant will detect the direction of the light and respond by growing more on the shaded side. This causes the shoot to bend towards the light, and seedlings show particularly rapid responses of this kind: it is usual to see obvious bending within 24 hours.

Roots need to grow downwards to anchor the plant, and they do this by a response to gravity which is exactly the reverse of that shown by shoots: the root of a seedling bean placed horizontally grows more on its upper side, so that it turns to grow downwards. Most roots do not respond to light. Children can see the responses of roots and shoots by deliberately planting beans upside down, i.e. with the seedling root pointing upwards, and recording the sequence of growth.

4.4: Photosynthesis

Unlike animals, plants do not have to take in high-energy foods, because they make their own. The process by which they do this is called photosynthesis. It is difficult to carry out useful investigations of photosynthesis at primary level, though children can sample and enjoy some of its products, but some understanding of it is important because it is the basis of all food-chains (5.7) and maintains the gas balance in the atmosphere (5.8). It can therefore be seen as a process on which almost all life on Earth depends.

The energy source for photosynthesis is light, normally light from the Sun. In most plants by far the greatest amount of photosynthesis is carried on in the leaves. Because the leaves are flat and thin, they allow the plant to have a very large area exposed to daylight, so that even if the light is not very bright the leaves have a large energy source available. Some of the light energy falling on the leaf is absorbed by the green pigment chlorophyll. Like other green-coloured substances, chlorophyll absorbs red and blue light and reflects the green (17.8). When an ordinary material absorbs light energy, it is simply heated as a result (17.5). What is unusual about chlorophyll is that most of the light energy it absorbs can be transferred as chemical-potential energy (12.2) in a complex series of chemical changes. These result in the formation of high-energy food chemicals, such as grape-sugar (glucose) and cane-sugar (sucrose).

The raw materials for photosynthesis are water absorbed by the roots from the soil and transported to the leaves by the stem, and carbon dioxide gas, taken in directly by the leaves from the air around them. The waste product is oxygen, which escapes from the leaf into the air. This exchange of gases, like the absorption of light energy, is made much more efficient by the flat, thin form of the leaves. Photosynthesis can be summarized chemically:

$$\text{carbon dioxide} + \text{water} \rightarrow \text{sugars} + \text{oxygen}$$

Plants and the gas balance. The summary of photosynthesis shows that in the light plants take in carbon dioxide, which is breathed out by animals and produced by the burning of fuels (9.4, 12.4), and exchange it for oxygen, which animals need for respiration and without which they would die. Life on Earth depends on the balance between the two gases (5.8), and photosynthesis is the only way in which it can be maintained.

Plants, like animals, use food as a source of energy for their living processes such as growth and reproduction. Like animals, they transfer energy by breaking down food by respiration (2.3), which requires oxygen. In bright light this process is hard to detect because the plant is making food by photosynthesis much faster than it is being used in respiration. In the dark, a plant respires and exchanges gases with the air much as an animal does, taking in oxygen and giving out carbon dioxide. Over a 24-hour period, however, the plant will take in more carbon dioxide than it gives out, and will give out more oxygen than it takes in, and end up with a surplus of food which can be used for growth or storage.

Transport, growth and storage of food in plants. Food made by photosynthesis is transported away from the leaves by the stem and distributed to all parts of the plant. Some of this food is used in shoots and roots for growth and the rest of it is stored. Like animals, plants need proteins to make new living tissue and grow, but unlike animals they can make proteins for themselves using sugars from photosynthesis and mineral nutrients from the soil. As part of their growth, plants also use food made by photosynthesis in quite a different way. Unlike animals such as humans, plants have no specialized skeleton to give them support. As they grow, the living tissues of plants develop built-in support from a tough, strong, fibre-forming chemical called cellulose, made from sugars. In soft tissues like leaves this support remains flexible, but in thick stems and roots which have to support a great weight of shoot it becomes hard and very tough: the material we call wood. Plant fibres such as cotton, which is almost pure cellulose, are also the products of growth using the foods made by photosynthesis as the raw material. Humans cannot use cellulose for food because they cannot digest it, though other, plant-eating animals can. It is, however, an important part of the human diet as dietary fibre (3.4).

Plants do not usually use all the food they make for growth: large amounts are often stored, and are an essential food source for humans and many animals. In this way, plants form the basis of food-chains (5.7, 5.8). As well as soft tissues which we can use for food, many plants store food in their wood and bark, not only in stems but in roots as well. Children can usefully observe and eat a range of raw plant foods. One of the commonest stored foods is starch, a carbohydrate, which we obtain mostly from potatoes (swollen underground stems) and cereal grains (seeds). Sugar-cane and sugar-beet store so much sugar that it can be extracted as the sugar we use, but carrots store enough sugar to taste quite sweet. Many plants store fats in the form of oil, particularly in seeds such as sunflower, peanuts and Brazil nuts. Sweet, fleshy fruits such as plums, oranges and strawberries are rather different, because their food-stores are not for the plant's use, but to attract animals which distribute their seeds (4.5).

4.5: Plant reproduction

Humans and nearly all animals children will observe can make more of their own kind in only one way: sexual reproduction. Plants reproduce sexually, but many also have other ways of increasing their numbers, more directly related to the ways in which they grow. The life-cycle of any living thing can be seen as a sequence of events or stages, centred on its reproduction. The life-cycle of plants, including both sexual and asexual stages, is summarized in Fig. 4.3.

Asexual reproduction. Any kind of reproduction which does not involve fertilization (see below) is asexual, i.e. non-sexual. Many plants with which children are likely to be familiar multiply in this way. The most obvious examples are plants which grow outwards rather than upwards, rooting as they spread: creeping buttercup, strawberry and bramble are examples. As their shoots touch the soil they form roots at the tips, and buds grow at the rooting points to form independent plants. Many more plants spread by way of creeping underground shoots, which grow

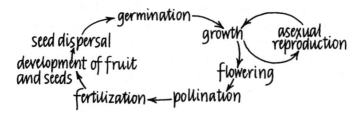

Figure 4.3 *Life-cycle of plants*

outwards and then send green shoots up into the air. Bindweed, stinging nettles, couch grass (twitch) and many other troublesome weeds are plants of this kind. Still other plants do not spread rapidly, but form dense colonies: daisies on a lawn and expanding clumps of daffodils or bluebells are examples.

The ability of plants to reproduce asexually is exploited by gardeners in propagating good varieties of plants by cuttings (cloning). These are most often pieces of shoot which are cut from the parent plant and placed in conditions which encourage root growth: usually warmth and a humid atmosphere. In some plants the shoot does not branch, so leaf-cuttings are used instead, as in African violets and begonias.

Sexual reproduction in plants. As in animals, sexual reproduction in plants involves the fertilization of a female egg-cell by a male sex-cell, which in plants is formed by the pollen grain. In plants, sexual reproduction involves four distinct phases: pollination, fertilization, the development of seeds and fruits, and seed dispersal. The plant's life-cycle begins again with germination of the seed (4.3).

Pollination. To be able to fertilize the egg-cell, the pollen grain has first to be moved from the anther which makes it, to the receptive stigma on the ovary (4.2). This is pollination. The pollen grain cannot move itself and so must be carried. The two commonest agents of pollination are insects and wind.

Insects are attracted to insect-pollinated flowers because they make a sugary liquid (nectar) on which the insects can feed. The nectar is often 'advertized' by brightly coloured petals, scent, or both. The pollen of these flowers is fairly heavy and sticky. The detailed form of flowers varies a great deal, but all of them make it likely that a visiting insect, on its way into the flower to feed on nectar, will brush against the stigma. If the insect is carrying pollen, the stigma is likely to pick some up from its body. The anthers are also positioned so that insects are likely to collide with them, covering themselves with pollen. Bees, which are important as flower pollinators, actually collect pollen and use it as a high-protein food in rearing their larvae.

Wind-pollinated flowers are quite different from insect-pollinated ones. Grass flowers are a good example: they are small, not brightly coloured and have neither scent nor nectar. Instead of the anthers and stigma being inside the flower, they hang outside to catch any air-current that is moving. The pollen is very light, dry and dust-like, so it is easily blown off the anthers and carried on the wind. When breathed in by some people, pollen of this kind causes hay-fever. The stigma of a grass flower is feathery, so it filters the passing air currents and has a better chance of catching a pollen grain of the right kind. Other wind-pollinated flowers children may find are the catkins (male flowers) of birch, alder and hazel; but those of willow ('pussy-willows') are pollinated by insects.

Fertilization. After pollination, the pollen-grain grows a very slender tube, visible only with a microscope, from the stigma into the ovary. The female egg-cells are in the tiny, undeveloped seeds (ovules) which can be seen by cutting open the ovary of a flower such as a bluebell. The pollen-grain makes a special sex-cell which is moved down the tube into the ovule and joins with the egg-cell it contains. This is fertilization, and if the egg-cell is not fertilized, the seed will not develop.

Seeds and fruits. After fertilization, many changes occur in the flower, often quite rapidly. The petals and stamens wither and fall off and the ovary begins to grow bigger. The fertilized ovules in the ovary grow to form the seeds, each seed being an embryo plant, with a food-store, in a tough protective coat (4.3). During development the seeds are protected by the ovary, sometimes called the seed-case. The sequence of changes can easily be seen in plants which have simple spikes of flowers, such as bluebell, snapdragon and willowherb.

The ovary or seed-case, with the seeds inside it, is the fruit. In many plants the seed-case develops in such a way that it helps to spread the seeds away from the parent plant once they are ripe (see below). Observing how fruits are related to the way that their seeds are dispersed is an excellent way to introduce the concept of adaptation (5.5, 5.6).

Seed dispersal. If all the seeds produced by a plant simply fell to the ground and germinated, there would be overcrowding, few would survive and the plant would spread slowly, if at all. This means that reproduction is more likely to be successful and ensure the survival of that kind of plant if the seeds are dispersed. There are many ways in which this can happen, each of which involves a special development of the seed-case.

Dispersal by animals: sweet, fleshy fruits (cherries, blackberries) are eaten by animals; the seeds remain undigested and are passed out with their faeces. Hooked fruits (goosegrass) catch on the fur of mammals and are carried away before they drop off or are removed.

Dispersal by wind: some fruits (dandelion, thistle) develop parachutes and others (sycamore, lime) a wing, so that when they fall the wind will carry them for some distance before they reach the ground. The fruits of poppies and campions are like pepper-pots: the small, light seeds are shaken out and scattered as the slender stems are moved by the wind.

Self-dispersal: some plants develop seed-cases which shrink as they dry, setting up large tension and twisting forces. When the fruit finally snaps, the seeds are thrown or flicked out over a wide area. Examples include gorse, broom, vetch, violet and cranesbill.

5

Variety, Adaptation and Interdependence

The ability to recognize animals and plants which occur locally, or which are learned about at second hand through reading, TV programmes or the internet, is useful for two reasons. First, it enables children to communicate effectively about living things which interest or concern them. Secondly, the ability to name even the broad group to which an animal or plant belongs makes it possible to gain access to stored information about it and so to identify it more accurately and learn about it in more depth and detail. This is particularly important when investigating the ways in which plants and animals are adapted to their ways of life (5.6) and the role which they play in their habitats (5.7), because detailed information can often be obtained only through long-term observation which children cannot carry out for themselves.

5.1: A variety of animals

In the summary of information given here, animals which children are likely to find in local habitats are listed, while those which they may know about from reading, TV, the internet, visits or holidays are given in square brackets. Related animals are listed on the same line, so each line represents a distinct group. The summary is followed by a brief description of each major group.

Animals are divided into two great groups: those which have backbones (vertebrates) and those which do not (invertebrates). Invertebrates are much more varied, so it is easiest to distinguish them by a process of elimination. If an animal is not a fish, amphibian, reptile, bird or mammal, it is an invertebrate.

Invertebrates. There are twenty-five major groups; children are likely to encounter only three. Keys to these are given in section 5.4.

Molluscs: slugs, snails [octopus, squid]
Annelids: earthworms, leeches
Arthropods: *crustaceans*: woodlice [crabs, lobsters, shrimps]
               arachnids: spiders [scorpions]

chilopods:	centipedes
insects:	dragonflies, damselflies
	grasshoppers [locusts]
	earwigs
	aphids, bugs
	ants, bees, wasps
	houseflies, bluebottles, craneflies
	butterflies, moths
	beetles

Molluscs. This group includes octopus and squid, but children will usually observe slugs and snails. These have slimy skins, no legs and move on a muscular 'foot'. Each animal has both male and female sex organs (is hermaphrodite), but they mate and lay eggs. They have simple eyes on stalks; most feed on living and dead plants, which they rasp with a toothed tongue. All slugs live on land; different snails live on land, in fresh water and in the sea.

Annelids are worms with no legs, slimy skins and round bodies divided into segments. Children may observe earthworms and leeches. Leeches live in fresh water by sucking blood from large animals or preying on small ones. They have a sucker on their hind end to anchor them while feeding, and can swim by passing waves along the body. Earthworms live on land, feeding on dead leaves which they grind up with soil in their gut. They are very important in soil formation and fertility (11.9). They are hermaphrodite, but mate and lay eggs.

Arthropods, the 'jointed foot' animals, are a very large and diverse group, which includes far more kinds of animal than any other. All, at least when adult, have jointed legs and a skeleton which is on the outside of the body. They grow by shedding this periodically and growing a new one. They have separate sexes and lay eggs. Children are likely to encounter four of the thirteen major classes of arthropods.

Crustaceans include crabs, shrimps and lobsters, but the most familiar ones are woodlice, which are the only land-dwelling members of the group. They have oval bodies distinctly divided into segments, with a pair of legs to each, and short feelers (antennae). They feed on decaying plant material. The female retains the eggs in a special pouch until they have hatched. Woodlouse behaviour may be studied as an example of adaptation (5.6).

Arachnids include spiders as well as scorpions. Spiders have bodies divided into two distinct parts. The front part (cephalothorax) includes the head and bears four pairs of legs. It is most often separated by a narrow waist from the abdomen behind. Nearly all spiders prey on other animals, but none eats solid food: they inject their prey with digestive juices and suck in the resulting liquid. Many spiders trap their prey in webs which have a beautiful pattern, but the ability to make these is not learned: it is an example of inborn (instinctive) behaviour.

Chilopods are the centipedes. They have long, narrow, segmented bodies with one pair of legs to each segment, and long antennae. They are fast-moving predators which live in the soil or under stones, and have poison fangs on the underside of the head.

Insects are a very large and diverse group. All have, at least when adult, a body divided into three parts (head, thorax and abdomen) with three pairs of legs on the thorax. Most also have two pairs of wings on the thorax, but flies have only one pair and worker ants have none, while in earwigs, bugs and beetles the fore-wings are thicker and harder, forming a case for the thin hind-wings. Insects have two main ways of developing. Dragonflies, damselflies, grasshoppers, earwigs and bugs hatch from eggs as nymphs, which have six legs and are obviously insects, though they may reach anything like the adult form only with their final moult. The other kinds of insect hatch into more or less worm-like grubs (larvae) which may be difficult to identify as insects at all. At the end of their growth the larvae enter an apparently dormant phase inside a special case (pupa). During this time they undergo pro-found changes (metamorphosis) to develop the form of the adult insect (imago).

Vertebrates. These are animals with backbones and skeletons inside their bodies, including a protective brain-case (cranium). In all except the soft-skeleton fishes, the skeleton is made of bone. There are five major groups; children are likely to encounter or learn about all of them. Keys to these are given in section 5.4.

Fish:	soft skeleton: [sharks]
	bony skeleton: stickleback, minnow, bullhead [ornamental and tropical fish]
Amphibians:	newts, frogs, toads
Reptiles:	[turtles, tortoises]
	[lizards, snakes]
	[crocodiles]
Birds:	ducks, geese
	hawks [falcons, eagles]
	domestic fowl, turkeys, partridge, pheasant
	gulls
	pigeons
	[parrots, budgerigars]
	owls
	[kingfishers]
	woodpeckers
	perching birds (includes all common garden and town birds not

Mammals:
 listed above)
 egg-laying: [platypus, spiny ant-eater]
 pouched: [kangaroos]
 placental: hedgehog, mole
 bats
 (primates): [apes] human
 [whales, porpoises, dolphins]
 hare, rabbit
 (rodents): mouse, rat, hamster, guinea-pig, gerbil
 (carnivores): dog, cat, fox, weasel [wolf, bear]
 [seals]
 [elephants]
 (single-hoofed mammals): horse [rhinoceros]
 (cloven-hoofed mammals): pig, cow, sheep, deer [camels, giraffe]

Fish. All live entirely in water and breathe by pumping water over gills at either side of the head. All lay eggs, but in some these are retained in the body of a parent until they hatch: guppies are an example. Sticklebacks are remarkable for nest-building and care of eggs and newly-hatched fry by the male.

Amphibians. Newts, frogs and toads live on land for most of the year, but all lose water easily by evaporation, so have to stay in damp places and hunt mainly at night. They breathe air with simple lungs but can also breathe through their skins. They breed in fresh water, laying eggs which are fertilized externally and protected by a coat of jelly. These hatch into a juvenile phase (tadpole) which breathes with gills until its lungs develop. Newts can be distinguished from lizards because lizards have a scaly skin which is quite dry.

Reptiles have dry, scaly skins which resist water loss, and breathe air with lungs. They breed on land, fertilization is internal and nearly all lay soft-shelled eggs which hatch into young resembling the adults in form. Children are not likely to encounter native snakes and lizards during fieldwork, but extinct reptiles (dinosaurs) are always of interest.

Birds have feathers, breathe air with complex lungs and maintain a high, constant body temperature (are 'warm-blooded'). Fertilization is internal and they lay hard-shelled eggs which are protected and incubated until hatching. Parental care is highly developed, involving feeding and usually teaching of skills and behaviour as well. Most birds can fly and many migrate long distances to exploit seasonal food supplies.

Mammals are warm-blooded animals whose females feed their young with milk. By far the biggest group of mammals are those which sustain the foetus in the uterus with a placenta (3.12). All have water-resistant skin; in most this is covered with fur which helps to maintain their high body temperature. Apart from the whales and their relatives, all mammals breed on land, and all show a very high degree of parental care.

5.2: A variety of plants

Plants are no more difficult to place correctly in their major groups than animals are; but the overwhelming majority that children will encounter are members of one group: the flowering plants. Dividing these into smaller groups (the equivalent of ducks and falcons among birds, or rodents and carnivores among mammals) is much more difficult, and for most purposes unnecessary at primary level, so is not attempted here.

Plants. There are four major groups; children are likely to encounter all of them. Keys to these are given in section 5.4.

Algae:	blanket-weed in ponds; bright green coloration on trees and walls	
	[seaweeds]	
Bryophytes:	mosses	
	liverworts	
Pteridophytes:	ferns	
	horsetails	
Spermatophytes:	*conifers*:	pines, spruces, firs, cedars
(seed plants)		cypresses [juniper]
		yew
	flowering plants:	monocotyledons
		dicotyledons

Algae are a very large and varied group, which probably includes several natural groups which are not closely related to each other. Most live in water, and those which children are likely to find are very simple, with no shoot or root structure at all. These include blanket-weeds in ponds and the green filament-weeds, looking like fine green hair, which grow on large plants, stones and the sides of aquarium tanks.

The commonest alga children may observe is one of the very few land-dwelling kinds: the bright green coloration on tree-bark and walls. This is made up of millions of microscopic, very simple plants (pleurococcus), which have a remarkable resistance to drought. Their distribution on trees and walls is usually controlled by moisture. If water runs down the trunk or branch they are washed off, and if it is too dry they cannot survive, so the most green colour is usually found in areas which stay moist for some of the year but don't get very wet.

On rocky seashores and harbour works, much larger algae are found in the form of seaweeds. The largest are the brown wracks and oar-weeds. These have a complex structure, and some have an internal transport system. They are anchored onto rocks or other hard surfaces, but do not have roots.

Bryophytes include two major plant groups: mosses and liverworts. Mosses are likely to be the more familiar. They have small leafy shoots which may be creeping and branching or upright, forming tufts and cushions. The shoots are much simpler in structure than those of ferns and seed plants, and they are anchored by hairs rather like root-hairs (4.2) rather than by true roots. Nearly all mosses live on land, mainly in wet or shady, damp places; but some are very resistant to drought and live on rocks and dry walls in full sun. When dried these do not wilt, but curl up, and when re-wetted they quickly expand and become active again. Some mosses of this kind are important in the early stages of soil formation (11.9). Mosses have no flowers or seeds. They reproduce by tiny spores, formed in small capsules which grow out of the shoots on slender stalks. The spores are dispersed by wind.

Liverworts are less familiar and widespread than mosses. The ones children may find are like green, branching ribbons, which may form mats and be flat or curly at their edges. They grow on bare soil or rocks, in damp, shady places in woodland, or in moist greenhouses.

Pteridophytes are an ancient group of plants often found as fossils in coal and other rocks, whose living members include ferns and horsetails. They may be distinguished from bryophytes because they have true stems, leaves and roots, but they produce neither flowers nor seeds. Ferns can be distinguished from flowering plants with divided, feathery leaves because leaves of all common ferns have brown scales on their stalks and midribs. The flowering plant leaves may have hairs, but not scales.

Nearly all ferns are land plants, and though adult plants of most kinds can withstand drought, they need moist conditions to reproduce, so they are more restricted in their habitats than seed plants are. Most live in woodland, and one (bracken) is a serious weed of heath and upland pasture. Ferns reproduce by spores which in most kinds are formed under the leaves in small cushion-like structures, or round the edge. The spores germinate to form a plant like a tiny liverwort, which requires water to grow and reproduce sexually, and from which a new fern-plant grows after fertilization.

The other common plants in this group are the horsetails, whose leaves are reduced to small brown scales. Photosynthesis is carried out by the green branching stems.

Seed plants. This group includes the overwhelming majority of larger land plants. They reproduce by means of seeds, which are formed after pollination and fertilization (4.5). There are two major groups. In the smaller and much more ancient group, the conifers (gymnosperms), the seeds are not enclosed in a seed-case (ovary), whereas in the larger group, the flowering plants (angiosperms), they are. Confusion is sometimes caused by reference to the cones and catkins of conifers as 'flowers': this should be avoided.

Conifers are all trees or shrubs. Most have leaves in the form of needles, except some of the cypresses in which they are scale-like. Most bear their seeds in cones, protected but not enclosed by the cone-scales. Pollen is produced by catkin-like shoots, and pollination (4.5) is by wind. After pollination the cones and seeds grow, often for a year or more, until the ripe cones open and the seeds are shed, to be dispersed by the wind. Two members of the group, juniper and yew, have seeds in fleshy coats: these are dispersed by birds.

Flowering plants bear seeds completely enclosed by a seed-case (ovary) which after pollination develops into the fruit. There are two main groups, which on a world-wide basis can be difficult to tell apart, but European plants can usually be placed in one group or the other with confidence.

Monocotyledons (seedlings have one seed-leaf). This is the smaller of the two groups. Almost all common plants of this group have sword-shaped or grass-like leaves; leaf-veins parallel; flower parts in threes or sixes. The only common exception is the highly-poisonous wild arum, which has broad, net-veined leaves. Monocotyledons include lilies, bluebells, daffodils, snowdrops, irises, crocuses, orchids, grasses, sedges and rushes. All the European members of this group are small plants; none forms a tree or shrub, though some Asian and tropical ones do (bamboos and palms).

Dicotyledons (seedlings with two seed-leaves). By far the larger of the two groups. Leaves of almost any form, but rarely sword-shaped or grass-like; typically broad and net-veined; most have flower parts in fours or fives. This group is very diverse in form and includes all trees and shrubs except conifers, and all the commonly-occurring plants not mentioned under monocotyledons.

5.3: A variety of other living things

Although the living things children are likely to be most aware of are animals and plants, there are others which influence their lives profoundly in a variety of ways, and which belong to neither group. Children may need to learn about three of them: bacteria, fungi and lichens.

Bacteria are microscopic organisms which have a much simpler structure than the cells which make up animals and plants. Bacteria are very small: typically a few thousandths of a millimetre long, and exist everywhere in the environment, even in our bodies, in enormous numbers. A few can make their own food using light or chemicals as their energy source, but most obtain their food by digesting dead or, more rarely, living material. The result of digesting dead material is decay, and the role of most bacteria is as decomposers (5.8), recycling material in the environment. When bacteria attack living material, either plant or animal, they cause disease. Other kinds of disease can arise when bacteria decaying food excrete poisonous waste which is then eaten by an animal. This danger is a major reason why food hygiene is important. It is worth emphasizing to children that very few of the many kinds of bacteria in the environment cause diseases in humans, but those that do can be very serious, so personal hygiene is also important.

Examples of bacterial activity which children may encounter include the spoilage of food already referred to. Decayed food usually has an offensive smell caused by the products of bacterial digestion: avoiding it is an instinctive (inborn, unlearned) defensive behaviour. They should also learn about the formation of bacterial plaque on teeth, and tooth decay (3.2); and may investigate the making of yogurt from milk (9.2), which uses different bacteria from those which make milk go sour.

Fungi are sometimes, and quite incorrectly, described as plants. They are a separate, distinct and very large group of organisms, most of which feed by digesting (decaying) dead remains of plants and animals. With the bacteria they are the main decomposers of the ecosystem (5.8). The body of most fungi is threadlike, spreading throughout whatever food they are digesting. The large 'fungi' which are frequently seen in autumn, such as mushrooms and toadstools, are simply the reproductive bodies of a much larger organism. Some of these are edible, but others which look quite like them are deadly poisonous and kill people every year. Children should be warned against eating any fungi not identified as edible by a competent adult. Some fungi attack plants, causing diseases such as blights and mildews, and a few cause diseases of animals.

When fungi digest food, they produce a range of chemicals as a result. Some of these are poisonous and offensive, but controlled decay by fungi gives many cheeses their distinctive flavours and textures (9.2). The most widely used fungus, however, is also one of the most unusual: yeast. Wild yeasts live in sugary liquids such as nectar and fruit juice. When their air supply is shut off they do not die, but respire by converting the sugar to alcohol, which is the basis of brewing and wine-making. Yeast grows very fast in a warm environment and gives out carbon dioxide gas as it respires. This is the basis of its use in dough to leaven it, making the bread lighter, easier to chew and digest and improving its flavour (9.2).

Lichens are not a single organism but a close association (symbiosis) between a fungus and a green alga (5.2). The alga can live without the protection of the fungus, but the fungus cannot live without the food made by the alga. Lichens are very diverse and are found in all parts of the world, partly because some of them can withstand extremes of heat, cold and drought. They have no roots, and are very important as the first colonizers of bare rock, which in many areas begins the process of soil formation (11.9). Most are slow-growing, and because they absorb water through their upper surface, are very sensitive to pollution in air and rain-water (5.9). As a result, they can be used as indicators of how clean the air is and how pollution levels are changing.

5.4: Classification using keys

Keys are devices used to classify or identify unknown members of a population. To classify things is to put them into groups which have something in common, such as stars, mountains or cathedrals, whereas to identify something is to distinguish it as a particular kind of thing within its class, or even as a unique individual. For example, my body classifies me as a male human, but my fingerprints and DNA (2.4, 5.5) identify me as an individual.

Anything can be classified and identified by making and using keys. Examples could include cars, foods, football teams and buildings; but here attention will be confined to plants and animals. Many books on plants, animals and other organisms concentrate on identification and most of these use keys. Because accurate naming is needed to gain access to information on particular kinds of living things, learning to use keys is a useful and important skill.

Two types of key. All keys work by requiring the user to make a structured sequence of observations and to take decisions on the basis of these. There are two main ways in which they can be constructed. The simpler but less useful of these is the deci-sion-tree, which is based on questions. At each stage, questions are posed which require a simple yes or no answer, and the layout is in the form of a diagram, so that the route through the key is easy to follow. Examples of decision-trees are given in Figs 5.1, 5.2 and 5.3.

The more complex form is the statement-key. At each stage the user has two (occasionally more) statements from which to choose, each of which leads either to an identification or to the number of the next section to be consulted. This is more complex, but also more accurate than the decision-tree, because more information is both available to and required from the user at each stage. The statement-key to invertebrate groups given below has exactly the same structure as the decision-tree in Fig. 5.1, so that the two can be compared.

Key to major groups of invertebrate animals

1. Has legs 2
   Has no legs 5

2. Has six legs . . . . .insect
   Has more than six legs 3
3. Has eight legs . . . . .spider
   Has more than eight legs 4
4. Body more or less oval, feelers short . . . . .woodlouse
   Body long and narrow, feelers long . . . . .centipede
5. Moves on a flat muscular foot; eyes on stalks . . . . .6 (mollusc)
   Body wormlike; does not move on flat under-surface . . . .7 (annelid)
6. Has spiral shell into which animal can retreat . . . . .snail
   Has no shell, or only a tiny one . . . . .slug
7. Sucker at hind end; lives in water . . . . .leech
   No sucker; lives in soil . . . . .earthworm

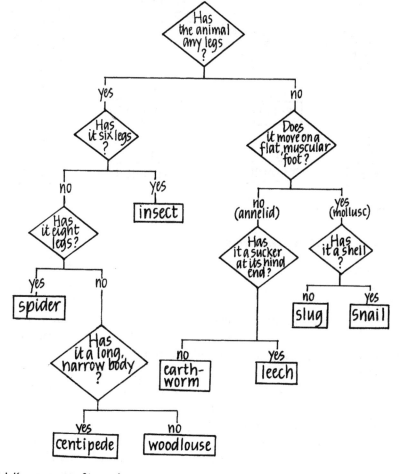

Figure 5.1 *Key to groups of invertebrates*

A corresponding pair of decision-tree and statement-key are given for vertebrate animals in Fig. 5.2, and on p. 72.

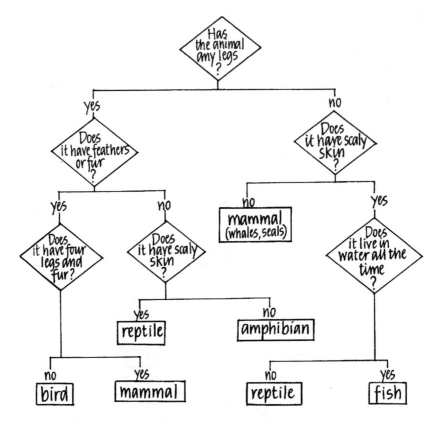

Figure 5.2 *Key to groups of vertebrates*

Key to groups of vertebrate animals

1. Has no legs 2
   Has legs 4
2. Has scaly skin 3
   Has no scales (large marine animals) . . . . mammal
   (whales and seals)
3. Lives all the time in water; breathes by pumping
   water over gills . . . . fish
   Lives on land (occasionally swims) . . . . reptile (snake)
4. Has body covering of feathers or fur. 5
   Has smooth, warty, slimy or scaly skin 6
5. Has four legs and fur (hair) on body. . . . . mammal
   Has two legs, two wings and feathers . . . . bird
6. Has smooth, warty or slimy skin . . . . amphibian
   Has scaly, dry skin (some also have a shell) . . . . reptile
   (lizards, crocodiles,
   tortoises, turtles)

The limitations of the decision-tree become more apparent as accurate separation of groups becomes more difficult; for example, when an attempt is made to classify all the plants children might find. One such attempt is given in Fig. 5.3. It would work for most plants, but a few such as duckweed and some heathers could be misplaced using it. The extra observation called for by the statement-key given below makes it more reliable, though it is more difficult to use.

Key to major groups of plants

1. Plant body not divided into different parts. 2
   Plant body divided into at least two different parts
   (stems, roots, leaves). 4
2. Grows under water . . . . alga
   Grows on soil, tree-bark or walls 3
3. Plant microscopic, forming green layer on trees and
   walls. . . . . alga (pleurococcus)
   Plant body ribbon-like and branching, 5–15 mm
   wide, often curly at edges . . . . liverwort
4. Plant has green leaves 5
   Leaves present only as tiny brown scales . . . . horsetail
5. Never has flowers, cones or catkins 6
   Has flowers, cones or catkins . . . . 7 (seed plant)
6. At least some leaves 2 cm long, usually much longer . . . . . fern
   All leaves less than 2 cm long, low tufted or creeping
   Plants. . . . . moss
7. Plant woody (tree or shrub) 8
   Plant not woody . . . . flowering plant
8. Leaves needle- or scale-like; may have catkins or
   cones but no flowers . . . . conifer
   Leaves broad or, if needle- or scale-like, with obvious
   flowers . . . . flowering plant

The keys given here are intended as illustrative examples, which may also be useful in classifying animals and plants into broad groups. When beginning to use keys, children should be given examples of the decision-tree type which are restricted in scope, concentrating on a small set of related variables such as the size and shape of leaves in a given range of commonly grown trees and shrubs, or the characteristics of wild flowers found around the school. To begin with, the selected plants or animals should be few in number and very easily distinguished. Progress can then be made by including an increased number of organisms which require more detailed observations in order to distinguish them. Only when children have developed the basic skills of using simple keys should they attempt broader classifications, such as the one given here, or the use of statement-keys.

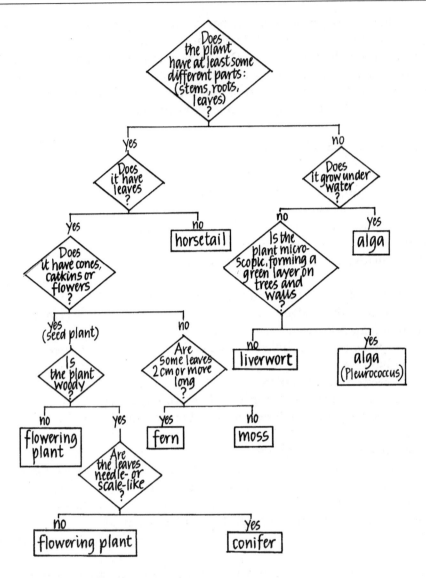

Figure 5.3 *Key to groups of plants*

5.5: Adaptation, evolution and DNA

Opportunities, problems and variety. As even a simple investigation of the plants and animals in an area shows, there is in many places a great variety of living things. In order to survive, any living thing has to exploit its environment to meet its needs, while solving the problems and withstanding the stresses placed on it. Most plants need soil for anchorage and as a source of water and nutrients; light and air to make their own food and, in some cases, animals to carry their pollen and distribute their seeds. Their main problems are likely to be lack of water and light, being eaten by animals, or disease. An animal needs food, water and, in most cases, shelter provided by a hiding-place, the security of a social group, or both. Its main problems are likely to be hunger, thirst, exposure, being preyed on and disease.

The variety of living things in any part of the world is a reflection of the range of opportunities offered by the environment and the problems it poses. In some parts of the Earth's surface such as the driest deserts and the middle of the Antarctic continent, the opportunities offered are so limited and the problems so severe that almost nothing lives there. Over most of the planet, however, both the opportunities and the problems are very varied and the variety of life is correspondingly wide. The same thing can be seen in miniature in many urban environments. In a tarmac playground surrounded by high walls the opportunities for living things to become established are few and their problems usually severe, so the variety of life is small, though often greater than many people imagine. In a wildlife garden next door, opportunities abound and problems are less acute, so a much greater variety of living things becomes established.

Adaptation. Life is a balancing act: if a living thing (organism) can exploit enough opportunities and solve enough problems, it lives and reproduces. If not, individuals or the whole population die out. A variety of organisms can live in most habitats because each tends to exploit different opportunities and solve different problems in order to survive. To do this effectively, organisms are specialized in their body structure, in their behaviour, or both. This specialization is called adaptation.

Adaptation is any feature of the body or behaviour of an organism which fits it for its environment and helps it to survive. Examples are all around us, but often they are difficult to understand because not enough is known about the opportunities and problems of the living things we observe. The concept needs to be established by looking at some very clear and simple examples. Perhaps the most useful set of adaptations for an introductory investigation are those shown by the beaks and feet of birds. Pictorial and written information about their structure and life-styles is readily available and their adaptations are clearly and obviously related to their feeding and movement. Children may also be able to follow-up some of their learning by first-hand observation if a bird-table is set up.

The main examples are:

insect eaters: robin, tits, wren, hedge-sparrow;
mixed diet: blackbird, song-thrush, starling;
small seed-eaters: finches (sparrow, chaffinch, greenfinch).

All the above are perching birds (passerines) with specialized beaks but unspecialized feet. All the following have both beak and foot adaptations:

predators: owls, hawks;
tree-climbers: tree-creeper, woodpecker;
fishing swimmers: gulls;
mud-sieving swimmer-divers: ducks;
waders: curlew, redshank.

Having used birds as an example to introduce the concept of adaptation, it can be further explored by way of case-studies made at first hand. Examples are suggested in section 5.6.

Evolution. Adaptations clearly do not come about by chance. They seem to be the result of changes brought about by interaction between living things and their environment over very long periods of time, a process known as evolution. What appear to be similar changes can take place much more quickly when humans deliberately breed and select plants and animals for particular purposes. Examples include all cereals, which have been developed from grasses; cabbages of many kinds including cauliflower and brussels sprouts, which come from one kind of wild cabbage; and the many breeds of different domestic animals such as dogs, cattle, pigs and sheep.

One of the results of sexual reproduction in both animals and plants is that the offspring vary: all closely resemble their parents, but none is exactly like them (see below, and 2.4). When breeding plants or animals for a particular purpose, humans select those which are most favourable, use them for further breeding and kill or eat the others. What seems to happen in the wild is that much the same kind of selection goes on, but much more slowly and haphazardly. Individuals which are more able to exploit opportunities and solve problems have a somewhat better chance of surviving long enough to breed, while those which are less well-adapted are less likely to live. This process is known as natural selection and its end result is the emergence of new kinds of animals, plants and other organisms. Examples of recent adaptation to a human-dominated environment include insects, bacteria and rats which have developed resistance to the chemicals which were used in the past to kill them.

Evolution is still problematic as a theory, partly because some people find it contrary to their interpretation of holy scriptures, and partly because scientific claims for its truth have in the past been greatly exaggerated. Like any scientific theory (1.1), that of evolution represents what is at present the best guess of scientists as to how the diversity of life on Earth came about. Most scientists believe that the outline of evolutionary theory is adequate to explain the facts as we know them, but that there are many details and inconsistencies which remain to be investigated and resolved.

Sources of variation. If the theory of evolution is accepted, it is evident that the process begins with, and depends on, variations between individuals and within populations which are passed down from generation to generation. The only source of this kind of variation in living things is change in the genetic information (DNA, 2.4) which controls the development and functioning of cells and organisms as they grow and interact with their environment. Change in DNA and the variation it brings about is not exceptional, but usual. Only in asexual reproduction such as the cloning of plants (4.5) are offspring identical to their parents. Changes in DNA always occur during the formation of sex cells as part of sexual reproduction (2.4, 3.12, 4.5) and the results can easily be observed: plants grown from seed and the offspring of animals look like their parents but are never identical to them. The variations in DNA which give rise to the differences we can see are of two basic kinds. One is an actual change in the DNA itself, known as a mutation. The other is a change in the combination of genes inherited by the individual.

Mutation and recombination of genes. A mutation is a change in the structure of the DNA which makes up a gene (2.4). A mutation will bring about a change in the particular aspect of the activity of a cell or organism which the gene controls. Mutation appears to occur at random and, because living processes are very highly organized (2.4), any haphazard change in the way they operate is likely to disrupt them and so prove a disadvantage to the organism. Examples of human diseases caused by mutated genes include cystic fibrosis and all forms of cancer.

Mutation occurs naturally in all organisms at differing rates, but can be greatly speeded up by factors in the environment such as ionizing radiation, ultra-violet light and some chemicals. This is why radioactive materials, excessive amounts of sunlight on unprotected skin and tobacco smoke are all very dangerous: exposure to any of them increases the risk of cancers, in which mutated body-cells multiply uncontrollably. Occasionally, however, mutations are advantageous. Examples include the development of resistance to antibiotics by many bacteria, and to pesticides by rats and many insects. These changes are advantageous to the organisms, but not to humans who are infected or have their crops destroyed and their buildings invaded.

Most genes do not operate independently but as part of a complex group. Because most genes exist in more than one form in a population, and complex organisms have thousands of genes, every individual's DNA is a unique combination of genes inherited from both parents. During sexual reproduction in both plants and animals the production of eggs and sperm, or egg-cells and pollen, involves a re-ordering or recombination of genes, so that new combinations are always being brought together at fertilization and in growing embryos. The results of gene recombination are usually more subtle than the sudden changes brought about by mutations, but are equally important as a source of variation within populations, and so to the process of evolution.

Artificial variation: genetic engineering and GM crops. According to evolutionary theory and a great deal of directly observed evidence, variations caused both by mutation and recombination are acted on during natural selection to produce changes in populations. Humans have exploited genetic variability for thousands of years through the controlled breeding and artificial selection of useful animals and plants, but this process has operated by selecting offspring from the variety which occurred spontaneously during cultivation. Knowledge of the role of DNA and development of the technology to work with it directly, has led to the ability to bring about genetic variation artificially in a controlled way. This is done by changing the DNA of organisms including bacteria, animals and plants using the techniques of genetic engineering.

Essentially, genetic engineering consists of changing one or more genes in an organism by adding, deleting or transferring DNA. For example, in some people with sugar diabetes, a gene has mutated so that they cannot make the hormone insulin. Using the techniques of genetic engineering, DNA which controls insulin production has been extracted from normal human cells and inserted into bacteria, which then start to produce insulin. Grown on an industrial scale, these bacteria are providing the insulin which diabetics need to survive. Other bacteria with added DNA are producing human growth hormone, used to help children with a deficiency of the hormone to grow more normally.

The possibility exists of changing or replacing defective mutant genes in humans themselves: a process known as gene therapy. Where diseases are caused by a single mutant gene which prevents the body from functioning normally, gene therapy offers the possibility of a permanent cure without the need to keep taking medicines, but although it has been attempted, it has not so far been successful.

The examples of genetic engineering which children are most likely to hear about are genetically modified (GM) crop plants. These have had their DNA altered to give them high resistance either to pests and diseases, or to weed-killing chemicals. They are highly controversial because very little is known about their long-term effects. These could include both direct effects on humans or animals which eat the crops and their products, or indirect effects on wildlife and the environment, for example if the GM plants cross-pollinate with related wild species.

5.6: Case-studies in adaptation

How children observe and learn about adaptation at first hand is likely to depend on the resources available. This is an example of an area where the case-study approach (1.1) is particularly useful. Brief notes are included here on three possible case-studies, which show the connection between observation and explanation needed in work of this kind.

Case-study 1: Skulls of mammals. The skull of any mammal gives more information about its life-style than any other part of its skeleton. This is because the major parts of its feeding mechanism (jaws and teeth) are in its head, and so are most of the major sensory organs. It is usually most productive to concentrate attention on the jaws and teeth, and on the position of the eyes as shown by the eye-sockets. Suitable skulls may usually be borrowed from museum loans services, and the most useful fall into two main groups:

hunting predators: dog, cat, fox
plant-eaters: cow, sheep, deer, horse, rabbit, squirrel, rat.

It is by no means necessary to have a wide range of specimens to make this study worthwhile: only two skulls of contrasting types, such as those of a dog or cat and a sheep or rabbit, are needed to observe the main adaptations.

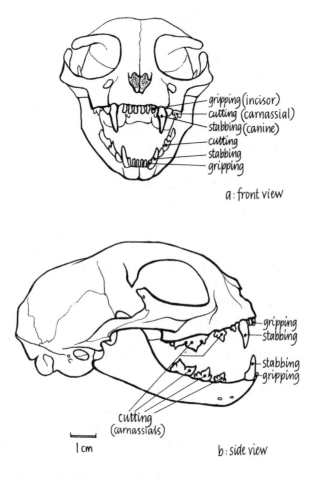

Figure 5.4 *Skull of a carnivore (domestic cat). Notice that larger carnivores such as dogs also have large crushing molars behind the cutting teeth*

Hunting predators have both eyes facing forwards. This is most clearly shown in the cat which, like humans, has a complete ring of bone round its eye-sockets. Forward-facing eyes enable the hunter to use binocular vision (3.10) to judge the distance of its prey accurately.

The jaws and teeth of hunters have many adaptations (Fig. 5.4). The jaw is specialized in two ways: it has a hinge-joint which does not allow much sideways movement, and the lower jaw (mandible) is narrower than the upper. When the jaw is closed, some lower teeth (canines, carnassials, see below) pass inside the upper ones to stab and slice. The teeth are of four main kinds, which from front to back are:

incisors:	rounded and fairly blunt; meet and grip for holding and tearing apart;
canines:	long, curved and pointed; pass and stab to kill the prey;
carnassial teeth:	sharp and saw-like; pass and cut to slice up flesh (skin is usually pulled and torn off);
molars:	blunt and knobbly; meet and crush for breaking up small bones; in some small carnivores such as cats (Fig.5.4) these are very small or absent.

The teeth are adapted for holding and killing prey, tearing it apart and cutting pieces off before swallowing them. The food is not chewed much, but this does not impair digestion because protein and fat are relatively easy to break down in the gut.

Plant-eaters have skulls which are more varied in structure than those of hunters, but all have adaptations in common (Fig. 5.5). The eyes are at either side of the head. This gives all-round vision and therefore a better chance of seeing a predator or other danger. As a result, plant-eaters have only a narrow field of binocular vision, but because they do not hunt, they have less need to judge distance accurately.

The jaws of plant-eaters are more loosely hinged than those of hunters, so as well as being moved up and down they can be rotated to give a grinding action. The lower jaw is only a little narrower than the upper, so the teeth meet rather than passing one another. All the plant-eaters have a wide gap between their front (biting) teeth and their cheek (grinding) teeth. This enables them to feed continuously, grinding up one mouthful of vegetation while biting off the next.

The front, biting teeth of plant-eaters are varied and different animals show three main adaptations: the horse has upper and lower teeth, which meet and cut as it bites. Sheep, cows and deer have only lower teeth in front, which they use to hold plants against the gum of their toothless upper jaw, pulling them off with a movement of the head. Rabbits, rats and squirrels have paired, chisel-like teeth, with which they nibble and gnaw (Fig. 5.5).

The cheek-teeth of plant-eaters are broad, with sharp ridges on top. These animals digest plant fibre for carbohydrate (3.4), but because this is difficult to digest it has to be ground up first. The cheek-teeth are specialized for this, but are themselves ground away in the process, so unlike the teeth of hunters (and humans) they keep on growing throughout the animal's life.

The approach used here, of focusing attention on particular structures then seeking to explain what has been observed, can be used equally well to study adaptations in other animal groups and habitats. Possible examples include swimming, breathing and feeding in aquatic insects. It is also the basis for what is known of the adaptations of extinct animals such as dinosaurs.

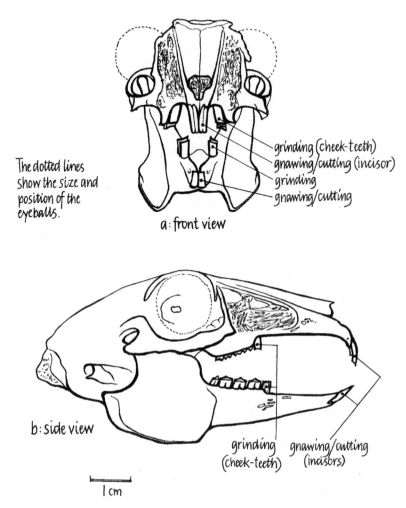

The dotted lines show the size and position of the eyeballs.

grinding (cheek-teeth)
gnawing/cutting (incisor)
grinding
gnawing/cutting

a: front view

b: side view

grinding   gnawing/cutting
(cheek-teeth)   (incisors)

1 cm

Figure 5.5 *Sketches of the skull of a herbivore (rabbit)*

Case-study 2: Behaviour of woodlice. Woodlice are one of the commonest invertebrate animals and the only land-dwelling crustaceans (5.1). They feed mainly on
decaying plant material, usually in dim light conditions at dawn and dusk. They are
always in some danger of death from water loss, so they have a strong preference
for humid, damp conditions. They do not, however, like wet conditions and can
easily drown if their living-places are flooded. Woodlice can easily be kept for a few
days in a small tank with a layer of damp, decaying leaves in the bottom. Pieces of
apple or carrot can be put in for food, though whether these are ever eaten is doubt-
ful, as they aren't usually decayed enough.

The adaptation of woodlice which children can investigate is not their structure
but their behaviour, which has obvious survival value. If twenty woodlice are put

onto a layer of damp, decaying leaves in bright light, they will quickly move down into the leaves and disappear. Asking children why they do this is a very effective way to generate a range of explanatory hypotheses (1.4). The most obviously testable hypotheses are likely to be those which relate to the adapted behaviour: they move as they do because they don't like strong light (or do like dark) and don't like dry conditions (or do like damp ones).

The easiest way to test these explanations is by using very simple choice chambers, which can be made from Petri dishes. If light–dark preference is being tested, half the lid of each dish should be painted black and conditions should be kept humid, for example by putting a layer of damp paper towel in the bottom of the dish. Ten woodlice are put into the dish, which is kept in bright light, and a record kept of how many can be seen at one-minute intervals. Usually they will show a strong preference for dim light. When testing for moisture preference, a plain dish should be used, with half the bottom covered with damp paper and half with dry. The light should be kept dim by putting a black card over the top. To observe the animals, lift the card slowly, count the number in each half and then replace it. Usually a strong preference for damp conditions is shown. The survival value of both observed behaviours can then be discussed and decisions made as to whether the original hypotheses have been upheld.

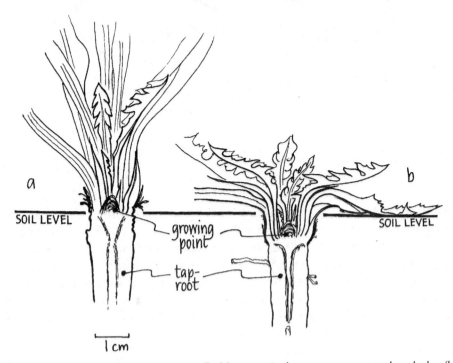

Figure 5.6 *Rosette weeds: dandelions cut vertically: (a) growing in short, unmown grass under a hedge, (b) growing in regularly mown grass*

Case-study 3: Adaptations of weeds. Weeds are opportunists: they exploit environments which other plants have not colonized. There are many reasons for their success: sometimes the environment is unfavourable for other plants, and in other cases disturbance has created a new environment which other plants have not yet exploited. One example of each is discussed here.

Rosette weeds are perennial plants adapted to colonizing heavily trampled soil and closely mown lawns. Examples include dandelions, hawkweeds and plantains. Their adaptation is one of structure: they can grow as a flat, round rosette of leaves from a single growing-point, so they suffer only minor damage when other plants would be crushed or cut to pieces (Fig. 5.6). They have very tough roots, so they are hard to pull up, and a main growing-point below ground level, so that even if their leaves are cut off or crushed they can quickly grow again. Interesting studies can often be carried out in early summer into rosette weeds flourishing in areas which are trampled bare in winter, such as goal-mouths and shortcuts between hard paving. Numbers of weeds can be related to intensity of trampling and the relative resistance of grass and weeds to trampling observed. Individuals can be dug up to see how their anatomy helps to ensure re-growth after damage.

Some weeds have adaptations of reproduction rather than structure, which enable them to exploit newly disturbed soil before other plants can become established. They usually grow from seeds and have very short life-cycles; germinating, growing, flowering and setting seed in two or three months. Two particularly useful examples are groundsel and bitter-cress. Plants can be dug up and grown outdoors in pots, to be observed as they flower and set seed, which can be collected and sown so that children can see the whole life-cycle. Very rapid seed production is only one of the adaptations: others include effective seed dispersal (by wind for groundsel and 'exploding' capsules for bitter-cress), rapid germination and very fast growth at almost any time of the year. All these adaptations help them to exploit environments which are available only for a short time, such as gardens in winter, the edges of fields and building sites.

Another aspect of plant life in which adaptation can readily be observed is the dispersal of seeds, discussed in outline in section 4.5.

5.7: Ecosystems: feeding relationships

Animals and plants living in a particular area are adapted (5.6), not only to environmental conditions such as climate and soil, but also to each other. Any part of the Earth may include a variety of areas (habitats), which may be natural or influenced by human activity to varying degrees. Examples which children might investigate include woodland, meadow, pond, stream, rocky seashore, wall, garden and field margin. Each habitat is distinguished not only by the environmental conditions in it, such as light, temperature, rainfall and soil type, but also by the range of living things which inhabit it. One of the greatest contributions of the life sciences during the past century has been the growth of an understanding that the living things in a habitat do not and cannot exist in isolation, but form a community whose members depend on each other. Understanding the interdependence of living things and their habitats is the aim of the ecologist. One way to develop this understanding is to investigate the relationships between members of a particular community. Such relationships are together known as an ecosystem.

Feeding relationships of humans. One of the most basic aspects of any ecosystem, and the one which children can most profitably investigate, is feeding relationships. This involves, for any organism, tracing its food back to its origins. An appropriate starting-point is the food which children themselves consume. Humans are animals which normally have a mixed diet (omnivores), including both plant and animal material. Tracing the animal material in the human diet back to its sources shows that all of it, and therefore all our food, has its origins in plants. Results can be shown graphically, using either pictures or words, for example:

$$\text{Human} \leftarrow \text{egg} \leftarrow \text{hen} \leftarrow \text{grain} \leftarrow \text{plant}$$

From the first, the fundamental point can be made that, in one way or another, we depend upon plants for all our food. This can then be linked to the concept of plants as living things which produce their own food by photosynthesis (4.4), using light from the Sun as their energy source (17.5).

Feeding relationships within ecosystems. Humans depend for their food on plants, but does the same principle apply more widely, to other animals in any habitat we might investigate? To find out, it is necessary to know the range of living things which inhabit an area, and use this to gain access to information about their diet, as well as observing them at first hand wherever possible. If children are successfully to do this at first hand, teachers need to select a small number of local, accessible habitats, research these in detail and use them as case-studies (1.1).

Food-webs, producers and consumers. Because observation of habitats may be difficult and their populations may change or fluctuate, it is often useful, in addition, to use second-hand information to learn about feeding relationships. As an example, a set of information on feeding relationships among larger animals in a garden is given in Table 5.1. This can be used in a variety of ways. One of the most productive is to make a set of labels for each animal or group, and plot feeding relationships by laying these out on large sheets of paper, to which they can later be glued if the chart needs to be made permanent. Plotting all the information in Table 5.1 on a single chart will show how complex feeding relationships within a habitat are likely to be, but is not otherwise very useful. It is more productive to find out where the food of a single animal comes from. As an example, the feeding relationships of a robin are shown in Fig. 5.7.

Table 5.1 Feeding relationships among larger animals in a garden ecosystem

Animal and group	Eats	Is eaten by
Birds:		
Tawny owl	mice, voles, sparrows, shrews, (? tits), snails, slugs, worms	
Blackbird	caterpillars, earthworms, fruit and seeds, soil-dwelling larvae	
Song-thrush	earthworms, snails, soil-dwelling larvae, caterpillars, fruit and seeds	
Finches (sparrow, chaffinch)	seeds, some caterpillars	tawny owl
Tits (blue and great)	aphids, caterpillars, some fruit and seeds	?tawny owl
Robin	caterpillars, earthworms, soil-dwelling larvae, fruits and seeds	
Mammals:		
Wood-mouse	snails, young plants, buds, fruits and seeds	tawny owl
Short-tailed vole	grass and other plant shoots	tawny owl
Common shrew	earthworms, woodlice, caterpillars	tawny owl
Hedgehog	earthworms, woodlice, caterpillars, snails, slugs, fallen fruit	
Soil dwellers:		
Earthworms	dead leaves	blackbird, song-thrush, tawny owl, robin, shrew, hedgehog
Soil-dwelling larvae	roots of plants	blackbird, song-thrush, robin
Woodlice	almost any dead and decaying plant material	hedgehog, shrew
Plant pests:		
Slugs	living and dead plant material	tawny owl, hedgehog
Snails	living and dead plant material	tawny owl, song-thrush, wood-mouse, hedgehog
Aphids	plant sap (by sucking)	tits
Caterpillars (insect larvae)	plant shoots of all kinds	blackbird, song-thrush, robin, tits, finches, shrews, hedgehog

A set of feeding relationships shown in this way is known as a food-web. Plotting the food-webs of different animals using the information provided shows that all their food, like that of humans, can be traced back to plants. Photosynthesis is the only source of food in any ecosystem, so plants are known as producers. Animals, because they rely on this food but do not produce any of their own, are known as consumers. The various roles which different animals play within the ecosystem are reflected in the way in which they appear at different levels in food-webs. Those which feed on plants (herbivores) are near the bottom, while those which eat other

animals (carnivores) are higher up, further away in terms of feeding from the production which maintains the whole system. Right at the top are predatory carnivores which are not themselves preyed on. They are often called top-carnivores, and
the main one in the garden ecosystem is the tawny owl.

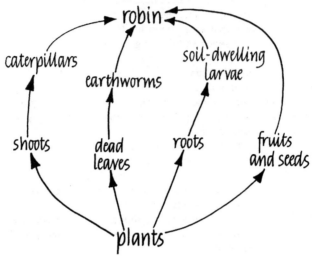

Figure 5.7 *Food-web of a robin*

Food-chains and pyramids. Other important ideas about feeding relationships can
be developed by concentrating on a single strand in a food-web. For example, one
such strand in the food-web of the robin is:

robin ← insect larvae ← leaves ← plants

This is known as a food-chain. Food-chains are useful because they can help us see
more clearly how plants and animals are related in the ecosystem. One way to do
this is to look at the actual amounts of material involved in a food-chain. For example, great tits feed themselves and their young mainly on insect larvae, which eat
plants, so their food chain is:

great tit ← larvae ← plants

Observations have shown that during the three weeks it takes to rear a brood of 8–10
chicks, they and the parents eat between 8,000 and 10,000 larvae. These are taken
from trees and other plants whose leaves together must weigh several hundred kilograms, since even a small garden can produce half a tonne (500 kg) of dead leaves a
year. Putting in the amounts of material involved, the food-chain looks like this:

great tits   ←   larvae   ←   plants
10–12   8,000–10,000   at least 500 kg

This shows what has been found in all food-chains of this kind: a small number of carnivorous animals prey on a much larger population of herbivores, which in turn feed on a very large amount of plant material. Because of this relationship, food-chains are sometimes called food-pyramids, with the large mass of plant material making up the base of the pyramid.

To develop a realistic idea of the feeding relationships within an ecosystem we need to chart food-webs to see the complexity, and food-pyramids to appreciate the numbers of living things and amounts of material involved. Together they emphasize not only the way in which all living things depend on the food produced by plants and therefore on light energy from the Sun (17.5), but also the way in which populations are naturally controlled. Each step of the food-pyramid must always be much smaller than the one below it, on which it depends. Great tits could never be as numerous as the larvae on which they feed, and a plague of caterpillars could not be sustained for a long period because they would destroy the plants and with them the means of food production. The food-pyramid also helps to explain the disastrous effects of some of the poisonous chemicals which pollute the environment (5.9).

5.8: Ecosystems: decay, recycling and interdependence

The feeding relationships of animals and plants make up the more obvious and conspicuous part of the ecosystem. The fact that there must be more to discover becomes apparent when we remember that no plant or animal lives for ever. Although living things have been living, dying and depositing waste material on the Earth for millions of years, we are not engulfed by their dead remains or their waste. When a living organism dies, its body undergoes changes similar to those which affect any non-living thing: it breaks down, becomes simpler and is dispersed into the environment (2.2). The only difference is that dead bodies and animal waste do not under normal circumstances undergo slow chemical and physical changes of the kind which result in the rusting of iron (9.5) and the weathering of rocks (11.8): most of their material is actively attacked and broken down very quickly because it is used as food by other living things: the decomposers.

Decomposers. Some animals in the ecosystem (scavengers) eat the dead bodies of other animals, and others such as earthworms specialize in eating dead plant material, an activity which is of great importance in soil formation (11.9), but most of the breakdown of dead bodies is carried out by micro-organisms, both bacteria and fungi (5.3), which together are known as decomposers.

In the ecosystem, decomposers are consumers because, like animals, they do not make food but rely, either directly or indirectly, on the food made by plants. They feed by making special chemicals (enzymes, 3.3) which digest dead material, much as we digest food in our gut. They then take in the liquid digested food and use it for growth and respiration (2.3). This process of digestion by decomposers is what we call decay, and sometimes produces chemicals which smell offensive to us (5.3), though most naturally decaying material simply smells earthy. Decomposers are found in very large numbers almost everywhere in the environment, particularly in the upper layers of most soils, and their spores float in the air like tiny particles of dust. Dead material is colonized within a very short time, the microbes begin to digest it and usually grow at a very fast rate.

Decay as a process of breakdown can easily be observed by carefully collecting dead leaves from undisturbed soil in garden or woodland and separating them into their different layers (Fig. 5.8). At the top are whole dead leaves; at the bottom a soft, dark brown, earthy material (humus, 11.9) in which no trace of leaves can be found; and in between are leaves in various stages of decay and disintegration. In the process of decay the plant fibre (cellulose, 4.4) is digested and the products respired by the decomposers, releasing carbon dioxide gas to the air and water to the soil. The decay of proteins is complex, but ends with the release of simple chemicals into the soil, which plants take up and use as mineral nutrients (4.3).

5 cm

Figure 5.8 *Stages in decay of leaves*

Decay as recycling. The essential role of decay in the ecosystem can now be seen clearly. It is natural recycling; the process by which material built into the bodies of living things by their growth processes is released again into the environment after their death, as carbon dioxide in the air and mineral nutrients in the soil. In this way the materials are made available to plants, to be taken up by them and re-used for photosynthesis and growth, so sustaining both them and all the consumers (animals and decomposers) in the habitat. Decay is often regarded by children and adults with distaste. It should rather be viewed as a process which is as essential in its way to the continuation of life on Earth as photosynthesis is. Without photosynthesis no food could be produced, but without decay the materials which plants need for photosynthesis and growth would be permanently locked away in dead bodies, unavailable for further use.

Interdependence. At primary level, children can learn in at least three different ways that all living things are dependent on each other. First, investigating feeding relationships by charting food-webs, chains and pyramids shows how animals as consumers depend on plants as producers. Secondly, finding out how decay occurs shows that both animals and plants depend on decomposers to recycle material, but also that the decomposers depend on the growth of animals and plants for a continued supply of food material. Learning about photosynthesis (4.4) shows a third aspect of interdependence. The respiration of nearly all living things relies on the oxygen produced by plants during photosynthesis, but it also produces carbon dioxide which is one of the raw materials used in that process, so the balance of gases in the atmosphere is conserved.

5.9: Human activity and ecosystems

Apart from the tops of higher mountains, very little of the landscape of Britain and Europe is natural, being the product of centuries of human activity. In large areas of land which are not cultivated in any way, ecosystems develop rather as individual plants and animals do: they become more complex until they reach maturity. In most of Britain, the mature natural ecosystem would be forest: mainly oak in the south, with increasing amounts of oak and birch further north, and pine-birch forest in Scotland. These natural forests would have a very wide range of plants and animals and extremely complex food-webs.

Any long-term human activity, whether hunting, forestry or farming, changes the ecosystem, usually making it simpler by killing off some kinds of plants and animals. The most vulnerable animals are always those at the top of their food-chain, so in Britain wolves, bears and wild boar have been hunted to extinction, while pine marten and wild cat are very rare. Foxes and badgers have a more varied diet and are more adaptable, so they have survived in much larger numbers though badgers are currently threatened with culling in some areas because they are suspected of transmitting a disease of cattle (bovine TB). Among wild birds also, large predators such as the golden eagle, osprey, peregrine falcon and red kite are still relatively rare though their numbers are increasing, while smaller birds have adapted to human-dominated conditions and survived better.

Forestry and farming as ecosystems. Forestry favours trees with valuable timber over those of little use, so it reduces the variety of trees in woodland. This destroys the food supply of some plant-eating animals, particularly insects, so the ecosystem of a managed forest becomes simpler and less diverse. This effect may not be obvious when the main forest tree is oak, because this one kind of tree supports a great diversity of insects, birds and mammals, as well as helping to produce a fertile soil, so pure oak woodland can still form a complex ecosystem. Where it does become apparent is when forestry becomes more like agriculture, with large-scale planting of exotic conifers (mostly spruce, pine and fir), grown in pure stands. Very few native animals can feed on these trees, which cast dense shade all the year round and change the soil, so that most of the ground plants beneath them are eliminated. The result is that the natural ecosystem collapses completely and the woodland area, apart from the crop trees, becomes very barren.

Farming and forest cannot exist on the same piece of land, since for crops to be grown or pasture to be established the forest has to be cleared. The object of farming is the opposite of natural diversity: the cultivation of one or a few kinds of animal or plant. Any animal which interferes with this, such as an insect or bird which feeds on the crops, is a pest, and any other plant which invades is a weed. Farming can therefore be seen as a human activity which artificially maintains a very simple, unnatural ecosystem in order to feed a very large population of a single animal species: humankind. This is not to say that agriculture is wrong, or that ecosystems in farmland, such as weeds at field margins, are uninteresting. What is called into question, as an issue of which children should perhaps be made aware, is whether the increased efficiency in modern farming achieved by mechanization, the increased use of artificial fertilizers and poisonous pesticides, can be sustained in the long term.

Pollution. Apart from the large-scale, long-term effects of forestry and farming, the human activity which causes most damage to ecosystems, and which children can investigate, is pollution. Because decomposers are so numerous and widespread in most habitats, waste and other materials added to the environment by human activity are usually broken down and recycled (5.8). When material which cannot be broken down naturally is added to the environment, the result is pollution.

It may be useful to think of pollution as being of two main kinds, though examples of pollution children can investigate for themselves are likely to include both. The first occurs when a material which normally would be broken down and recycled within a habitat is added in such a large quantity that the decomposers cannot decay it as they normally would. Examples of this are the pollution of a pond by runoff from a manure-pile, and of a river by sewage. The second kind of pollution occurs when a substance which the decomposers cannot decay at all is added to a habitat. Examples include oil-slicks and persistent pesticides in the food-chain (see below).

Children can learn about pollution both through first-hand investigations and from news items and TV programmes. There are two main examples of pollution which they are likely to be able to investigate for themselves: litter and air pollution. Most litter comes from packaging of food and drink. An investigation of the problem can usefully begin with a survey of a local area and classification of litter according to the materials in it (usually paper, plastic, steel, aluminium and glass). The dangers created by litter can be explored and experiments conducted over a 3 or 6 month period to compare rates of breakdown of the different materials when buried in soil. Litter is likely to include pollutants of both kinds: paper, at least in small quantities, will decay fairly rapidly, whereas the other materials break down slowly, if at all. Work in this area can easily be linked to cross-curricular themes such as environmental education, citizenship and health education.

Particularly in an urban environment, air pollution may be a serious problem. Pollutants include solid particles in the form of smoke and dust, and poisonous gases. Solid pollutants can be collected by exposing strips of adhesive tape (double-sided tape stuck onto card is best) in various locations for 24 hours, and comparing the amounts of material sticking to them. It is important to ensure that all the cards are either laid horizontally or fixed vertically to ensure fair comparisons. When the solid pollutant particles are seen under a microscope or magnifier it will come as no surprise to learn that they can irritate the lungs, causing coughing and bronchitis (3.13). Solid pollutants also collect on leaves, and are particularly evident on evergreens, most of whose leaves live for several years. By sampling leaves of the same age from evergreens in different localities and wiping the deposits from them onto white, absorbent paper, levels of pollution can be compared.

The two main poisonous gases which pollute the air are carbon monoxide, which is difficult to detect, and sulphur dioxide. Both are harmful and both are produced by petrol and diesel engines. Sulphur dioxide is also produced in large quantities by coal-burning power-stations (9.4), and is the main cause of acid rain in Britain and Europe. Pure water is not acidic: it has a pH of 7. Raindrops dissolve sulphur dioxide in the air, forming a dilute acid (sulphurous acid), so rainwater collected in city centres is usually distinctly acidic, with a pH of well below 7 when tested with universal indicator paper. When polluted air is breathed in, sulphur dioxide dissolves on the moist lining of the lungs and irritates them, making any chest condition such as bronchitis worse. Acid rain causes extensive damage to some building stones (11.8) as well as poisoning trees, plants and water-dwelling animals in badly affected areas.

Pollution in food-pyramids. Children may already be aware that some pollutants have a disastrous effect on animals high up in food-chains. The classic example is the effect of some insecticides such as DDT and dieldrin (both now illegal in the EU), which after killing insects remain in the soil and get into ground-water. At the bottom of the food-pyramid concentrations of these chemicals are very low, but because they cannot be broken down in an animal's body and may be stored in fat tissue, the concentration rises with each step of the pyramid. For example, one earthworm eats large amounts of dead leaves, one shrew eats hundreds of earthworms and one owl eats hundreds of shrews in a year. At low concentrations these chemicals are harmless to mammals and birds, but the pyramid effect means that if they get into the bottom of the food-chain they may be concentrated enough to be poisonous when they reach the top. Many predatory birds such as falcons, hawks and owls suffered badly in Europe during the 1960s and 1970s because pesticides prevented their eggs from developing properly, though the position has now improved so that populations are rising again and some species are extending their range.

6

States of Matter and Physical Change

6.1: Solids, liquids and gases

Most materials and objects which children encounter in everyday life are fairly obviously in one of the three states of matter: solid, liquid or gas. Investigating changes between these three states is essential if concepts of them are to be developed and established firmly. Changes between solids and liquids are easy to show, but those between liquids and gases can be rather more difficult to investigate and understand.

An object is usually thought of as being solid if it has a shape of its own which it retains when unsupported by a container. A liquid, on the other hand, has no shape of its own. If it is in a container it takes up the container's shape, but otherwise it runs out, forming a thin layer on a level surface or collecting in pools on an uneven one.

When investigating the differences between liquids and solids, examples of solids made up of small particles, such as sand, sugar and salt, should be included. In large numbers, the particles fill the bottom of a container and if this is tilted they can be poured out, appearing to flow rather as a liquid does. It is important, therefore, not to over-emphasize ease of flow as a property of liquids, since these solids seem to share it. A better approach is to concentrate on the individual particles with a hand-lens and pencil-point, observing that each grain has its own form and keeps it when pushed or squashed, unlike a drop of liquid. It is also helpful to point out that solid particles form a heap when poured out onto a flat surface, which liquids do not. Beginning with coarse particles such as sugar or sand, children can go on to see that finer powders such as flour or baking-powder are also solids. It is important to develop the concept of particulate solids before investigating solutions and suspensions (6.5).

It is less easy to develop a firm concept of the difference between liquids and gases. One way is to think about how a solid, a liquid and a gas behave in a container with a lid on. The solid keeps its shape and the liquid fills the bottom of its container. The gas, like the liquid, has no shape of its own but it fills the container completely and unlike the liquid does not collect at the bottom.

Showing that gases are real and have substance needs thought and care because nearly all gases are invisible and those which are not are highly poisonous. With young children especially, a range of experiences such as blowing to feel a wind and propel things, playing with fans, sails, balloons and windmills can all help to estab-lish this concept. The way in which a gas fills the whole container in which it is confined can be shown by inflating a balloon. The squashed (compressed) air inside stretches the balloon evenly, so it must be pushing out equally in all directions and filling the whole space inside. This can be contrasted to a little water in an air-filled balloon, which collects at the bottom. Another piece of evidence is to point out that if air settled at the bottom of a room, as water does at the bottom of a swimming-pool, one would not be able to breathe up near the ceiling. However, it can be observed that when a light-bulb or tube is changed, whoever climbs up to do it does not need breathing apparatus, so the air in the room must fill it up.

6.2: Changes of state: melting and freezing

Changes of state between solid, liquid and gas are usually associated with heating, cooling and changes in temperature (12.3). An explanation of these changes, though not generally thought of as being part of the primary science curriculum, is given in Chapter 8. Evaporation (6.3) and solution (6.5) are special cases which should be care-fully distinguished from apparently similar changes of state (boiling and melting).

A solid changing to a liquid is said to melt; a liquid changing to a solid is said to freeze. Both changes can easily be observed by allowing an ice-cube to melt and then re-freezing the liquid water. There are, however, two important differences between this example of changing state and others with which children are likely to be familiar. The first is that when ice melts and water freezes there is no inter-mediate state between solid and liquid. Children will be familiar with, and should investigate, more gradual changes of state in foods and other chemicals. The second difference is that ice and water change size in a very unusual way when freezing and melting (see below).

Gradual changes between liquid and solid. Many foods and other chemicals, espe-cially when heated or cooled slowly, show a gradual change of state between liquid and solid. Chocolate shows a reversible change of this kind very well when heated gently over a water-bath, for example when making chocolate crispies. Less easily reversible but even more gradual changes can be seen as ice-cream slowly melts and jelly, cornflour custard and blancmange become cool and set.

The setting of plaster and concrete is rather different from that of jelly or custard in that it is brought about by chemical changes (9.1) rather than cooling, but both show a similar gradual change of state. Most paints which children use are solid-liquid mixtures (suspensions, 6.5) which lose water by evaporation (6.3) and gradually solidify as they dry up.

The freezing and melting of water. Liquid water and ice have some very unusual properties. One of these is the change in volume when ice melts or liquid water freezes. Most substances become smaller when cooled and larger when heated (12.3), but as water freezes into ice it expands. This can be shown by filling a plastic drinks bottle completely with water, screwing the top on tightly and putting it into a freezer. As the water freezes, the expansion of the ice will split the bottle.

Water normally freezes at 0°C, but if chemicals such as salt are added to it, the freezing-point is lowered so it has to be much colder before ice will form. This explains why crushed rock-salt is used on icy paths. The salt starts to dissolve on the surface of the ice, but the ice is much warmer than the freezing point of the salt solution. The result is that instead of the salt solution freezing, more liquid forms, more salt dissolves and so on. When used on roads, the salt is usually mixed with grit to give vehicle tyres more grip (friction, 14.3) on partly melted snow and ice.

If the temperature continues to fall below 0°C, ice continues to expand. This expansion has had two profoundly important effects on the Earth and living things. The first is that as water seeps into cracks in rocks in the cold regions of the world and freezes, the expanding ice opens up cracks in the rock. The freeze–thaw cycle, which may be repeated every day for much of the year, is a major cause of the breakdown or weathering of rocks (11.8) and so of soil formation (11.9). The other effect of the expansion of ice is even more important. Because ice expands as it freezes, a kilogram of ice takes up more space than a kilogram of water at 0°C (i.e. the ice has a lower density). The result is that ice floats, so in the cold parts of the world, where lakes, rivers and even the sea freeze over, living things can remain active under the ice, which also insulates them (12.3) from extreme cold. If ice sank, lakes, rivers and the sea would freeze from the bottom up and life in cold waters would be much more restricted than it is.

6.3: Changes of state: boiling, condensation and evaporation

Boiling. If water is heated to 100°C and heating is continued, the temperature does not continue to rise, but the water begins to boil. Boiling is the process of a liquid being changed to a gas by heating, and for any liquid it normally takes place at a characteristic temperature: the boiling-point. Unlike evaporation (see below), boiling does not take place only at the surface of a liquid, and gas bubbles can form anywhere. If a metal saucepan of water is heated, bubbles of gas (steam) usually form on the bottom, but that is only because the heating effect is strongest there. Children may notice that when cold tap-water is heated in a pan, bubbles form and rise to the top, long before the water boils. These are bubbles of air which was dissolved in the water (6.5), but which comes out of solution as the water is heated up.

Observing the boiling of water provides good opportunities to discuss safety in the kitchen. One way to emphasize this is to point out that boiling water kills and cooks human skin just as it kills and cooks anything else such as potatoes, and does it very quickly. Dissolving chemicals in water causes its boiling-point to rise, so that it is hotter than 100°C when it begins to boil. This explains why pasta and rice cook faster in salted than in unsalted water. When a lot of a chemical is added to water, as for example sugar is added when making jam, the boiling liquid is so hot that a special high-temperature thermometer is needed. Boiling syrups and jams are particularly dangerous because they are sticky: a splash on the skin is not only very hot but also does not run off, so it causes much worse scalding than boiling water would do.

When a liquid boils it turns to gas. Water turned to gas by heating is called steam, and is completely colourless and transparent, which means that it is invisible. Only when steam cools down does it form the hot cloud which is usually called 'steam'. This can be shown by looking at water boiling in a pan. The gas above the surface is invisible and only when it rises is it possible to see the 'steam'. What happens is that as the steam rises, it cools to below 100°C and liquid water re-forms (condensation, see below), but in the form of tiny droplets which are so small that they can remain suspended in the air as a mist or cloud. When steam comes into contact with a cold surface, liquid water forms by condensation very quickly. The process of boiling a liquid, collecting the gas, cooling and condensing it is known as distillation, and is often used as a method of extracting and purifying liquids (6.5).

Evaporation and condensation. Boiling is not the only way of converting a liquid into a gas. If a dish of water is left exposed to the air, the water will seem to disappear gradually, but it has not been heated to a high temperature, so it has not boiled. It has simply 'dried up' or evaporated. Evaporation occurs when a liquid changes to a gas at its surface. Some liquids do this much faster than water, for example the surgical spirit used to clean the skin before an injection, which dries up almost instantly. It can easily be shown that evaporation takes place at the surface of a liquid, by measuring 10 ml of water into a shallow dish and tipping another 10 ml onto a cloth which is then hung up to dry. The water on the cloth will evaporate much faster than that in the dish because it has been absorbed and 'spread out' (6.6), so that it has a much larger surface exposed to the air.

When water or any other liquid evaporates, it does not actually disappear, but turns into a gas which mixes with the air. This cool gas phase is called a vapour. The gas formed when water evaporates is not called steam, because it is not hot, but water vapour. Air is a mixture of many gases, of which water vapour is one, colourless and invisible like the rest. If the air contains a lot of water vapour it is said to be moist or humid. The evaporation of water from the Earth's surface, especially the oceans, and its condensation as clouds and precipitation, are the basis of the water cycle and of much of the weather which we experience (11.4).

When any gas is cooled sufficiently it changes into the liquid state by the process of condensation. If humid air is cooled, the water vapour in it may condense as tiny droplets, rather as steam does, and remain suspended as fog, mist or cloud (11.4). If the humid air comes into contact with a cold surface it will condense as liquid water. The air which animals breathe out is warm and very humid. In buildings with a lot of people inside, humidity builds up until water begins to condense on cold surfaces, such as windows in winter, so that these mist over and may have 'condensation' running down them. In cars, condensation from moist air breathed out can impede the driver's vision, so devices such as hot air blowers and electrically heated rear windows are used to re-evaporate the water and give a clear view.

Although evaporation can often continue at low temperatures, it gets faster as the temperature rises. This can be observed by comparing the rate at which puddles dry up on hot and cool days in summer and the effect of a hot air blower on a misted window. The difference comes about because evaporation depends on a transfer of energy (latent heat, 12.2) from the liquid to the vapour, so that the liquid tends to become cooler as a result. When the temperature is high, this transfer of energy can take place faster so the rate of evaporation goes up, and if evaporation is very rapid the cooling effect is much more marked. This can be shown by putting a drop of rapidly evaporating but harmless liquid such as surgical spirit onto the skin. It will feel much colder than a drop of water, and colder still if air is blown onto it. The cooling effect of evaporation is important in the avoidance of overheating of the body in many mammals, such as humans (sweating, 3.9) and dogs (panting).

6.4: Physical changes, mixtures and their separation

Melting, freezing, boiling, evaporation and condensation are all examples of physical changes. Physical changes may alter the appearance and other physical properties of materials and objects, but the actual substances involved remain the same. For example, ice, water and steam are all the same substance, water, and changes of state between them do not alter this. Any change which does result in the formation of a new kind of substance is a chemical change (9.1). An important part of the concept of physical change is that however fundamentally the materials seem to change, they do not change in themselves at all. This is likely to seem contradictory to children who have a great deal of experience of bringing about physical changes in a wide range of objects and materials. Because physical changes are very varied and so commonly encountered in everyday life, it is useful to think of them as falling into three broad groups: changes of state caused by heating and cooling (6.2, 6.3); changes of shape caused by applying forces to objects and materials (Chapter 7, 10.2); and changes caused by mixing.

Mixtures. A mixture is made when two or more substances are physically combined or mixed together to make what appears to be a single substance, while remaining chemically distinct. For example, air is a mixture of gases, mainly nitrogen and oxygen. It has more or less the same composition throughout the atmosphere, but the different gases are not chemically combined. Mixtures are made by physical changes and can, at least in theory, be separated by physical changes, though this may be very difficult. For example, to separate the gases in air it is necessary to make the gas so cold that it condenses into a liquid (at about –200°C) and then allow it to warm up gradually so that the different gases boil off in turn as their boiling-points are reached. This is the main way in which nitrogen and oxygen are produced for industrial use.

In order to understand their properties it is necessary not only to make mixtures and observe the changes this brings about, but also to use, and if necessary devise, a variety of methods to separate them again. The main kinds of mixture which children may encounter, use or investigate are:

solid dispersed in solid: particulate mixtures;
solid dispersed in gas: smoke, dust suspension;
liquid dispersed in liquid: emulsion;
liquid dispersed in gas: aerosol;
solid or gas dispersed in liquid: solution, suspension (6.5);
liquid dispersed in porous solid: absorption (6.6).

Solid–solid mixtures. These are made when granules or powders are mixed together. If the particles are of different sizes it is usually possible to separate them, at least to some degree, by sieving. This is a useful method for rough analysis of some soils, particularly sandy and stony ones, and is commonly used in the building industry to assess the suitability of gravels and aggregates for particular kinds of concrete (10.2). Sets of sieves with different meshes are available for this purpose. If the particles are finer and will not dissolve in water it may be possible to separate them by sedimentation. The solid mixture is shaken up with water and left to settle. The smaller the particle the longer it takes to sink, so fractions of the mixture with different particle sizes are separated into layers when the sedimentation is complete. This is a standard method of soil analysis (11.9) which is also used in the purification of sewage and in the refining of clay for pottery.

If a mixture is made of two solids, one of which will dissolve in a liquid while the other will not, they can be separated by shaking the mixture in the liquid, then filtering out the one which will not dissolve. The dissolved solid can then be recovered by evaporating or boiling away the dissolving liquid (6.5). A mixture of sugar and sand can be separated in this way. It is, however, much more difficult to separate a mixture of two substances which both dissolve in water, such as salt and sugar. This is in fact a useful example because it serves to emphasize that some simple physical changes can be very difficult to reverse.

If one of the ingredients of a solid particle mixture is magnetic (15.3), it can be extracted from the others using a magnet. Ceramic magnets (15.7) are particularly useful for this, and children can use them to separate iron filings from (dry) sand. This is best done with the magnet inside a thin plastic bag, so that the iron powder does not cling to it directly. Industrially this method is used to separate iron and steel from other metals in loads of mixed scrap.

Solid–gas mixtures. A suspension of very fine solid particles in a gas is known as a smoke. The solid particles in a smoke are so fine that they do not settle out, so if they are breathed in they go right into the lungs and are likely to irritate and damage them. Tobacco smoke is particularly harmful because it is not only irritant but also contains many chemicals which can cause cancer (3.13). Smoke, mixed with larger solid particles suspended in the air, is also part of the air pollution produced by vehicle engines and some industries. Unlike the smoke, the larger suspended particles will settle out slowly, but can still be very harmful, not only by creating a dirty urban-industrial environment, but also by contributing to bronchitis and other respiratory diseases when they are breathed in. Larger solid particles separating out of the air can be trapped and used as a measure of air pollution (5.9).

Liquid–liquid mixtures. A suspension of very small droplets of one liquid in another is known as an emulsion. The emulsion children will be most familiar with is milk, which is a suspension of fat droplets in water. In whole milk, some of the fat droplets are large enough to separate, and rise to the surface to form a layer of cream, which may be skimmed off to make butter. As a result, skimmed milk has a much lower fat content than whole milk. Another example of an emulsion is PVA or white glue, made by dispersing a synthetic resin in water.

Liquid–gas mixtures. A suspension of liquid droplets in a gas is known as an aerosol. Pressurized cans which produce aerosols are very commonly used to spray liquid chemicals, including hair lacquer, car paint and household insecticides. By far the most common and widespread aerosols, however, are natural suspensions of tiny water droplets in air, usually known as cloud, mist or fog (11.4).

6.5: Solutions and suspensions

When a solid is mixed with a liquid, the mixture produced is either a solution or a suspension, depending on whether or not the solid will dissolve in the liquid. To understand what is meant by dissolving it is useful to compare the properties of two mixtures, one of which forms a true solution while the other does not. Suitable substances to use are red pottery clay (terracotta) and instant coffee, mixed separately with water and stirred until no lumps remain. Both mixtures are brown, but the clay–water mixture is cloudy, whereas the coffee–water mixture is clear. After a while the clay will probably begin to settle out at the bottom of its container, but the coffee never will. Finally, if the clay–water mixture is filtered through filter paper or paper towel, the clay will remain in the paper whereas the coffee mixture passes through the paper unchanged and leaves no solid residue in it. This simple investigation shows three characteristics of a true solution (coffee) as opposed to a suspension (clay):

a *solution* is clear, will never settle out however long it is left, and is unaffected by filtering;

a *suspension* is cloudy, usually settles out to give a sediment and can be separated by filtering.

A solution is formed when a substance (solute) dissolves in a liquid (solvent). Any substance which will dissolve is said to be soluble; one which will not is said to be insoluble. The differences between a true solution and a suspension arise because the suspension is a mixture of very small, solid and insoluble particles in a liquid. These scatter light passing through the mixture, so making it appear cloudy, and are usually large enough to sink and settle out. In any case they can be removed by filtering, which is in effect a kind of sieving process. A true solution, on the other hand, consists of individual chemical particles (molecules, 8.1), which are thousands of times smaller than the smallest solid particle. It should be emphasized that dissolving a substance such as sugar or salt in water simply makes a mixture: the solid has not disappeared and no new substance has been made. This can easily be shown by tasting the solutions, using short disposable straws to ensure hygiene.

Separating solutions. Because a true solution cannot be separated by filtering, other physical changes have to be used. Most if not all the solutions children make at primary level use water as their solvent, so, for them, separating a solution consists simply of recovering the solute, since there is no need to recover the solvent. This can usually be done either by evaporation or, if necessary, by boiling. For example, a concentrated salt or sugar solution is left exposed to the air in a shallow dish, with a sheet of paper supported about 1 cm above it to exclude dust. As the water evaporates the solute will recrystallize, but gentle heat (for example from a room heater) will usually be needed to make the last of the water evaporate. This kind of solute recovery is used on a large scale in the extraction and refining of salt and sugar, but on a very small scale it is also exactly what happens when fibre-tipped and other pens with liquid ink are used. The ink is a solution of dyes, and when deposited on the paper the solvent, usually water, evaporates and leaves the solute as a visible mark.

If it is necessary to recover the solvent from a solution, the solution is boiled or evaporated and the gas or vapour collected, cooled and condensed. This is the process of distillation, and is used not only to recover industrial solvents from processes such as dry-cleaning (see below) but also to produce pure fresh water from sea-water or contaminated supplies, particularly in dry areas of the world where the process can rely on heating from the Sun.

Having made solutions and suspensions in water and separated the solutes and solids from them, children can experiment with the separation of more complex mixtures such as salt and sand, sugar and chalk or instant coffee and cornflour.

Solubility. If increasing amounts of a solute such as salt are added to water and stirred, a point will be reached at which no more will dissolve. For any solute there is a definite amount which can be dissolved in a certain volume of solvent. This is a measure of another property: its solubility. When as much solute as possible has been dissolved, the solution is said to be saturated. In nearly all cases solubility increases with temperature, so far more sugar or salt can be dissolved in 100 ml of hot water than if the water is cold. This can be shown by making a saturated salt solution in a small volume of hot water. When this is allowed to cool, solid salt will recrystallize, even though the solution has lost very little water by evaporation in such a short time.

Speed of dissolving. When a solid dissolves, it does so only at its surface. Because of this, a single lump of solid will dissolve much more slowly than the same amount crushed to powder. This can be shown by taking two similar small lumps of soap, cutting one into tiny pieces and comparing the amount of time these and the larger lump take to dissolve in the same amount of water at the same temperature and stirred to the same degree. The difference shows why soap powder is preferred for washing clothes and a lump of soap for personal hygiene. A similar investigation can be done by using crystals of rock-salt or coffee-sugar: two similar crystals are selected, one is crushed and the time taken for the two samples to dissolve is compared. This also explains why sugar lumps dissolve much faster than one might expect. They are porous (6.6), made up of small grains of sugar pressed together, with air in between them. Water gets between the grains, softens and breaks up the lump, and then dissolves the individual grains very quickly.

Solvents other than water. Many useful substances which cannot be dissolved in water, such as fats, waxes, resins, oils and gums, can be dissolved by other solvents which evaporate much more quickly. Various resins, both natural and synthetic, form the basis of fast-drying glues and varnishes, which are very useful technologically but whose solvents can, if inhaled, cause permanent injury or death. Many are also highly inflammable, and for these reasons their sale to children is restricted or prohibited. Perfumes, eaux-de-toilette and colognes are made by dissolving oils, some of which are distilled from flowers, in alcohol (ethanol). Dry-cleaning is a process which uses and recycles a powerful fat solvent capable of removing deep-seated dirt and stains without damaging fabrics which would be ruined by water-based cleaning.

Soap and detergents. Most of the dirt on our clothing comes from our skin, which is greasy. Fats and greases will not dissolve in water and are in fact water repellent (6.6). Soap and detergents can clean clothes and skin because they are able to break up a film of greasy dirt into tiny droplets which are then washed away in suspension by the water.

Gases dissolved in water. Gases as well as solids can dissolve in water and other solvents. Air dissolves in water, but unlike solids such as sugar and salt, much more air can dissolve in cold water than in hot. This explains why bubbles of air appear in cold tap-water when it is heated up. Fish and most other water-dwelling animals rely on oxygen dissolved in water for respiration. Fish breathe by taking water in through the mouth and pumping it over the gills on either side of the head. The warming of water by electricity generating stations and the dumping of waste such as sewage can reduce the amount of dissolved oxygen in river water to the point where fish and other animals die.

Children will also be familiar with carbon dioxide gas dissolved in water, in the form of fizzy drinks. Because the gas is put in under pressure, much more can dissolve than normally would do at that temperature. When the bottle is opened, the pressure is released and the excess gas comes out of solution as bubbles which make the drink fizzy.

6.6: Absorbency, chromatography and waterproofing

Many common materials, both natural and manufactured, are solid in that they keep their form when unsupported, but have many small cavities in them which can be filled with liquid or gas. Such materials are described as being porous and include paper, cloth, sugar lumps, most woods, soil and soft rocks such as chalk, some sandstones and limestones. All these materials, in differing degrees, have the property of absorbency, which means that when in contact with a liquid they will soak it up or absorb it. The properties of an absorbent material can easily be seen by cutting a strip from a paper towel and dipping one end into water. The water does not simply wet the paper in contact with it, but moves up the strip to a much higher level. This happens because the water is attracted to the paper fibres. The narrower the gaps in the paper, the greater the force of attraction will be and the higher the water will rise. When a material has absorbed a liquid in this way, it has in effect formed a mixture in which the liquid is dispersed in the solid. Because the liquid is attracted to the solid it tends to stay dispersed in it, and this property is used in towels and babies' nappies. If the wet material is squashed or twisted the liquid may be removed, as for example when squeezing a wet sponge or spinning washing in a spin-dryer. Paint-brushes are specially made to exploit this effect: paint is held in the small spaces between the bristles while these are relaxed, but when they are bent and squeezed together the paint is forced out.

Absorbency is an important property in many materials. In paper towels and kitchen rolls it is an advantage, and children can devise fair tests to measure and compare the absorbency of different kinds and brands. In other materials such as brick (10.2), absorbency is a disadvantage. A porous brick will absorb water and so may allow rising damp to penetrate up into the walls of a house. If a porous brick which has absorbed water is frozen, the ice will expand inside it (6.2) and may cause it to crack or flake.

The ability of porous solids to hold liquids is very important to life on Earth, because most land plants depend on it for their water supply. Soils are porous, and water can move into them both from above (rainfall) and from below (ground-water). Plant roots grow into the soil, and root-hairs (4.2) penetrate between the particles, into the spaces where water is held. They are then able to take up water for use by the plant. The spaces between the particles of clay soils are much smaller than those in sandy soil, so the forces holding water in them are much larger. As a result, clay soils hold more water and dry out much more slowly than sandy soils do (11.10).

Chromatography. Separating solutions with more than one solute, such as sugar and salt dissolved in water, can be very difficult. Some solutions of this kind can be separated by a method which depends on absorbency, known as chromatography. Chromatography means, literally, writing with colour, and the best way for children to investigate it is to separate mixtures of water-soluble dyes. Some interesting mixtures are to be found in felt- and fibre-tipped pens with non-waterproof inks. The first stage is to put a concentrated spot of dye on to a white absorbent paper such as blotting-paper, by repeatedly loading the spot with ink and letting it dry. The paper is then dipped into water, or water is carefully dripped onto the spot of dye. As the water spreads across or outwards, it dissolves the dyes and carries them over the paper, but at different speeds. As a result, the different dyes in the mixture become separated into spots or rings. In this way, children can do their own detective work to see whether different manufacturers use different dye mixtures. Comparing black inks is particularly interesting and the technique has been used to investigate forgeries.

Different dyes are carried over the paper at different speeds because they are attracted to the paper fibres to different degrees. A dye which is strongly attracted to paper will move only slowly and leave a streak behind the main spot, whereas one which is attracted more weakly will move more quickly and leave no streak. Chromatography is a very important technique in industry, research and forensic science for separating complex mixtures of chemicals in solution.

Waterproofing. Sometimes we need to use a porous material such as cloth or paper but do not want it to absorb water. To make a porous material waterproof it has to be coated, or the spaces in it filled up, with another material which will not attract water but repel it. Wax is an example of a material which repels water very strongly. This can be seen by dropping water onto leaves which have a waxy coating, such as those of cabbage or nasturtium. The water can neither wet the wax nor spread out over it, and either runs off or contracts into a round globule. A similar effect can be seen by dropping water onto the feathers of water-birds. If a porous material such as paper is coated with a water-repellent substance it can be made waterproof. Children can experiment by waterproofing paper with a layer of wax crayon, testing it to see how long water takes to seep through and comparing it with untreated paper.

7

Mechanical Properties
of Materials and Objects

7.1: Forces, materials and objects

When forces act on an object, they may bring about two sorts of change: changes in the way the object is moving (Chapter 14) and changes in its shape. The way in which materials and objects respond when forces are applied to them determines and in many cases limits the uses to which they can be put, and so is of great importance in everyday life. Collectively, the properties which govern how materials and objects respond to forces are known as mechanical properties. Investigating and understanding mechanical properties has a reputation for being complex and difficult, but much of the difficulty comes from a confused use of language, particularly in relation to properties such as strength and flexibility. Once the basic mechanical properties are distinguished and understood, and language is being used correctly, most if not all the difficulties can be resolved.

Material properties and object properties. Any object has a range of mechanical properties, but these properties are themselves of two kinds, and it is essential to understand the difference between them. A material property is a property of the stuff of which the object is made. It is unaffected by the size and shape of the individual object under investigation. The material properties discussed in this chapter are: compressibility, hardness, elasticity, plasticity, brittleness and toughness. In contrast to these are object properties. These depend not only on the material of which the object is made, but also on its size and shape. Only two object properties are discussed in this chapter, but both are very important: stiffness and strength. The difference between the two kinds of property can be understood by considering two objects made of steel: a strip 20 cm long, 2 cm wide and 1 mm thick; and a bar 20 cm long, 2 cm wide and 2 cm thick. Both would be equally difficult to scratch, so their hardness is the same: this is a material property. The strip, however, would need a much smaller force to bend it than the bar would. This is a measure of its stiffness, so stiffness is an object property.

Table 7.1 Summary of mechanical properties of materials and objects

Type of shape change	Material property	Object property
Dent/scratch surface	**Hardness:** measure of how easy/ difficult it is to dent or scratch.	
Deformation	When force is no longer applied to deformed material, it: • returns to original shape: **elastic**; • retains new shape: **plastic**.	Object cannot be deformed: it is **rigid**. Object can be deformed: it is **flexible**. Measure of resistance to deformation is **stiffness** (specify whether in compression, tension or bending).
Fracture	How (in what manner) does fracture occur? • suddenly (cracks spread easily): **brittle**; • slowly: **tough**.	Size of force required to cause fracture is measure of **strength** (specify whether in compression, tension or bending).

In discussing compressibility (7.2) we are concerned mainly with gases, but also with liquids and solids. All the other properties discussed in this chapter are shown only by solids, and are summarized in Table 7.1.

7.2: Compressibility

The major differences between solids, liquids and gases are discussed in sections 6.1–6.3. Another important difference is seen when squashing (compression) forces are applied to gases and liquids in closed containers. This can be investigated by using a bicycle-pump or a large plastic syringe with a finger held tightly over the hole in the end. When the plunger is pushed in, the air in the barrel is squashed into a smaller space: it is compressed. Compressed gas pushes outwards on the vessel containing it, so if the plunger is released it springs back. Children are likely to have experience of compressing air, through inflating bicycle tyres and balloons. The property of compressibility means that gas-filled bags and tubes can act as shock absorbers, an effect made use of in car and bicycle tyres, air-beds, inflatable cushions and the air-bags fitted in cars to prevent the driver hitting the steering-wheel in the event of a crash.

It can easily be seen and understood that when a gas is squashed, its volume decreases. It is equally easy to see that attempts to squash a solid block of metal or hard plastic bring about no detectable change in volume or shape. For all purposes and observations of everyday life, these solids are incompressible. Because liquids change shape very readily, it may be less obvious that they are just as incompressible as solids are. The incompressibility of a liquid is, however, very easy to experience. If water is drawn up carefully into a plastic syringe so that there are no air bubbles in it, and a finger is placed firmly over the end, it is impossible to push the plunger in. Similarly, if a plastic drinks bottle is completely filled with water and the top screwed on, squeezing it has very little effect: it changes shape a little but then cannot be squashed any more. This can be compared with the amount by which the same bottle can be squashed when filled with air. If an elastic container such as a balloon is filled with water and squashed it changes shape, but does not become smaller as it would if filled with air.

Care should be taken to distinguish between compressibility and the changes of shape which some solids undergo when they are squashed. For example, it is possible to squash a plastic eraser out of shape using one's hands, but this does not involve a change in volume: the eraser is still the same size and, like a water-filled balloon, it is incompressible. The same is true of clay and other similar materials.

There are some solids which can be puzzling because they do seem to be compressible. Balsa wood is one example with which children may be familiar, and corks in wine bottles remain tight because they are compressed as they are inserted. The behaviour of these materials when they are squashed can be explained by remembering that although they behave as solids, they are porous (6.6), with microscopic cavities in them which are filled with air. When they are squashed the air in them, like that in a dry sponge, is either compressed or squeezed out so the solid parts move closer together and the volume of the object decreases. The cork, when released, usually recovers its shape, but squashed balsa wood will not spring back fully. This is the difference between an elastic and a plastic material (7.6).

7.3: Hardness and its estimation

Hardness is a measure of how easy or difficult it is to dent or scratch the surface of a material. It is a material property (7.1) and so does not depend on the size or shape of the object under test. It is not necessary to measure hardness precisely, but useful comparisons can be made between a range of common materials. At its simplest, comparing hardness consists of attempting to dent or scratch one material with another. In this way, objects such as a lump of modelling clay, a stick of chalk, a piece of wood and a steel nail can be placed in a rank order of hardness. The modelling clay can be dented by all the others so it must be the softest. The steel nail can dent all the others but cannot be dented by them, so it is the hardest. The investigation can be extended by trying to find materials which are softer than the modelling clay (e.g. jelly) and harder than the nail (e.g. a hard steel file or a piece of flint). When working with the harder materials children will not be able to produce dents, so the better criterion of scratching one material with another can be introduced.

Since 1820, the hardness of rocks and minerals has been measured by scratching them, according to a standard scale known as Moh's scale of hardness. The details of the original scale are not relevant, but values vary from 1 (softest: talc) to 10 (hardest: diamond). Some typical hardnesses on Moh's scale are: finger-nail 2–2.5;

'copper' coin 3; steel knife-blade 5.5; window glass 5.5; hard steel file 6–7. With the scratching test, these 'standard' materials can be used to find rough hardness values for groups of common materials such as plastic, metal, wood, brick and stone and, if necessary, to compare a range of specimens from each group.

Some care may be needed to distinguish between scratching and the rubbing off of material. For example, a steel nail will not scratch a flint pebble or a piece of granite, but metal can be rubbed off onto the stone. Seeing this, children may ignore the scratches on the nail and conclude, wrongly, that it is the harder of the two.

7.4: The application of forces: compression, tension and bending

Changes in shape are one of the main ways in which we can tell that forces are acting on an object. Such changes are of two kinds: the object may be pushed or pulled out of shape (distortion or deformation), or it may break (fracture), or both may occur, distortion being followed by fracture.

When investigating the effects of forces on objects, it is essential always to be aware of the way in which the forces are being applied and to make this clear in any report. In developing children's knowledge and understanding of how objects respond by changing shape, it is useful to begin with forces which they can apply themselves, with their bodies. They should experience applying forces to a variety of materials with their hands and simple machines such as scissors (14.9). Six ways of applying forces are illustrated by Fig. 7.1. By experimenting with strips of plastic foam it is possible to build up first-hand knowledge of different ways of applying forces and at the same time the idea can be developed that some responses of an object are related to its size and shape as well as to the material of which it is made.

Wherever possible, investigations into forces and their effects should involve measurement, using either standard or non-standard units. The standard unit of force is the newton (symbol: N) which is roughly equal to the weight of 100 g, so 1 kg presses down, on Earth, with a force of about 10 N (15.2). Forces can be measured using weights or forcemeters. In general, weights are easier to measure with but more difficult to use, whereas forcemeters are easier to use but have scales which children may have difficulty in reading. Non-standard measurement of forces, for example by adding yogurt-pots of dry sand, is a useful way to begin measuring and comparing forces in the early years. It is also helpful to begin, even with older children, by helping them to make rough comparisons based on their senses. More precise measurements of forces using weights and forcemeters, and the changes these bring about, are likely to lead to a better understanding of materials and their properties if they grow out of simpler and more direct observations.

In the remainder of this chapter, attention will be focused on the ways in which materials and objects respond to forces applied in three ways: squashing (compression), stretching or pulling (tension) and bending (Fig. 7.1a–d).

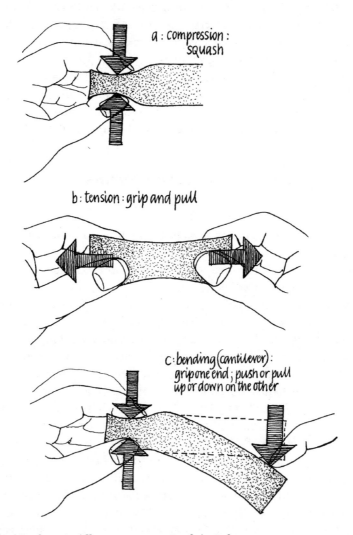

Figure 7.1 *Applying forces in different ways to a strip of plastic foam*

7.5: Stiffness and flexibility

An object which showed no change when forces were applied to it would be perfectly rigid. In reality, even objects which seem to be rigid, such as bars and blocks
of steel, do change shape very slightly when quite small forces act on them, but the
changes are so small that they are very difficult to measure. However, rigidity is still
a useful idea because as far as children are concerned a lot of objects such as bricks,
thick metal bars and wooden beams are rigid: their shape cannot be changed by any
force the children can apply.

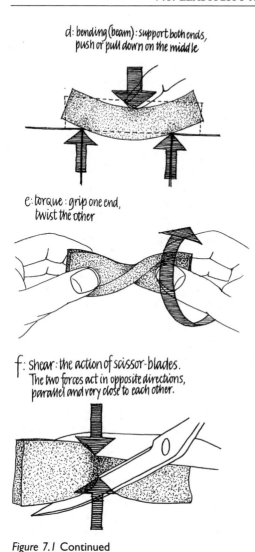

d: bending (beam): support both ends, push or pull down on the middle

e: torque: grip one end, twist the other

f: shear: the action of scissor-blades. The two forces act in opposite directions, parallel and very close to each other.

Figure 7.1 Continued

There is also a need for a concept which will enable children to describe the behaviour of objects whose shape can be changed, but only by applying quite large forces to them. This concept is summed up in the property of stiffness, which is a measure of how difficult it is to change the shape of an object: the more the object resists changing shape, the greater the stiffness it shows. Thus a thick steel wire has high stiffness in bending, whereas a thin wire has low stiffness: it is flexible. Stiffness as a property is quite distinct from strength, though the two are often confused, especially when children talk or write about making objects change shape (7.7).

Flexibility can be thought of as the property opposed to rigidity and stiffness, but simply to describe an object as 'flexible' can be misleading. As always, it is necessary to know how the forces which made it change its shape were applied. A piece of string, for example, is highly flexible (it has very low stiffness) in bending, but in tension it resists changing shape and will not get longer, so it shows high stiffness. It may seem odd to refer to a material such as string as being stiff, but a taut string is, and feels, much less flexible and much stiffer than a slack one.

Stiffness and flexibility depend on the size and shape of the object as well as on the material of which it is made, so they are both object properties (7.1). For example, a cardboard tube may be very stiff or even rigid when an attempt is made to bend it; but if it is cut down longways with a knife, the cardboard of which it is made is quite flexible. It is the cylindrical shape of the tube which gives it its rigidity.

7.6: Elasticity and plasticity

Changes of shape in a flexible object when forces are applied to it are of two kinds, depending on what happens when the forces are removed. If the object is springy and returns to its original shape when released, as a rubber band does, it is said to be elastic. If, on the other hand, the object retains its new shape when released, as modelling clay does, it is said to be plastic. Elasticity and plasticity are material properties (7.1), but they are not mutually exclusive: most common flexible materials show a combination of the two.

When forces are applied to a flexible object, it begins by changing shape elastically and, up to a point, it will carry on changing that way, going back to its original shape when released. This can be seen by repeatedly bending and releasing a piece of thin, stiff card, increasing the force applied and the bending a little each time, and observing what happens when it is released. Up to a point the card regains its original shape, but if it is bent more than this it will not go back all the way: it has changed plastically and part of the bend in it is permanent.

Materials such as modelling clay which seem to behave in a completely plastic way simply have very little elasticity: they start to become permanently distorted almost as soon as a force is applied to them, and they spring back hardly at all when released. Any non-springy flexible object, such as string which is not under tension, shows plastic deformation as its shape is changed.

Plasticity and elasticity as properties are independent of stiffness and flexibility, but to describe how real objects behave it is usually necessary to refer to both. For example, a rubber block and a thin rubber band are both highly elastic, but the block is much stiffer than the band, because larger forces are needed to change its shape. Similarly, cold modelling clay is much stiffer than warm, though both show almost perfect plasticity. This principle also works the other way round: the amount of distortion which any object undergoes depends on how large a force is applied to it. This is another aspect of the principle, very important when investigating forces and movement, that 'the bigger the force, the bigger the change' (14.1). It can be investigated using both elastic and plastic materials. If the length of a rubber band is measured as it is stretched by increasing weights, it will be found that the length increase is a steady one over most of its range, so that if length is plotted against weight applied, we would expect the graph to be a straight line. If plasticine is slightly softened by warming and then made into spheres, these will show plastic distortion when dropped onto a hard surface. The amount of distortion, shown by the size of the flat circular face produced by the impact, increases as the ball is dropped from an increasing height (14.6). This is a particularly suitable investigation for young children because measurement of the distortion is unnecessary: they can make a permanent record of their results by coating the flattened face of the ball with paint and printing it.

Many processes in school and industry exploit a combination of plasticity and elasticity. Making models in card and pop-up books in paper both require sheets of materials to be creased and bent permanently (plastic deformation) while relying on their springiness (elasticity) to retain or make shapes. In making vehicle body panels, sheet steel is permanently pressed into shape using large forces, but still remains somewhat flexible and springy.

7.7: Strength

'Strong' and 'strength' are words with a complex set of interrelated meanings for both adults and children. Even if one excludes such everyday uses as 'a strong smell' or 'a strong argument', and concentrates on 'strength' in the context of forces acting on objects, neither the uses of the word nor the concepts behind them are simple. Children are likely to use 'strong' in at least four ways, to express four different concepts:
1. 'He can lift a heavy weight. He must be strong.' (Concept: the ability to exert a large force.)
2. 'She gave the trolley a strong push and it went faster.' (Concept: the large force itself.)
3. 'It's a strong spring. I couldn't squash it very much.' (Concept: the property of withstanding a large force with little change of shape.)
4. 'The thread is thin but very strong. We hung 6 kg on it before it broke.' (Concept: the property of withstanding a large force without breaking.)

Of these four examples, the first two clearly are not concerned with the way objects respond by changing shape when forces are applied to them, and so can have nothing to do with the scientific concept of 'strength'. The third and fourth examples are more problematic. The word 'strong' appears to mean much the same thing in both; but in fact each example represents a distinct scientific concept.

It is the fourth example which uses 'strong' correctly in the accepted scientific sense. Scientifically, strength is a measure of the forces which an object can withstand before it breaks. The greater the force withstood, the stronger the object. Squashing the object until it breaks gives a measure of its compression strength, while pulling or stretching it shows its tensile strength and bending its bending strength. Strength is an object property (7.1): it depends on the size and shape of the object as well as on the materials of which it is made. This means that if we wish to compare the strength of two materials, such as the bending strength of two samples of concrete, it is essential in order to make the test fair that the objects tested should be of the same size and shape, as well as being tested under the same conditions.

The third example given above uses the word 'strong' in a potentially confusing way, because it refers, not to strength in the scientific sense, but to a property already discussed: that of stiffness, which indicates how large a force is needed to change the shape of an object. Confusion between stiffness and strength is very common, and comes about partly because the two are often associated: many useful objects such as steel nails and wooden beams are both strong and stiff, whichever way forces are applied to them. The confusion can be avoided by remembering that stiffness is related not to strength but to flexibility. For example, compare a rubber band which stretches a lot and can support a load of 50 N (5 kg) with a cotton thread which does not stretch but can support only 25 N (2.5 kg) before it breaks. The band has low stiffness (it stretches easily) and higher tensile strength, whereas the thread has high stiffness (it resists getting longer) but only half the tensile strength of the band: the two properties are quite independent of each other.

7.8: Brittleness and toughness

Strength as a property is a measure of how large a force an object can withstand before it breaks, but it tells us nothing about the way in which the fracture is likely to occur. Clearly, this is an important issue: to use materials which break suddenly and without warning could be (and all too often is) disastrous. Two properties which can help us to understand and predict the breaking of materials are brittleness and toughness.

A brittle material characteristically breaks suddenly and completely, as a china plate may do if it is dropped onto a hard floor. There is no halfway state: either the material breaks, or it does not. Another characteristic of brittle materials is that fractures in them are usually fairly smooth and 'clean', not rough, splintery or jagged. This gives a clue to the nature of brittleness: it is caused by the way in which cracks spread through a material. Once a crack has started in a brittle material, only very small forces are needed to make it spread until the fracture is complete. This can be seen when window-glass is cut to size. The glazier uses a glass-cutter (made of a very hard material) to make a light, even scratch on the surface of the glass. Once the glass has been scratched, only a very small force, in the form of tapping on the underside, is needed to spread the fracture through the glass and so break it.

There is a common tendency to think of brittle materials as being weak and easily broken, in other words as having low strength. This is not always true. It may take a large force to make the first crack in a brittle material and if so, the material is strong. Glass and the very hard steel used in files are examples of strong materials which are also very brittle: they break suddenly if they are bent, but it takes a large force to do it. Similarly, there is a tendency, both among children and adults, to think that all materials which break suddenly are hard. This association probably comes from experience with brittle materials such as glass, china and brick, but it is false.

Dried, uncooked pasta and board chalk are not hard, but both are brittle materials which are useful because children can experiment with them safely and observe how they break. There are, however, much softer brittle materials. A plastic eraser, for example, is springy when squashed (elastic in compression) and may appear to be quite tough, but if it is bent it shows elastic deformation up to a point and then cracks suddenly with no warning. The crack spreads very quickly into a clean fracture which splits the eraser in two. An even softer material is jelly. It may seem odd to refer to it as being brittle but, as many cooks attempting to turn jelly from a mould can testify, once a crack has started the weight of the jelly alone is usually enough to make it spread until the mass falls apart.

The property which contrasts with brittleness is toughness. In a tough material, cracks will not spread easily, so the material breaks more slowly and often shows signs of breaking before it fractures completely. A good way to study the breaking of a tough material is to hold a thin garden cane (made from bamboo) in both hands and bend it slowly, watching it carefully until it breaks. Cracks can be seen, and sometimes heard, long before the final break, which usually happens slowly. The fracture itself is very ragged and splintery, quite unlike the clean break characteristic of brittle materials.

Polythene sheet is also useful as an example, because it shows very clearly that cracks do not spread readily in a very tough material. Cut strips 2 × 20 cm from a polythene bag, make a small cut in one long side and pull the ends apart. The fracture will spread from the cut, but only very slowly, in complete contrast to the behaviour of glass and other brittle materials. Polythene also provides an example of deformation which is partly elastic and partly plastic. The stretched strip will recoil a little when it is released, but most of the increase in length is permanent.

In nearly all materials brittleness is a disadvantage, and can be seen as the price paid for other useful properties such as the hardness of steel files, the transparency of glass and the easily cleaned surface of china. Toughness, on the other hand, is very often a major advantage. Much of the usefulness of materials such as wood, cloth, string, paper, polythene and many metals comes from their toughness.

In buildings toughness can be critical (10.2). Wood is very tough and good for smaller buildings, but in comparison with other materials such as steel and concrete it is not very strong in relation to its size. Concrete on its own, however, is not a good material for beams (in ceilings, or over windows and doors) because it is very brittle and under bending forces it can break entirely without warning. As a result, concrete used for pillars, beams and floors in large structures such as multi-storey buildings and bridges is reinforced with rods or meshes of steel, which not only increase its bending strength but also its toughness, so that if it does crack, the cracks should not spread right through. It also means that the structure should give warning signs long before it actually breaks.

7.9: Linking the properties of materials to their uses

Once a basic knowledge of the properties of materials has been built up, it is possible to understand much more clearly how and why materials and objects are used in different ways. An effective way to do this is firstly, to identify the materials which are used together for a particular purpose. Secondly, identify the properties which make each one useful and list them under 'advantages'. Thirdly, identify any properties which may limit the usefulness of each material and list them under 'disadvantages'. It is then possible to compare the contribution which each one makes with the way in which it behaves and changes.

For example, if one wished to send a glass bowl (a very brittle object) in a parcel by post, one might use plastic foam 'chips' for packing, a cardboard box, strong brown wrapping paper, adhesive plastic tape and string. These materials can be assembled in the classroom and children asked to investigate and list their properties as described above. A set of results is given in Table 7.2.

This investigation can act as the starting-point for many other enquiries such as: what would happen if some of the properties of the materials were changed and, for example, string and paper became elastic? Where do all the materials come from? Are they natural (10.1), and if they are not, how are they made? How does packing a glass bowl in this way protect it? Similar investigations can be carried out into many sets of materials. Those used in houses (10.2) and bicycles are particularly interesting and have the added advantages that children are already acquainted with many of them at first hand, and work on them can be linked up to many other areas of the curriculum.

Table 7.2 *Comparing the properties of packing materials*

Material	Advantages	Disadvantages
Plastic foam 'chips' (packing)	Very soft, flexible, compressible, elastic; tough, very cheap and lightweight.	May shift in transit, so need to be packed firmly in a thick layer.
Cardboard (box)	Fairly soft; strong and rather stiff in bending and compression; tough.	(Not waterproof)
Soft polythene sheet	Soft; very flexible in bending and tough; waterproof	Not very stiff in tension; may deform plastically
Brown paper (wrapping)	Fairly soft, very flexible and mainly plastic in bending; very stiff and fairly strong in tension; tough.	(Not waterproof)
String (tying up)	Soft, very flexible and plastic in bending; very strong and stiff in tension; very tough; not affected by water.	(None)
Plastic adhesive tape (sealing)	Soft, flexible in bending; strong and fairly stiff in tension; adhesive (sticky).	Not waterproof; glue may come off if wetted; very brittle

8
Explaining Physical Changes

Investigating materials by finding out how they respond and change in different ways, and linking their properties to their everyday uses, will enable the majority of pupils at primary level to learn as much as they need to about the properties of materials and physical changes. There are, however, two reasons for including a chapter on explaining physical changes in the present book. The first is that there will always be pupils who can and need to go deeper into explanations than the majority. The second is that in order to begin developing an understanding of why materials behave as they do, it is necessary to make the acquaintance, in a very simple form, of one of the most powerful ideas in science: the particulate or atomic theory of matter. This theory is also essential to an understanding of chemical change (Chapter 9) and electricity (Chapter 13).

8.1: Atoms and molecules

The atomic or particulate theory of matter is not only one of the most powerful and far-reaching ideas in science: it is one of the most rewarding. In return for developing a few simple concepts, an extraordinary diversity of everyday events and scientific observations can be explained. In its simplest form, the atomic theory of matter is the idea that all material things, whether solids, liquids or gases, are made up of very large numbers of very small particles called atoms. According to the theory, matter is not continuous, as it appears to be, but particulate. As a basic idea, the theory is very ancient: it seems first to have been proposed by the Greeks Leucippus and Democritus about 450 BC.

The word 'atom' comes from the Greek for 'cannot be cut', and to help understand what was meant, Democritus proposed an ingenious thought-experiment, beginning with a small piece of pure gold and an exceedingly sharp knife. We have to imagine that the knife is used to cut the gold in half, then to cut one half into quarters, a quarter into eighths, and so on. Even when the piece of gold becomes too small to see, Democritus wants us to imagine what would happen if we could carry on cutting it. Finally there would come a time when we had reached the smallest piece of gold there can possibly be. This cannot be cut in two, because if it were, it would not be gold any more. That smallest possible piece, says Democritus, is that which cannot be cut: an atom.

The Greeks had several other ideas about atoms which scientists now believe to be correct; for example, the idea that they can join together in groups. Today such groups of atoms are called molecules. They also realized that atoms and molecules are very small, and they are in fact so small that it is difficult to gain a clear idea of their size, so two or three different ways of trying to do this may be useful. If we start with a length of 1 metre, then one thousandth of a metre (10^{-3}m) is a millimetre, still within the range of ordinary measurement. One thousandth of a millimetre (10^{-6}m) is called a micrometre and objects of this size, such as many bacteria and microbes, can be seen with powerful microscopes. But to get to around the size of a molecule of sugar, we have to go a thousand times smaller still, to 10^{-9}m, called a nanometre which is one millionth part of a millimetre. As molecules go, those of sugar are quite large, being made up of 45 atoms of three different kinds. Molecules of water, each with only three atoms, are much smaller.

Another way to gain some idea of how small atoms are is to imagine things enormously enlarged. One elegant example was given by Andrade and Huxley over fifty years ago: 'If we could magnify a copper wire, of the thickness of a hair, until it was big enough to fill a wide street, the atoms of which it is made would be the size of small specks of dust.'

Another ingenious thought-experiment is attributed to the great physicist Lord Kelvin, who devised it about a century ago to show how small molecules are by giving an idea of how many there are in a glass of water. He asks us to imagine a drinking-glass of water, whose molecules are labelled so that each one of them can be recognized and counted when mixed with ordinary water. (This would be very difficult, if not impossible, even with modern technology.) In the imaginary experiment, the glass of 'labelled' water is tipped into the sea and left for a very long time (several thousand years) until the labelled molecules are evenly mixed throughout all the oceans of the world. An investigator then goes to the sea and takes from it one glass of water. What are the chances that one or more of the labelled molecules would be taken up? Lord Kelvin calculated that each glassful of water, in all the seas and oceans, would on average contain not one, but a hundred of them!

Two other basic ideas need to be introduced at this stage. The first is that, in all materials and at any temperature we normally experience, the molecules are not still, but are moving, constantly and very rapidly. The other is that together with this constant movement there are basic differences in the ways molecules are arranged and how close together they are. Both these ideas will be developed by using them to explain the properties of gases, liquids and solids.

8.2: Explaining the properties of a gas

A gas is in some ways the simplest kind of material to think about and investigate, because it has no form or structure at all. In the air around us, the average distance between molecules is about ten times their own size, so they can move between each other freely, except when they collide. However, because they move very fast, each molecule collides with others very frequently: in the order of a thousand million times each second. On a tiny scale, any gas is a very violent and chaotic material, and its basic properties at the molecular level help to explain many of the properties which children can observe and investigate.

Because molecules of gases move so fast and are free to move away from each other, they fill any container (such as a room) completely and do not settle at the bottom as a liquid does. It is only on the scale of the whole planet that the weight of the air is enough to keep it in a layer around the Earth. The distance between gas molecules means that any gas is about 99.9 per cent empty space. This explains why gases are compressible. When a gas is squashed, its molecules are pushed closer together and this has clearly observable effects. If the molecules are closer together, more of them will collide with each square centimetre of the container every second, so the force pushing out on it will increase. If the container is elastic, like a balloon, it will stretch. If air is squashed into a rigid container such as a sealed syringe or bicycle-pump, the walls will resist the extra force, but the piston will feel springy: a force has to be applied to keep it pushed in. Compressed gas is in fact an example of an elastic material (7.6), because when the squashing force is released the gas goes back to its original size.

Heating and cooling affects a gas (and indeed any material) by changing the speed and violence of molecular movement. As a gas is heated, its molecules move more and more violently, and this can have two results. If the gas is not sealed in a container and is free to expand, the distance between its molecules, and so its volume, will increase. This thermal expansion (12.3) means that every litre of hot gas will have fewer molecules in it than a litre of cold gas, so it will weigh less. (Technically, it would be said to have a lower density.) This explains why heated air rises and hot air balloons can float in the cooler air around them (14.10). On the other hand, if the gas is in a sealed container the molecules will move more rapidly as it is heated up, so they will collide more frequently with each other and with the container, pushing outwards on its walls.

An example of this occurs when car tyres become 'hard' and over-inflated, which is likely to happen on a hot day when driving at sustained high speed, for example on a motorway. The tyre heats up and this causes the compressed air inside to exert an even bigger outward force on the tyre. This may make the tyre change shape so that it does not grip the road effectively and there is less friction between them (14.4), which can be dangerous. Cooling a tyre has the opposite effect: the movement of the molecules becomes less rapid and so the force they exert on the container decreases. In very cold weather, car tyres may become under-inflated and too 'soft' to grip the road properly. It is usual, when measuring the effect of compressed gas on a container such as a tyre, to measure not force but pressure, which is the force acting on each unit area. Pressure is not a construct usually required in primary science, but it may be useful for teachers to remember that it is a force, not pressure, which keeps tyres inflated and liquids such as water and blood flowing through pipes.

8.3: Explaining the properties of a liquid

When a gas is cooled to a low enough temperature, it turns into a liquid by condensation (6.3), for example when steam turns into liquid water. When this happens, there is a very large decrease in volume, and the liquid occupies only about one-thousandth of the space that the gas did. This can more readily be shown in reverse. If a pan of water is boiling, the bubbles which rise to the surface are steam, i.e. water in the gas phase. Even without measuring, it can easily be seen that a very large volume of steam is given off with no detectable drop in the water level. The change in volume as a gas condenses shows that in a liquid the molecules are very much closer together, and it is thought that every molecule is in contact with at least some others. Although molecules in a liquid are still moving, they cannot move between each other nearly as freely as molecules of a gas can.

Molecules in a liquid, instead of travelling at very high speed between collisions, can be thought of as jostling very rapidly but able to move position only slowly, rather like people in a dense, excited crowd. The closeness of the molecules and the restriction of movement which this brings about can help to explain many properties of liquids. Because the molecules are not free to move away from each other even though they can move between each other, a small amount of liquid cannot fill a large container and simply lies at the bottom. Because its molecules are not moving freely and colliding violently with the container, a liquid does not press out on the walls in the way that a compressed gas does. The outward force of water on a container, which can be clearly felt in a water-filled balloon, comes simply from the weight of the water. However, because its molecules can slip past each other, a liquid has no shape of its own and its own weight will make it flow downwards if it is free to do so.

In a gas, it is easy to squash the molecules closer together, but in a liquid they are already very close and some are in contact with each other. Once molecules are in contact, very large forces are needed to make them move closer still, and this explains why liquids are, for all everyday purposes, incompressible. However, liquids do change in volume when they are heated and cooled, for exactly the same reason that a gas does: heating makes the molecules move more rapidly, so the average distance between them increases slightly and the whole liquid expands. Cooling reverses the process, and these changes are used in liquid thermometers to measure temperature (12.3).

Explaining evaporation is slightly more complex. The key idea is that if a liquid is at the same temperature throughout, all the molecules will on average be moving at the same speed, but at any instant some will be moving faster and others slower than this average. If a fast-moving molecule happens to be at the surface of the liquid it may escape into the air above, and it is this escaping of molecules which is evaporation. The hotter the liquid is, the more rapidly its molecules move and, if other conditions are the same, more of them will escape and the rate of evaporation will increase. However, a faster-moving molecule also has a higher-than-average energy level, and as it is always these molecules which escape, evaporation results in a transfer of energy from the liquid, which causes the cooling effect characteristic of evaporation (6.3).

8.4: Explaining the properties of a solid

If a liquid is cooled to a low enough temperature it will solidify or freeze and form a solid. What happens is that as the liquid cools, the molecules within it move less and less violently and rapidly, and finally become joined together as the solid forms. In a solid, the molecules (or atoms) are moving rapidly by vibrating as they do in a liquid. The critical difference is that in a solid, the molecules are not free to move past each other. Because the speed of molecular movement is affected by temperature, solids expand on heating and contract on cooling just as liquids and gases do.

Most liquids shrink a little as they solidify, so molecules in a solid are somewhat closer together than those in a liquid (water is peculiar in that it expands as it freezes, 6.2). As a result, solids are incompressible as far as any normal uses are concerned, just as liquids are. However, the obvious differences between solids and liquids do not come about because the molecules are more tightly packed in a solid, but because they are bonded together. It is this bonding between molecules which gives solid materials the definite shape which liquids lack, and many of their mechanical properties (Chapter 7). For example, in order to scratch a material its surface has to be penetrated and the bonds between molecules broken. The molecules of different materials are bonded in different ways, and greater forces are needed to break some bonds than others. The more difficult it is to break the bonds between molecules by scratching the surface, the harder the material is.

8.5: Explaining the properties of some flexible materials

When forces are applied to a material, they are resisted by the bonding between the molecules which make it up. The stronger the bonding, the more the material will resist changing shape. If the force is large enough, molecular bonds can be broken and the material may fracture, either partly or completely. The concept of bonding between molecules can help us to explain at least some of the properties of common flexible materials (7.6).

Flexible materials such as threads, fabrics, wood, paper, card, rubber and plastics are made up of large molecules which are like very long, thin chains, either straight or branching. Each chain molecule is made up of several thousand small molecules joined end-to-end in a repeating pattern. These materials are called polymers and they are worth considering in some detail, because they show the connection between mechanical properties and molecular structure very clearly, in ways that children can investigate. Large forces are needed to break these long chain molecules in tension, but the way they are arranged in the material can vary in two main ways. First, they can be straight and mostly lined up in the same direction (as they are in a cotton thread, for example), or they can be tangled up, rather like long threads all bundled together. Secondly, they can be bound sideways onto each other to a greater or lesser degree.

Rubber bands. Rubber is elastic because it has tangled molecules which are only weakly bonded to each other. When the band is pulled, the tangled molecules begin to straighten out. Only a small force is needed to do this and make the band stretch a lot. If it is released at this stage, the molecules relax and curl up again so that the band shortens to its original length, showing the property of elasticity. If a greater force is applied, however, more and more molecules are straightened out and it becomes harder and harder to make the rubber stretch: its stiffness increases. Finally, the rubber will not stretch any more because all the molecules are fully straightened out, though if a large enough force is applied the molecules will be broken and the band itself will snap.

Cotton thread. Cotton is a plant fibre made of cellulose (4.4). It has long, straight chain molecules which are mostly lined up along the thread but which are not strongly bound to each other, so that the thread is very flexible. When it is pulled, however, the thread is very stiff: it stretches hardly at all because the force is not tending to straighten molecules out as it is in the rubber band (they are straight already), but pull them apart. Finally, if the force is big enough it will overcome the bonding in the molecular chains and snap the thread, giving a measure of its tensile strength.

Wood. The fibrous structure of wood is also based on the long, straight chain molecules of cellulose, lying along the grain and similar to those in cotton thread, except that in most kinds of wood they are very strongly bound to each other. This means that the wood not only resists tension as the thread does, but is also stiff in bending, tough and difficult to split.

Polythene. This widely used plastic material is made in many different grades. In the soft kind used for making bags, the long chain molecules are mostly lined up with each other in the same direction as the faint ridges on the surface of the sheet. They are only weakly bonded together, and the behaviour of a strip of polythene when it is pulled depends partly on the direction of the pull. This can be shown by cutting strips about 1 × 10 cm from a bag, some along the ridges and others at right angles to them. If the pull is in the same direction as the ridges (and so the molecular chains) the strip is quite hard to stretch, and unless it is pulled very gradually it is likely to snap. This is because the force is breaking some of the bonds between groups of molecules, which are slipping past each other. This cannot happen quickly, and in many materials such as the cotton thread it cannot happen at all. If the force is applied too suddenly, larger fractures occur and the strip comes apart.

If a pull is applied, again gradually, at right angles to the ridges and molecular chains, the strip stretches under a much smaller load, usually by forming a narrow 'neck' or stretch zone. This happens because bonding at right angles to the molecules is much weaker than it is along them, so they are easily pulled round and lined up in the direction of the pull. In the process, the stretch zone becomes much longer and thinner and, like the first test strip, it is hard to stretch further because all the molecules are lined up along it. In all cases almost all the stretching undergone by the strips is irreversible; an example of plastic deformation.

8.6: Crystals

When evaporating solutions of materials such as sugar and salt, particularly if this is done under a microscope, children will see a form of solidification which does not result from cooling and which involves the formation of crystals. The definite shape of crystals (those of sugar and salt are both cubic) comes about because, as the solute comes out of solution, its molecules become stacked in a very orderly way onto those which have already formed a solid. The process seems to begin in a very strong solution when tiny particles of insoluble solids such as dust form centres for crystal formation to start. Once it has begun, the orderly stacking of molecules continues with no outside interference. Because all the molecules of any chemical substance are the same size and shape, the structure of a crystal is extremely regular and highly ordered and, with very few exceptions, all the crystals of the same substance have the same basic shape.

Crystals are also formed when many substances, which have been melted by heating, cool and solidify. All metals form crystals in this way, and any metal is a mass of interlocking crystals. These are usually small, but sometimes are large and easy to see, for example the flat crystals of zinc on galvanized iron. When forces are applied to metals and they change shape, the crystals do not break but slide past each other in various ways, much as the molecules in a strip of stretched polythene will do. Because the metal crystals slide past each other rather than breaking, metals show very distinctive physical properties: they can be hammered into sheets, drawn into wires and most of them are very tough. When metals are mixed as alloys and worked by heating and hammering, their crystal structure changes and with it their mechanical properties.

9
Chemical Changes

9.1: The nature of chemical change

Many of the processes which change materials, and with which children are familiar, are physical. These include changes brought about by mixing (6.4, 6.5), by applying forces to change shape (Chapter 7) and changes of state caused by heating and cooling (6.2, 6.3). Such changes may alter many properties of the material or object, but do not result in any new or different kind of material being formed. A change which does result in a different kind of material from that which was present before is a chemical change. Children will also be familiar with many processes which involve chemical changes, and which affect their lives in a variety of ways. Cooking (9.2), for example, is useful, whereas the rusting of steel (9.5) is a serious nuisance. Other chemical changes such as decay (5.8) and burning (9.4) are useful in some circumstances and destructive in others. Observing and describing these and other processes gives children a context, firmly based in their own experience, in which to continue developing such fundamental concepts as change, no-change, sameness, similarity, difference, cause and effect, through basic strategies such as comparing and contrasting. It needs to be clearly understood, however, that at primary level, investigating processes which involve chemical change cannot lead to an understanding of the nature of chemical change itself.

Chemical and physical change. Because they result in the formation of materials or substances different from those which were present before they occurred, chemical changes are fundamentally different from physical changes. In the past there have been unproductive attempts to set up hard-and-fast criteria which would enable teachers at primary level to distinguish in simple ways between chemical and physical changes. Such attempts are very often misleading, because it is not the observable characteristics of a change, such as reversibility, transfer of energy or the appearance of the products which distinguishes chemical changes from physical ones. There is no foolproof way for teachers or children at primary level to show whether or not a new material or substance has been formed as the result of any change, and it will often not be possible to say, just by looking, whether any particular change is chemical, physical, or involves both.

This means that to put a lot of effort into trying to teach the nature of chemical change at primary level is unproductive, because it takes children's learning and inquiry away from their own experience and observations. This does not mean, however, that chemical changes should be ignored and their investigation neglected. The productive strategy is for the teacher to adopt the case-study approach (1.1), researching processes and materials which children are likely to encounter and selecting relevant examples which are known to involve chemical changes. Attention can then be concentrated on observing what is changed and under what conditions, the changes themselves and the products which result, in the context of the children's own lives, experience and interests. The remainder of this chapter is taken up with three examples of case-studies. Other chemical changes are discussed more briefly in Chapter 10, in the context of manufactured materials.

9.2: Chemical changes, cooking and food

Like most of the major groups of materials we use, food is a range of natural and manufactured substances. In preparing many kinds of food, natural raw materials are cooked to make them more palatable, more digestible, or both, and most cooking processes involve at least some chemical changes. Basic cooking relies, at least in part, on changing raw ingredients by heating.

Of the three major kinds of food chemical (carbohydrates, fats and proteins, 3.4), the most interesting chemical changes which children can investigate affect proteins. Boiling water does not affect a fat such as olive oil at all. A dry starchy carbohydrate such as pasta or rice swells up, becomes soft and therefore more easily chewed and digested, but the changes it undergoes are largely physical and can be reversed simply by drying. In contrast, a high protein food such as egg-white is changed chemically by heating, and the changes are obvious, drastic and irreversible.

Boiling an egg. When heated, the proteins in foods change chemically and irreversibly: they become coagulated, which means that their structure becomes tighter and they cling together in a mass much more firmly than before. Egg-white, composed mostly of water with about 9 per cent of protein (albumen) in it, is a very useful material to investigate. Coagulation of the protein is easily shown by dropping a little egg-white into hot water. Children can carry out controlled observations to find the lowest temperature at which it will occur by making small boats of aluminium foil, putting a little egg-white into each and floating them on water at different temperatures. It is also possible to investigate coagulation by comparing the textures of eggs poached or boiled in their shells for different lengths of time. Up to a point, coagulation is a progressive process. The longer an egg is boiled, up to about 10 minutes, the firmer and tougher (and therefore more indigestible!) its white will be. Lightly coagulated protein can hold a lot of water, but if extra water is added and the mixture is overcooked, coagulation and shrinkage are likely to proceed so far that water is squeezed out, which happens in overbaked egg custard.

Cakes and baking powder. Cakes and breads have a distinctive texture: they are spongy, with a firm but soft 'skeleton' trapping thousands of small, gas-filled bubbles. This texture is not simply pleasant to eat: it makes the food much easier to chew and provides it with a large amount of surface area on which digestive juices (3.3) can work effectively. The 'skeleton' of bread and cakes is made mainly of proteins which are present in the flour and coagulated in baking. In some cakes, protein from eggs also helps to make a firm, soft structure. Wheat flour makes the 'lightest' (i.e. the most bubble-filled) bread and cakes, because it contains more proteins with particular chemical properties. When wheat flour is mixed for cooking, these proteins combine with water to form an elastic substance called gluten, a physical process which gives a well-made bread dough its springiness.

The process of making bubbles in the dough or cake mixture is traditionally known as leavening. In a naturally leavened mixture, for example that used to make sponge cakes, air bubbles are incorporated by beating eggs and sugar until they make a foam, adding the other ingredients and cooking immediately. The light, soft texture produced results from a combination of chemical and physical changes. During the cooking the air bubbles expand (physical change) and are made larger by steam produced from water (physical change) squeezed out of the gluten as it coagulates (chemical change), to form the structure of the cake.

In baking which does not use eggs, an alternative way of providing gas bubbles is needed, which uses a second set of chemical changes in addition to the physical ones and the coagulation of protein. The simplest way of doing this is to use mixtures of chemicals (known collectively as baking powder) which, at some stage in the process, undergo a chemical change to produce bubbles of carbon dioxide gas within the mixture. This can be seen by putting a spoonful of baking powder into very hot water. There is a wide variety of chemical mixtures in use, but all of them use 'bicarbonate of soda' (sodium hydrogen carbonate) as the source of carbon dioxide. The commonest kind of baking powder is a mixture of sodium hydrogen carbonate, with acidic chemicals such as 'cream of tartar'. When mixed into the dough, both chemicals dissolve in water and react with each other, giving off carbon dioxide. The carbon dioxide expands and mixes with steam just as the air in a naturally leavened mixture does, and again the gas bubbles are trapped as the protein coagulates. Commercial baking powders also contain starch, which helps to keep the active chemicals dry, preventing them from reacting with each other during storage. Some kinds of flour for domestic use are sold with baking powder already mixed with them in the correct proportion. These are known as self-raising flours.

Yeast and bread. To be easily digestible, bread needs to have the same light, bubble-filled texture as cakes. As when using baking powder, the bubbles in bread are of carbon dioxide mixed with steam, but they are generated in a different way, using chemical changes brought about by yeast.

Yeasts are a group of microscopic fungi (5.3) which in natural conditions live in sugary fluids made by plants, such as the nectar of flowers. The yeast used in making bread is baker's yeast, which has been used and kept in cultivation by bakers and brewers for centuries. It can feed on starch as well as sugar as long as it is moist, though it grows more slowly, partly because the starch has to be digested to sugar before the yeast can use it for food. Yeast normally uses sugar or starch as a source of energy in almost exactly the same way that a human does, by bringing about a complex sequence of chemical changes (respiration, 3.6) which can be summarized like this:

$$\text{sugar} + \text{oxygen} \rightarrow \text{water} + \text{carbon dioxide} \ (+ \text{energy})$$

Yeast has an unusual ability: it can live and grow in a sugary liquid even if there is no oxygen. It still feeds on the sugar, but uses a different set of chemical changes and makes alcohol (ethanol) as a waste product. This is the basis of the alcoholic fermentation of sugar used in the making of beer and wine, but it does not occur in the making of bread.

Bread rises because the yeast, feeding on starch, makes bubbles of carbon dioxide which are trapped by the dough. Steam is also produced as the dough cooks, and the gases expand as the loaf heats up, so the bubbles become bigger and the texture lighter. To produce a properly risen loaf it is necessary to use 'strong' or bread-making flour, which has a higher protein content than ordinary plain flour (12 per cent as compared to about 8 per cent). When the gluten made by the proteins and water coagulates in baking, it makes a strong 'skeleton' which traps the gas bubbles made by the yeast very efficiently, and gives the loaf a firm texture. Active or dried yeast should always be mixed with tepid water. Temperatures above 43°C will kill it, and cold water will prevent it becoming active. When the bread dough has been mixed and kneaded, it is left in a warm place to 'prove' for 1½–2½ hours. During this time the yeast grows, producing quite large bubbles. The dough is kneaded again before finally being shaped, to remove these bubbles and redistribute the yeast.

Bread is baked at about 230°C and during the first 20 minutes the yeast warms up and grows very rapidly, before it is killed and the gluten is coagulated as the temperature rises higher. Looking at a crusty loaf cut in two shows how the cooking proceeds. The yeast on the outside is killed first, so the bubbles in the crust are small and the texture dense. The hardness of the crust is caused by partial drying during the latter stages of baking. The yeast in the middle of the loaf is heated up more slowly and keeps growing for longer, so larger bubbles and a lighter texture are produced. Because the middle of the loaf is still expanding when the crust is hardening, the top of the loaf often splits, and this can be controlled by cutting the dough across just before baking.

Cheese and yogurt. The making of cheese and yogurt, like that of bread, depends on the coagulation of proteins. There are, however, important differences. In making cheese and yogurt the proteins in milk are coagulated, not by heating but by other chemical changes which produce acids. Acids are a very large class of chemicals, all of which have a characteristic sharp taste: the sharpness of lemon juice, for example, is caused by citric acid. Some acids are dangerous and corrosive, but many milder ones are found in foods. Acids, like heat, make proteins contract and coagulate, and the ones which give cheese and yogurt their solidity and texture are made by microbes (bacteria, 5.3).

Milk is a complex mixture which is an emulsion (6.4) of fat droplets in water which also contains a variety of chemicals in solution, including sugars and proteins. Milk also contains microbes, although in the milk we drink most of them have been killed by the process of pasteurization, called after Louis Pasteur, who first devised it for killing off harmful microbes in French wine. In treating milk, pasteurization consists of heating the milk enough to kill microbes but not enough to coagulate the proteins in solution. Not all the microbes are killed in this way, and enough remain to turn the milk sour through chemical changes, mainly by feeding on the sugar lactose and producing lactic acid as a waste product, which gives sour milk its sharp taste. If souring goes on for long enough the milk proteins will be coagulated by the acidic conditions and the milk will curdle, separating into a solid part (curds) and a liquid part (whey). In making cheese, the souring process is made faster by introducing into the pasteurized milk a culture of specially chosen and cultivated bacteria which make lactic acid. After pressing out the whey, the curds are commonly inoculated with other microbes which feed on the proteins and in doing so produce chemicals which give particular cheeses their different flavours. In some ('blue') cheeses, the microbes are fungi (moulds) which can be seen in veins or cavities within the cheese. Examples include Stilton, Gorgonzola, Danish Blue and Roquefort.

Making yogurt is a process of controlled souring of milk, which results in the proteins being coagulated, but not in the separation of curds and whey. In making yogurt, milk is first sterilized by bringing it to the boil, then it is cooled to 43°C and a culture is added of two or three other harmless bacteria in the form of a spoonful of 'live' (not pasteurized) yogurt. These particular bacteria flourish in warmer conditions than most microbes, since 43°C is the lethal limit for baker's yeast. If kept at that temperature for several hours they create moderately acidic conditions (pH 4.4–4.6) which coagulate the remaining milk proteins, so that the milk thickens and turns to yogurt. If incubation is continued too long, conditions become more acidic and the proteins may coagulate further, resulting in a separation of whey from the thickened yogurt.

The acidity of yogurt not only gives it its characteristically sharp taste, but also means that many other microbes cannot live in it, so it keeps well. At 7°C live yogurt can be stored for 15 days, and at 1°C (the temperature in a refrigerator) it stays edible for 30 days.

Food spoilage. The action of yeast in bread and yogurt-making bacteria in milk are examples of controlled and beneficial chemical changes brought about by microbes feeding on edible materials. There are, however, many more uncontrolled and harm-ful chemical changes brought about by microbes on food than there are useful ones. Human food is, on the overall scale of substances in the environment, very easy to digest: compare bread with wood, for example. As a result, it is possible for many microbes to digest our foodstuffs and grow on them very rapidly, so that the food becomes decayed (5.8) and unfit to eat. Work on chemical changes and food prepa-ration can usefully be linked to the decay of food as a major human problem, and its prevention as an important branch of food technology. Both useful and harmful chemical changes in food brought about by microbes involve enzymes: natural chem-ical accelerating agents which are discussed in relation to digestion (3.3).

9.3: Reactions with oxygen

Like all changes, chemical reactions involve transfers of energy (12.1). Some reac-tions transfer energy to the environment, usually as thermal energy (12.2), for example the warming of plaster of Paris when it is mixed with water. Others require a transfer of energy from the environment, for example the reaction between citric acid and sodium hydrogen carbonate in fizzy sweets and sherbet powder, in which the reacting chemicals are heated by the mouth, which is thus cooled down. Some reactions require a very large input of energy to bring them about, for example the smelting of iron from iron oxide (10.2). In that case, heat is supplied by another reaction which gives out very large amounts of energy: the burning of coke.

Chemical changes which release energy are an essential part of everyday life, and children will be familiar with at least three kinds, all of which involve reactions with oxygen in the air. One of these is respiration (3.6), the process by which living things, including the children's own bodies, transfer energy from food chemicals through a complex controlled sequence of chemical changes. The other two kinds of change are burning and rusting which, although they have a superficial similar-ity in that both involve oxygen in the air, are in most ways examples of very dif-ferent kinds of chemical reaction. Investigating them together can, however, be useful. By comparing the two kinds of chemical change it is possible to understand more clearly the conditions under which each occurs and the ways in which they may be controlled or prevented.

9.4: Burning and its prevention

Burning is the general name for a very large variety of chemical changes, all of which require three factors in order to occur: fuel, oxygen and a high temperature, the-so-called 'triangle of fire'.

Fuel is the general name for any substance, apart from oxygen, involved in burn-ing. Fuels vary a great deal in their chemical nature, but all have one thing in common: their chemical structure is such that they have large amounts of chemical-potential energy (12.2). When they combine chemically with oxygen in burning, this energy is transferred to the environment as thermal energy, usually with light energy as well.

Oxygen. Oxygen is the name which the French chemist Lavoisier gave to the part of the air which is needed for a fuel to burn. This is the same part which humans and other animals need for respiration (3.6). About one-fifth of the air is oxygen, and it is believed that it was released into the atmosphere by photosynthesis (4.4) carried out by plants over millions of years early in the history of the Earth. The Earth is the only planet in the Solar System with free oxygen in its atmosphere, which is a mixture of gases, containing about 78 per cent nitrogen, 21 per cent oxygen and 1 per cent other gases, including a very small proportion (normally 0.03 per cent) of carbon dioxide. The proportion of carbon dioxide in the air is normally kept very low by plants, which use it as a raw material in photosynthesis (4.4, 5.8).

Temperature and activation energy. When fuels are in contact with oxygen they are always liable to react with it, but at normal room temperatures a fuel such as candle-wax seems quite stable: fuel and oxygen can be present together without burning taking place. Before the chemical changes which make up the burning process can begin, the temperature of the fuel has to be raised to the point at which it begins to break down chemically and react with oxygen. The energy needed to start a chemical reaction is called activation energy. In the case of a fuel with oxygen the activation energy is usually supplied by heating, which raises the temperature and completes the 'triangle of fire'. The higher the temperature needed to start the burning reaction, the more difficult it is to set fire to the fuel. Once the fuel has started to burn, some of the energy released in the chemical reaction heats more fuel, causing it to break up and combine with oxygen, so that the reaction continues.

The wax candle: an example of burning. The changes involved in burning can be observed safely using wax candles fixed firmly, using molten wax, to metal lids or dishes. Loose clothing, particularly sleeves, should be avoided and pupils with long hair should tie it back securely. It is also helpful to begin with a partly burnt candle rather than a new one, because the wick is already saturated with wax. The burning of a candle is a complex process which involves physical as well as chemical changes. When a match is applied to the wick, the heat of its burning causes the wax first to melt, then to vaporize (physical changes) and finally to burn (chemical change).

A burning candle is a complex system (Fig. 9.1), which rewards close observation. Any flame is a region of burning gases. When a candle is first lit, the flame is usually small because only a little wax vapour is available. This, however, produces enough heat to melt the wax in the exposed part of the wick and then in the top of the candle. Because the heating effect is greatest near the wick, a 'cup' forms in the top of the candle, which becomes filled with molten wax. As wax is vaporized and burnt at the top of the wick, more hot liquid wax moves up by capillary action (6.6). After the candle has been burning for a short time, the flame usually becomes bigger than at first, because the melting of the wax in the main part of the candle increases the fuel supply. Sometimes the heat released by the small flame is insufficient to begin melting the main part of the candle. If this happens it will usually be found that the wick has been broken off short. The burning process is starved of fuel, the flame becomes smaller and finally goes out. Some burning may continue in the smouldering wick, which is interesting as an example of incomplete burning which produces smoke (see below).

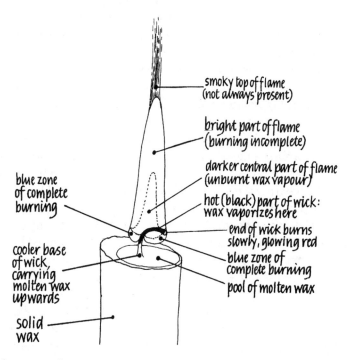

smoky top of flame
(not always present)

bright part of flame
(burning incomplete)

darker central part of flame
(unburnt wax vapour)

hot (black) part of wick:
wax vaporizes here

end of wick burns
slowly, glowing red

blue zone of
complete burning

pool of molten wax

blue zone
of complete
burning

cooler base
of wick,
carrying
molten wax
upwards

solid
wax

Figure 9.1 A burning candle

As the candle burns, heat from the flame sets up a pattern of movement in the air around it. Heated air, together with gases produced by the burning process, rises in a vertical stream above the flame, while at the same time cool air is drawn in at its base. The flame itself is quite complex, with three main parts which need to be noticed. The dark area immediately around the wick is occupied by hot wax vapour which has not begun to burn and so does not give out any light. At the base of the flame is a small blue zone, where the oxygen supply is greatest because air is being drawn in towards it. Here the burning process is rapid and complete. In the main, bright part of the flame, wax is at first only partly burnt because the oxygen supply is lower. The first part of the burning process produces tiny, very hot particles of solid carbon, which carry on burning, glowing brightly as they do so. It is this second, slower phase of burning which causes the candle flame to give out light. The presence of carbon in the flame can be shown by holding a tin lid in the bright part of it for a few seconds. Carbon particles are cooled and deposited as soot. Very finely divided carbon of this kind (lamp-black) is still used to make ink, for example by Muslim scribes.

Burning other fuels. Wax will burn only when it is heated enough to melt and then vaporize, whereas some other fuels such as wood and coal seem to burn as solids. What happens is that as these fuels are heated they begin to break down chemically and give off inflammable gases (wood gas and coal gas) which can burn with a flame. When all the inflammable gases have been given off and burnt, the solids which are left (embers or charcoal) carry on burning more slowly with little or no flame, until the only solid remains are ashes.

In contrast to solid fuels, some liquid fuels change into gases very easily by evaporation (6.3). All liquid fuels are dangerous, and children should never use or play with methylated spirit, petrol (gasoline), paraffin (kerosene), diesel oil or white spirit (turpentine substitute). The main example of a liquid fuel with which children will be familiar is also one of the most dangerous: petrol. Petrol evaporates fairly quickly at room temperature, forming a heavy vapour which can sink to the floor of a room and form a layer. When petrol vapour mixes with air, the mixture can be ignited very easily and burns so quickly that it explodes. This is why there should be an absolute ban on smoking in any part of a garage or petrol filling-station. When used as the fuel for a motor car a petrol-air mixture, made by the carburettor or fuel injection system, is drawn into the engine cylinder, compressed by the piston and ignited by a spark from the sparking-plug. The mixture explodes, driving the piston down, turning the crank-shaft and so generating the forces (14.1) to make the car move.

Complete and incomplete burning. If wax or a liquid fuel such as petrol or paraffin (kerosene) are burnt completely, there are no solid remains at all: the only products of the burning process are two gases: carbon dioxide and water vapour. If wood is burnt completely, a little solid residue is left as ash, but the main products are the same. Burning coal is more complex. All coal has some sulphur-containing chemicals in it, and some kinds have large amounts of them. When coal is burnt completely, ash, carbon dioxide and water vapour are produced, but so is another gas: sulphur dioxide. If this gas is allowed to escape into the air, as it is from most coal-fired power stations, it becomes a serious pollutant as the major cause of 'acid rain' (5.9).

If fuels have to be burnt, rapid and complete burning causes the least possible pollution, so that in listing its products one is considering the best possible case as far as environmental damage is concerned. In reality, the overwhelming majority of burning processes are not complete, usually because the burning is not properly controlled. This was especially true of poorly designed fires, stoves and industrial burners in the nineteenth and early twentieth centuries, giving rise to severe atmospheric pollution such as 'smog'. If too much fuel is available, it will be broken down by heating faster than the available supply of oxygen will allow it to burn, for example in a candle which is burning with too long a wick. So much wax vapour is available that not all the carbon can burn in the bright part of the flame, so some of it is given off as a sooty smoke (6.4). A different kind of incomplete burning gives the smelly smoke characteristic of a smouldering candle wick when the flame has been blown out. Incomplete burning is a major cause of air pollution (5.9), and while redesigning furnaces in power stations, correct engine adjustment and improved design in motor cars have all contributed to significant reductions in emissions, it remains a major problem.

Preventing and controlling fire. As with most destructive processes, the best way to avoid damage from uncontrolled burning is to prevent it happening in the first place. For any fire to start fuel must be heated, so children should be protected from heat sources such as matches and electrical appliances, and inflammable materials should, as far as possible, be stored securely. The greatest danger to children is probably their failure to realize that many everyday things around them can act as fuels and may become lethal if they are ignited. Clothing on fire heats and kills the skin, while burning furniture may produce very large quantities of smoke through incomplete combustion. If inhaled, this smoke is likely to cause damage to lungs even if its effects are not fatal.

There are two main ways of controlling or stopping the burning process and so putting a fire out. The traditional method of pouring or spraying water onto a fire to extinguish it works by reducing the temperature of the fuel, but is often of limited use and is sometimes very dangerous. Water is most effective in controlling solid fuel fires such as burning paper or wood. It should never be used on fires caused by an electrical fault, because water in a jet or on a floor will conduct electricity and this may lead to electric shock or electrocution (13.13); nor should it be used on fires involving petrol, oil or burning fat. Burning oil and petrol merely float on water and spread more quickly, while water thrown onto burning oil or fat in a pan is likely to explode by turning almost instantly to superheated steam, flinging very hot, sticky liquid all over the room. Modern water-based fire extinguishers use compressed gas (either air or carbon dioxide) to propel a jet of water through a flexible hose.

The second main method of extinguishing fires depends on reducing or preventing contact between the burning fuel and oxygen in the air. The best way of extinguishing fire in a pan of burning fat, for example, is simply to put a lid on it. Special fireproof blankets may also be used for this purpose, but their main use is to smother flames in burning clothing. The victim is rolled in the fireproof blanket, which also protects the rescuer. Electrical fires can be extinguished safely only by spraying a special dry powder, which forms a crust over the burning surface, so cutting off its air supply. When fighting large oil or petrol fires (including crashed aircraft), large quantities of foam are sprayed over the fire and the surrounding area. This will float even on burning petrol, smothers the fire by excluding air and at the same time prevents it spreading.

9.5: Rusting of iron and steel

Corrosion is the general term used to describe chemical changes which 'eat away' metals. There are many different kinds of corrosion, but most of those observed in everyday life occur when metals are exposed to weathering. Rusting is one example of corrosion, which affects impure iron and steel. Economically and technologically it is by far the most important kind of corrosion in the industrialized world, causing enormous amounts of damage and dilapidation to installations, machinery, civil engineering works, shipping and buildings both public and private. Great amounts of material and labour are expended annually on trying to prevent rusting or even slow it down.

Tarnishing and corrosion. When investigating the chemical changes at the surfaces of metals, it is useful to distinguish between corrosion and tarnishing. Any of the commonly used metals except gold (i.e. steel, copper and its alloys, aluminium, zinc and silver) become dull when a freshly polished surface is exposed to the air, even in conditions which seem quite dry. This effect is one form of tarnishing, caused by a chemical reaction between the metal and oxygen in the air, which results in the formation of a very thin layer of metal oxide on the surface. Other reactions cause different forms of tarnishing. For example, a silver or silver-plated spoon used to eat boiled eggs will become tarnished with silver sulphide. The layer of tarnish dulls the characteristic lustre of the metal, but can be removed by the fine abrasives in metal polish. In commonly used metals tarnishing is not destructive, because the oxide layer will protect the metal from further change as long as it is not broken down to expose the metal surface once more. If, however, conditions such as weathering break down the oxide layer, the destructive changes which we call corrosion are likely to set in. When investigating the rusting of steel, the main interest lies in finding the conditions under which the corrosion occurs and ways in which it may be prevented or slowed down.

Investigating the conditions in which rusting occurs. The chemical changes which cause iron and steel to rust are complex and a great deal of scientific and technological research has been devoted to finding out about them, but the conditions under which they occur can easily be investigated. Rusting is a chemical reaction in which iron metal combines with oxygen and water to form a chemical complex of iron oxide and water, similar chemically to much of the ore from which iron is obtained by smelting (10.2). It is a reaction in which energy is transferred to the environment, but because it takes place slowly, no heating effect is detectable. Everyday experience shows that steel is likely to rust when exposed to air, but investigating the conditions needed in some detail will help children understand more about rust prevention, as well as providing excellent opportunities for prediction, 'fair testing' and the use of controls.

It is useful to choose a standard material to investigate: 2.5 cm (one inch) steel nails are cheap and convenient. Before each test, the nails used should be cleaned with fine abrasive sheet until they are shiny. The detailed approach and method of investigation will depend on the context in which it is undertaken, but the main variables which need to be considered may be summarized as follows. Newly cleaned nails suspended in dry air (for example, over a heater) will tarnish slowly but will not rust. This shows that air alone will cause tarnishing but not corrosion in steel, and provides an opportunity to distinguish between the two. Only when the steel is in contact with both water and air will corrosion set in, and it is then likely to be rapid. A nail in a little water at the bottom of an open jar will be rusty within 24 hours, and the first signs may be visible much sooner. The contact between liquid water and steel does not, however, need to be direct: rusting will occur in humid air. A nail suspended in air above water in a sealed jar will rust rapidly even though no liquid appears to touch it, because very small amounts of water vapour condensing (6.3) on the metal are enough to start the process of cor-rosion. In contrast, a nail in water with no air dissolved in it will not rust. This can be shown by boiling water for ten minutes to drive off all the dissolved air, cooling it, pouring it gently into a jar, dropping in a nail and then sealing the water surface with cooking oil. Air cannot penetrate the oily layer to dissolve in the water, so the nail will not rust. A control set up using unboiled tap water with a sealing layer shows some rusting, though this is limited by the small amount of oxygen dissolved in the water. Once this has all been used up, no further rusting can occur.

A variety of factors in the environment can speed up the rusting process. Con-stant wetting of steel which is not actually immersed in water (for example, by high and frequent rainfall) gives the greatest contact between metal, oxygen and water and so the most rapid rusting. Chemicals such as salt dissolved in the water will also speed up the process, so steel exposed to sea-water or spray rusts very rapidly indeed; a major problem for ships with steel hulls and superstructure.

The difference between steel and metals such as copper and aluminium, which tar-nish quickly but corrode much more slowly, is that the oxide layer formed as steel tar-nishes is very easily broken, allowing water and air into contact with the metal. Rust forms a loose and flaky layer which is very easily broken and disturbed by stress and bending, so that it cannot protect the metal in the way that copper and aluminium are shielded by their oxide layers. As a result, water and air continue to penetrate and the steel continues to corrode, particularly if the rust layer is disturbed in any way. If unchecked, this is likely to continue until all the tough, strong, flexible metal is con-verted to brittle and weak rust, with potentially disastrous consequences.

Control and prevention of rusting. It is very difficult if not impossible entirely to prevent rusting in any steel object which is in use, but there are several different ways in which the process can be slowed down. Those which can be investigated at primary level involve a protective coating which seals the surface of the steel and so impedes or prevents contact between water, air and the metal.

To be effective, protective coatings have to be waterproof and adhere closely enough to the steel to prevent oxygen reaching it. Most are relatively short-lived because if the steel object is in use it will be subjected to abrasion which wears any coating away, bending which will tend to loosen or crack it, or both. Apart from other metals plated onto the steel (see below), the main coating materials are paints, oils and greases. Paints are relatively cheap and flexible, but most have low resistance to impact or abrasion. It is also very difficult to make paint adhere well to the surface of steel, so that complex surface treatments and multiple coatings are needed, as in car body finishing, if paint on steel is to be durable for more than a short time. Without such special treatments and materials, paint on steel or ironwork exposed to weathering requires regular renewal if destructive rusting is to be avoided.

Table 9.1 Summary of the differences between burning and rusting

Aspect of chemical change	Burning	Rusting
Energy transfer to environment	Large and usually very rapid in the form of heat and light	Very slow: no detectable heating
Temperature of reacting materials	Usually 500–1,500°C	Air temperature, i.e. rarely over 40°C
Products	Oxides, usually gases; some ash	Iron oxide-water complex; no gases or ash
Role of water	Slows down or stops reaction	Necessary for reaction to occur

Grease and oil are very effective in rust prevention as long as the steel is completely covered. If the objects are in use this usually means that they have to be enclosed, as for example ball-bearings in a bicycle, or the protective layer will quickly be wiped off. Grease is, however, very effective in preventing rust in stored steel machines and tools, because the protective layer is not disturbed.

Steel can also be protected by coating (plating) it with other metals which corrode less easily. When steel is plated with zinc, it has a double protection. Zinc is a soft metal which tarnishes quickly but corrodes quite slowly when exposed to weathering, so it forms an effective protective layer. If the layer is scratched or cracked, a second, chemical kind of protection starts to operate. Although zinc on its own corrodes more slowly than steel does, when the two are in contact, as in 'galvanized iron', the zinc tends to corrode more readily than the steel does, so that rusting is slowed down and may be prevented for a long time, by 'sacrificing' the zinc.

Comparing rusting and burning. Rusting and burning are both chemical changes which involve oxygen from the air, produce chemicals containing oxygen (oxides) and transfer energy to the environment. In all other ways, however, they are very different. It can be an instructive exercise for children to work out the differences from their own observations and experience. The main differences are summarized in Table 9.1.

10

Obtaining and Making Materials

10.1: Natural and manufactured materials and objects

When investigating materials, their origins and ways in which they are used in relation to their properties, a useful way to begin is to distinguish natural materials from manufactured ones. Natural materials are substances which are produced by natural processes and changes, either chemical or physical (9.1). Examples include animal materials such as bone, ivory, wool and silk; plant materials such as cotton, wood and olive oil; and mineral materials such as granite, salt and slate. Natural materials may be changed physically and shaped by human activity in a wide variety of ways to make them useful (see below), but the nature of the material itself is not changed. In contrast to these are manufactured materials, made by processes which result in a raw material being transformed into a different kind of substance by chemical changes. In a few cases, chemical processes are used to make materials which occur naturally but are rare: the smelting of some metals such as copper is an example; but most manufactured materials do not occur naturally at all.

When investigating mechanical properties (Chapter 7), it is necessary to distinguish carefully between the material or substance of which an object is made, and an object which is made of one or more materials shaped in a certain way. This distinction is also very useful in avoiding confusion when thinking about and distinguishing the natural and the manufactured. For example, stone is a natural material, and a stone pebble on a beach is also a natural object, because it was not shaped by human activity. A cut stone building-block or a roofing slate, on the other hand, are manufactured objects, although both are made of natural materials. Manufactured materials which children investigate are likely to be in the form of manufactured objects, such as bricks, polythene bottles or cardboard boxes. Naturally formed objects of manufactured materials are less common, and are usually worn away or corroded, such as heavily rusted steel or beach pebbles of brick and glass.

Natural materials may be changed physically in a wide variety of ways to make them usable, and care may be needed to distinguish such changes from the chemical changes involved in making manufactured materials. Examples children may be familiar with include:

cutting, carving and splitting: wood, slate and stone;
crushing and grinding: clay, chalk, metal ores, coal, roadstone, foodstuffs
    (especially cereals and spices);
sieving and sorting: sand, gravel, roadstone, flour;
sedimentation: clay for ceramics;
spinning, weaving and knitting: cotton, wool, linen, silk;
dissolving, filtering and evaporating: extraction and purification of salt and sugar;
pulping and sieving: paper (glue is also added).

In order to understand something of how and why materials are used as they are, it is necessary to obtain information about both their properties and their origins. This could be done for the materials used in a wide variety of activities, but the most productive enquiries are likely to be those which concentrate on processes and products with which the children are already familiar and in which they have an interest. Here, as elsewhere in primary science, the case-study approach (1.1) is useful. As an example of a case-study into the properties, origins and uses of natural and manufactured materials, the remainder of this chapter concentrates on the main constructional materials used in house-building.

10.2: Constructional materials used in house-building

The origins of each material are described in outline, together with the chemical and physical changes involved in making and using it, and its mechanical properties (Chapter 7) are summarized. These are then related to the way the material is used in building a house.

Wood is the major natural material used in house construction. There are two main groups of woods. Softwoods, such as spruce and pine (deal), come from coniferous trees (5.2); hardwoods, such as beech and oak, from broadleaved trees. Wood is shaped before use by sawing, planing and other cutting processes, and softwoods may be treated with chemicals to preserve them against attack by insects and decay by fungi.

Woods vary in hardness, but in comparison with materials such as brick and stone, they are all fairly soft. Although there are exceptions, softwoods generally are softer than hardwoods, though they may be just as strong and, if properly treated with preservatives, equally durable. In relation to their size and weight, most woods are very strong and stiff in compression and tension; moderately stiff and elastic in bending. Their elasticity in bending is a result of their fibrous nature, which is also responsible for their other outstanding property: toughness. Wood is fairly difficult to split along the grain and very difficult indeed to split across it, so if used as a beam and overloaded it will usually sag and crack long before it actually breaks. The moderate hardness, elasticity and toughness of woods make it possible to shape them by cutting with steel tools such as saws, chisels and planes. It also means that when nails or screws are driven into wood, they are gripped very securely and the wood does not usually split open. Wood is a very poor thermal conductor (12.3), so it helps to conserve energy when used in doors and window-frames.

Softwoods generally are very much cheaper than hardwoods. Sawn softwood is used for constructional timbers in roofs and load-bearing joists in floors; planed softwood boards are used for flooring. All these uses exploit the strength and stiffness of wood and its elasticity in bending. Its softness and toughness mean that the timbers and boards can easily be cut to size and shape, and can be joined securely with nails. Hardwoods are used for high quality joinery, such as exterior doors and door-sills, where durability and appearance are important, and for decorative work. Very high-quality building may include hardwood block flooring.

Slate is a natural material, still used for high-quality roofing, mainly in conservation areas. Slate is a metamorphic rock (11.7) which is quarried, sawn into blocks and then split into sheets with a thin steel wedge rather like a wide chisel. In one direction (the direction of cleavage or splitting) slate is weak and brittle, but at right angles to this it is much stronger and tougher, so that it can be drilled for fixing and once in place is a very durable roof covering. Good slate is non-porous (6.6) and therefore is completely water- and frost-proof.

Tiles are of two kinds. Traditional ceramic tiles are of fired clay, a material similar to brick. Modern interlocking tiles are made of concrete. Both materials are discussed in more detail below.

Brick is made of fired clay, a manufactured material. Traditional roof tiles and drainage pipes are made of basically the same material. The raw material is natural clay, quarried and ground to a paste with water. Pottery clay of the kind which children may use in school is further refined by being mixed with water to form a suspension and allowed to settle out in tanks (6.5), but for brick-making this is not necessary. The stiff paste of ground-up clay is shaped in moulds, or by being pushed out (extruded) through a rectangular die and cut into bricks with a wire. The soft, damp bricks are dried for several days before being fired. All the changes in the clay up to this point are physical and reversible. Firing the clay, which involves heating it to around 800°C for about 48 hours in gas-fired kilns, brings about chemical changes which are not reversible. Fired clay is a much harder material than dried clay, and it cannot be softened by water. It consists of mineral particles bound together with a glass-like substance.

The colour and properties of brick are very variable, depending on the kind of clay used and the way it is fired. In general, brick is fairly hard, rigid and very strong in compression, but much weaker in bending, and brittle. This means that although brick is a very strong and durable walling material, it can crack suddenly if the walls are not properly supported. As a result, windows and doors must always have strong beams (lintels) over them, and house foundations must be deep and stable. Brick is a fairly good thermal insulator (12.3), but energy loss from a building is greatly reduced by cavity-wall construction and insulating materials within the wall. Brick walls are also effective as soundproofing barriers (16.4).

A very variable property of brick is its porosity (6.6). Soft, porous bricks (commons) can absorb water by capillarity, so if used on an outside wall they are likely to crack or flake in frosty weather (6.2). They are good for internal walls, but harder, less porous bricks (facing bricks) are needed for walls exposed to the weather. Even harder bricks with very low porosity (engineering bricks) are used in contact with soil and for damp-proof courses in houses, to prevent rising damp (6.6).

Glass is a manufactured material. Of the three basic ingredients of window-glass, two are natural: sand, which is quarried and cleaned by washing and sieving, and limestone, which is quarried and ground to powder. The third ingredient is soda-ash (sodium carbonate), a manufactured chemical. These are heated together until they melt at about 1,200°C. A chemical change results in the formation of glass, which can be drawn out into sheets while still liquid, and cut into usable pieces when it has cooled and become solid. This process leaves the glass sheets with very smooth surfaces, but some window-glass has patterns moulded into it.

Glass is a hard material, which in the form of sheets is very strong and stiff in compression and tension, but flexible, elastic and very brittle in bending. Its outstanding properties are transparency, which allows it to transmit light very well, and hardness, which together with its smooth surfaces makes it very easy to clean. Glass is a moderately good thermal insulator (12.3), but energy loss through windows is greatly reduced by double or secondary glazing. Windows are much less effective as soundproofing barriers than brick walls are (16.4), but here again a double layer of glass is helpful. The main disadvantage of glass is brittleness, which makes it vulnerable to accidental damage and vandalism.

Insulation. A variety of materials is used for thermal insulation (12.3) in both walls and roofs. The most widely used are plastic foams and fibres such as rockwool and fibreglass. Fibrous materials in sheets are laid in lofts to insulate ceilings or are blown as particles into cavity walls. Plastic foams can be injected into cavity walls in older buildings or built into new ones in the form of lightweight slabs. These have metal foil faces which increase their efficiency. What all these materials have in common is that they trap a thick layer of air, which is a very poor thermal conductor (12.3).

Plastics include a very wide variety of materials, all of which are manufactured. Almost all modern plastics are made from chemicals derived from oil (petroleum). Types used in buildings include moderately soft, flexible and very tough materials such as PVC (polyvinyl chloride) used in rainwater pipes, guttering and to insulate electric cables, and polythene sheet used to make a waterproof membrane in foundations. A group of much harder plastics are the synthetic resins of various kinds used in laminated work-surfaces and for electrical plugs, sockets and switches.

Plaster. Modern wall plaster is a manufactured material based on the naturally occurring mineral gypsum and is basically similar to plaster of Paris, with which children can experiment. Even when perfectly dry, gypsum contains water chemically bound into its structure. When heated to just over 400°C most of this chemically bound water is driven off and the gypsum forms a powder, which is the plaster we buy. This is a chemical change, but it is easily reversible. When water is added to plaster, gypsum re-forms as long, needle-shaped crystals (8.6) which lock together as they grow to form a solid mass, which is fairly soft but also fairly tough. Because the setting process is the result of a chemical change, the change of state from semi-liquid to solid is gradual rather than sudden. Even so, plaster of Paris sets much too quickly for it to be used in building. Builder's plaster has chemicals added to it which slow down the setting process, so the plasterer has time to smooth a layer onto the wall before it becomes solid.

Plaster is used to make a smooth surface on interior walls, which can then be covered with paint or wallpaper. Because good plaster is soft but fairly tough, it is possible to drill through it for wall fixings without cracking it or breaking it off the wall.

Steel and other metals used in buildings are all manufactured by smelting them from naturally occurring minerals called ores. In some older buildings, window and door fittings may be made of brass (alloy of copper and zinc) or even bronze (copper and tin), while aluminium and its alloys are used for a wide range of components in modern buildings, including window-frames and door fittings. By far the most widely used metal in buildings, however, is steel, which is an alloy of iron.

Most iron ores are, chemically, similar to rust (9.5). The iron metal is chemically combined with oxygen, and however strongly the ore is heated, the two cannot be separated. To smelt the metal, something has to be found which will combine with the oxygen and hold it even more strongly than the iron does. At the same time the mixture must be made very hot for the chemical change to take place. Carbon, in the form of coke made from coal, is used both to remove the oxygen and as the fuel for heating the furnace.

Early iron-smelting relied on carbon in the form of charcoal, but today iron is produced in tall, chimney-like furnaces 30–40 m high. In addition to air, three raw materials are used. Iron ore and ground limestone, which are natural, are mixed with coke made from coal before being fed into the top of the furnace, and pre-heated air is then blown in at high pressure through jets near the bottom. This gives these iron-smelters their common name of blast-furnaces. Inside the furnace two chemical changes take place, producing molten iron metal which runs to the bottom. The limestone is needed to combine with impurities in the iron ore so that these can be separated from the molten metal as the waste material known as slag. The molten iron is run out of the tap-hole, usually into a truck which takes it to a steel plant nearby, and slag is removed through the slag-hole. Because the solid raw materials can be fed into the top of the furnace while iron and slag are removed from the bottom, blast-furnaces can be kept in continuous production for long periods of time, thus saving a lot of fuel.

Newly smelted iron contains 4–5 per cent carbon. Steel-making involves removing most but not all of this. There are many specialized steels, but the kind most used in construction is fairly hard and, in relation to its size and weight, very strong and stiff in compression and tension. Depending on how it is shaped, steel can be flexible in bending, as in a cable, or rigid, as in a girder. The steel used in construction is fairly hard but very tough and, like most metals, it can be shaped in many different ways. Its strength and toughness make it very useful for girders and lintels to span gaps in buildings, because it will support a large weight, but if overloaded will bend rather than breaking suddenly. For the same reason steel rods are used to reinforce concrete (see below and 7.8). Hardness, toughness and ease of shaping are also the properties which make steel very useful for fixing devices such as nails, screws and bolts. The main disadvantage of steel is that it is very easily corroded by rusting (9.5), and if it is to be long-lasting, protection against this must be provided.

Cement, mortar and concrete. Strictly speaking, 'cement' means any material which binds other materials together. In the context of building work, 'cement' is often used, incorrectly, to refer to the cement mortar which is used to bond bricks into walls. Cement mortar is made from a mixture of sand, water and cement powder, which is properly known as Portland Cement. Cement powder is a manufactured material. The natural raw materials for making it are limestone or chalk, and clay or shale (11.7). These are quarried, crushed and ground to fine powders before being mixed together and heated in huge kilns like large, rotating steel barrels. At about 1,300°C, chemical changes occur which produce a hard mass (clinker), which when cooled and crushed is ground again to a fine grey powder which can then be used in construction.

Cement is used in two main ways in buildings: in cement mortar and in concrete. Both are made of natural materials (sand, gravel, stones and water) mixed with the manufactured cement powder. Cement mortar is used in bricklaying to bond the bricks together. It is made from one part of cement to about six parts of building sand, mixed dry before the water is added to make it into a smooth, semi-liquid paste. Concrete is made from one part of cement mixed with about eight parts of aggregate, made up of coarse, sharp-grained sand, often mixed with gravel and stones. Both the sand and aggregate are quarried and sorted by a sieving process (screening, 6.4) to produce mixtures suitable for various applications.

When water is added to cement powder and sand or aggregate, a series of chemical changes begins which make the mixture change from a semi-liquid paste to a hard solid which is unaffected by water. It is this change of state which makes it possible to use cement mortar for bonding bricks, and concrete for pouring and moulding. As it sets, the cement binds the sand or aggregate into a single hard, solid mass, but the process is quite a gradual one. Cement mortar and concrete may seem hard after a day or two, but they carry on becoming harder and stronger for at least a year, a process known as curing.

Both cement mortar and concrete are fairly hard materials, rigid and very strong in compression but much weaker and brittle in bending, so they may crack and fracture without warning. This means that they are very good materials for supporting large loads, as long as they themselves are fully supported from below. If concrete is used to span a gap, as in bridge-building or for a lintel over a window or door, it must be reinforced with steel rods, which are much tougher and more flexible, to avoid the danger of sudden and catastrophic fracture (7.8).

11

Earth Science: Weather, Rocks and Soils

11.1: An overall view of the Earth, weather and climate

Investigating the properties of materials, together with the chemical and physical changes involved in their making and use, enables children to begin developing an understanding of how and why things are made as they are and work as they do. The same basic concepts can be used when observing and learning about the much larger-scale natural changes and processes which affect the planet as a whole. A useful way to begin is to think of the outer parts of the Earth, which we can observe directly, as made up of three parts, corresponding to the three states of matter: solid, liquid and gas. Although the interior of the Earth is very hot and at least partly liquid, its outer rocky crust or lithosphere on which we live is cool and solid. About two-thirds of the lithosphere is covered by liquid water with many chemicals dissolved in it, forming oceans, lakes and rivers (the hydrosphere); while the outermost part of the planet is the mixture of gases we call the atmosphere. Added to these are living things, which collectively are sometimes known as the biosphere, a term which is often taken to include soils, the active surface layer of the lithosphere.

Some of the chemical and physical changes which shape the face of the planet are caused by very large-scale forces, movements and transfers of energy generated by heating deep within the Earth. Examples are volcanoes, earthquakes and some kinds of rock formation, which are not discussed in detail here. Attention is focused in this chapter on materials which children are likely to find in their environment, on changes which they can investigate and whose results they can observe at first hand. The changes come about when the lithosphere, hydrosphere and atmosphere interact in a variety of ways, as a result of energy transfer between the Sun, the Earth and space, together with the activities of living things. The processes which result from these interactions include weather and climatic patterns, the weathering, erosion and deposition of rocks and the formation of soil.

Weather and climate. Weather is the name given to the events and changes which take place from day to day within the Earth's atmosphere, as it interacts with the hydrosphere, lithosphere, biosphere and incoming radiant energy from the Sun

(12.2). Although weather in many parts of the world (including Britain) is often very changeable and difficult to predict in detail, broader patterns and repeated changes can be observed. Short-term changes and events are referred to as weather; longer-term changes and patterns describe the climate of a region.

When investigating weather it is necessary, in order to begin developing an understanding of what is observed, to interpret observations in terms of the properties of liquids and gases (6.1) and changes of state (evaporation, condensation, freezing and melting, 6.2, 6.3). One effective overall strategy is to begin by concentrating on changes the children can observe for themselves and to develop explanations of them (11.2–11.5). These can then be used to develop an understanding of the water cycle as it is experienced both locally and on a wider scale (11.5), and to interpret common short-term weather patterns such as depressions, anticyclones and thunderstorms (11.6). The aspects of weather which children can usefully observe, and for which explanations can be developed, include temperature; wind (direction and speed); cloud (type and amount of cover); condensation at ground level; and precipitation (type and amount).

11.2: Temperature

Temperature, measured in degrees Celsius (°C, 12.3) is a measure of how hot or cold things are. In weather study, it is the temperature of the air which is usually measured. Air temperature has profound effects on children's lives, which they can describe and understand. These effects are both direct (comfort, clothing, patterns of activity) and indirect (use of heating in home and school). Broad seasonal variations in air temperature are caused by changes in the amount of energy reaching any particular part of the Earth's surface from the Sun throughout the year (18.4). At all times of the year it is useful to record air temperature at intervals during the day and, if possible, to record maximum and minimum temperatures for a succession of 24-hour periods using a special thermometer. Any measurement of air temperature must be made in the shade, so that the thermometer is not directly heated by sunlight, and well away from buildings, particularly sources of hot air such as flues and chimneys from heating systems. This information can then be related to observations on cloud cover and other weather conditions.

The difference between the maximum and minimum air temperatures during a 24-hour period (the daily temperature range) varies much more widely over land than over the sea. This is because the land surface is heated up much more quickly during the day by incoming solar radiation (sunlight) than water is, but also cools down much more quickly at night. Daily temperature range may also depend partly on cloud cover. Under clear skies by day the land will be heated up, unless the solar radiation is reflected by snow cover, so that in much of Britain, even in winter, air temperatures are likely to rise significantly during the day. At night, however, the air temperature usually drops sharply under clear skies as the land surface cools rapidly, so minimum temperatures are low. At all seasons of the year cloud cover moderates both effects: it absorbs much of the incoming solar radiation, so reducing the heating of the land surface and maximum air temperatures by day, while at night it acts as an insulator, preventing rapid cooling of the air and earth beneath it, so keeping minimum temperatures higher (see also 18.4).

11.3: Wind

Wind is the name given to any movement in the atmosphere. Children can make two main kinds of observations and measurements of wind: its direction and its speed. Both are likely to be affected near the ground by obstacles such as buildings, trees and hedges. Measurements should therefore be carried out in large open spaces wherever possible. Wind direction is measured by finding the compass point from which the wind appears to be blowing, using a windsock or weathervane, both of which can be made by the children themselves. Wind speed is measured using an anemometer. Accurate portable anemometers are very expensive, but if one can be borrowed they are very useful for calibrating simpler instruments. Designing and making an anemometer is an effective technological exercise, and at least two basic kinds can be made by children: those which are deflected by the wind (flaps, flags and windsocks) and those which rotate (propellers or cups on arms).

Wind speed, like other speeds, should strictly speaking be measured in metres per second (ms^{-1}) , but children may be able more easily to visualize the speed if it is quoted in kilometres or miles per hour, which they can then compare with speeds they have experienced when watching or travelling in cars or trains.

The speed of the wind is directly related to the forces it exerts on objects in its path, such as buildings and trees, and on the surface of water in lakes and at sea. This in turn is related to effects which children experience and can observe. In 1806 a naval officer, Commander (later Admiral Sir) Francis Beaufort, devised a twelve-point scale which linked the speed of the wind to the effects which it is likely to have, at sea and on land. The Beaufort Scale is still used to communicate predicted wind speeds in shipping forecasts, and is very useful for estimating wind speed when accurate measurement is not possible. A simplified version, with the effects likely to be observed on land, is given in Table 11.1.

Winds are streams of air which move because some parts of the Earth's surface, and so the air above them, are heated more than others. When air is heated it expands, becomes less dense and tends to rise. This kind of movement, whether in a gas or a liquid, is called convection (12.3). Convection currents in air can easily be detected above room heaters (make sure any fan or blower is switched off!) using paper spirals hung from thin threads, which spin as the warmed air moves up past them. On the large scale of North Atlantic weather systems, warm air rising over the ocean creates an area of low pressure, often called a depression, several hundred kilometres across (11.6). At the same time, hundreds or even thousands of kilometres away, cool air will be sinking downwards from higher in the atmosphere. This cool air is more dense (each cubic metre weighs more) than the air around it. This not only makes the air sink, but also causes it to press down with a greater force (weight) on each square metre of the Earth beneath, setting up a large area of high pressure, often called an anticyclone. Air moves outwards from the sinking high-pressure air mass towards the low-pressure area, replacing the warm air as it rises. The air currents set up in this way are what we call winds.

Winds rarely if ever blow in straight lines between areas of high and low pressure. In the northern hemisphere, winds blowing inward towards an area of low pressure

Table 11.1 *Modified Beaufort Scale for estimating wind speed*

Beaufort number	Seaman's term	Speed mph (kph)	Observed effects
0	Calm	under 1 (under 1)	Calm; smoke rises vertically
1	Light air	1–3 (1–5)	Smoke drift indicates wind direction; weathervanes do not move
2	Light breeze	4–7 (6–11)	Wind felt on face; leaves rustle; weathervanes begin to move
3	Gentle breeze	8–12 (12–19)	Leaves and small twigs in constant motion; light flags extended
4	Moderate breeze	13–18 (20–29)	Dust, leaves and loose paper raised; small branches move
5	Fresh breeze	19–24 (30–39)	Small trees in leaf begin to sway
6	Strong breeze	25–31 (40–50)	Larger branches of trees in motion; whistling heard in wires
7	Moderate gale	32–38 (51–61)	Whole trees in motion; resistance felt in walking against wind
8	Fresh gale	39–46 (62–74)	Twigs and small branches broken off trees; progress impeded
9	Strong gale	47–54 (75–86)	Slight structural damage; slates blown from roofs
10	Whole gale	55–63 (87–100)	Seldom experienced on land; trees broken or uprooted; considerable structural damage occurs
11	Storm	64–72 (101–115)	Very rarely experienced on land; widespread damage
12	Hurricane	73 or more (116 or more)	Violence and destruction

Note: Wind speeds are given first in miles per hour (mph), followed by speeds in kilometres per hour (kph) in brackets.

move in an anticlockwise spiral, sometimes at high speed. One unusually violent example of this was the storm of 16 October 1987, which generated force 12 winds and destroyed an estimated 15 million trees in southern England. Winds blowing from an area of high pressure in the northern hemisphere spiral outwards in a clockwise direction, usually much more slowly and gently, as the air-mass sinks down. In the southern hemisphere the directions of rotation are reversed. Depressions and anticyclones are associated with well-marked patterns of weather, which children can observe (11.6).

11.4: Water in the atmosphere

When liquid water is exposed to air it usually 'dries up' or evaporates (6.3), and is converted to water in the cool gas phase, known as water vapour. Air containing a lot of water vapour is said to be humid. If evaporation continues for long enough, a point will be reached at which the air can hold no more water vapour and is said to be saturated. Exactly how much water vapour is in saturated air depends on the temperature: the higher the temperature, the greater the amount. This means that if saturated air is cooled, it will not be able to hold all the water vapour in it and some will change back to liquid water by condensation (6.3). For condensation to occur, humid air must be cooled. In the atmosphere this occurs in two main ways: first, when humid air comes into contact with a cold surface (for example, condensation on cold windows) and secondly, when the warm, humid air is itself cooled (for example, breathing out on a cold day; vapour trails from jet aircraft). Cooling a humid air-mass leads to the formation of tiny water droplets. These are so small that they do not fall down through the air and settle out, but remain suspended in the atmosphere as a natural aerosol (6.4) known as cloud, mist or fog. If the air is cold enough, the cloud will consist not of liquid water droplets, but of tiny crystals of ice.

Cloud is the general name for an air-mass, well above ground or sea-level, in which water vapour has condensed to form tiny, suspended droplets of liquid water or crystals of ice. For cloud formation to occur, a humid air-mass has to be cooled, by rising up into the atmosphere, by coming into contact with cooler air, or by both at once. Observing cloud formations and the ways in which they change gives information both about conditions in the atmosphere and about the weather which is likely to be experienced at ground level. Cloud formations are very varied, but the commoner kinds can readily be observed, recorded and to some extent interpreted by children. A useful strategy is to begin observations, whenever possible, on a day when there is some clear sky, so that the overall forms of the clouds can more readily be seen.

The standard names of cloud types are derived from Latin, and though they may appear complex, all common cloud formations are named using combinations of only five words:

cirrus (a lock of hair);

cumulus (a heap);

stratus (a layer);

alto- (high; which means between 2 and 6 km, not higher);

nimbus (a rainstorm or shower).

There are various classifications of clouds, each with a different purpose. The simplest, and likely to be the most useful for primary teachers, is based on the kind of air movement and cooling which cause the cloud to be formed. There are two main types. The first is brought about by the gentle uplift of air, for example during contact between warm and cool air-masses. The resulting clouds are mainly or wholly in horizontal layers. The second type is caused by stronger upward air-currents (convection currents) and so has much more vertical development, giving the clouds a heaped-up or towering appearance. There is no sharp distinction between these two basic cloud types, but once they can be recognized and linked to different patterns of air movement, intermediate forms are more likely to be observed and interpreted accurately.

Layer-clouds vary in form according to their height. The highest (cirrus) are wispy or look like feathers. They are composed entirely of ice crystals, and no rain or snow falls from them. Layer-clouds forming at intermediate heights of between 3 and 6 km (altostratus, altocumulus) are usually denser than cirrus, but again little or no rain and snow falls from them. Lower-level layer-clouds (stratus) form from quite low down to heights of 2–3 km. They are often dense enough to hide the sun completely and give dull, overcast days with light rain or snowfall for many hours. Very dense, low-level layer-clouds (nimbostratus) give heavier prolonged rain and are very frequently associated with depressions.

Clouds which form as a result of upward convection currents have much more upright and billowing forms than layer-clouds, reflecting the more rapid and sometimes turbulent upward movement of the air-mass within which they form. Gentle upward movement produces the more or less isolated 'cotton wool' clouds usually called fair-weather cumulus, from which no rain falls. Stronger convection currents produce more rapid upward air movement and the formation of full cumulus clouds, which may produce rain or snow showers, particularly after a depression has passed. Very strong convection currents result in thunderstorms with cumulonimbus clouds, the tallest cloud type of all (11.6). Cumulus and cumulonimbus clouds form when warmer, humid air is made to rise rapidly. This can happen in two ways: first by local heating of the Earth's surface, most commonly over land in the summer; secondly, when cold air and warm air meet in such a way that the warm air becomes unstable and begins to rise quickly.

Condensation at ground level: mist, fog, dew and frost. If humid air near the ground is cooled enough, some of the water vapour in it will condense. This can happen in two ways. The first, known as mist or fog, is in some ways very like cloud formation, but just above ground level. However, whereas cloud is produced by warm air rising and becoming cooler, mist and fog condense when cool air sinks towards the ground or sea and becomes colder still. The most obvious effect is that light passing through the air is scattered (17.2), reducing visibility and making it difficult or impossible to see distant objects clearly. If visibility is between 1 and 2 km the cloud is referred to as mist; if it is less than 1 km, as fog.

The second kind of condensation occurs when humid air comes into contact with cold surfaces at or near ground level, particularly in still air conditions. The form which the condensation takes depends on the temperature of the air and the surfaces with which it is in contact. If both are above 0°C, condensation from clear air, usually at night, produces dew, while in misty or foggy conditions fog-drip is likely. If the ground temperature is below 0°C but the air temperature is just above there will be a ground-frost. Frost is formed when water vapour condenses directly into ice without forming liquid water first. If both ground and air are below 0°C there will be an air-frost, and condensation in the form of hoar-frost may form not only at ground level, but also on trees and telephone wires well above it. Frost is always most likely when the air is still, cold and stable; conditions associated with clear skies and rapid cooling of the land surface at night. If a fog forms at ground level when surfaces are below 0°C, the cloud droplets may freeze onto them to form rime, often in the form of ice-flags which face into the wind. This is very frequent in mountains in winter, but at low altitudes is rarer, sometimes being called freezing fog.

11.5: Precipitation and the water cycle

Precipitation is the general name for water falling to the ground from clouds in the atmosphere, either as solid or as liquid, including rain, snow, sleet and hail. Outside the tropics, almost all precipitation begins to form inside clouds as very small ice crystals. Once these tiny crystals have formed, they grow quickly as water vapour freezes onto them, and growing crystals may cling together as they collide. Inside the cloud, the air is rising. While the ice crystals are small, the upward movement of air prevents them from falling, but as they grow a point is reached at which this is no longer possible. What happens as the ice crystals fall depends on the height of the cloud and the air temperature. If the ice crystals fall for long enough through air above 0°C they will melt and fall as raindrops, whereas if the air is cold enough, they will reach the ground as snowflakes. Children may be able to observe how the size of snowflakes is related to temperature: powdery snow is associated with colder conditions than large, feathery flakes. When melting flakes pass through a layer of very cold air near the ground they may re-freeze, forming sleet; a term which is also used to describe mixed rain and snow falling when the air temperature is about 1.5°C.

Raindrops lose water by evaporation as they fall below the cloud. This explains why it is sometimes possible to see a thick veil of rain (virga) beneath a cloud, when no rain falls to earth. The intensity of rainfall (i.e. how much water falls in a period of time) depends mainly on the size of raindrops, which in turn depends on the speed of the upward movement of air within the clouds which produce them. At one extreme is a very fine drizzle, which may last for several hours, from layer-cloud produced by gentle uplift of air. At the other is the brief, intense downpour of very large raindrops, from a thunder-cloud produced by violent upward air-currents (11.6).

Thunderstorms may also produce a distinct kind of precipitation: hail. There is no general agreement among scientists as to how hailstones form inside clouds, and there may well be more than one process at work. The most generally accepted theory is that a hailstone begins its growth, as a raindrop does, as a particle of ice, but is circulated round inside the thundercloud by the violent air-currents, repeatedly carried up and then falling. With each cycle it develops more layers of ice, until it is too big for the updraught inside the cloud to support it, when it falls to the ground.

The water cycle. Earth is the wet planet. Its character and the conditions on its surface are largely a result of the abundance of water, which in the form of seas and oceans covers about two-thirds of its surface. As living things, children need to know and understand something of the processes which create the conditions making life on Earth possible. Some of these processes: weathering, soil formation and weather, are discussed in this chapter, but underlying all of them is a much larger-scale pattern of changes, to which all of them contribute and without which none of them could continue. This is the circulation of water between the hydrosphere, atmosphere and lithosphere which is known as the water cycle.

In outline, the water (or hydrological) cycle is simple, though the details of how water moves in and on the land in any particular area are likely to be very complex. Water evaporates from the ocean into the atmosphere, the energy required for evaporation (latent heat, 6.3) coming from the Sun. Sooner or later the water vapour condenses as cloud, which may produce precipitation in a liquid form (rain) or a solid form (snow or hail). Precipitation falling into the ocean (about 77 per cent of the total, worldwide) is recycled directly, but the remainder which falls on land returns by less direct routes which may be rapid or take a very long time to complete. In mountains and polar regions, for example, snow turns to ice in glaciers and ice-caps where it may remain, slowly moving downwards or outwards towards the sea, for thousands of years before it melts and re-enters the active part of the water cycle.

Apart from weather and precipitation, the parts of the water cycle which affect the lives of children most obviously are likely to be those which influence water supply and human activities such as farming. Water falling on land may be recycled to the atmosphere very quickly by evaporation from the soil surface and from the leaves of plants. Some of the water which goes deeper into the soil will move sideways, draining into lakes or rivers, including the artificial lakes we know as reservoirs. Much of this will return to the sea in a relatively short space of time – a few weeks or months – even if it is diverted on the way for human use. In areas with porous rocks, however, water often percolates much deeper and remains, in some cases for a very long time, as ground-water which may be extracted by drilling boreholes and pumping it to the surface.

The pattern of water supply, use and replenishment varies widely in different parts of Britain and Europe, but in densely populated areas all the major sources (rivers, lakes, reservoirs and ground-water) are exploited. In Britain there is a particularly clear pattern of population in relation to water supply. In general, the highest concentrations of people live in the areas of low rainfall, while areas of high rainfall are relatively sparsely populated. This has given rise to the need for large-scale storage of water in reservoirs and its long-distance transportation by pumping through pipes. Children should be aware of the need to conserve water and the dangers of pollution and overexploitation, both of rivers and ground-water resources.

11.6: Patterns of weather

Particularly at the upper end of the primary age range, knowledge and understanding of weather can be developed, and children's own observations given more relevance, by studying patterns of weather over periods ranging from a few days to a few hours. An effective strategy for studying weather patterns in the medium term is to use television forecasts, recorded end-to-end for a period during which the children themselves are making observations and measurements. The forecasts can then be viewed as a continuous sequence and compared with the first-hand data to see how accurate the forecasting process is. In following such a programme, well-marked patterns of weather are likely to be experienced, two of which, the depression and the anticyclone, are discussed here.

Depressions are low-pressure zones and the weather systems associated with them. The depressions which affect Britain originate to the west, over North America or the Atlantic Ocean, when warm, moist air from the south and cold, dryer air from the north begin to interact. A large, wedge-shaped mass of warm air is squeezed by the denser cold air and begins to rise. This rising of the warm air causes the atmospheric pressure around the point of the wedge to fall and a depression is formed. Two patterns of weather associated with depressions can be observed by children: one of winds and one of cloud and precipitation.

Because air moves towards a zone of low pressure, winds begin to blow inwards towards the centre of the depression in an anticlockwise spiral. The whole system, which may be 2,000 km across, moves eastwards and as it does so the low pressure area often intensifies so that the winds spiral into it at increasing speed. As a depression crosses with its centre to the north of Britain it is often possible to record a clear pattern of change in wind direction, from southerly, through south-westerly to westerly and north-westerly, which reflects the spiral path of winds blowing into the centre. In trying to observe such wind-patterns it is worth remembering that winds at ground level may be misleading and watching the movement of clouds may give more reliable information.

The pattern of cloud and precipitation associated with a depression is often equally clear. Most of the rain or snow is generated at the boundaries (fronts) between the warmer and colder air-masses. The wedge-shaped mass of warm air usually gives rise to two fronts (Fig. 11.1a) at both of which cold air lifts the warmer air, causing condensation, cloud formation and precipitation (Fig. 11.1b). The sequence of cloud-forms and precipitation as a depression approaches and a warm front passes over can be observed and interpreted during the course of a single day if the timing is favourable. The commonest sequence is: cirrus, cirrostratus, alto-stratus (light rain begins), nimbostratus (heaviest rain), stratocumulus (rain decreases), stratus (light rain or drizzle). As the depression passes over and the cold front approaches, winds often become more violent and blustery because the cold air behind moves in faster than the depression travels, causing the warm air to rise sharply. This causes dense cloud formation leading to rain or snowfall, and is also one cause of thunderstorms (see below). When the cold front has passed over, the wind direction usually changes to the north-west and cooler, finer but showery weather follows.

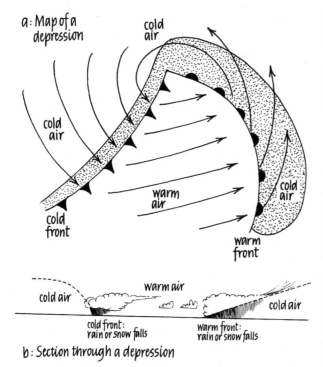

a: Map of a depression

b: Section through a depression

Figure 11.1 A depression (Northern Hemisphere). On the map, the arrows show wind directions. The shaded area shows where rain or snow are likely to fall, as warm air is lifted by cold air moving in beneath it

Anticyclones are in many ways the opposite of depressions. A depression, caused by low pressure and rising, unstable air-masses, gives wet, windy and changeable weather. An anticyclone, on the other hand, caused by high pressure and falling, stable air-masses, is characterized by settled fine weather and light winds. Because air in an anticyclone is falling and becoming warmer, there is usually little tendency for clouds to form, so skies are often clear and even if they are overcast there is little or no precipitation. The winds, blowing outwards from the centre of the high-pressure zone in a clockwise spiral, are usually light. As a result, there is often a very marked daily pattern in the weather under an anticyclone, which changes with the seasons. In summer, clear skies give hot, sunny weather, with nights which are warm because they are too short for the land to cool down very much. In autumn the days are still quite warm and the humidity of the air is often high, but the nights are longer and colder than in summer because clear skies allow the land to cool down rapidly. As a result mist and fog are very frequent. In winter, the days are often sunny but very cold, because during the long nights the land cools down well below freezing-point, giving severe frosts.

Thunderstorms create a third pattern of weather which children may be able to observe, much more short-lived than depressions and anticyclones, but also more spectacular. Thunderstorms are generated by cumulo-nimbus clouds, which are formed when warm, moist air becomes unstable and rises very rapidly by convection. In Britain there are two main ways in which this can happen. The first occurs in summer when the sun is heating the land. This heating causes the air just above the surface to become heated and to rise, but is always uneven. If very moist air is strongly heated and begins to rise rapidly, cooling and cloud formation may set off a violent sequence of events which leads to a thunderstorm. The second cause of thunderstorms is the rise of warm air associated with a depression. In most depressions which cross Britain the rise of warm air, caused by colder air moving under it, is fairly gentle and gradual, but sometimes the cold air moves in so fast that the warm air is made unstable, begins to rise much faster than usual and thunderstorms are generated. This can happen at any time of the year, not just in summer, which explains why thunder, lightning and hail may be experienced in autumn and even, occasionally, in winter.

There is much about thunderstorms which is not understood, but their violence, which children can observe at first hand, can be explained. As warm, moist air rises in the atmosphere, water vapour condenses and cloud forms. This transfers energy (latent heat, 6.3) to the air, warming it, causing it to expand, become less dense and so rise even further, leading to more condensation. If the rising air is much warmer and moister than the air around it, condensation, cloud formation and the heating it causes occur much more quickly, so the upward movement of air within the cloud becomes more and more violent. This can often be seen simply by watching a thundercloud develop. In the early stages of its development, it is these violent updraughts within the cloud which prevent ice particles from falling and allow them to circulate and grow to form hailstones. Later, in part of the cloud, rain or hail will begin to fall. They set up strong downward movements of air. Because this air comes from high up in the cloud it is much colder than the air at ground level, and can often be felt as a cold wind blowing outwards from the approaching thunderstorm.

The exact cause of lightning is not known, but very large electrical charges are built up within thunderclouds. In any thunderstorm, most lightning occurs inside the clouds and may be visible as sheet lightning. Cloud-to-ground lightning occurs when a downward discharge, like a faint lightning stroke, is met by a small upward one as it nears the surface of the Earth. When the two meet, a pathway is created down which the bolt or stroke of lightning, like a gigantic spark, can travel. This lasts for less than 0.1 sec., but in that time it generates very high temperatures (estimated at 25,000°C, much hotter than the surface of the Sun), causing the air to glow white-hot and giving the flash of lightning which we see. The lightning conductors on buildings are an attempt to provide a route through which the very large current generated by the cloud can travel harmlessly to Earth.

The intense local heating of the lightning flash causes the air around it to expand violently, sending out the shock-waves which we hear as thunder. Light from a distant lightning-stroke reaches the eye almost instantly, but sound travels much more slowly; at about 300 metres per second (300 ms^{-1}). This means that if the time between seeing lightning and hearing the resulting thunder is measured, the distance between lightning-strike and observer can be estimated quite accurately (3 sec. = 1 km). It also explains why distant thunder is heard as a rumbling, whereas thunder nearby is heard as a loud crack. A lightning-stroke is several kilometres long, so sound generated along its length at the instant of discharge takes different amounts of time to reach the observer (16.1).

11.7: Rocks and their formation

An outline of the main concepts used in classifying rocks is given here, together with information on particular types of rock which are used as materials and with which children are likely to be familiar. It is, however, clearly impossible to give detailed information on all the rock types which might be found and used in any area, or which children may handle as specimens. When studying rocks, as when investigating habitats and ecosystems, an effective strategy is to research one's locality in some detail rather than attempting a comprehensive survey. The materials found in buildings and the landscape can then be used as the basis for case-studies of how rocks are formed, used and changed.

The solid, rocky crust of the Earth is made up of a great variety of chemical substances. Each distinct chemical substance is called a mineral, and many minerals are important natural and raw materials. Examples referred to in Chapter 10 include gypsum used for making plaster of Paris, and clay minerals used for bricks and other ceramics. Most minerals form crystals (8.6), some of which when cut and polished are prized as gemstones. Examples include diamond, a rare crystalline form of carbon, and rock crystal, which is the pure mineral form of silica or silicon dioxide, familiar in a less pure form as grains of silver sand.

Rocks are made up of mineral particles bound more or less tightly together. Some rocks are made wholly or mainly of one mineral, for example chalk and limestone which are almost entirely composed of the mineral calcite, a form of calcium carbonate. Other rocks are made of a mixture of minerals. Often the individual mineral particles are very small, but sometimes, as in the case of granites, they are large enough to be seen easily.

There are three main groups of rocks: igneous, sedimentary and metamorphic. All of them had their origin in molten material from within the Earth which cooled and solidified at some time in the past. What makes the three groups different is the way in which the materials making up each kind of rock have been changed since they first became solid, perhaps many millions of years ago.

Igneous rocks. Rocks which have not changed since they cooled and solidified from molten material are called igneous, from the Latin word for fire. There are two main groups of igneous rocks: those which solidified slowly deep within the lithosphere and those which cooled much more quickly at its surface.

Igneous rocks which cooled deep within the lithosphere are called plutonic or intrusive rocks. As very hot liquids, they were forced up into the solid lithosphere under very high pressure from deep within the Earth. Because they were insulated by the solid rocks around them, the hot liquids cooled slowly and the various minerals in them separated out as distinct crystals. The slower the cooling, the longer the crystals had to grow and the larger they are. The most familiar rock of this kind is granite, but other rocks formed in a similar way from different mixtures of minerals include diorite, gabbro and peridotite.

Igneous rocks which were forced out as liquids from the surface of the lithosphere are called volcanic or extrusive rocks. Because they are able to transfer heat rapidly to the air or water around them, volcanic rocks cool quickly and so have much finer textures than plutonic ones, with very small or microscopic crystals. One of the most widespread volcanic rocks is basalt, which forms the Giant's Causeway in Antrim and Fingal's Cave on the island of Staffa. The hexagonal columns in these basalts are not crystals, but were formed when cracks appeared in the cooling and contracting rock mass.

Many volcanic rocks, both plutonic and volcanic, are very hard. Traditionally used for building, some of them have during the past hundred years been extensively quarried for roadstone. In complete contrast are volcanic rocks such as pumice, which is soft and will float in water even though it has the same chemical composition as granite. Pumice is soft and floats because it is a solidified froth, full of gas bubbles trapped when it cooled very quickly.

Sedimentary rocks. With the exception of materials such as coal, which are formed directly from the remains of dead plants, sedimentary rocks are made up of material from other rocks (which may be of any kind), broken down by the chemical and physical processes of weathering (11.8). The products of this breakdown may be transported over large distances by water, wind or ice, but sooner or later are deposited, usually in layers called strata. These sediments may then undergo hardening by physical changes such as compression by the weight of later deposits on them, or chemical changes such as cementation (see below), so that they turn into sedimentary rocks.

Table 11.2 Simple classification of sediments and sedimentary rocks

Particle size (mm)	Name of particle	Name of sediment (particles separate)	Name of rock (particles joined together)
over 300	boulder	boulder gravel	boulder conglomerate
50–300	cobble	cobble gravel	cobble conglomerate
5–50	pebble	pebble gravel	pebble conglomerate
2–4	granule	granular sand	granular sandstone
0.1–2	sand	sand	sandstone
0.005–0.1	silt	silt	siltstone
under 0.005	clay	clay	shale

Note: less formal definitions may be useful when working with the small particle sizes. A widely used one is that if individual grains can be distinguished they must be silt grade or larger; whereas if the sediment does not feel gritty on the teeth, it is clay.

Sediments and sedimentary rocks made up of solid rock fragments (clastic sediments) usually contain particles of different sizes. They are roughly classified according to the size of the particles which make up the bulk of the sediment, and whether these are separate or have been joined together to form a solid mass. A simple classification is given in Table 11.2.

Sediments, whose particles are not joined together, form a wide range of valuable natural materials, ranging from the very fine particles which make up clays, to sands and gravels which are often quarried together for the aggregate needed to make concrete (10.2). Grains of sand may vary in both shape and mineral composition, so that different sands have a range of properties which are exploited by industry and the building trade. Silver sand is made up almost entirely of the mineral quartz, a form of silicon dioxide or silica.

Sedimentary rocks, formed when the particles of a sediment are joined together, have properties which vary according to the size of its particles, their chemical nature and the way they are held together. Shales are formed from clay-sized particles compacted by the weight of later deposits. They are mostly soft, fine-grained rocks which split easily into thin layers along their original strata or bedding-planes, in contrast to slates (see below). Shales often contain chemicals such as oil, which may be exploited as valuable resources.

Sandstones are formed when ground-water, seeping through sand, deposits minerals between the grains, forming a natural cement which locks them together. The more complete this cementation is, the less porous (6.6) the rock will be and, in general, the more slowly it will weather (11.8). The two main cementing minerals are calcium carbonate and silica, which form calcareous and siliceous sandstones respectively. Many sandstones are coloured brown or greenish-grey by iron-containing chemicals, which may be abundant enough to use as ore for the smelting of iron metal (10.2).

Some sediments (chemical sediments) are deposited from materials dissolved in water. Like clastic sediments, they may be changed to form rocks. Children are likely to be familiar with two examples: rock-salt, which is a mineral sediment, and chalk or limestone, which are rocks.

Rock-salt, an impure form of sodium chloride, is an example of the class of minerals known as evaporites (another is the gypsum used to make plaster, 10.2). It was deposited when sea-water evaporated, probably in shallow lagoons which were periodically flooded and then overlain by later sediments. Salt for use in cooking is obtained by drilling into a salt-bed and forcing hot water into it under pressure through a pipe. The brine formed as the salt dissolves is pumped back to the surface where the water is evaporated to obtain solid salt. The brown rock-salt used on roads and paths to melt ice (6.2) is mined directly, and in use is often mixed with grit to give more friction (14.4).

Chalk and limestone are both formed from calcium carbonate, which will not dissolve in water. Many marine animals such as shellfish, crabs, lobsters and sea-urchins, as well as a wide variety of microscopic animals, can make calcium carbonate from other chemicals dissolved in sea-water, and use it as the main hardening material for their shells or exoskeletons. When they die their soft parts decay, but the shells fall to the sea floor and under some conditions form an ooze made largely of calcium carbonate. Chalk is a soft rock formed from very thick beds of this chemical sediment, hardened by pressure, while greater age and hardening form limestone. Most chalk is too soft for use as building stone, but a wide variety of limestones is used. They are vulnerable to chemical weathering, especially when this is accelerated by acid rain (5.9), which poses major conservation problems in much of Europe. Both rock types are often very rich in fossils and are valuable raw materials, used for example in the manufacture of cement and the smelting of iron (10.2).

Metamorphic rocks. After their formation, rocks of any type may be further changed by heat and pressure during periods of movement and activity within the lithosphere. Rocks changed in this way are called metamorphic (from the Greek for 'changed in form'). The three metamorphic rocks with which children are likely to be familiar are slate, marble and graphite, all of which are formed from sedimentary rocks.

Slate is formed from shales in which the clay particles have been changed both physically and chemically by intense compression and heat. The resulting rock can be split into thin sheets, but the direction of the cleavage is related to the forces which modified the rock, not to the original bedding of the sediments. As a result, slates are often found with bands of different colour running across them. Slates are harder and stronger than shales, fine-grained, impervious to water and weather very slowly. These properties, coupled with their cleavage, have led to slate being used as a roofing material in many parts of Britain and Europe (10.2).

Marble is a metamorphosed limestone, in which the calcium carbonate has become recrystallized under heat and pressure to form a fairly hard and coarse-grained rock which, unlike slate, is very tough and resistant to splitting. Pure marble is white, but other minerals may give it a wide range of colours and patterns (imitated when 'marbling' walls and paper with paint). Marble is soft enough to be carved but hard enough to take a fine finish, and in clean air weathers only slowly. These properties, coupled with its colour and toughness, have made it highly prized as a material for building and sculpture since before 2000 BC. Like all carbonate rocks, marble is very vulnerable to the accelerated chemical weathering caused by acid rain and other forms of atmospheric pollution (5.9), which is a serious problem in many ancient monuments, for example in Athens.

Graphite is a form of carbon, formed when coal is subjected to intense heat and pressure. Pure graphite is a soft, silvery-black solid which has three interesting properties: it leaves a mark when rubbed onto a surface such as paper, it conducts electricity, and its surface is curiously smooth and slippery. Graphite is most familiar as the main ingredient of the 'lead' of pencils. To make an ordinary pencil such as an 'HB', graphite is ground up and mixed with clay and water to form a paste which is then moulded and baked before being put into an outer casing. The greater the clay content, the harder the 'lead' and the greyer the line it makes. Pure graphite is used for very soft, black drawing pencils and graphite sticks; soft 'leads' for propelling pencils can be used for investigating electrical conductivity (13.8).

11.8: The weathering of rocks

In comparison with human time-scales, large landforms such as hills and valleys seem permanent, but neither they nor the rocks of which they are made last for ever. Rocks break down and disintegrate, but usually the process is so slow that is impossible to detect, especially since most rocks in Britain are covered with a layer of soil which conceals and to some extent protects them. However, where rocks have been used as materials for buildings, kerbstones, gravestones and other artefacts exposed to the weather, changes are often much more rapid and easy to detect. In cities, stone often becomes discoloured by sooty deposits from smoke, and may suffer severe damage from atmospheric pollutants such as sulphur dioxide dissolved in rainwater (5.9). Even in areas not badly affected by atmospheric pollution, flaking and crumbling of rocks in buildings and other artefacts is often evident.

Breakdown in the structure of a rock may come about through physical changes, chemical changes or a combination of both. Collectively these changes are referred to as weathering. It may be useful to distinguish between weathering on the one hand and erosion and transport on the other. Weathering is the actual process of breakdown, whereas erosion and transport remove the products of breakdown and, in some cases, carry them over long distances.

Physical weathering, also known as mechanical weathering or disintegration, is the process by which a rock is reduced to smaller fragments without any changes in its chemical composition. A wide variety of natural processes bring about physical weathering, but the ones whose effects children may observe are frost, water, wind and plant roots.

Water has the very unusual property that when it freezes, it expands (6.2). This expansion brings about weathering by frost. If the mineral particles which make up a rock are not completely cemented together (11.7), there will be holes or pores between them into which water can seep, and even a non-porous rock is likely to have cracks and joints which can become filled with water. If water in pores or cracks freezes during frosty weather, the rock structure will be subjected to large forces tending to crack it apart or break off pieces at its surface.

The rocks and manufactured materials most vulnerable to frost weathering are soft, with weakly cemented particles and high porosity, used in situations where they are frequently saturated with water and cannot dry out easily. The commonest sign of frost weathering on buildings is surface flaking, which can often be observed in soft porous sandstones and limestones, as well as manufactured materials such as soft brick and mortar mixed with too little cement. Frost weathering may also affect slate when it is of poor quality. Compact rocks with very low porosity, such as hard sandstones, marble and granite, are usually very resistant to frost weathering, both because they take up very little water and because their particles are cemented together very strongly.

The breakdown of rocks caused by water is usually regarded by geologists not as weathering but as erosion (i.e. removal of debris); but the action of sea and river water on cliffs and beaches is usually a combination of the two. The most obvious breakdown products are sand, gravel and pebbles which form beaches at the edges of rivers, lakes and the sea. They are formed by abrasion, as rock fragments are moved and rub against each other, and ancient deposits of this kind are quarried for building materials (10.2). Weathering by wind, like that caused by water, is usually classed as a form of erosion. Although it is very important in many desert areas of the world, children in Britain are unlikely to see wind acting as an agent of rock-weathering unless they visit sand-dunes.

In contrast, weathering brought about by plant roots and, indirectly, by animals, is widespread and very important in soil formation (11.9), but is usually difficult to detect. Occasionally, however, tree roots can be seen penetrating cracks in rocks. As they grow, the tough, woody roots can exert very large forces, widening the cracks and so exposing more of the rock to the effects of frost and chemical weathering.

Chemical weathering. Chemical weathering, also known as decomposition, is brought about by chemical changes in the rock. These may take place within the mineral particles which make up the bulk of the rock, the material which cements them together, or both. Whereas physical weathering simply produces smaller pieces of rock, chemical weathering, like all chemical change, produces different substances with different properties (9.1). There are many kinds of chemical weathering, but children are likely to encounter only two of them. One of these is weathering by solution, which occurs naturally but is greatly accelerated by acid rain pollution (5.9); the other is organic weathering, caused by the activities of living things.

Weathering by solution affects carbonate rocks such as chalk, limestone and marble, and calcareous sandstones (11.7). In all of them, the material dissolved is calcium carbonate (dolomitic limestone, which contains both calcium and magnesium carbonates, is much less common). Calcium carbonate is insoluble in pure water, but rainwater, even in the absence of pollution, is very slightly acidic and can dissolve it, though very slowly. In this way, carbonate rocks will weather and may crumble over long periods of time. Solution weathering of carbonate rocks is greatly speeded up by acid rain (5.9) caused mainly by the burning of coal and oil, but also naturally through volcanic activity. This has inflicted major damage on historic buildings in most industrialized countries, including Britain.

Organic weathering of rocks is of great importance as one of the main processes leading to soil formation (11.9), but is usually so slow that it is difficult to observe. Children may, however, be able to observe the results of two kinds of organic weathering. The first is to be seen at the base of many soils, where subsoil rests on the rock beneath. In most areas this is exposed only by major earthworks such as road-building or quarrying, but if it can be seen it will usually be observed that the rock immediately beneath the soil is looser, broken up, discoloured and softened. Decaying plant material at the soil surface and the humus it produces (11.9) release acids into the soil water and these bring about much of the weathering, which tends to make the soil deeper, so making it easier for the roots of large plants such as trees to penetrate and break up the rock still further.

It is much easier in most localities to find examples of the second kind of organic weathering, but its results may be more difficult to detect. It is brought about by lichens growing on bare rock or manufactured structures. Lichens (5.3) are a group of living things made up of two different kinds of organism, a fungus and a microscopic green plant (alga), growing in close association. Many lichens can withstand very wide variations in temperature and prolonged drought. Partly because of this, they are able to colonize hostile environments such as bare rock and hard, durable manufactured materials such as brick, mortar, concrete and tarmac. Part of their process of becoming established consists of making acidic chemicals which dissolve part of the surface of the material on which they are growing. This literally etches and eats the material away, rather as an acid may corrode and dissolve a metal, and though it happens very slowly, it eventually creates a habitat in which small plants such as mosses can begin to grow. Even in inner-city areas it is often possible for children to see stages in the colonization of mortar joints in walls, beginning with very tiny lichens, continuing with larger lichens which are gradually replaced by mosses. If the wall remains undisturbed for a long time, the mosses quite often build up enough soil to support larger but still very tough and hardy plants such as ferns and willowherbs.

11.9: Weathering and soil formation

Over most of the Earth's land masses, where the lithosphere is exposed to the atmosphere, rocks have weathered and become altered to form a thin surface layer of extraordinary variety, complexity and importance: the soil. Thought of on a global scale, soil is no more than a very thin film on the Earth's surface, yet all land-based life depends on it. Soils are formed by the interaction of rocks, the atmosphere and living things. They are so varied and complex that no detailed advice can be given here on what children are likely to find when investigating them. As when studying local rock types, the most practical strategy for the teacher is likely to be researching local soils with the help of specialists and using these as case-studies.

Soil formation. Soil formation begins when plants and animals colonize bare rock or newly deposited sediments. Colonization of bare rock (usually by lichens followed by mosses, 11.8) is a very slow process, whereas on some sediments, such as river gravels or dune sand, plants may be found growing only a year or two after the material has been deposited.

Soil is formed as dead plant material decays at the soil surface and is mixed, mainly through the activity of soil-dwelling animals, with mineral particles formed by weathering of rock. The decaying plant material has three important properties. First, as it decays it releases plant nutrients (4.3) into the soil water, which further encourages plant growth. Secondly, decaying plant material retains water in the soil while remaining loose with plenty of air in it, making it easier for plants to colonize and survive periods of drought. Thirdly, the process of decay produces acids which are carried downwards by soil water and speed up the chemical weathering of the rock or sediments on which the soil is forming (11.8).

Apart from plants, which contribute their dead remains to the soil, and microbes which decay them, the most important living agents of soil formation in Britain are earthworms. They feed on dead plant material and, having no teeth, take soil into their gut and use it to grind up the fibrous plant remains. They eat (and therefore grind up) large volumes of plant material, because its food value to them is low. The result of this feeding is worm casts: a paste of soil mixed with finely ground plant material which can be attacked by microbes and decayed (5.8) much more rapidly than whole leaves. At the same time, earthworms mix the soil, both carrying material from the surface downwards and leaving some of their casts at the surface.

Decay and humus in soil. In areas populated by animals and plants but not cultivated, a layer of decaying vegetable matter forms the uppermost layer of the soil. This is well-developed in most woodland, where the process of decay and breakdown can be traced by observing the disintegration of leaves and their conversion to humus (5.8). If the earthworm population is high, as for example in oak woodland, decay is fairly rapid and the humus produced is a dark brown, crumbly material which is moderately acid (pH 5–5.5) and rich in plant nutrients. If the earthworm population is low, as in heathland and conifer forest, decay is slow, the humus produced is black, greasy and much more acidic (pH 3.5–4.5), so the soil is poor and infertile.

In grassland, particularly if it is mown, and on cultivated areas, less dead plant material reaches the soil each year than in a woodland. These soils usually support a very large earthworm population and have an active community of micro-organisms near the surface, where there is a good supply of oxygen. Together these ensure that any dead plant material on the soil surface is broken down, decayed and recycled very rapidly. One result of this is that grassland and cultivated soils often have little or no distinct humus layer. What they usually show when undisturbed is a dark topsoil, coloured by humus mixed into it by earthworms.

11.10: The properties of soil in relation to plant growth

Between the surface layer of decaying plant material and humus (if this is present) and the subsoil, is the middle layer of the soil which, confusingly, is often called topsoil. It is made up of weathered mineral particles with varying amounts of humus mixed with them. Although the topsoil may be only a few inches deep, it is vitally important in farming because it supports nearly all the roots of crop plants and in most soils contains about 90 per cent of the plant nutrients available to them.

The texture and fertility of topsoil depend on many factors. One of the most important, which children can investigate, is the range of size among the mineral particles which make it up. (A list of particles and their sizes is given in Table 11.2.) Before trying to analyse soil samples it is helpful to investigate their texture and consistency in a very simple and direct way, because these qualities are closely linked to drainage and how easy or difficult the soil is to cultivate. Useful comparisons can be made simply by taking a small handful of each kind of soil and squeezing it in the hand as hard as possible. When released, a sandy soil treated in this way will fall apart and crumble very easily, whereas a clay loam will have been moulded into a compact, plastic mass which clings together and has to be pulled apart. Soils with varying proportions of sand, silt and clay will have textures between the two, and natural soils can be compared with the extremes of damp silver sand on the one hand and pottery clay on the other.

Having compared textures, it is then useful to carry out a simple analysis of particle size in the same soils, by suspension and sedimentation (6.5). Each weighed sample is put into about twice its own volume of water in a jar with a secure lid. After any lumps have been broken up, the mixture is shaken vigorously and left to settle. Because large particles settle out faster than small ones it is usually possible, if similar containers are used, to make accurate visual comparisons of the particle range in the different soils. The range of particles, shown by the depth of the various layers, can then be linked to the earlier observations on texture.

The range of particles in a soil can help to explain not only their texture, but also many of their other physical properties. Most of the particles in sandy soils are relatively large, so they have an open, porous structure from which water drains quickly. Sand grains do not cling together strongly even when wet, so that these soils are usually 'light', easy to cultivate and well aerated. The very small particles which make up most of a clay loam, on the other hand, cling together strongly, so that these soils are 'heavy' and may be very difficult to dig or plough. The small particles of clay have very small spaces between them, through which water can drain only slowly, so that the soil may become very wet during periods of heavy rain and in winter. In this state the soil may have very little air in it, so that root growth may be prevented and some crops may die. Both the amount of air in drained soil and the speed with which water will drain through it can be investigated by children and compared with observations on texture and particle sizes.

Clay loams have physical properties very different from those of sandy soils, and are also different chemically. Because sand grains are hard and inert, sandy soils have little capacity for storing the soluble chemicals (nutrients) which plants take from the soil and use for growth (4.3). As water drains rapidly through, the plant nutrients tend to be washed (leached) out very rapidly and lost in the ground-water, so that sandy soils tend to be 'hungry' and infertile. One result is that it may be impossible to farm such soils profitably, so that areas such as the Dorset Heaths and Breckland in East Anglia remain as heathland or are planted as conifer forest. Some kinds of clay particles, on the other hand, can actually capture and store plant nutrients, which can then be extracted by plant roots. This means that, although they are often difficult to cultivate and 'cold' (i.e. slow to warm up in spring), clay soils are often very fertile and support rich pasture.

12
Energy

12.1: Energy and change

Most of science as a whole, and the overwhelming majority of investigations carried out by children at primary level, are concerned with change. Observing and learning about change enables us to distinguish living things from non-living (2.1), to find out how the human body works (3.2–3.12), how plants grow, feed and reproduce (4.3–4.5) and how living things interact to form communities (5.7–5.9). The properties of materials, both physical and chemical, are concerned almost entirely with how they change, or can be made to change other things (Chapters 6–10), while Earth science investigates change and its results in the atmosphere, lithosphere and hydrosphere (Chapter 11).

As even such a brief list shows, observing, describing, measuring and understanding changes are an essential part of science. Understanding change in the world we observe, the world of material things, is impossible without a concept of energy. It is often said that energy is an abstract idea which is difficult to define; that it is easier to say what energy is not than what it is. This attitude is both unhelpful and misleading. The basic concept of energy is very simple and straightforward, and one which can be used to link many areas of science in ways which are meaningful to children. Though it may at times be difficult to apply the concept of energy to some of the changes children observe and investigate, developing and using it is an essential part of their education in science, without which much of what they experience can be neither explained nor understood.

Energy is the property of material things (or, more properly, of systems) which enables them to change. This property shows itself in different ways in different objects and systems, so that these are said to have different forms of energy (12.2). In this context, 'system' means a group of objects which interact as changes take place, for example the Solar System, which is made up of the Sun, planets and other objects. The forms and amount of energy in an object or system determine the kind and extent of the changes it can bring about or undergo. When a change occurs, energy is transferred from one part of the system to another, often in a different form. For example, when a battery (an object) is connected to form part of a circuit (a system) which includes a lamp, chemical changes in the battery cause some of its energy (chemical-potential energy, 12.2) to be transferred to the rest of the system as electrical energy. Most of this electrical energy is transferred in turn to the filament of the lamp as thermal energy (12.2), making it so hot (12.3, 13.7) that it glows. The hot filament transfers energy to its environment as light and by heating the air around it.

Any change in any object or system, whether it be a microbe or a motor car, a person or a planet, involves transfer of energy, and the same is true in reverse: any transfer of energy brings about change. Another way of saying this is that the changes we observe in the material world and the transfer of energy are two aspects of the same happening or phenomenon.

In thinking and communicating about change, energy and energy transfer, it is important to avoid the suggestion that energy is a substance which is generated, moved around and transformed as changes occur. For example, a battery in a circuit does not generate energy when the circuit is switched on. What it does generate is electric current (13.3). Because current is flowing, the circuit has the property that it can bring about changes, such as making a lamp light up, so we say that energy has been transferred to the circuit from the battery, in the form of electrical energy.

The fact that energy is a property and not a substance is also shown by the way in which some energy transfers do not change objects at all, but simply their position or the way they are moving. If a person lifts a brick from the floor by pulling it up on a rope, energy from food (chemical-potential energy, 12.2) is transferred to the muscles of the arms (by way of respiration, 3.6) as energy of movement (kinetic energy, 12.2), and from them to the brick, which is lifted and gains energy as a result (gravitational-potential energy, 12.2). The energy in the person's body has been reduced; that of the brick has been increased. If the brick which is suspended from the rope were allowed to fall down, it could bring about changes which it could not do while on the floor, so it has the property we call energy in greater degree, but all that has changed is its position in relation to the Earth. As a material object the brick has not changed at all. The higher the brick is raised, the more energy it gains and the more change it can bring about. If, for example, the brick fell onto your foot from a height of 1 cm you would feel it but it would be unlikely to hurt, whereas if it fell from a height of 1 m you would suffer severe pain and probably some injury as well.

Energy, forces, work and measurement. Lifting a weight is an example of a very important kind of change which involves forces. When the movement or shape of an object is changed by forces (14.1), energy is transferred, as it is in all changes. It is, however, important to realize that transfer of energy is not the cause of change. Like other changes we can observe more easily, it is an effect. It is especially important not to confuse the concept of energy with that of force (14.12). Forces are causes: they make things happen. They determine whether and how objects move or stay still, and may determine their shape. When the movement or shape of an object changes, this is an effect caused by forces acting.

Energy, on the other hand, is a property of the system on which the force or forces are acting to cause change, and transfer of energy is an inevitable part of that change. The particular kind of change involved in lifting a weight is called work. Work is done when a force is exerted so that a change is brought about in the shape of an object, its position or the speed or direction in which it is moving. A car which is being driven by its engine, an electric drill which is rotating, moving a barrowload of bricks and stretching an elastic band all involve forces, work and different kinds of energy transfer.

The concept of work is very important and useful, because it enables us to measure energy. When doing work, the energy transferred is equal to the force applied (measured in newtons, symbol: N), multiplied by the distance it is moved, measured in metres (m). For example, if a brick has a mass of 3 kg, it will take a force of about 30 N to lift it. If is lifted to a height of 2 m, the work done is 30 × 2 Newton-metres (Nm), and this is also a measure of the energy transferred to the brick. It is convenient to have a special unit to measure both work and energy, and this is the Joule (symbol: J), 1 J being equal to 1 Nm. If a heavier weight is lifted, or the same brick is lifted to a greater height, more work will be done and, as we have already seen, more energy will be transferred to it. For example, 5 kg of bricks lifted 3 m involves a force of 50 N moving over 3 m, so 50 × 3 = 150 J of energy is transferred to them.

The concept of work is useful because it has led to a measure of energy which can be used when investigating any kind of change, but it can create problems for teachers at primary level. In the language of science and technology, 'work' has the very precise meaning outlined above, but children and adults use the word in a wide variety of ways. This means that in scientific activity, care is needed to use the word 'work' in the correct way and to emphasize what it means in this context. The other problem is more wide-ranging. Because energy transfer when doing work provides a measure of both work and energy, energy itself has come to be defined, in the context of secondary science, as 'the capacity to do work'. This definition is useful in physics and engineering, but is too specialized and restricted to be helpful in primary science, because children observe and may seek to explain many energy transfers, such as a fire burning or an electric lamp being lit, which have no direct connection at all with work, either in terms of forces and movement or the way in which the word is commonly used. Because of this, the wider concept of energy as the property which enables systems to change has been developed here.

12.2: Forms of energy

When energy is transferred from one part of a system to another as a change occurs, it may change in form. Examples involving a simple electrical circuit and lifting a brick have already been mentioned in section 12.1. In some books on physics such changes are referred to as the transformation of energy, but this term should be avoided because it tends to reinforce the misleading idea that energy is a substance. A better approach is to use the 'describe-explain' strategy (1.8), concentrating first on the observable changes which are taking place and then explaining these in terms of the transfer of energy.

The main forms of energy involved in changes which children are likely to investigate and learn about at primary level are:

kinetic energy;
thermal energy;
electrical energy;
light energy (one form of radiant energy);
gravitational-potential energy;
elastic-potential energy;
chemical-potential energy;
nuclear energy.

Kinetic energy. In order to make an object move, energy has to be transferred to it by doing work (12.1). The object can then bring about changes because it is moving, which it could not do if it were at rest. Because a moving object can bring about changes, it must have energy. This is the energy which was transferred to it when it was made to move, and is called energy of movement or kinetic energy. The heavier the object and the faster it is moving, the more energy has been transferred to it in making it move and the more kinetic energy it has.

Kinetic energy is most obvious when something impedes the movement of an object, slowing it down or stopping it. When this happens, kinetic energy is transferred to another part of the system. For example, water in a pond is at rest and has no kinetic energy, but water flowing downhill has kinetic energy which can be transferred to water-wheels or turbines (again as kinetic energy) and used to bring about changes such as the grinding of grain or generating electric current. Other systems which transfer kinetic energy include windmills, which are becoming increasingly important for the generation of electricity (12.4), electrical generators, which when they are rotated transfer kinetic energy to electrical circuits as electrical energy, and any object which makes a sound (16.1).

The most widespread transfer of kinetic energy occurs when two moving objects or materials come into contact. Its effects are most obvious when solid surfaces slide over one another, but it also occurs when objects move through air or water. When two surfaces or materials move past each other, there is a force (friction, 14.3) which impedes their movement and slows them down. The most obvious effect of this is that the moving objects and their surroundings are heated (12.3). This happens because kinetic energy is transferred to the objects in the form of thermal energy (see below) as the movement becomes slower. A familiar example is the braking of a bicycle (14.9). As the brake-blocks grip the wheel and slow the bicycle down, kinetic energy is transferred to the blocks, the wheel-rims and the air around them, which are heated as a result. The heating effect of working to overcome friction can be felt even more simply, by rubbing the hands together.

Large masses of moving material have very large amounts of kinetic energy, which can bring about catastrophic changes. Apart from war and famine, most disasters are brought about by changes of this kind. Natural examples include landslides, earthquakes, high seas, flooding rivers and storm-force winds, while manufactured systems can be very destructive if they move out of control: car, train and aeroplane crashes are all-too-familiar examples.

Energy is transferred as kinetic energy to any object while it is made to move. Children will be familiar with systems in which energy is transferred in this way from a variety of sources: chemical-potential energy in food (moving animal) or fuel (internal combustion or steam engine); gravitational-potential energy (falling water is an important example); elastic-potential energy (spring, catapult and air-gun) and electrical energy (electric motor).

Thermal energy. All materials are made up of very small particles (atoms and molecules, 8.1), which are constantly moving. In a gas they move about freely and collide with one another, whereas in a liquid they are in contact and move past each other much more slowly. In a solid the particles cannot move past each other at all (this is why it is a solid), and simply vibrate. If energy is transferred to a material its molecules move more, and move faster. In most situations the most obvious effect of this is that the temperature of the material goes up and it becomes hotter (12.3). The exceptions are when changes of state are occurring, by melting, boiling or evaporation (6.1–6.3). In such a situation, the energy transferred to the material results in a change of state rather than a rise in temperature. This 'extra' energy transferred to the material is known as latent heat.

A hot object can bring about change by heating whatever is around it, which a cold object cannot do, so it must have more energy. This is usually called the thermal energy of the object, though it is sometimes referred to as internal energy or, quite incorrectly, as heat. The more violently its molecules are moving and the higher its temperature, the more thermal energy an object has. Heating, cooling, thermal energy and temperature are discussed further in section 12.3.

Electrical energy. When an electric current (13.3) is generated, energy is transferred to a circuit in the form of electrical energy. There are two main ways of doing this: by batteries (13.4) which have chemical-potential energy, and by generators which transfer kinetic energy as electrical energy when work is done to make them move. Lightning (11.6) is a violent event in which electrical energy is transferred to the environment as light, thermal energy and kinetic energy in the form of sound. Electrical energy is widely exploited in technology because electric current can activate appliances which bring about a wide variety of useful changes and transfers of energy. Examples include transfer of energy as kinetic energy by electric motors, as thermal energy by heaters (13.7) and as light energy by filament lamps and fluorescent tubes. Electric current and its effects are discussed in Chapter 13.

Light energy is the form of radiant energy with which children are most familiar: others include radio waves, microwaves and X-rays. Light is a very important form of energy to us, partly because we can detect it directly through the activity we call vision (3.10) and so gain information about the world around us. Because of this, understanding how light interacts with materials is a major branch of science (Chapter 17). Light also demonstrates that energy can be just as real as material things, and is not imaginary or simply an idea invented to explain changes. The major source of energy for the Earth is light from the Sun, which reaches us across 150 million kilometres of space: not much imaginary about that!

When materials are heated to a high enough temperature they glow (become incandescent) and transfer energy to the environment as light. The colour of the light emitted depends on temperature. Light from a star like the Sun, whose surface temperature is about 6,000°C, is white, while cooler stars appear yellow or red and hotter ones appear blue. A lightning flash generates temperatures comparable with those of the hotter stars, about 25,000°C, and so the light it emits also appears blue. The same effect can be seen in an electric lamp. If the current for which the lamp was designed is passed through it, the filament is heated to about 2,300°C and gives a yellow light. If the current is reduced (13.3), the filament is at a lower temperature and so appears dimmer and more red, whereas a larger current gives a whiter light but overheats the filament, which usually breaks in a short time.

Fluorescent tubes, neon strip-lights and yellow (sodium vapour) street lights work by passing an electric current through a mixture of gases in a tube. The gas molecules are activated (excited) by the electrical energy and transfer some of this energy to the environment as light, a process known as gas discharge. The colour depends on the gases used in the tube, not the temperature to which they are heated. Light is also emitted at much lower temperatures by chemical changes carried out by living organisms, including animals (glow-worms, fire-flies and some jellyfish), and a few fungi and bacteria. This is known as bioluminescence.

Light energy can be transferred in a variety of ways. It may be absorbed as thermal energy so that the material is heated as in the solar panels on some houses, in which water is heated by sunlight. Light falling on water can also evaporate it (6.3). Transfer of energy in this way makes possible the series of changes in the atmosphere and hydrosphere which we know as weather and the water cycle (11.2–11.5). Materials are now made which can generate electric current when light falls on them, transferring some of the energy to circuits as electrical energy. These are solar cells, used in calculators, in satellites such as the Hubble space telescope and unmanned spacecraft for exploring the Solar System. They may become important as energy sources in the future (12.4). As far as life on Earth is concerned, however, by far the most important transfer of light energy occurs during photosynthesis (4.4), in which light is absorbed (17.5) as part of a process which produces foods with high chemical-potential energy (see below). It is almost the only way in which energy can be transferred to the biosphere, so nearly all life depends on it (5.7).

Potential energy and energy storage. The four forms of energy discussed so far are all characteristic of systems which are undergoing change. If a change is taking place in a system, one more of these forms of energy is involved. There are, however, other forms of energy which are characteristic of materials and systems which, while they are capable of change (because they have energy), are not changing at the moment. Examples include suspended weights, coiled springs, foods and fuels. Energy of this kind is referred to as potential energy.

When energy is transferred to an object or system as potential energy it is in effect stored, but in referring to storage of energy, care is needed to avoid any suggestion that energy is a material. It is more accurate and less misleading to say that through the transfer of energy, the system has acquired the property of being able to change under certain conditions, for example if the weight is made to fall, the spring to uncoil or the fuel to burn.

Gravitational-potential energy. Like kinetic energy, this form of energy is connected with movement and work, but is a result of an object's vertical position within a system rather than its movement. For example, a brick suspended from a rope has gravitational-potential energy, transferred to it as work was done in pulling it up. The heavier the object and the higher it is lifted, the more energy is transferred to it in the lifting and the more gravitational-potential energy it has.

Any object or material moving spontaneously from a higher to a lower level in relation to the Earth, whether falling, rolling, sliding or flowing, is transferring some of its gravitational-potential energy to the system as kinetic energy. Some will also be transferred as thermal energy, because friction and heating are always involved in any movement. Gravitational-potential energy is already an important renewable energy source (12.4), in hydro-electric installations and tidal barriers, both of which use water flowing downwards to rotate turbines.

Elastic-potential energy. An elastic object is one which regains its original shape when the forces deforming it are released (7.6). This is a change, so the deformed object must have potential energy. This is part of the (kinetic) energy transferred to it when work was done in changing its shape, and is known as elastic-potential energy. The greater the force needed to deform the object and the greater the change of shape, the more energy is transferred to it during deformation and the more elastic-potential energy it has. Examples of familiar elastic objects include bouncy balls (elastic in compression), rubber bands (elastic in tension) and the springs of clockwork toys (elastic in bending).

The energy transfers involved in dropping a ball and allowing it to bounce are summarized in Table 12.1. When an elastic object regains its shape, some of its potential energy is transferred as kinetic energy, but not all. This is shown by the bouncing ball, which will never bounce as high as the point from which it was dropped, because some of its potential energy has been transferred as thermal energy, both as air-resistance (friction) is overcome, and as the ball is deformed and recoils. This is an example of the principle of the conservation of energy (see below), and is particularly useful because changes in the energy of the ball can easily be observed. Theory predicts that the ball would be very slightly warmer after it had bounced than before, and this has been detected using very sensitive temperature probes.

Table 12.1 *Summary of the main energy transfers in a falling and bouncing ball*

Position and movement of ball	Forms of energy: arrows show energy transfer		
	Gravitational-potential	Kinetic	Elastic-potential
Ball held suspended	→maximum$_1$	0	0
Ball falling	decreasing	→increasing	0
Ball hits floor and is deformed	0	decreasing	→increasing
Ball fully deformed and momentarily at rest	0	0	maximum$_2$
Ball recoils	0	increasing	←decreasing
Ball rises	increasing	←decreasing	0
Ball at top of bounce	maximum$_3$	0	0

Note that the potential energy of the ball decreases with each change and energy transfer, so maximum$_1$ is the greatest and maximum$_3$ the least. The energy is transferred as thermal energy in the ball and its surroundings.

Chemical-potential energy. All chemical changes involve transfer of energy, either to or from the environment (9.3). Any chemical substance which transfers energy to the environment as it undergoes chemical change has chemical-potential energy and some are very widely used as energy sources both by humans (for example batteries and fuels) and by all living things in the form of food.

Batteries are small, sealed tanks of chemicals (13.4), which generate electric current when connected as part of a circuit, transferring energy to the circuit as electrical energy. As they do this, their own chemical-potential energy is reduced until the chemical changes are complete and current can no longer be generated. In some batteries the chemical changes can be reversed by passing current through the battery in the reverse direction, transferring electrical energy to it as chemical-potential energy so that it is 'recharged'. Note, however, that no kind of 'rechargeable' battery is safe for use in primary schools (13.4).

Fuels are chemicals, produced by the activities of living things either recently (wood) or in the past (fossil fuels, 12.4), which can be chemically combined with oxygen in the chemical changes known as burning (9.4). Burning transfers energy to the environment or the system very rapidly, so that it is characterized by powerful heating and high temperatures. The internal-combustion engine is a special case of burning, in which a compressed mixture of vaporized fuel and air is burnt in a chamber. The burning is so rapid that it is in effect an explosion, producing very hot gas which expands rapidly (12.3), transferring energy to the pistons as kinetic energy.

Foods are complex chemicals which are used as a source of energy by living things, in the process of respiration (3.6). This is quite unlike burning, because it is a low-temperature process in which chemical-potential energy is transferred in a complex series of controlled chemical changes, to produce a simpler high-energy chemical known as ATP. All living cells use ATP as their source of energy for such processes as movement and the building-up of new living material in growth and tissue replacement. All foods have their origin in the process of photosynthesis (4.4), in which light energy is absorbed by plants (17.5) and transferred as chemical-potential energy by building up substances such as sugars, starch and oil.

In discussing or investigating any of these or other common examples, it is important to avoid any confusion between energy itself and the objects or materials which are energy sources. One way to do this is to emphasize that fuels, foods and batteries are materials and objects, whereas energy is not a material, but a property which some materials and systems have. For example, both petrol and water are liquids, and both sugar and sand are particulate solids, but petrol and sugar have an important property which water and sand do not: they have a lot of chemical-potential energy. This energy means that petrol can be used as a fuel and sugar as a food, whereas water and sand cannot be used as either. The fuel and food are materials which happen to to be sources of energy, but they are not the energy itself.

Nuclear energy, sometimes incorrectly called 'atomic' energy, is different from the other energy sources considered in this chapter. In all the examples discussed so far, energy is transferred to a system by work or some other kind of change, and sooner or later is transferred from it again as further changes take place. In the changes which result in the transfer of nuclear energy, instead of one form of energy being transferred as another form, a very small amount of matter is transformed into a very large amount of energy, so that after the changes, the mass of material involved has been very slightly reduced. There are three main ways in which nuclear energy affects the lives of children: radioactive decay, and two kinds of nuclear reaction: fission and fusion.

In the late nineteenth century it was found that some naturally occurring minerals emit radiation which, among other effects, will change photographic plates as light does, but in complete darkness. The properties of these materials led to their being called radioactive. All radioactive materials are changing by a process known as radioactive decay, which under natural conditions within the Earth results in the slow transfer of nuclear energy as thermal energy. This is the process which is thought to cause the heating of the Earth beneath its crust. Children will have seen pictures of some of the results of this heating, in the form of earthquakes and volcanic eruptions.

Nuclear reactions are different from the decay of radioactive materials. They involve sudden and drastic changes in the structure of the central part or nucleus of atoms. Nuclear reactions, unlike radioactive decay, do not occur naturally on Earth. They are of two kinds. Nuclear fission involves the splitting in two of the atomic nuclei of certain radioactive materials. This occurs in a very rapid, uncontrolled and catastrophic way in atomic bomb explosions, and in a much slower and (hopefully) more controlled way in atomic power stations.

Nuclear fusion occurs when two light atomic nuclei join to form one heavier one. In both hydrogen bombs and the centre of the Sun the nuclei fused are those of hydrogen and the material produced is helium. The process needs very high temperatures so it has not yet proved possible to use it technologically as a controlled energy source. The Sun is in effect a gigantic nuclear fusion bomb, which does not explode because it is so massive: its intense gravitational field (15.2) holds it together. The Sun is the major energy source for the Earth (internal heating being the only other one) and the radiant energy transferred from it includes light, which is the only source of energy for almost all living things.

Energy transfer and conservation. Dropping an elastic ball and observing it as it bounces provides an easily understood example of an important scientific principle. As the ball bounces, each successive bounce is lower, which means that the potential and kinetic energy of the ball is reduced with each bounce and transfer of energy. When scientists and engineers were carrying out research into forms of energy in the nineteenth century, accurate measurement of energy transfers in a wide variety of changes revealed two important facts.

First, most changes are like the bouncing of the ball, in that they seem to result in energy being lost from the system. To show this, it is necessary to measure the total energy transferred to the system (input) and compare this with the useful energy transferred from the system (output). For example, if 100 J of electrical energy are transferred to the filament of a lamp, only about 20 J are emitted as light, so we say that the lamp is 20 per cent efficient. By comparing input and output, a car engine is found to be about 25 per cent efficient, whereas an electric motor is about 65 per cent efficient. There is only one kind of energy transfer which is 100 per cent efficient, and that is when the output is thermal energy, causing heating of the system, as in an electric heater.

The second important fact revealed by careful measurement was that the energy which seems to disappear from systems during change is not lost at all, but is transferred in the form of thermal energy, raising the temperature of the system and its surroundings. This applies not only to hot objects such as electric lamps and car engines, but to any moving system such as a windmill, turbine or generator, to chemical changes (rise in body temperature during exercise is an example) and to the absorption of light energy (solar cells are only about 10 per cent efficient). Only when heating is itself the intended outcome can an energy transfer be completely efficient.

These and many other observations and measurements have led to the theory known as the principle of the conservation of energy. Put very simply, this states that energy never disappears, and the total amount of energy in any system and its surroundings remains the same. The apparent loss of energy occurs because every change results in some energy being transferred from the system to its surroundings as thermal energy, causing a rise in temperature.

A car burning fuel is a familiar example of this. The burning process transfers chemical-potential energy as thermal energy to hot gases in the engine. About 75 per cent of this is transferred to the environment, directly by emission of hot exhaust gases and indirectly by way of the cooling system. Twenty-five per cent is transferred to the engine, transmission and wheels as kinetic energy. This is transferred as thermal energy to the moving parts of the car, the tyres and the road, and from them to the environment, as work is done to overcome friction and keep the car moving. At the end of the journey, the kinetic energy of the car is transferred as thermal energy to the brakes as they slow the car down, and from them to the environment.

Thermal energy is always transferred from the hotter parts of a system to the cooler ones (12.3), so it tends to spread out into the environment from a hot object. The cooling of a hot drink or a car engine, and the warming of air and water by power-stations (thermal pollution) are examples. This tendency for thermal energy to spread out means that it is usually impossible to make use of it once it has been transferred to the environment. It is possible to slow this transfer down, for example by thermal insulation (12.3), but it can never be prevented altogether.

12.3: Heating, cooling and temperature

During any change, some energy is always transferred as thermal energy (12.2), making the molecules of an object or system move more violently, and so making it hotter. Once one part of a system has been made hotter than the rest, there is always a tendency for thermal energy to be transferred from the hotter parts to the cooler ones. This is the process of heating, which can take place in three ways: conduction, convection and radiation (see below). There is much confusion over how such changes should be thought of and described. The best way to avoid this is always to use the word 'heat' as a verb, not a noun. One may quite correctly describe objects as being hot or cold, observe that they are made hotter or colder by heating and cooling, and link these properties and changes to the thermal energy of the object. What should be avoided is speaking as if objects contained heat, or as if heat were gained by or lost from a system, because this suggests that energy is a substance.

Heating and expansion. When an object is made hotter, its thermal energy is increased, making its molecules (8.1) move more violently. In a gas this means that the molecules move faster and collide with each other, and whatever the gas is contained in, more frequently. In liquids and solids, whose molecules are in contact, the molecules move or vibrate over greater distances as the material is made hotter, so that on average they are further apart. If the material is cooled, the reverse happens: the movement of the molecules is reduced and they are closer together. The result of these increases and decreases in molecular movement is that the size of an object changes with temperature. Almost all materials become bigger (expand) as their temperature rises and smaller (contract) as it falls. The only common exception is water, which expands as it freezes (6.2). Expansion and contraction are important in understanding energy transfer by convection and the use of liquid thermometers to measure temperature.

Temperature and thermometers. Temperature is a measure of how hot or cold an object is, and an indicator of its thermal energy. Three temperature scales are in common use, the most useful for primary science being the Celsius scale, sometimes incorrectly referred to as the centigrade scale. Temperature is measured in degrees with reference to fixed points, which in the Celsius scale are the freezing- and boiling-points of water. The difference between them is divided into one hundred degrees, so we say the water freezes at 0°C and boils at 100°C.

Thermometers are devices which measure temperature. Although the human skin registers sensations of hot and cold, it responds mainly to differences in temperature and so is very unreliable as a thermometer (3.10). The most commonly used thermometers in primary science are the liquid-in-glass type. These are made of a thick-walled glass tube with a very narrow bore, sealed at one end and with a thin-walled reservoir of liquid at the other. Because the reservoir is thin-walled, the liquid inside responds rapidly to changes in the temperature of its surroundings as energy is transferred by conduction (see below). Changes in temperature cause the liquid to expand or contract, so it rises or falls in the tube. Because the bore of the tube is very narrow, even a very small change in the volume of the liquid in the bulb produces a visible rise or fall in the tube, which is engraved or printed with a scale of degrees. Modern glass thermometers are filled with a non-toxic coloured liquid mixture. Mercury-in-glass thermometers should never be used in primary schools. If they are found, for example among old stock, they should be removed and handed to the local safety agency for safe disposal.

Digital thermometers work by measuring changes in an electrical circuit as it is heated or cooled and giving a readout on an LCD display. They are expensive, but those with a probe and flexible connection are particularly useful for children who cannot read scales, and where use of a glass thermometer is difficult, for example in environmental measurement. Children may also encounter strip thermometers, in which coloured digits become visible at different temperatures. These have only a limited working range but are useful for measuring temperatures in controlled environments such as rooms and tropical fish-tanks.

Heating by conduction. If the violently vibrating molecules of a hot material are in contact with those of a cooler material, thermal energy will be transferred until the temperature of the two is uniform. This is known as thermal conduction. As a result of conduction, thermal energy always tends to spread throughout a system. How rapidly this occurs depends on the temperature difference and the materials involved. Materials such as metals which transfer thermal energy very rapidly are said to be good thermal conductors, whereas materials such as wood and air, which are very poor conductors, are known as thermal insulators.

How hot or cold a material feels to the skin often has as much to do with its conductivity as with its temperature. Because a metal can transfer energy to or from another object very rapidly, hot metals feel hotter and cold metals feel colder than a material such as wood which is at the same temperature. This can be experienced by placing wooden and metal objects in a refrigerator for an hour, or hot water for a few minutes, and simply holding them. Simple comparisons of the conductivity of different materials can be made using hot water: flames or heaters should never be used. Suitable objects for comparison include large (15 cm) steel nails, wooden dowels and plastic utensils of about the same length. Stand these in a mug so that they lean outwards. Place a small blob of margarine or other fat near the end of each, at the same height and facing outwards. Pour very hot water into the mug. How quickly the fat melts shows how good a thermal conductor each material is. This information can be linked both to the use of materials as related to their properties, and to work on safety in the home, for example by examining a variety of kitchen utensils.

Heating by convection. When heating occurs by conduction, no movement of material is evident. Heating in liquids and gases, however, usually gives rise to a pattern of movement called convection. The movement is set up because materials expand as they are heated. This means that a certain volume of liquid or gas weighs less when hot than it does when cold. The result is that when a liquid or gas is heated by conduction, hotter material tends to rise through the cooler material around it. If the system is being cooled, movement is set up in the reverse direction and cooler material sinks down through warmer layers. The movements set up in this way are called convection currents.

As material moves by convection, hotter material will transfer energy, mainly as a result of mixing, with the cooler material around it. Convection currents circulate on a very large scale in both the atmosphere and oceans, redistributing much of the energy reaching the Earth from the Sun, and playing a major part in the generation of the changes we call weather and climate (11.3–11.6).

On a small scale, both storage heaters and central heating systems which circulate hot water through 'radiators' rely on convection to transfer and distribute thermal energy in rooms. The 'radiators' in such systems would more logically be termed convectors. Convection currents in both air and water can be observed in the classroom. Rising currents in the air above heaters can be detected using paper spirals suspended from threads. Patterns of convection currents in water can be shown by filling a heat-resistant glass beaker with water, heating it gently on a hot-plate and then dropping in a few grains of dye powder.

Heating by radiation. All warm and hot objects transfer energy by radiation. They do this by emitting a form of radiant energy called infra-red radiation, which behaves like light although we cannot see it. Infra-red emitted by a hot object does not heat the air through which it passes, but is absorbed by solid objects in its path, which are heated as a result. This explains why a large fire can be felt even when one is too far away from it to be affected by the hot air rising from it. Heaters such as electric fires transfer some energy by conduction and convection, but far more by radiation, with the result that they can give an immediate sensation of warmth to someone sitting in front of them while the room itself remains cold.

Thermal insulation slows down the transfer of thermal energy from hotter parts of a system to colder ones. This can include both reducing the rate of energy loss from a hot object such as a person, an oven, a hot-water tank or a house, and reducing the rate of energy gain by a cold object such as a refrigerator or freezer. Apart from reflective foil layers (see below), most common insulation systems work by slowing down conduction and convection, which usually occur together, and rely on materials which are very poor thermal conductors.

The ideal constructional material is one which combines high durability and good strength properties (7.5, 7.7, 7.8) with poor thermal conductivity. Wood, brick and glass are the most commonly used examples (10.2). One way to improve the insulation of a building is to reduce conduction by making a basic element of construction double-layered, with air trapped in between: cavity walls and double or secondary glazing are examples. The effectiveness of this is limited, however, because air can still circulate in the cavity and so transfer energy by convection between the inner and outer layers.

Even more effective is the kind of insulation referred to by engineers as lagging. This consists of one or more layers of fibrous or foam material, itself a poor conductor, which traps a thick layer of air, prevents it moving and so reduces convection as well as conduction to a minimum. The most familiar form of lagging is warm clothing, while examples in the home include carpets and underfelt, loft insulation, jackets for hot-water tanks and insulation of pipework to prevent freezing. Oven-gloves provide an example of lagging working in the opposite way, as a protection against burning. Double-wall construction can be made much more effective by filling the cavity with fibre or foam material, because this cuts down convection as well as conduction (10.2). Houses and ovens use this method of insulation to reduce the rate at which they cool down, and refrigerators to reduce the rate at which they warm up. All kinds of domestic insulation are of great importance in view of the need to reduce consumption of fossil fuels and the demand on energy resources generally (12.4).

Slowing down energy transfer by radiation requires a different kind of insulation. The aim is to reflect the infra-red radiation and so prevent it being absorbed. This is usually achieved by using a very thin layer of metal foil. For example, a substantial proportion of the energy transfer from the human body to the environment occurs by radiation. If the infra-red is reflected back to the body it is re-absorbed, energy loss is substantially reduced and skin temperature rises. This explains the use of reflective 'space blankets' (foil-lined plastic sheets) to treat victims of hypothermia, shock or accidental injury. The foil facing on insulating materials used in the form of thick sheets in walls and roofs of modern buildings increases their efficiency in a similar way (10.2).

The most efficient thermal insulation children are likely to encounter is the vacuum ('Thermos' or Dewar) flask. This is a double-walled glass vessel with the inside of the cavity silvered like a mirror. After shaping, the air between the walls is sucked out by a vacuum pump. This means that there is nothing in the cavity to transfer energy by conduction or convection, and the silvering reflects outgoing or incoming infra-red. Transfer of energy is very slow, being limited to conduction through the insulated stopper and the glass walls around it. Stainless steel vacuum flasks, though robust, are less efficient because the metal walls are much better thermal conductors than glass walls are.

12.4: Energy sources and resources

The economies of industrialized nations and the lifestyles of their citizens are heavily dependent on the availability of cheap and convenient energy sources. All energy sources are limited, either in terms of their overall amount, such as fossil fuels, or in terms of availability, such as direct solar radiation. Detailed consideration of the geographical, economic and political issues arising from energy supply are beyond the scope of primary science, but concepts of energy transfer are essential in reaching an understanding of them. Discussion of this major issue is therefore limited to a summary of the main energy sources, together with some of the possibilities which may be more extensively exploited in the future.

Coal and oil. Both are fossil fuels, formed from the partly decayed remains of plants (coal) and marine animals (oil). Both are non-renewable and, even at twice the present cost of extraction, it seems unlikely that supplies of oil will last far beyond the middle of the twenty-first century, though coal may not be exhausted for another century after that.

Oil and its products such as petrol (gasoline) have a very high energy value in relation to weight and, being liquids, can be moved by pumping. Using appropriate safety measures they can easily be stored and transported (in the fuel-tank of a car, for example), and so provide a very readily exploited and versatile fuel. Other fuels produced from oil include butane gas and the liquefied petroleum gas (LPG) used as a fuel for cars. Both are compressed so that they become liquid and are stored in pressurized tanks. Coal's energy value in relation to weight is lower than that of oil, and while it is more difficult to transport it requires much higher temperatures to ignite it and so is much safer in transit and storage. Both coal and oil can generate high temperatures when burnt in furnaces, which means that they can be used both directly for industrial heating and for the generation of electric current by way of steam turbines.

Apart from being non-renewable, both coal and oil have significant disadvantages, particularly in terms of pollution (5.9). As well as smoke, burning them releases extra carbon dioxide gas into the atmosphere, which may contribute to global warming. Both contain sulphur compounds, which when burnt produce sulphur dioxide, a serious atmospheric pollutant and the main cause of acid rain.

Natural gas is usually associated with oil and has the same origin. Because it can be pumped easily, extraction and transport costs are at present low in relation to its energy value, though its safe storage requires expensive installations. It can be used in a very wide range of industrial processes as well as for domestic heating. It shares the disadvantages of coal and oil, except that it can be made largely sulphur free and so is a much 'cleaner' fuel, contributing little if at all to acid rain pollution.

Nuclear energy. As recently as 1980 it seemed likely that nuclear energy would be the major energy source for industrialized nations by the mid-twenty-first century. Four factors now make this unlikely. First is the very high and steeply rising cost of nuclear power stations, their relatively short working lives and the high cost and difficulty of decommissioning them after use. Second is the technical difficulty and escalating cost of disposing safely of large quantities of radioactive waste. Third is the impossibility of guaranteeing the safety of nuclear power stations and the extremely serious and widespread consequences of major accidents. Fourth is the failure to develop controlled nuclear fusion, the process by which matter is transformed into energy in the Sun and hydrogen bombs and the need to rely on fission, which produces materials such as plutonium which can be used in nuclear weapons. The likely failure of nuclear energy to provide a safe, clean and affordable source of energy means that increasing attention is, belatedly, being paid to the development of so-called 'alternative' and renewable resources.

Kinetic and gravitational-potential energy. It is perfectly possible to transfer some of the kinetic energy from moving wind and water to devices such as electric generators. As very large-scale energy sources, all kinetic energy projects share two major disadvantages. The first is that in order to match the energy values of fossil fuels, very large amounts of moving material and so very large installations are required, so both the cost of setting-up and the environmental impact are likely to be correspondingly high. Secondly, and more seriously, in only one of the four available methods can the rate of energy transfer be both fully controlled and continuous: the others can operate only discontinuously or intermittently. This is a serious disadvantage, because large-scale storage of energy using existing technology is extremely expensive and new alternatives have yet to be fully developed. The four methods of kinetic energy transfer are: hydro-electric generators, tidal barriers, windmills and wave-driven generators.

Hydro-electric generation is by far the best-established of the four. Once installed, running costs are low and the process is pollution-free, though changing water-flow may affect wildlife and farming downstream. It has the great advantage that water-flow and electricity generation can be fully controlled and continuous. The main disadvantages are that the cost of installation is very high and use is in the main limited to mountainous areas with high, reliable rainfall. Environmental damage is high and, in the tropics especially, the long-term effects on ecosystems have proved to be severe and unpredictable.

Tidal barriers work rather like very large hydro-electric installations, by allowing water to flow in as the tide rises, then out through turbines as it falls. The disadvantages, however, are formidable. Their use is limited to estuaries or inlets with abnormally high rise and fall of tides. Very large-scale installations are needed: for example, a barrier across the mouth of the River Severn is under investigation. These are likely to have severe and unpredictable consequences for navigation (silting-up), fishery, wildlife, leisure use and pollution. Operation is possible only during fixed, though predictable, periods, and for about eight out of every twenty-four hours.

Wave-driven generators are undoubtedly possible and prototype installations are under test. They would be pollution-free and have no predictable environmental impact. Their use would be limited to areas of sea which have more or less continuous wave movement and are away from shipping lanes. Very large and costly installations would be required and these would probably need a high level of maintenance and renewal.

Wind-driven electric generators are becoming more familiar, both on land and off-shore. They have the great advantage that they can be used singly or in groups, are non-polluting apart from noise and for appropriately exposed and windy sites are a possibility for private enterprise. In relation to energy transferred and electric current generated their installation is expensive, and there are many complaints that they are unsightly and noisy, though it may be worth remembering that very similar complaints were made about windmills in the seventeenth and eighteenth centuries when they too were the new technology. The main disadvantage of wind-driven generators, however, is that possible sites are limited and even in those, their activity is intermittent and unpredictable. Again the problem of energy storage is a major limitation.

Radiant energy (including light). The use of radiant energy from the Sun, transferred as electrical energy by solar (photo-electric) panels, is familiar through the
use of solar-powered calculators and watches and, more remotely, as the energy
source for satellites and space-stations. Transferring radiant energy as thermal
energy is technologically much simpler, and children may be familiar with the solar
heating panels used in houses to contribute to space- and water-heating. Radiant
energy is clean, possible, practical and unlimited in amount. There are two major
limitations to its use on a very large scale. The first is that photo-electric panels are
at present only about 10 per cent efficient, so to transfer energy on a large scale a
very large ground array is needed. The second limitation is that the world's largest
energy users, the industrialized nations, are mostly in climatic zones where intense
sunlight is seasonal, unreliable and unpredictable. Again the central problem is not
so much the availability and transfer of energy, but rather its storage and transport.

The second form of radiant energy use is by way of photosynthesis (4.4), which
is entirely non-polluting and transfers energy in potentially its most easily used
form, as chemical-potential energy. Many investigations are under way to find efficient ways of using plant products such as wood and straw as fuels, and of converting them into sugars which can be fermented by yeast to yield alcohol, a
perfectly practical and very 'clean' fuel, or to decompose them to yield methane
(natural gas). Oil from oil-seed rape is being converted to a diesel oil substitute.
Some of these schemes are operating as pilot studies, but none on a large scale yet.

Thermal energy of the Earth. This is an essentially limitless heating resource,
already exploited in some parts of the world such as Iceland and New Zealand, for
domestic and industrial heating. Its use is at present limited to land-based zones of
crustal fracture, where hot rocks are close to the Earth's surface. Technologically it
could be used on a larger scale to deliver superheated steam and drive electric generators, but again the limitation is its very localized availability and the fact that
energy is very expensive to store and transport.

Chemical-potential energy. The main source of chemical-potential energy to sup-
plement conventional sources is waste. Solid waste can be used directly as a fuel in
specially designed furnaces; liquid waste (sewage) can be subjected to controlled
decay to yield methane gas. Both methods are extensively used on a local scale to
reduce energy costs to communities, and the limitations to their wider use are usually political and social rather than technological. It seems unlikely, however, that
such methods could do more than provide a minor, though useful, source of energy
in the future.

Long-distance transfer of energy resources. In all the 'alternative' and renewable
energy resources discussed, large-scale operation is limited, either by cost of installation and environmental impact, by availability in terms of amount, locality and
time, or by both. The problem is not so much that energy is not available; rather

that it is very difficult to transfer it as potential energy to a system which can then be transported over large distances, as for example we transport oil today. Direct large-scale storage of electrical energy remains a dream, but there are possibilities for transferring it as chemical-potential energy. One of the most promising of these is the generation of hydrogen gas, which can be burnt as a fuel whose only waste product is water vapour. It can be generated in limitless quantities by passing an electric current through water, the other product being oxygen. The major limitation on the use of hydrogen is its storage and transport. This can be achieved in high-pressure tanks but is very costly and dangerous, so research is being carried out into safer alternatives.

It seems unlikely that there will be any single overall solution to the problems of energy supply in the next century. Eventually the answers will probably come, if they come at all, through a much more economical use of existing resources coupled with a diversity of alternatives adapted to local needs, opportunities and problems. There can, however, be little doubt that supply and use of energy will be one of the major issues facing today's primary school children and their children, which is why the concepts involved have been discussed here in some detail.

13

Electricity

When working with electricity in the primary school, the emphasis is usually on building simple circuits, finding out what their properties are and learning about the safe use of mains electricity. There is a wide range of interesting and useful activities which can enable children to build up knowledge and skill in this area, but reaching an equal level of understanding may be more difficult. This is because the basic concepts needed to understand current electricity (electron, charge, electrical forces and charge separation, for example) cannot easily be related to the children's own experience, and the concepts which they and teachers can use to explain and predict how circuits behave (current, voltage, resistance) are not basic. In this situation, achieving a degree of understanding becomes much easier and confusion less likely if, alongside first-hand investigation, a clear mental picture or model of electric current can be developed (13.3, 13.4).

13.1: Simple circuits

First-hand work on electricity is likely to begin with the construction of very simple circuits. Fig. 13.1 shows a simple electrical circuit, represented by a drawing (a) and a diagram (b). When communicating about circuits it is useful to be able to show their layout in the form of diagrams. These do not show details, such as the actual shape of the circuit, the lengths of the wires or whether crocodile clips have been used, but they do show the positions of the essential components in relation to one another. Electrical engineers have developed a wide range of symbols for use in circuit diagrams, but only a few are needed in primary science. These are shown in Fig. 13.2.

Fig. 13.1 shows a circuit with the switch open. When the switch is closed (Fig. 13.3a), the circuit is 'switched on' and the lamp gives out light. This obvious change means that energy is being transferred to the environment (12.2) and children will probably identify the battery as the source of energy. It appears that something reaches the lamp from the battery which leads to energy transfer (13.4), but can reach it only when the switch is closed. If either wire is detached from the battery

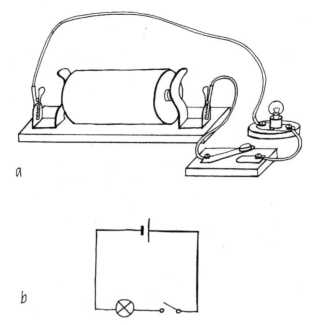

Figure 13.1 A simple circuit represented by a drawing and a diagram

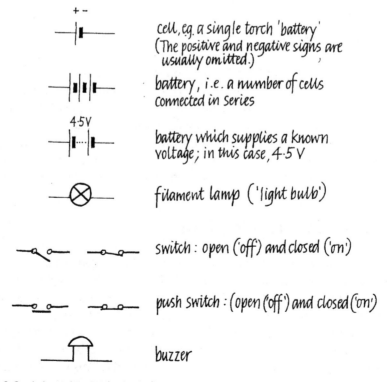

Figure 13.2 Symbols used in simple circuit diagrams

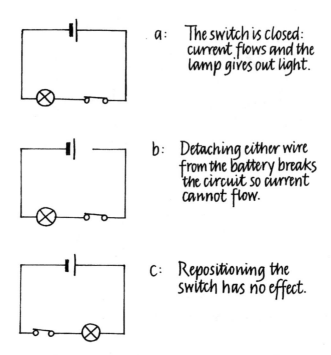

a: The switch is closed: current flows and the lamp gives out light.

b: Detaching either wire from the battery breaks the circuit so current cannot flow.

c: Repositioning the switch has no effect.

Figure 13.3 *Changing a simple circuit*

(Fig. 13.3b) the lamp goes out, and repositioning the switch (Fig. 13.3c) makes no difference to the way it works. A great variety of similar and related experiments can be used to develop the idea that a complete pathway is needed from the battery, through wires, (closed) switches and devices such as lamps, motors or buzzers, before anything will 'work', i.e. before energy transfer can take place. This complete pathway is an electrical circuit, and once the concept of the circuit as a complete pathway has been established, other concepts can more easily be developed.

13.2: Conductors and insulators

Materials which can form part of an electrical circuit are called electrical conductors. A wide variety of materials can be tested to find out whether they are conductors or not, using a simple circuit with a gap in it instead of a switch (Fig. 13.4). Bridging the gap with various materials and observing whether or not the lamp glows allows a simple classification to be made. Children will find that all the metals they test are conductors, and that nearly all non-metals are not. One exception which they can usefully use is graphite, in the form of thick pencil 'leads'. This will act as a conductor, but it is not a very good one and it may be observed that the lamp is dim. This is a useful observation when developing the concept of electrical resistance (13.6).

Materials such as wood, plastic, rubber and paper, which cannot form part of an electrical circuit, are called electrical insulators. Some insulators, especially plastics, are very important technologically because they allow mains electricity to be used safely (13.13). An incomplete circuit with an open switch or a gap in it will not 'work' because air is an insulator.

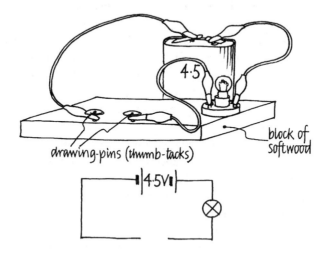

Figure 13.4 *Testing electrical conductivity*

13.3: Electric current

In a complete circuit it is the flow of electric current, brought about by the battery, which transfers energy to devices such as lamps, motors and buzzers, causing them to emit light, move or make a noise. The use of terms such as 'energy', 'electricity' or 'electric power' to refer to electric current should be avoided. To understand something of what electric current is and to begin building up a useful mental model of how it behaves, it is necessary to know a little about atomic structure. All matter is thought to be made up of very small particles called atoms (8.1), each of which consists of a central nucleus surrounded by a cloud of very rapidly moving, even smaller particles called electrons. In electrical conductors such as copper, about 4 per cent of the electrons are free to move from atom to atom. Normally they do not do this, but if they are acted on by forces (electrical forces) they can be made to move. It is the flow of these so-called 'free' electrons, acted on by electrical forces within a conductor, which is electric current.

Developing this basic concept into a mental model of current flowing in a circuit can be difficult, and like most difficult ideas it cannot be built up all at once, but develops as one makes sense of experience and begins to see how observations relate to each other. There have been many attempts to make easily understood models of electric current by using analogies, such as suggesting that it is like water being pumped around in pipes. The problem with such models is that while each makes it easier to understand part of the behaviour of current and circuits, they all tend to produce confusion somewhere else, so on balance it is probably best to avoid them.

Investigating three properties of electric current. Once the basic properties of electrical circuits are understood (13.1, 13.2), older and more able children can learn more about electric current by investigating three of its properties. Although these investigations are simple in themselves, a certain amount of logic is needed to understand their significance. Once children understand the meaning of what they observe, this can help to overcome some common misconceptions about electric current, for example that it flows in part of a circuit only, or in different directions in the same simple circuit.

The first property to investigate is that current flows in all parts of the circuit. This can be shown simply by moving the lamp in a simple circuit (Fig.13.1) to the five possible positions in relation to the battery and switch. The lamp lights up in the same way regardless of where it is, so current must flow in all parts of the circuit.

The second property is that current has direction. This can be shown using a buzzer or electric motor instead of a lamp, and a different battery may be needed as well. Most buzzers sound only when connected correctly. If the connections are reversed, no current flows and there is no sound. If a buzzer is placed in different positions in a simple circuit (Fig.13.1) and correctly connected it will sound every time, showing that current flows in the same direction throughout. This can also be shown using small electric motors. These will rotate whichever way they are connected, but if the connections are reversed, so is the direction of rotation (clockwise or anti-clockwise).

The third property of current is that it can be varied in amount. Electric current flowing in a conductor such as a wire is invisible. Electrons are so small that they can move slowly through the solid structure of the conductor without changing its appearance at all, unless they make it very hot (13.7). The greater the rate and speed of electron flow, the greater the current; the greater the current, the greater the rate at which energy can be transferred to devices such as lamps, motors and heating elements. The heating of a lamp filament when current passes through it is a particularly important example. As current in the circuit is increased, the filament begins to glow and becomes hotter and brighter, changing colour from black (no light given out), through red to yellow and finally to white. These changes in brightness and colour are very important for investigating electricity in primary science because they mean that the lamp can be used as a simple current measuring device. If a lamp is moved to different positions in a simple circuit, its brightness will not change. This shows not only that current flows in all parts of the circuit, but also that the amount of current is the same throughout. Lamps used as simple current measuring devices also make it possible to compare the behaviour of different circuits (13.9, 13.10).

How much current flows in a circuit is the result of two other factors: the forces making electrons move (measured as voltage, 13.5), and opposition to their movement around the circuit (resistance, 13.6). Before discussing how voltage and resistance affect current, however, it is necessary to develop the concept of electric current further by learning something of how batteries work.

13.4: Batteries and electric current

The batteries used to generate current in experiments with electricity in the primary classroom are small sealed tanks of chemicals. When these react together, they produce a concentration of electrons in one part of the battery (the metal base of the case) and a deficiency of electrons at another (the metal stud in the middle of the other end). If electrons come close together, a very strong force makes them repel each other and move apart. When a battery is connected to a circuit, the concentration of electrons in the case (the negative terminal) repels the 'free' electrons in the conductors of the circuit, pushing them away from the battery. This electrical force acts all round the circuit almost instantly, so as soon as the circuit is completed (switched on), current is moving in all parts of it (13.3). The flow of electrons is from the negative terminal to the positive, so the same number of electrons flows into the battery at the positive terminal (which has a deficiency of electrons), as is forced out from the negative terminal.

The chemical reactions which enable the battery to make electrons move continue only as long as the circuit is complete. As soon as it is disconnected or switched off and current ceases to flow, the chemical changes stop. Once the chemical changes in the battery are complete it can no longer generate current and must be replaced. The generation of current is a useful example of energy transfer (12.1). Chemical-potential energy in the battery is transferred to the circuit by way of chemical changes and the movement of electrons. It should be emphasized that the battery does not generate energy: it generates electric current and in so doing causes energy to be transferred. Rechargeable batteries, in which the chemical reactions are reversible, should not be used in primary schools because they can become very hot if short-circuited (13.11).

It may be helpful at this point to address two common misconceptions about electric current. The first point to make is that current does not 'get into the circuit' from the battery. Electrons which can be made to move are already in all the conductors of the circuit. What the battery does is to generate a force which makes them move, setting up a flow of current. When they are moving in the circuit, the electrons can transfer energy (12.1) as they pass through devices such as lamps and motors, producing changes such as light, heating and movement. The second point to make is that electrons do not move round a circuit very fast. The electrical force making them move is propagated round the circuit with almost the speed of light, but the electrons themselves move through the solid structure of the conducting materials only slowly: a few millimetres each second at most. A similar effect can be seen by lining glass marbles up along a metre rule, almost touching one another, then giving the end one a sharp push. Each marble moves hardly at all, but the one at the other end will move out almost immediately, showing that the force has been transmitted very quickly.

A final point about batteries is that the single 'battery' is properly called a dry cell. A battery is made by joining two or more cells together, usually so that they can produce a higher voltage or current (13.5).

13.5: Voltage

In order to concentrate electrons at its negative terminal (the case), a battery has to exert an electrical force on them. Because electrons repel each other, this force in turn acts on the 'free' electrons in the conductors of the circuit, making them move and so generating current. The bigger the force, the faster the electrons move through the conductors (though they always move quite slowly) and the bigger the current. The property of the battery which determines the size of the 'push' is electromotive force (emf) but because this is measured in units called volts (symbol: V), it is easier to use the commoner term voltage. Voltage is an important concept because it is one of the factors affecting current in a circuit which children can control.

The 'push' which a battery can give to current, that is, the voltage it supplies, is shown on it in volts (V). A standard dry cell generates current at about 1.5 V. If more than one cell is joined correctly (in series, 13.9), with the negative terminal of one connected to the positive terminal of the next, the electric forces they produce reinforce each other and the voltages across the terminals simply add together, so that a battery of three 1.5 V cells produces a total of 4.5 V, and one of six cells, 9 V. Special symbols are used in circuit diagrams to show that batteries of this kind are being used (Fig. 13.2).

If two cells are connected the wrong way round, with negative or positive terminals joined (Fig. 13.5), the electrical forces they produce will be in opposition and cancel each other out, so no current will flow in the circuit.

13.6: Resistance

Conductors vary a great deal in how easy or difficult it is to make current flow through them. In a good conductor such as copper wire, current flows very easily, so the conductor is said to have low electrical resistance. In a poor conductor such as graphite, current will still flow but much less readily, so graphite has much higher resistance than a copper wire of the same thickness. Insulators, which will not let current flow at all, can be thought of as having very high resistance indeed. Resistance is an important concept because it is a major factor affecting current flow in circuits which children can control (13.12).

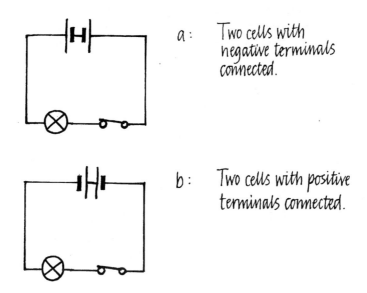

a: Two cells with negative terminals connected.

b: Two cells with positive terminals connected.

Figure 13.5 *Connecting cells incorrectly: In both cases the electrical forces exerted by the two cells are in opposition, so no current flows*

The resistance of a conductor does not depend only on the material of which it is made: it is also affected by shape and size. A long, thin wire will have higher resistance than a short, thick one of the same material. This is important when developing ideas about the heating effect of current (13.7) and fuses (13.13).

13.7: The heating effect of electric current

When electrons are made to move through a conductor as electric current, they do not move entirely freely. Their movement is impeded by the solid structure of the material through which they are moving. The movement of the electrons causes vibration in the structure of the conductor, so transferring energy to it and heating it. If the conductor has low resistance (good conducting material, thick wire or strip) it does not impede the current much, so there is little heating and the rise in temperature may be undetectable. This is likely to be the case for connecting wires in the circuits which children investigate. If, on the other hand, resistance is high (poor conducting material, thin wire), the current is impeded much more, energy is transferred rapidly and the temperature of the conductor rises. Examples with which children will be familiar are the filaments of lamps and the heating elements of electric fires and toasters.

For any particular conductor, the rate of heating and therefore the rise in temperature depends on the current and resistance: the larger the current and/or the higher the resistance, the hotter the conductor becomes. It is this relationship which makes it possible to use the brightness of lamps as a simple measure of current, as long as the lamps used for comparison are of similar type (13.3). If the current is large enough, even a copper wire can become hot enough to start a fire (13.13).

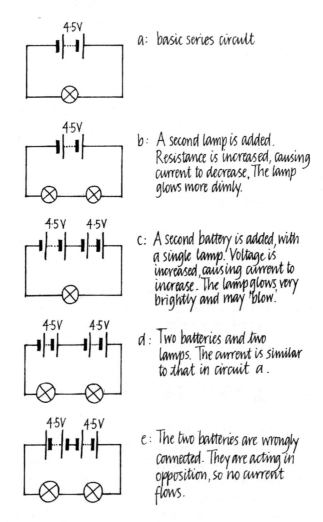

a: basic series circuit

b: A second lamp is added. Resistance is increased, causing current to decrease. The lamp glows more dimly.

c: A second battery is added, with a single lamp. Voltage is increased, causing current to increase. The lamp glows very brightly and may 'blow'.

d: Two batteries and two lamps. The current is similar to that in circuit a.

e: The two batteries are wrongly connected. They are acting in opposition, so no current flows.

Figure 13.6 *Simple series circuits*

13.8: The relationship between voltage, resistance and current

At primary level, most investigations of circuits, apart from those concerned with control (13.12), are aimed at finding out about their properties by measuring current, which can be done in a simple, non-standard way by comparing how brightly lamps glow (13.3). It is important to understand that in simple circuits, the amount of current is determined by the voltage (a property of the battery) and the resistance (a property of the whole circuit), and not the other way round. To put it another way, voltage and resistance are causes and the current is the effect they produce between them.

The voltage of the battery determines the size of the 'push' the battery gives to electrons in the circuit, so if the rest of the circuit stays the same (i.e. if resistance remains constant), increasing the voltage will cause an increase of the current. Resistance is a measure of how difficult it is to make current move in the circuit, so if the voltage stays the same (i.e. the battery is not changed or run down), decreasing the resistance will increase the current and vice versa.

At least in the early stages of finding out about the properties of circuits it is very helpful if children observe the rules of fair testing (1.7). This means that for any particular design of circuit they should experiment by changing either the voltage (number or type of batteries) or the resistance (e.g. the number of lamps) but not both at once. They should also make sure that all lamps used for making comparisons are of the same type. Once some understanding of the relationship between voltage, resistance and current has been developed, it can be extended by investigating circuits in two general ways: from effect to cause (observe a change in current and seek the cause of it) and from cause to effect (change the properties of a circuit and predict what the result will be).

13.9: Unbranched (series) circuits

The simplest type of circuit which children can usefully investigate has a single pathway for current: it is an unbranched or series circuit. When investigating any kind of circuit it is a useful strategy to keep a simple series circuit set up (Fig. 13.6a), which gives a standard of brightness against which lamps in other circuits can be compared. Having established the principle that the brightness of a lamp is a rough measure of the current flowing through it (13.3), it is possible to investigate the behaviour of circuits by adding components to them and observing the results. To explain what happens, however, it is necessary to understand the relationship between voltage, resistance and current (13.8).

The filament of a lamp heats up when current flows through it because it has a fairly high resistance. This means that adding a second lamp in series with the first (Fig. 13.6b) increases the total resistance of the circuit. The voltage of the battery is unchanged, so current is reduced and the lamps glow more dimly. Because the current is reduced, the battery will 'last' (i.e. continue to generate current) for longer than if only one bulb were in the circuit. Notice, however, that adding the second lamp does not change the basic character of the circuit: it is still unbranched, so the lamps are said to be connected in series. In this, as in all series circuits, removing a component (lamp or wire) will create a gap so that current ceases to flow throughout the whole circuit.

If two cells or batteries are connected in series, the total voltage is equal to their separate voltage values added together. Adding a second battery to a circuit with a single lamp (Fig. 13.6c) means that the voltage and so the current will be greater than in the simple circuit (Fig. 13.6a). The single lamp will glow very brightly and will probably overheat, so that the filament and therefore also the circuit are broken. If a second lamp is added to the circuit, however (Fig. 13.6d), the resistance is increased, so the current is reduced to about the same level as that in the simple circuit (Fig. 13.6a) and the lamp will be as bright. It is also useful to show the effect of reversing one battery, giving the arrangement shown in Fig. 13.6e. Because the electrical forces generated by the two batteries are in opposition, they cancel each other out and no current flows in the circuit.

Once it is understood that the relative brightness of the lamp(s) can be used to compare current (13.3), the different circuits can be used to investigate and establish a simple, logical, cause-and-effect relationship between the number and type of batteries and bulbs on the one hand and current on the other. Once this has been established it is possible for pupils, either then or later, to develop the concepts of voltage and resistance, together with an understanding of their relationship to current.

13.10: Branched (parallel) circuits

The second basic type of circuit which children need to investigate includes more than one pathway for electric current. This is achieved by making the circuit branch. A simple branched circuit is shown in Fig. 13.7a. As the diagram shows, there are two possible conducting pathways, and if the circuit is built it is found that current flows in both. This is called a parallel circuit and the lamps are said to be connected in parallel. What may be unexpected is that each lamp glows as brightly, and therefore has the same current flowing through it, as the single lamp in the simple circuit (Fig. 13.6a). This should be contrasted with the behaviour of two lamps connected in series (Fig. 13.6b).

The behaviour of the parallel circuit can be explained by remembering the relationship between voltage, resistance and current (13.8). The brightness of the lamps shows that each branch of the parallel circuit has the same current flowing through it as flows in the simple circuit, so the current at points A and B in Fig. 13.7a must be twice that in the simple circuit. Since the voltage has not changed, the increase in current must have been caused by reducing the resistance of the circuit. This can be explained by remembering that resistance is a measure of how difficult it is for current to flow in a circuit and that, if two pathways are provided rather than one, current can flow more easily.

If children find it difficult to understand how a circuit with two lamps can have a lower resistance than a circuit with one, an analogy with one-way traffic in a city may be useful. Fig. 13.8 shows a model of current flow. In the model, the two-lane roads represent the unbranched, low-resistance wires in the circuit and the single-lane roads, the lamps with higher resistance. In slow, nose-to-tail traffic, will more vehicles be able to pass points A and B if both single-lane roads are open, or if only one is open? Obviously, if both are open; but opening or closing the road at point C will not affect the amount of traffic which can pass point D. If in an electrical circuit there are two lamps through which current can flow, the resistance of the whole circuit is lowered and the battery can make more current flow through it. This does mean, however, that the chemical changes in the battery will take place faster, so it will have only about half its normal active life. When working with parallel circuits it is important always to use fresh batteries, since those near the end of their active lives cannot generate a large enough current to make both lamps glow brightly, even if resistance is low.

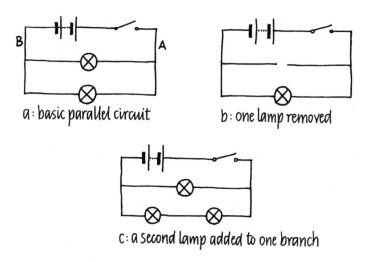

a: basic parallel circuit   b: one lamp removed

c: a second lamp added to one branch

Figure 13.7 *Simple parallel circuits*

Another property of parallel circuits, which children can investigate, is that their branches behave as if they were independent circuits, so changing one branch has no effect on the others (unless one branch is a short circuit, 13.11). One obvious example of this is provided by removing the lamp from one branch of a parallel circuit (Fig. 13.7b) and observing what happens in the other. There is no change: the lamp continues to glow and its unchanged brightness shows that the current through it is the same as before, because the active part of the circuit is now behaving just as a simple series circuit does. The same principle is shown when a slightly more complex circuit is built (Fig. 13.7c). The single lamp continues to glow as brightly as before, but the two in the other branch behave exactly as we would expect of two lamps in series (see Fig. 13.6b): both glow, but more dimly. It is also noticeable that removing a lamp from one branch has no effect on the lamp(s) in the other. If removing a lamp from a parallel circuit does affect the brightness of those in other branches, the probable cause is that the batteries being used are nearly exhausted.

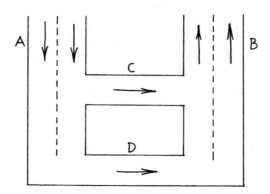

In a crowded one-way traffic system, more traffic can circulate
past points A & B if both single-lane roads C & D are open.
C & D are like lamps in a circuit, which limit current.
Two lamps in parallel allow more current to flow (as at
A & B in Fig 13.7a) than one.

Figure 13.8 *Modelling current in a parallel circuit*

13.11: Short circuits

If the terminals of a dry cell or battery are directly connected by a low-resistance conductor such as a length of copper wire, the resistance of the circuit is very low, so a
large current can flow in it. This situation is called a short circuit and should normally
be avoided for a number of reasons. First, the short circuit allows the battery to generate a large current so that it will rapidly be discharged and rendered useless. Secondly, the conductor itself will be heated by the large current and may become hot
enough to burn the skin. The effect of a short circuit can be shown by building a simple circuit (Fig. 13.6a) and connecting the terminals of the battery with a length of
copper wire for a moment (not more than a second). This makes what is in effect a
parallel circuit, but because the resistance of the wire is so low, nearly all the current
flows through it rather than through the lamp, which goes out.

Children need to be aware of short circuits because they are not merely wasteful and
frustrating: they are frequently dangerous and should always be avoided. Some batteries discharge very quickly and generate large currents when short-circuited, because
the chemical changes which generate current in them can be very rapid. If this happens, both the battery and the conductor short-circuiting it are likely to become very
hot, with a danger of severe burning. This is one reason why 'rechargeable batteries'
(nicad cells) and car batteries should never be used in primary schools. Many of the
dangers of using mains electricity are associated, in one way or another, with short
circuits, and most of the measures needed to use electric appliances safely are aimed
at preventing them or limiting damage if they do occur (13.13).

13.12: Controlling circuits

Circuits are controlled by regulating the flow of current in them. There are two main ways of doing this: first, by using some kind of switch to allow or prevent the flow of current; secondly, by changing the resistance of the circuit and so increasing or decreasing the current.

Simple switches. A simple switch is a gap in the circuit which can be closed by a conductor. Switches work because air is an insulator and will not allow current to pass across the gap. Commercially made switches are useful, but to understand the principle of switching children need to make their own from materials such as paper fasteners, paper-clips and drawing-pins mounted on card. In a series circuit the position of the switch is immaterial (Fig. 13.3a, c): it switches the whole circuit on or off wherever it is. In parallel circuits, however, switches can be positioned to operate the whole array or any part of it. This is the basis of control in circuits such as traffic-lights and motor car lights.

Pupils who are designing circuits may also find it useful to experiment with more complex switches. Two- or three-way switches, for example, can be made by using a swinging arm (such as a paper-clip) between two or three contacts, so that as one circuit is switched on, another is switched off. Designing switches to operate circuits in particular ways provides a useful link between science and technology.

Variable resistors. Switches give all-or-nothing control of current in a circuit: either the current is flowing or it is not. A different kind of control can be exercised by changing the resistance of the circuit. This makes it possible to vary the current gradually and continuously. The principle of variable resistors can be shown by bridging a gap in a simple circuit (Fig. 13.4) with varying lengths of fairly high-resistance conductors, such as graphite (pencil 'leads'), or nichrome wire, and observing the effect on the brightness of the lamp. The greater the length of material inserted, the greater the resistance, the lower the current and the dimmer the lamp.

Commercial variable resistors work by rotating a contact on a coil of wire or a strip of material containing carbon. By moving the contact, a variable length of the high-resistance conductor is included in the circuit, controlling the current. Devices such as volume controls on audio equipment use variable resistors in this way.

13.13: Mains electricity and safety

All the work on electricity discussed so far has used batteries and low voltage current. Apart from short circuits (13.11) and the possibility of heating a very thin wire, these are perfectly safe: there is no danger of fire or electric shock. In their homes and at school, however, pupils regularly use electric appliances whose energy source is mains electricity. They do not need to understand the difference between battery current (DC) and mains current (AC), but they do need to know and understand enough about mains electricity to use it safely. This means knowing the main causes of danger, the basic safety measures built into circuits and appliances, and some simple rules for using them safely.

The first thing to emphasize about mains electricity, without being alarmist, is that potentially it is lethal. When properly used with well-designed and maintained appliances it is safe, but when safety measures fail it can and does kill people, directly through electric shock, and indirectly through causing fires. One reason why mains electricity can be dangerous is that the voltage is much higher than that generated by batteries. In Britain, mains voltage is 240 V, which means that even quite a small current can transfer a large amount of energy very quickly. This helps to make electricity supply efficient: the faster the current can transfer energy, the smaller the current needed to meet a particular demand and the less the circuit heats up. (In grid supply this principle is carried much further: main 'power lines' on pylons carry current at up to 40,000 V.) The two main dangers of mains electricity, of which children need to be aware, are electric shock and fire.

Electric shock. Because the human body contains a large amount of water in which chemicals such as salt are dissolved, it can act as an electrical conductor, particularly if the skin is wet. If an electric current passes through the body it will bring about changes which, depending on the size of the current and how it moves through the body, may range from a slight tingling sensation to uncontrollable jerking and spasm of muscles, severe pain, burning, heart failure and death. Apart from burning, electric current has this effect because it disrupts the normal control of the body by the brain, spinal cord and nerves.

Electric shock can occur only if there is a conducting pathway through the body, usually to the earth. There are two common causes of this: touching bare wires or faulty appliances with a metal object or bare hands, especially if they are wet, and using appliances in damp or wet conditions. Impure water conducts electricity sufficiently well to provide conducting pathways between a mains circuit, the body and the earth. Because of this, it is extremely dangerous to use electrical appliances in a bathroom unless, like electrically heated showers or electric razors, they have been specially designed and installed for that purpose. If a mains appliance such as a radio or TV were to fall into a bath while switched on, anyone in the water would receive a severe and probably fatal shock.

Fire caused by electricity. Electric current passing through a conductor heats it (13.7). If a mains circuit or appliance is faulty and a short circuit develops (13.11), a large current may flow, causing wiring or other metal to be heated, so that inflammable material in contact with it may ignite. The main precautions against fires caused by electricity are the regular testing and inspection of appliances and wiring, and the use of correctly rated fuses (see below).

Basic concepts of control. The purpose of mains electricity and the technologies which depend on it is the transfer of energy. When this is controlled, appliances are safe. When control fails or is rendered ineffective by wrong usage, a dangerous situation is always created. When electrical circuits and appliances are properly installed, maintained and used, accidents are very rare. The overwhelming majority of danger and accidents associated with mains electricity result either from incorrect installation or neglect, so that the circuit or appliance is faulty, or from carelessness and deliberate misuse.

There are three basic means of controlling mains electricity and so ensuring safety: insulation and earthing; the use of circuit breakers and fuses; and correct usage of circuits and appliances.

Insulation and earthing. Mains electricity has been described, perhaps a little over-dramatically, as being like a raging giant who has been imprisoned and is always trying to get out. The 'prison' is insulation. If conductors are properly insulated, current cannot reach the outside of the wiring or appliance, so they can be touched safely. If insulation is damaged there is always the danger of a short circuit leading to electric shock, or fire, or both. In modern circuits and appliances the commonest insulators are plastics where the working temperature is low, and ceramics where it is high.

The examples of insulators with which most children will be familiar are the rigid insulating covers of plugs, sockets and switches, and the flexible covers of supply leads and cables. Any signs of wear or damage to insulation should be taken seriously. If the damage is to a plug or lead this should be replaced, but if it is to a socket, switch, circuit or appliance this should not be used until it has been checked and if necessary repaired by a qualified electrician.

Some appliances which children may use include uninsulated wires. The most familiar examples are the heating elements of electric fires and toasters. When the appliance is switched on these are not only very hot, but are carrying large currents and so should never be touched. Electric fires, like all open fires and heaters, should be shielded by a complete cage, and it is very dangerous to try to dislodge burning crumbs from a toaster while it remains switched on.

If insulation fails, the whole appliance may become 'live', that is, connected to the mains circuit and capable of carrying current. Touching the casing of the appliance could then result in a short circuit through the body to earth and electric shock. There may in addition be the danger of a short circuit, heating and fire within the appliance. To help prevent this, many appliances are earthed. This means that the casing is connected to the third (long) pin on a standard mains plug. This in turn is connected, through the earth wire in the mains wiring, to the earth. Failure of the insulation in the appliance sets up a short circuit by way of the earth wire, through which a large current flows to earth, overloading the circuit breakers or fuses (see below) so that they break the circuit, cutting off the main current and preventing further damage.

Circuit breakers and fuses. These are essentially damage-limitation devices, designed to break the circuit if the flow of current becomes too high, thus cutting it off altogether. Circuit breakers are always used in modern wiring at the distribution box which is the point of origin for all the mains circuits in a building such as a house. If there is a surge in current the circuit breaker detects this, a switch is opened and that particular circuit is deactivated. This can happen if a device fails, a short circuit occurs or the circuit is overloaded. The circuit can be reactivated only by closing the switch at the distribution box.

Older wiring and individual appliances are protected by fuses. These work by overheating and breaking if too large a current flows in a circuit. If circuits and appliances are properly installed, maintained and used, mains fuses should never be activated. Simple fuses are lengths of thin wire in a cartridge made of heat-resistant and insulating ceramic material, inserted into a circuit. They are an example of using a potentially dangerous effect to help ensure safety. When current flows in a circuit, the conductors are heated (13.7). If a short circuit occurs (13.11), the current could increase, possibly to a dangerous level, if the circuit were not protected. Because the fuse wire is very thin in relation to the current it carries, it has enough resistance to heat up and melt if it is overloaded, so breaking the circuit and effectively switching it off.

There are two kinds of fuse in domestic use. The distribution box of a house is likely to include wire fuses with three ratings, corresponding to the maximum current which various circuits are designed to carry, together with the main switch for controlling the supply of current to the whole building. Current is measured in amperes (abbreviated to amps; symbol: A). Lighting circuits are rated at 5A, power circuits serving wall-sockets and heaters at 13A and those for electric cookers and shower units at 30A. Each circuit is protected by a fuse of appropriate rating.

Children are likely to be more familiar with the second type of fuse: the cartridge fuses used in standard three-pin plugs. These are the 'front-line' defence, giving protection from short circuits arising in individual appliances. Domestic power circuits are rated at 13A, which is therefore the maximum current which they should carry. Many appliances require much smaller currents than this, and fuses should be used in their plugs which match their maximum requirement. For example, a TV set needs a maximum current of less than 2A. If it developed a short circuit and had a standard 3A fuse fitted, this would quickly 'blow', breaking the circuit, but if a 13A fuse were fitted, a faulty set would probably overheat and might catch fire before the fuse melted. Plugs are usually sold fitted with 13A fuses. These should be replaced when plugs are fitted to appliances which require a smaller current. To calculate the kind of fuse required, find the power rating of the appliance in watts (W) and divide this by the mains voltage (240V). This gives the current in amps (A): use the next highest rating of fuse. For example, a microwave oven rated at 650W will have a current of 2.7A, so should be fitted with a 3A fuse.

Safe use of mains circuits and appliances. Once the basic principles are understood, using mains electricity safely becomes a matter almost of commonsense. The following is simply a list of the major points as they relate to children. More comprehensive advice and information can be obtained from electricity supply companies.

1. Never use improvised or damaged plugs; make sure that plugs are correctly wired and are fitted with fuses of the correct rating.
2. Never use appliances with damaged leads.
3. Never poke anything into a mains socket. If a socket is seldom used it should be protected by a dummy plug-cap.
4. Never try to use mains electricity to operate a home-made circuit or one designed for use with batteries.
5. Never use appliances in wet conditions or with wet hands.
6. If anything seems to be wrong with an appliance (e.g. strange noise, malfunction, smell of burning) switch off immediately and unplug it. Do not use it again until it has been checked and repaired if necessary.
7. Always switch off before changing a light-bulb; always switch off and unplug before changing an attachment to a power tool.

14

Forces and Their Effects

Like all scientific concepts, those concerned with forces and their effects are used to help us explain what has been observed and predict what might happen in the future. Scientific concepts of forces are used to help us explain and predict the movement and shape of objects, both when these change and when they remain the same. Scientists cannot say what forces are, only what they do, so in order to learn about them, their effects have to be experienced. This chapter is mainly about how forces make things move or stay still. More discussion and investigation of how forces change the shapes of things will be found in Chapter 7.

14.1: Pushes and pulls: the basic properties of forces

In order to learn about forces, their effects have to be experienced. One commonly used idea of forces is, simply, that they are pushes and pulls. Particularly with young children this is a good starting-point, because it is easy to develop a simple and intuitive concept of forces in relation to one's own body and the forces exerted by it to affect things. For example, I can push or pull a table and move it, or squash clay and change its shape.

By using our bodies to make us aware of the forces applied to objects, familiar activities in physical education and art can be used to show how forces are involved every time we move something, including ourselves, or change its shape. Such activities can also help to establish two basic and very important properties of forces. These are that forces have both direction and magnitude.

Forces act in particular directions. If an object is pushed or pulled, any changes in its movement or shape occur in the direction of the forces acting on it. Children experience this in many ways every day. Any ball game involves pushing the ball by throwing, kicking or hitting it. Especially when the ball is still to begin with, as in a shot in netball or a penalty, corner or free kick in football, it can clearly be seen and felt that the ball travels in the same direction as the force with which it is kicked or thrown, though it is also affected by gravity (14.5; Fig.14.4c).

In writing and drawing, the pen or pencil moves in the direction in which it is pushed or pulled, so what is drawn or written is a visible record of changes in direction of the forces applied to it. If plastic or elastic materials are squashed or stretched (7.6), their changes of shape also show the direction in which forces acted on them.

Forces have magnitude. Forces can vary not only in direction, but also in magnitude: they can be bigger or smaller, resulting in bigger or smaller effects. The connection between change and the magnitude of the forces bringing it about can be observed very directly by walking, running or jumping, and by throwing and kicking balls. In all these activities, the greater the force exerted by the body, the faster or further the body itself or the ball moves. Similarly, when changing the shapes of objects, for example by squashing clay, stretching an elastic band or pressing on a brush to squeeze paint out, the greater the force applied, the more the object changes shape. Experiences of this kind should lead directly to the important principle that 'the bigger the force, the bigger the change it brings about'.

Measuring forces. Still without going beyond the simple, intuitive concept of forces as pushes and pulls, it is possible not only to experience forces of different magnitudes but also to measure them. The basic unit of force is the newton (symbol: N). The formal definition of this unit is not important at primary level: what is important is to link it to experience. At the Earth's surface, gravity pulls down on a mass of 100 g with a force (weight, 15.2) of about 1 N, so that holding a range of masses ('weights') and weighed objects enables children to experience a range of forces directly: 100 g presses down with a force of about 1 N, 1 kg with a force of about 10 N and a 3.2 kg brick with a force of about 32 N, so it is possible to use both standard masses ('weights') and other objects to exert forces measured reasonably accurately.

Forces can also be measured using forcemeters, which are in effect spring-balances. By pulling on the forcemeter a spring is extended, the length of extension showing how large a force is applied. Forcemeters are very useful, but are often difficult to read. A simplified paper scale stuck onto the barrel may help this.

14.2: Pushing, pulling and pairs of forces

The apparently simple concept of pushes and pulls is the basis for thinking about forces in science and engineering, and in the early years can be a very useful starting-point. Beyond such early experiences, however, it can give rise to significant problems for the primary teacher. There are three reasons for this. The first is that very often we are investigating situations where forces are clearly acting, but nothing is obviously pushing or pulling anything else. A moving trolley being slowed down by friction is an example (14.6).

The second difficulty is that any pushing or pulling action does not involve one force, but a pair of forces acting in opposite directions. A push is a force applied towards the object being pushed; a pull is a force applied away from the object. A pushing action involves two forces acting towards each other. For example, if I push a trolley, whether it moves or not, the trolley pushes back at me with exactly the same force as I exert on it. A pulling action involves two forces acting away from each other and sometimes this can be experienced directly. When I am carrying the shopping, for example, gravity pulls down on the bag while my arm pulls up on it. The two forces are in balance so the bag neither rises nor falls (14.3; Fig. 14.7b).

The pair of forces involved in a pushing action can also be experienced directly, by way of simple body experiments using things that will not move. If I push on to a wall, the wall does not move, but I do, in the opposite direction. Similarly, if I want to jump up, I have to push down on to the floor with my legs and feet. My body moves in a direction opposite to the one I am pushing in because when I push on the floor or wall, it pushes back at me, and the object which moves is the one which is free to move, in this case my body. (See also the discussion of walking in section 14.4).

The third difficulty of working in terms of pushing and pulling actions is the problem of correctly identifying the pair or pairs of forces involved. This problem is most likely to arise when only one of the forces involved in an action can be observed and measured. For example, when the Earth pulls an object towards it with a gravitational force so that it falls, no second force seems to be involved. What actually happens is that a falling object pulls on the Earth with the same force that the Earth pulls on it, but because the Earth is so massive there is no detectable effect on it. As far as our experience goes, only the falling object moves. In a similar way, when I throw a small object I push it, but I am not usually aware that it is pushing me with an equal and opposite force, because I am much more massive than it is. In both examples, as in any change of movement, pairs of forces (pushes or pulls) are involved, but showing this in a convincing way is far from straightforward.

At primary level this problem cannot easily be solved, but it can quite legitimately be avoided by adopting an alternative approach, not to contradict the idea of pushes and pulls but to work alongside it. To do this, we need to look in more detail at how forces are related to change. The starting-point is to realize that we never normally experience a situation in which no forces are acting.

14.3: Forces in and out of balance

Because we live on Earth, everything in our world, including ourselves, is affected by gravitational force (15.1), and everything that moves encounters forces which resist its movement (friction, 14.4), generated by contact with the solid, liquid or gas around it. This means that the movement and shape of all the things we experience, whether they are changing or not, is a result of the forces acting on them.

In some ways, this makes understanding what we observe easier, because there are, basically, only two situations to consider. Either the forces acting on an object are in balance and so cancelling each other out, or they are out of balance.

Forces out of balance. The forces acting on an object are out of balance if:

- its movement changes in speed;
- its movement changes in direction;
- its movement changes in both speed and direction;
- its shape changes.

Forces in balance. The forces acting on an object are in balance if:

- there is no change in its movement, either in speed or direction. (This includes both remaining stationary and moving at a constant speed in a straight line.);
- there is no change in its shape.

It should be clearly understood that on Earth we never experience a situation in which no forces are acting. Children are likely to hear from time to time about spacecraft which, having passed the planets, continue travelling out into deep space at a constant speed. They do this because, if no forces are acting on a moving object, it simply keeps moving, in a straight line at a constant speed. On Earth, however, a no-change situation does not mean that no forces are acting on the object, but that the forces acting on it are balanced, bringing about no change in shape or movement (14.7, 14.8).

Thinking about forces in and out of balance can often be made easier by following two simple rules. First, identify clearly the object and the change (or no-change) which is the focus of interest. Secondly, remember that it makes sense to speak of forces being in or out of balance only if they are acting on the same object (Figs.14.7–14.10).

The two basic situations of forces in and out of balance can be explored in relation to movement very simply by using a symmetrical beam balance. The main forces involved are the weights of whatever objects are put into the pans, weight being the force with which an object is pulled towards the Earth by gravity (15.2). The object on which the weights act is the beam of the balance. If the weights in the pans are equal, the beam remains level and at rest: the forces acting on the beam are in balance and there is no change. The beam moves only when the force on one side is changed, either by adding weights or taking them away, showing that it is forces out of balance which cause change of movement. The beam balance is also useful because it shows that the change of movement always takes place in the direction of the larger force: it is always the heavier weight which moves down. The investigation of static friction (14.4) also shows forces in and out of balance very clearly.

The same principle applies to change of shape. This can be shown by stretching a rubber band between the hands. When the band is stretched and held, the pulls inward by the band and outward by the hands at either end are equal: the forces acting on the rubber band are in balance and nothing moves. Only when the pulling action of the hands is increased or decreased does the shape of the band change so that it becomes longer or shorter, and this can be felt directly. Changes in the forces and the response of the band can be measured using a forcemeter at one end. As the hands pull harder or relax, the change in length of the band can be experienced directly and measured at the same time. Such observations can also help to reinforce the important concept (14.1) that the bigger the force applied, the bigger the change it brings about.

In using the idea of forces in and out of balance to interpret the changes we see or bring about ourselves, there are basically four situations to consider:

- forces out of balance, object stationary;
- forces out of balance, object moving;
- forces in balance, object stationary;
- forces in balance, object moving.

These are discussed in sections 14.5–14.8. First, however, we need to understand more about the force which, with gravity, has the greatest effect on the way we live: friction.

14.4: Friction

Friction is a force which tends to oppose or impede the movement of objects and materials past each other, regardless of whether they are solids, liquids or gases. Friction has a profound effect on the lives of everyone. This is because, first, with very few exceptions, it affects all moving objects on the Earth, including those in the atmosphere; and, secondly, because a great deal of technology is directed towards reducing friction where it is a nuisance and exploiting it where it is useful.

Friction between solids: static friction. Much basic understanding of friction can be developed using an arrangement such as that shown in Fig. 14.1. 'Sliders' are similar pieces of wood or laminated chipboard, which can be loaded with weights and covered with a variety of materials such as sandpaper, polythene sheet and carpet. They can be moved by hand, or by using a string, pulley and bucket as shown, or with forcemeters pulling horizontally. Particularly when they are moved with the hands, the resistance to movement as the slider is pushed or pulled can be felt and is usually audible. Simple comparisons of friction generated by different pairs of surfaces can be made, first by feeling and then by measuring. Finally, the force needed to make the slider move in each case can be recorded.

a. General view

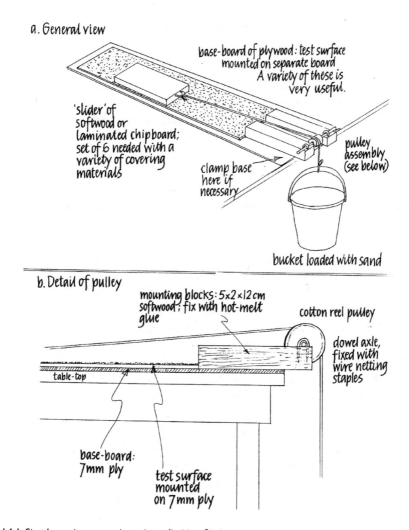

base-board of plywood: test surface mounted on separate board
A variety of these is very useful.

'slider' of softwood or laminated chipboard; set of 6 needed with a variety of covering materials

clamp base here if necessary

pulley assembly (see below)

bucket loaded with sand

b. Detail of pulley

mounting blocks: 5×2×12 cm softwood; fix with hot-melt glue

cotton reel pulley

dowel axle, fixed with wire netting staples

table-top

base-board: 7mm ply

test surface mounted on 7mm ply

Figure 14.1 *Simple equipment to investigate limiting friction*

If two surfaces are in contact and an attempt is made to start them moving by pushing or pulling, this will be resisted by friction. Because the surfaces are not moving this is called static friction. The least possible force which will start one surface moving past the other is a measure of how much resistance to movement there can be between the two. This is known as the limiting friction. When a small pulling force is applied to the string attached to a slider, static friction and pulling force are in balance (14.3), so nothing moves. The slider will not move until the pulling force is increased so that it is greater than the limiting friction. At that point, friction and pulling force are not in balance (14.3) so the slider begins to move. As the pulling force is exerted, the string becomes taut. This shows that the friction force and the pulling force are acting in opposite directions: the pull is forwards and friction acts backwards, opposing movement as friction always does. This observation is useful when trying to understand why moving things slow down and stop (14.6).

Moving sandpaper-covered surfaces over each other provides a helpful model of friction between solid surfaces. All surfaces, however smooth they appear to be, have tiny irregularities on them. These catch on each other, just as the grains on the sandpaper do, and so impede movement. If the surfaces are pressed more closely together, for example by loading a slider or trolley, the limiting friction will be increased and a larger force will be needed to make the object move. If, on the other hand, the surfaces can be held slightly apart by a film of liquid, friction will be reduced and much smaller forces will be needed to move objects. This is the basis of lubrication, which is difficult to demonstrate with sliders but whose benefits are clearly felt in machines such as bicycles (14.9).

Making use of static friction. In many situations friction is a nuisance and much technological effort, such as lubrication and special bearings, is directed towards reducing it. Without friction, however, our normal modes of movement and transport would be impossible. When walking, the sole of the foot or shoe is placed on the ground. Because it is pressed down by the weight of the body, the limiting friction between foot and ground is high, so the foot will not slip unless a large sideways force is applied to it. This can be experienced by trying to slide one foot across the floor while standing: it cannot be done until the friction between foot and floor is reduced by transferring most of the body's weight onto the other foot. This high-friction contact without sliding is the key to walking and running. When we walk, the leg is pushed backwards, and because the foot does not slide over the floor, the body is moved forward as a result. This may be difficult to understand because walking is so habitual. If so, try walking backwards: the pushing action of the leg and the friction forces between the floor and the feet will be much more apparent.

Observations on walking can usefully be linked to simple experiments on pushing, pulling and body movements (14.2). Walking is possible because (and only when) the push force exerted by the leg is less than the limiting friction between the foot and the ground. The foot does not move but becomes for a second or two a fixed point at which the push force of the leg acts on the floor. The result is like pushing against a wall or jumping: the foot pushes against the immovable floor, and the floor pushes back on the foot. The body moves away from the fixed point (the foot) in a direction opposite to its own pushing action.

A similar effect makes bicycles and cars move. Forces applied by pedalling or by the engine make the wheels rotate. The rubber tyres, pressed down by the weight of the rider or the vehicle, make a high-friction contact with the road. The limiting friction between tyre and road is greater than the force needed to move the vehicle forward, so as the wheels rotate and push backwards, the road pushes on the wheels with an equal and opposite force and the vehicle moves forward. This action of the wheel on the road is a combination of rolling friction (see below) and high-friction contact. The tyre in contact with the road at any instant is the point at which the pushing force is being exerted. This may be easier to understand with a tracked vehicle such as a toy tank or bulldozer. The part of each track in contact with the ground is stationary. As a backward pulling force is exerted on the tracks by the driving wheels, high-friction contact prevents the tracks moving, so the body of the vehicle moves forward over them.

It is significant that both walking and the movement of vehicles exploit static friction rather than being hindered by it. This is possible because in good conditions the foot and the tyre slide over the ground little if at all, but are lowered into contact with it and then lifted again. How essential high-friction contact is to both walking and road transport becomes apparent when it is lost, for example on slippery floors or wet, icy and snow-covered roads. Feet slip, wheels spin and normal forward movement becomes difficult or impossible. High-friction contact is equally important when trying to slow down, stop or change direction. If it is lost, control is usually lost with it, resulting in skidding and accidents to both pedestrians and vehicles.

Friction between a tyre and the road can be increased by pushing the body of the vehicle down, towards the road surface. This is achieved in racing cars by a wing at the rear which acts as the reverse of an aircraft wing (see below), creating downforce rather than lift as it is moved through the air. On wet roads, the patterned tread on tyres allows water to be squeezed from between the contact surface and the road. When the tyre is excessively worn, the channels of the tread are no longer deep enough to remove the water and the vehicle 'aquaplanes' – rides on a film of water which acts as a lubricant, so there is insufficient friction to prevent skidding if an attempt is made to brake or corner sharply (see section 14.6 under 'Changing direction').

Friction between solids: rolling. If spheres (marbles) or cylinders (rollers made from thick dowel) are placed between a slider and a hard surface, friction is greatly reduced, so a much smaller force is needed to make the slider move. If all the surfaces involved are hard, rolling friction is usually very much less than sliding friction, because there is very little sliding of surfaces over one another. As the curved surfaces rotate, they move towards and away from the flat ones with only a tiny area in contact at any moment. On soft surfaces such as carpet, much of the advantage of rolling friction may be lost because friction forces are generated as the rollers or marbles deform the material by compressing it. The reduction of friction by rollers, wheels, and later by ball- and roller-bearings, is of great importance both historically and in present-day technology.

Some modern toy cars have very low-friction wheel assemblies. Tests can be carried out using a standard push force from a catapult (Fig. 14.3) to see whose toy car is best (least friction, travels furthest), or with one toy car to compare the friction generated when it runs over a variety of surfaces.

Solid–liquid friction: streamlining. When a solid object moves through a liquid or gas it experiences friction forces which tend to slow it down. This resistance occurs not only because there is friction as the liquid or gas moves over the solid surface, but also because the solid body pushes fluid aside. The overall resistance of this kind is known as drag. The less the solid disturbs the liquid or gas through which it passes, and the smoother the flow over its surface, the less the drag will be.

Friction between solid and liquid can be investigated using an arrangement such as that shown in Fig. 14.2. Model boats of the same area and thickness but of different shapes can be pulled along, and the drag on each compared by measuring the force needed to keep it moving. This can lead to simple ideas of streamlining. If very fine sawdust is sprinkled onto the water surface, the pattern of movement caused by the different models can be seen and linked to the shape of each and the drag which it experiences. The more swirls and eddies the moving solid creates, the greater the drag will be.

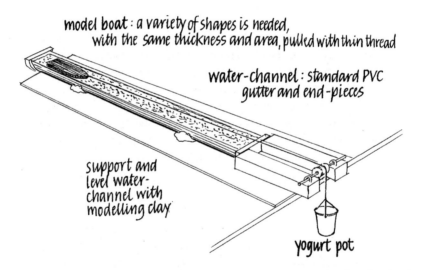

Figure 14.2 *Simple equipment to investigate friction between solids and water: baseboard and pulley are similar to those shown in Fig. 14.1; load yoghurt pot with 10 g, 5 g and 1 g weights*

Solid–air friction: parachutes. When an object is falling through air, it experiences friction forces which give rise to drag, just as a solid moving through liquid does. This opposes the gravitational force of the Earth and so tends to slow the rate of fall. If the drag can be increased the rate of fall will be reduced, and so will the impact when the object finally reaches the ground. One way to achieve this is by using a parachute (see Fig. 14.10).

The behaviour of parachutes as they fall is very complex. The main variables, load and size of canopy, are obvious; but there is a third important factor, stability, of which teachers need to be aware when making, modifying and improving model parachutes. If a simple canopy is made by attaching strings to the corners of a square of fabric or plastic sheet, it will slow the fall of an object attached to it, but as it falls the load will probably swing wildly: the parachute is unstable. In real life this would probably result in injury or damage to the person or object being dropped, so it needs to be corrected. A simple parachute is usually unstable because air trapped in the canopy cannot escape easily and the canopy tilts to release it, making the load swing like a pendulum. This is particularly noticeable in parachutes made with plastic sheet, which allows no air to flow through it. The problem can usually be cured by making one or more small holes in the centre of the canopy, or by using a fabric which allows a slow flow of air through it. Once this is understood, experimenting with parachutes offers almost limitless possibilities and variations.

Parachutes are particularly useful when working on forces because they show clearly that when forces are out of balance, it is the difference between them which determines how fast change occurs. The drag created by the parachute acts against the pull of gravity. The higher the drag, the smaller the difference between the two forces and the slower the rate of change. This is explained diagrammatically by Fig. 14.10.

When an aircraft glides down in a shallow descent its rate of fall is slowed, but this is achieved in a different way from the slow descent of a parachute. In a parachute, gravitational force is opposed by the friction (drag) between the canopy and the air. In an aircraft, the forward movement of the wing through the air creates an upward force under the wing known as lift, which opposes the pull of gravity and slows the rate of descent. Unlike the parachute, which if stable will fall vertically, the gliding aircraft will continue to descend slowly only as long as it keeps moving forward through the air, because it is this movement which generates lift. Powered aircraft are propelled through the air by their engines, so that much more lift is generated than when gliding. The lift is greater than the weight of the aircraft so the imbalance of forces is reversed and it can gain height.

14.5: Forces out of balance, object stationary

If unbalanced forces act on a stationary object it will either move, or change shape, or both. Changes of shape are discussed in Chapter 7.

Movement from rest. When a stationary object is acted on by unbalanced pushing or pulling forces it will begin to move, always in the same direction as the larger force. This can be shown very simply by holding up a ball and dropping it (Fig. 14.7d), but pushing and pulling in a more obvious way is likely to be easier to understand. The effect of pulling an object at rest can be observed with the 'sliders' used to investigate friction (14.3, Fig. 14.1). The pulling force and the friction force between slider and base-board act in opposite directions. When the pulling force becomes greater than the friction the two are no longer balanced and the slider begins to move.

The action of a pushing force on an object at rest can be investigated using a simple trolley propelled by a rubber band (Fig. 14.3). Toy cars can be used instead but are more difficult to observe in detail. When the trolley is fitted to the rubber band, pulled back and held, the situation is one of no-change, showing that the forces acting on the hand, the rubber band and the trolley are all in balance. When the trolley is released the rubber band straightens out, exerting a pushing force on the trolley. This is much greater than the friction forces tending to impede the trolley's movement, so it moves forward in the direction of the push force.

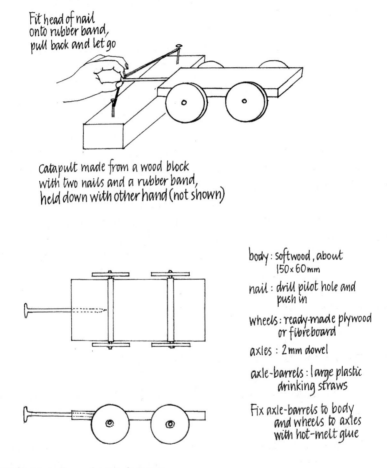

Figure 14.3 *Simple trolley and catapult system*

By varying the amount by which the band is stretched, and by loading the trolley with modelling clay, two important aspects of movement from rest can be observed. The first is that the bigger the pushing force, the faster the trolley travels. The second is that the greater the weight of the trolley and its load, the larger the force needed to make it move at the same speed. The reason for this is twofold: increasing the weight of the trolley increases friction, which tends to impede movement (14.4), but the greater mass of the trolley (15.2) also needs a greater force to get it moving. What happens when the trolley slows down and stops is discussed in the next section.

14.6: Forces out of balance, object moving

Three kinds of change in movement. When a moving object is acted on by unbalanced forces, its movement will be changed. How the movement changes depends on the direction and size of the forces in relation to the way the object is moving. This can be very complex, but basically there are three situations which children at primary level are likely to experience and investigate, and which are summarized by Fig. 14.4. When observing and trying to explain changes in the movement of objects, the 'describe-explain' strategy (1.8) provides a useful framework within which to operate.

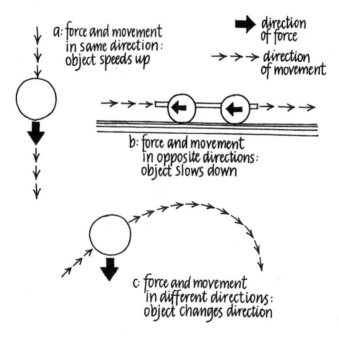

Figure 14.4 *Unbalanced forces acting on moving objects: in a and c the unbalanced force is gravity; in b it is friction*

1.   Force acts in the same direction as the object is moving. Result: the object speeds up, but does not change direction, i.e. it continues to move in a straight line (Fig. 14.4a).
2.   Force acts in the direction opposite to the object's movement. Result: the

object slows down, but its direction does not change (Fig. 14.4b).

3.   Force acts in a direction different from the object's movement. Result: the
     direction of movement is changed and, depending on how large the force
     is and its direction, speed is likely to change as well (Fig. 14.4c).

Of these three situations, the second is for most children and many adults the most
difficult to understand. The essential point is that if an object is slowing down in a
straight line, then a force must be acting on it in the opposite direction, opposing
movement. This is discussed further below, in the context of objects slowing down.

Speeding up. If an object moving in a straight line speeds up without changing
direction, then an unbalanced force is acting on it in the direction in which it is
already moving (Fig. 14.4a). If nothing else changes, the longer the force continues
to act on the object, the more its speed will increase. This can be shown by investigating the effect of gravity (15.2) on the speed of falling objects. Gravitational force
acts on everything on Earth all the time, so as an object falls its speed increases,
although air resistance means that it will finally reach a constant speed (Fig. 14.10).

   This speeding up can be seen by dropping spheres of soft modelling clay from different heights between 0.5 and 2 m on to a hard, level surface. A longer fall means
that gravitational force acts on the sphere for a longer time, so that it is moving
faster on impact. This in turn means that the force of the impact will be greater so
the sphere will be squashed more. Spheres of the same size dropped from different
heights will have differently sized flat faces after impact, which can be recorded by
brushing them with paint and printing them on a prepared chart.

   A similar effect can be seen by dropping a steel ball-bearing from different heights
into a layer of dry silver-sand 2 cm deep in a shallow box. The size of the splash
crater depends on the force of the impact and so varies with the length of the fall
and the speed of the ball-bearing.

   Dropping objects in this way shows that the amount by which a moving object
speeds up depends on how long the force acts on it; but change in speed also
depends on how large the force is. Gravitational force on a mass (i.e. its weight,
15.2) is constant, but the effect of changing the force and the time it is acting can
be shown when riding a bicycle. Pedalling hard makes one speed up much more
rapidly than pedalling gently, and, other things being equal, pedalling for a minute
or two results in greater speeding up than pedalling for only a few seconds, because
the force has been acting for a longer time.

Slowing down. If an object moving in a straight line slows down without changing
direction, then an unbalanced force is acting in the direction opposite to its movement (Fig. 14.4b). When a simple trolley is moved from rest by a rubber-band catapult on a level floor (Fig. 14.3) it rolls across the floor, getting slower all the time
until it stops, and then does not move any more. Explaining what happens when
the trolley is released and is moved from rest is very simple (14.5). The critical ques-

tion, and the one which makes this a very useful investigation is, Why does the trolley slow down and stop?

The answers given to this question can usually enable the teacher to deduce at least something of the children's own concepts of forces and their ideas about why things move. The misconception most commonly met with is that if an object is moving, a force must be acting on it to keep it moving. Given our everyday experience of moving loads (14.8) this is an understandable assumption, but it is quite wrong. It is most often expressed in an answer such as 'The trolley slows down because it is running out of push', or some variant of it. The investigation itself provides evidence to argue against this interpretation and the mistaken idea which lies behind it. Once the trolley has moved forward away from the elastic band, nothing is pushing it, so it cannot be running out of push, and there is no force at all acting on it to keep it moving. To explain what happens, go back to first principles. The trolley's movement is changing, so the forces acting on it must be out of balance. It is slowing down, so there must be a force acting on it which is opposing its movement, i.e. acting in the opposite direction.

To find out what the slowing-down force might be, do a simple thought-experiment, which could be carried out in reality. Imagine you are pedalling your bicycle on a level road. You stop pedalling: no force is now acting to move you forward. What happens? You gradually slow down, as the trolley does. How could you slow down more suddenly, in a shorter distance? By putting the brakes on. Because the brakes change your movement, making you slow down more suddenly, they must be exerting a force on the bicycle and you, as they grip and rub on the wheel-rims (14.9). This is the force called friction (14.4), which tends to slow down moving things by acting in the direction opposite to movement, i.e. backwards (14.4, Fig. 14.1). Even without the brakes on, there are other friction forces acting on you and your bicycle, so you slow down. One of these is air resistance, which can be felt pushing backwards as you and the bicycle move forwards. When these ideas are applied to the simple trolley, children can usually see quite readily what could be generating friction: mainly the axles rubbing on the body as they rotate.

As with speeding up (see above), the greater the force opposing movement, the more rapid and obvious its effect will be; and the longer it acts, the more the moving object will be slowed down. Again this relates to children's own experience with bicycles and as passengers in other vehicles. If the brakes are applied gently, the force opposing movement is small so the bicycle slows down more gradually, and usually more safely, than if braking is fierce. The reverse is also true: if a vehicle is travelling fast it will take longer for braking forces to stop it than if it is moving more slowly, and it will travel a greater distance while it is slowing down. All these observations have fundamental relevance to education in road safety.

Changing direction. If an object moving in a straight line changes direction, then a force must be acting on it in a direction different from the one in which it is travelling. The curved path of a ball thrown or kicked into the air is a very familiar example of this effect (Fig. 14.4c). As the ball travels through the air there are no forces propelling it forward, though air resistance (friction, not shown in Fig. 14.4c) is tending to slow it down. Gravity, however, is acting vertically downwards all the time, so the ball's direction is continually changing and it moves in a curved path. This change of direction continues until the ball is falling vertically (i.e. in the same direction as gravity) or it hits something.

Rolling balls across a floor so that they collide with each other or fixed objects provides another example. The ball moves in a straight line until it hits something, which it will push, and be pushed by, at the same time (14.2). Unless the push is in a direction exactly opposite to its movement, the ball will move off at an angle in a new direction. This is the principle which underlies games such as snooker, billiards and pool.

Road vehicles use forces acting at an angle to their direction of travel to change direction. When cars or bicycles are steered round a corner, their front wheels are turned so that they are at an angle to the direction of movement, while continuing to rotate. This generates friction forces between the tyre and the road which push the front of the vehicle sideways, making it change direction. If this sideways force becomes greater than the friction forces between the tyres and the road (wheels turned too much, speed too great), the car or bicycle will skid out of control.

14.7: Forces in balance, object stationary

When the movement and shape of an object on Earth remain the same, the forces acting on it are in balance. Three examples of forces in balance acting on stationary objects have already been discussed: a beam balance in relation to movement, a stretched elastic band in relation to shape (14.3), and a 'slider' pulled too gently to overcome static friction (14.4).

The commonest and often the most puzzling case, however, is when an object is simply at rest, as when a book sits on a table. The difficulty is usually to convince children that any forces at all are acting on the object. A useful line of argument is to ask, 'What would happen if the table did not support the book?' (It would fall to the floor.) 'What prevents it falling?' To find out, support a heavy object such as a brick in your hand. To keep the brick steady, you have to press up on it. This means that you are exerting an upward push force on it. This force opposes the downward pull of gravity and if the two are in balance the brick does not move. If you either relax your muscles or push harder, the forces are out of balance and the brick moves down or up.

The next stage is to measure the force needed to support the brick, with a top-pan spring balance. The weight of the brick compresses the spring, changing its shape until it pushes up with an equal force, and the mechanism tells us how large that force is. But the weight of the brick stays the same, so the table must exert an equal force to keep it from falling. The only reason why this and many other such balanced forces are difficult to detect is because most of the structures we live among are rigid as far as normal forces are concerned (7.5) and so show no apparent response when loads are placed on them. Much useful reinforcement of the basic idea of forces in balance can be achieved through work in physical education, by pushing and pulling on partners, tug-o'-war contests and work on balance, both on the floor and on apparatus.

The principle of balanced forces is exploited in all devices for measuring weight. Rubber bands can be used as simple forcemeters by carefully measuring the extension produced when known weights are suspended from them. If a card scale is constructed using these measurements it can be used with the band to measure unknown weights or forces, remembering that the weight of a 100 g mass is about 1 N (14.1). The changes of shape involved also make two important points. The first is a reminder that the bigger the force applied to a system, the bigger the change it will bring about. The second is that when forces are out of balance, what often happens is that the system changes until the forces are in balance again, when change ceases. In this case, the longer the rubber band, the greater the inward pulling forces it exerts and the greater the outward pulling forces needed to balance them. Every time the pulling forces applied to it are changed, the band changes in length until the opposing forces are equal again. Floating, a very important example of forces in balance with no movement, is discussed as a separate topic in section 14.10.

14.8: Forces in balance, object moving

If an object is moving in a straight line and at a constant speed, its movement is not changing. This implies that the forces acting on it must be in balance. Model parachutes provide an example of this, with the downward force of their weight balanced by the upward force of air resistance which inflates the canopy, though it is difficult to be sure that they are moving at constant speed. Cyclists, however, can experience constant speed when freewheeling down a gentle slope. The gravitational force of the Earth moves the cycle and rider forward and would, if unopposed, cause their speed to increase (14.6). Friction forces in the cycle bearings, and from air resistance, oppose the forward movement and, while the two forces are in balance, speed remains constant. If either changes, for example because of a change in the slope or wind-speed, the speed of the cyclist will change. If the change is a slight one, the forces may come into balance again and movement at a constant speed may be re-established, either faster or slower than before.

A similar situation arises whenever a car is driven at a steady speed in a straight line. If the road is level, the pushing force from the road on to the wheels making the car move forward (14.4) is balanced by friction and air resistance, so the speed does not change (Fig. 14.9b). This situation can usefully be contrasted with that of a trolley, with no propulsive force, being slowed and stopped by friction (14.6).

14.9: Forces and machines

A 'machine' is the general term for a device which, by applying and transferring forces, enables a person to do something they cannot do unaided. Most hand tools are examples of simple machines, which whenever possible should be investigated by actually working with them. A useful starting-point is to remove a tightly fitting can lid with a screwdriver. The friction forces holding the lid in place and resisting its movement are much too large to be overcome by the unaided hand. The screwdriver is used as a lever, pivoting on the rim of the can (Fig. 14.5a), and shows most of the properties of a simple machine. A force is transferred from one place (the screwdriver handle) to another (the lid of the tin). The force applied to the machine (the effort) is changed to a much larger force in order to overcome the friction forces between the tin and the lid (the load), but to do this the effort has to be moved through a much greater distance than the load. In the example shown, the effort moves about 12 times as far as the load, so the force used to move the load is about 12 times the effort.

Another good example is to use a claw hammer to pull a nail from a piece of wood (Fig. 14.5b). The load is the friction force between the nail and the wood, the effort being the force applied to the hammer handle. Using a typical hammer the effort moves through about 300 mm to pull a nail 30 mm out of the wood, so the machine generates a force of about ten times the effort in order to move the load. The hammer is acting as a lever, its pivot being the curved surface of the head in contact with the wood. It is also noticeable that the effort required to move the load is least when it is applied at the end of the handle; that is, as far away from the pivot as possible.

The importance of applying the effort to a machine at the right point can be shown by using a spanner to loosen a nut tightened onto a bolt holding two pieces of wood or metal together. Again the effort required is least when it is applied at the end of the spanner away from the nut. If it is applied part way along the spanner and so nearer the nut, a larger effort will be required and it may not be possible to turn the nut at all. Another example of a lever-based machine is a pair of scissors, whose pivot is the rivet on which the blades turn, and whose load is the resistance of whatever is being cut. Scissors show another principle of lever-based machines: that while the effort needs to be as far away from the pivot as possible, the load needs to be as near the pivot as possible if the machine is to be effective. If the load is considerable, as for example when cutting thick card, the scissors cut most effectively when it is at the angle between the blades and as near to the rivet as possible. A similar effect can be observed when cutting thick wire with pliers or wire-cutters.

All the machines mentioned so far have the property that they can, as it were, multiply force, having as their input a small force moving over a large distance, and producing as their output a larger force moving over a shorter distance. There are other ways of doing this: pulley systems and gears are examples children can investigate. Screw threads are another class of machine. but they are more complex because they always involve a second device, usually a lever, to operate them, for example the spanner which tightens a nut. In all cases, remembering that loads and efforts are forces, the questions to ask are:

What does the machine do (i.e. what is the load moved)?
How big is the load compared with the effort (estimate) and how far does each move (measure)?
How does the machine transfer force from one place to another?

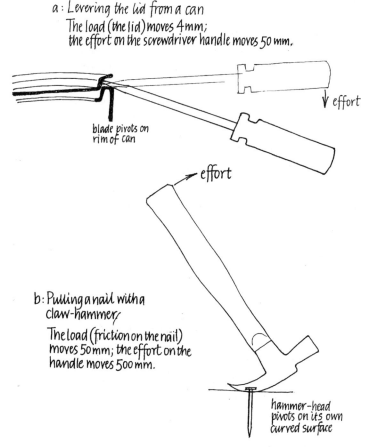

a: Levering the lid from a can
The load (the lid) moves 4mm;
the effort on the screwdriver handle moves 50 mm.

↓ effort

blade pivots on
rim of can

→ effort

b: Pulling a nail with a
claw-hammer;

The load (friction on the nail)
moves 50mm; the effort on the
handle moves 500 mm.

hammer-head
pivots on its own
curved surface

Figure 14.5 *Two simple lever systems*

Most simple machines children can investigate are useful because they change a small force into a much larger one: we could call them force-multipliers. Some, however, work the other way round, and could be called distance-multipliers. Their input is a large effort moving over a short distance and their output is a smaller force moving over a larger distance. The most familiar examples are the limbs of animals. The human arm is a lever system in which a very small shortening of the biceps muscle (3.5) brings about a very much larger movement of the hand. Gear-systems can be used to do the same thing: rotary egg whisks and bicycles (see below) are examples.

The bicycle: a more complex machine. Many basic concepts on forces and machines can be consolidated by investigating how a more complex machine works. A very useful example which many children experience at first hand is the bicycle, which is a complex system made from an assembly of simple machines. At primary level, attention can profitably be directed to two functions of the system: the transmission of propulsive force and the brakes.

The force to move the bicycle is generated by the leg-muscles of the rider. The leg is a distance-multiplying lever system, in which a very small movement of the muscles produces a much larger pushing movement of the foot. The foot presses down on the pedal, causing the crank and chainwheel to rotate. Teeth on the chainwheel engage the chain-links, pulling the upper part of the chain loop forwards. The chain transmits this pulling force to a smaller cog on the rear wheel, causing it and the wheel to rotate. The tyre makes a high-friction contact with the road, transmitting a backwards pushing force. Because the road is immovable and the tyre does not slip, the road pushes forwards on the tyre, so the bicycle and rider move forward.

It may be interesting to work out whether the bicycle is overall a force- or a distance-multiplying machine. This can be done by comparing the distance moved by the effort in one complete turn of the pedals with the distance moved by the bicycle as a result. For example, the cranks on my bicycle are 175 mm (0.175 m) long, and it moves 6.4 m for each complete turn of the pedals:

length of crank (r)   = 0.175 m
diameter of circle travelled by pedal (d) = 0.35 m
distance travelled by pedal in one turn (πd) = 1.1 m.

This shows that the bicycle is a distance-multiplier: for every 1.1 m the effort moves, the rider and bicycle move 6.4 m. The exact relationship between the two varies quite widely with different bicycles and gears.

The brakes of a bicycle are a double lever system which is a force-multiplier. A small pulling force on the brake lever is changed to a large pulling force on the brake cable. The pulling force is transmitted by the flexible cable, running inside a sheath lubricated by grease, to the brake mechanism. This is another lever system, which in most cases further increases the force as it moves the brake blocks into contact with the wheel-rims. The blocks push inwards, gripping the rims and generating large friction forces as they slide past, so slowing the movement of the cycle and rider.

14.10: Floating and sinking

Floating as arrested fall. When an object floats in a liquid or in air (as a hot-air balloon does), it neither rises nor falls, so the forces acting on it must be in balance. In developing an understanding of floating it is helpful to overcome a habit of thought created by language. Floating is not a case of something happening, as our use of the word suggests, but of something not happening: the floating object is prevented from falling. To begin with, this is most easily understood by investigating objects floating in water. For example, if a table-tennis ball is dropped into an empty bowl, it falls to the bottom. If the bowl has water in it, the ball falls to the water surface but then does not fall any further, because the water holds it up. This state of arrested fall is what we call floating. Because the floating object does not continue to fall, the water must be exerting an upward force on it, which balances the weight of the ball.

Displacement and upthrust. To find out how water exerts an upward force on a floating object, stand a bucket in a bowl and fill the bucket completely with water. Gently push a plastic football into the water. As the ball is pushed down, it pushes the water away and occupies part of the space within the bucket, so the water overflows. This displacement of the water causes the remaining water in the bucket to exert an upward force on the ball, known as upthrust. The upthrust can be felt, because it is necessary to exert a downward push in order to balance it and keep the ball still. As the ball is pushed further down, the displacement and the upthrust increase: more water overflows and a larger push is needed to prevent the ball rising. This shows that displacement is related to upthrust. In order to understand floating and sinking in terms of forces, it is necessary to find out what that relationship is.

The relationship between displacement and upthrust. This can be shown by a simple investigation. Cut the top part from a 2- or 3-litre plastic bottle, pour 1 litre of water into the bottom part, stand it on a level surface and mark the water level carefully with a waterproof marker. 1 litre of water has a mass (15.2) of 1 kg, and a weight (is pulled down by gravity with a force of) about 10 N (14.1). Empty the cut-down bottle, dry it and place 1 kg dry sand in the bottom. Now float the loaded bottle upright in water. It will float with the marked line level with the water (Fig. 14.6). The downward force acting on the bottle and its contents is their weight: about 10 N. Because the loaded bottle is floating, the upthrust must be equal to this. Because the line on the bottle is level with the water surface, 1 litre of water has been displaced, but 1 litre of water has a mass of 1 kg and a weight of about 10 N. In other words, the upthrust on an object is exactly equal to the weight of the water it displaces. This is known as Archimedes' Principle.

One prediction which can be made on the basis of Archimedes' Principle is that when the weight of a floating object is changed, displacement and upthrust change until the system is in balance again. This can be shown by changing the load in the marked bottle. If the weight is reduced, the bottle rises so that displacement and upthrust are also reduced. If the weight is increased, the reverse happens and the bottle sinks deeper. This self-adjusting property explains why similarly shaped pieces of different materials float with different proportions under the surface. If weight is very low in relation to volume, as in expanded polystyrene foam for example, a small amount of displacement generates enough upthrust to support it, so very little of the object is immersed. If the weight is greater in relation to volume, more upthrust is needed to support it and the object sinks deeper, displacing more water.

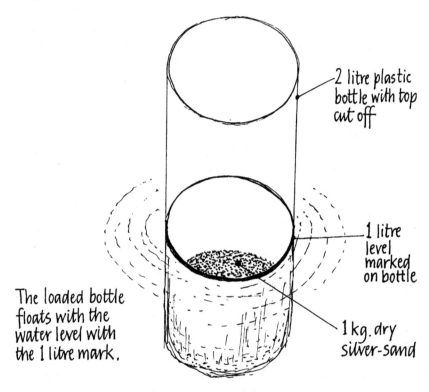

2 litre plastic bottle with top cut off

1 litre level marked on bottle

The loaded bottle floats with the water level with the 1 litre mark.

1 kg. dry silver-sand

Figure 14.6 *The relationship between displacement and upthrust*

Sinking – and more floating. Any object has to displace a weight of water equal to its own weight in order to remain afloat. If it cannot do this, weight will be greater than upthrust, balance of forces will not be achieved and the object will continue to fall: in other words, it will sink. Objects in water sink because the water cannot give them enough support. This can be shown by suspending an object which sinks, such as a ball of modelling clay, from a thread attached to a forcemeter, and lowering it into water. The weight of the object appears to be reduced. Actually it is unchanged (15.2): the change in the reading on the forcemeter is caused by the upthrust of the water on the object. But because the upthrust is less than the weight of the object in air (this can be checked using the forcemeter), the water cannot support it fully and it sinks.

Modelling clay is particularly suitable for this investigation because its shape can be changed. Although it sinks when a solid lump, it is often possible to make it float if it is formed into a hollow cup shape, as thin-walled and large as possible. Its weight is unchanged, but in a cup shape it can displace more water than when it is a solid lump, so gaining more upthrust and, if it is large enough, remaining afloat. Similar experiments can be carried out with aluminium foil, and help to explain why ships made of steel can not only float, but carry heavy cargoes as well.

Floating in air. Because air has weight, if it is displaced by an object it will exert an upthrust on the object just as water does. Most objects are so heavy in relation to the air they displace that this effect is not noticeable, but if an object is light enough in relation to its volume it will float in air. The examples children are likely to see are balloons filled with helium, a gas which, litre for litre, is much lighter than air, and hot-air balloons.

When air is heated, it expands, so a litre of hot air weighs less than a litre of cold air, and hot air rises (12.3). If air is heated and the rising warm air is trapped in a very large balloon, this can be inflated and eventually will float in the cooler air around it. As with any object warmer than its surroundings, the balloon loses thermal energy by heating the air around it and becomes cooler (12.3), so the burner has to be ignited periodically to raise the temperature of the air inside the balloon and keep it afloat.

14.11: Diagrams of forces

Because forces have both magnitude and direction (14.1), it is possible to represent them graphically in the form of diagrams. The usual way to do this is to draw the forces as arrows. The direction of the arrow shows the direction of the force, the length of the arrow shows how large a force it is, and its position shows where the force acts. Once the basic concepts of forces in and out of balance have been developed, force diagrams can be helpful in understanding particular situations, though they do need to be used carefully.

Fig. 14.7a is a simple diagram of the forces acting on a ball at rest. The diagram shows that the forces acting on the ball are acting in opposite directions and are in balance. Diagrams of forces should always be used with an awareness of possible misunderstanding. Balanced pulling forces are shown in Fig. 14.7b. Notice, however, that although gravity acts on the whole of the brick, the force acting downwards (the weight of the brick) is represented by a single arrow from its centre. Also, only one pair of forces is shown, although similar pairs would be acting between the string and the hook, and between the hook and the beam above.

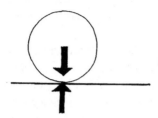

a: ball on floor

downward force: weight of ball

upward force: resistance of floor

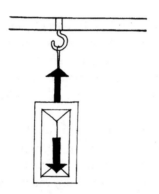

b: suspended brick

upward force: pull of string
under tension

downward force: weight of brick

c: book on table

downward force: weight of book

upward force: resistance of table

Note that the forces shown are the result of all the forces acting on the book and the table. The forces act over the whole area of contact, not at a single point.

d: falling ball, which has just been released

upward force: air resistance (friction)

downward force: weight of ball

Figure 14.7 *Simple diagrams of forces*

Another common example is seen when a book rests on a table. The forces involved act over the whole area of the book in contact with the table. When representing this situation in a diagram, however, it is usual to represent all the upward and downward acting forces by single arrows, as in Fig. 14.7c, so that the relationship between them can be seen. Unless this is clearly understood, the diagram could result in misconceptions about how forces act.

a: Trolley at rest

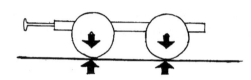

b: Trolley is pushed to the right

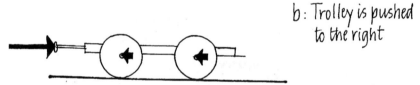

Force tending to make the trolley speed up: the push on the nail.
Force tending to make the trolley slow down: friction, mainly between the axles and the body.
Result: trolley speeds up and moves to the right.

Figure 14.8 *Forces acting on a trolley*

When an object falls for a small distance through the air, it is acted on by forces which are out of balance. A diagram (Fig. 14.7d) is useful for showing this, and to emphasize that movement takes place in the direction of the larger force. Again the diagram shows the results of forces acting on the ball from both directions, but should not be seen as implying that the forces act at a particular point: they act on the ball as a whole.

Diagrams representing the forces acting on moving objects can present other problems of which the teacher needs to be aware. For example, if a trolley is at rest, the forces acting on it could be shown by a diagram such as Fig. 14.8a. When the trolley is moving these forces continue to act on it in the same way, but to include them might make the diagram too complex and confusing. To simplify the diagram they are usually omitted and only the forces affecting the movement of the trolley are represented (Fig. 14.8b, c). Once this convention is understood, such diagrams can be very useful. Figs 14.6b and c, for example, emphasize that friction forces opposing the movement of the trolley act in the direction opposite to its movement, and that when it is rolling across the floor, no force is tending to make it speed up, and only the friction forces are affecting its movement (14.6).

Once their limitations are understood and accepted, diagrams can be very helpful in reaching an understanding, particularly of sequences of changes which otherwise

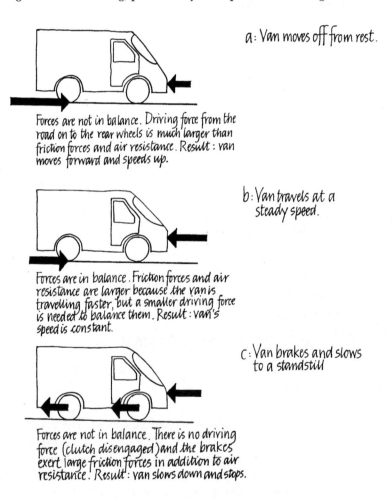

a: Van moves off from rest.

Forces are not in balance. Driving force from the road on to the rear wheels is much larger than friction forces and air resistance. Result : van moves forward and speeds up.

b: Van travels at a steady speed.

Forces are in balance. Friction forces and air resistance are larger because the van is travelling faster, but a smaller driving force is needed to balance them. Result : van's speed is constant.

c: Van brakes and slows to a standstill

Forces are not in balance. There is no driving force (clutch disengaged) and the brakes exert large friction forces in addition to air resistance. Result : van slows down and stops.

Figure 14.9 *Forces acting on a van which affect its movement. The total of all friction forces and air resistance are shown acting on the front of the van in (a) and (b). In (c), friction forces in the brakes are shown separately*

a: The sky-diver has just jumped from an aircraft.

Forces are not in balance.
Downward force : weight of sky-diver
Upward force: air resistance.
Result : speed increases rapidly as free-fall begins.

b: The sky-diver is in free-fall.

Forces are in balance.
Air resistance has increased with increasing speed until is equal to the weight of the sky-diver.
Result : free-fall at about 50 ms⁻¹ (metres per second).

c: Parachute canopy has just opened.

Forces are not in balance.

Weight remains constant, but air resistance is greatly increased by the drag of the parachute canopy.
Result : rate of fall is reduced.

d: The sky-diver is about to land.

Forces are in balance.

Air resistance (drag) on the parachute has been reduced as rate of fall has slowed.
Result : sky-diver is falling at a constant speed of about 5 ms⁻¹.

Notice that the forces acting in (b) and (d) are the same. The difference made by the parachute is to reduce the speed at which the sky-diver's weight is balanced by air resistance.

Figure 14.10 Forces acting on a sky-diver

would be difficult to describe. Two such sequences are shown in Figs 14.9 and 14.10, which use most of the concepts discussed in this chapter to explain the changes observed.

14.12: Forces and energy

The main role of scientific concepts, at least at primary level, is in explanation and prediction, not in description (1.8). In some investigations it is possible to produce two equally valid explanations for what has been observed using different sets of concepts. The most obvious examples of this are changes of movement and shape, which can be explained using concepts of force, or of energy. For example, the speeding up and slowing down of the trolley discussed in sections 14.5 and 14.6 in terms of forces, could also be explained in terms of energy transfer (12.1, 12.2) between the various parts of the system: the body of the operator, the elastic band, the trolley and the environment. Clear and useful explanations of these and many other changes can be arrived at using concepts either of energy transfer or of forces. Neither explanation is better than the other, and which is used should depend on the teacher's objectives for children's learning. What is almost always unwise and confusing is to attempt an explanation using concepts from both sets.

The words 'force' and 'energy' are used very precisely in science to denote concepts which are quite distinct, though connected to each other, and which are related to different aspects of change. Care should be taken to avoid confusing them. Energy is a property of a system which enables it to change (12.1). Forces, on the other hand, act on systems, either to change them or to keep them the same (14.3). Any change in a system involves transfer of energy, so all the actions of unbalanced forces discussed in this chapter could be explained in these terms (see, for example, kinetic energy in section 12.2).

The distinction between forces and energy can be seen most clearly when balanced forces are acting so that there is no change in shape or movement. When a book is resting on a shelf, for example, it is stationary only because balanced forces are acting on it (Fig. 14.7c), but there is no change of energy going on at all. Lifting the book onto a higher shelf involves both unbalanced forces and transfer of energy. Once resting on the higher shelf, energy transfer ceases and though the book now has more gravitational-potential energy (12.2), balanced forces keep it stationary just as they did before. In a similar way, unbalanced forces and energy transfer are involved in stretching an elastic band over pegs on a board, but once it is in place, with a higher level of elastic-potential energy than before, balanced forces continue to act on the band and the pegs, even though energy transfer has ceased.

In everyday speech 'force' and 'energy' are used much more loosely than in science, but this is a language habit education should seek to overcome rather than reinforce, at least in the context of scientific investigations. For similar reasons, concepts which show the relationship between force and energy, but which cannot be developed with understanding, should never be introduced at primary level. The main one to avoid is momentum, and the scientific concept of work (12.1) should be used only if children's investigations and questioning make it necessary. The introduction of these concepts before they are needed, like any premature use of specialized scientific language, is likely to lead away from productive experience, not towards it (1.8).

15
Gravity and Magnetism

15.1: Action-at-a-distance

When investigating the forces we experience in everyday life and their effects (Chapter 14), much of our attention is directed towards finding out how objects interact when they are in contact with one another. From very early in life, however, we become aware that not all changes of movement are caused by things directly pushing or pulling each other. If an object is held above the Earth's surface and released, its movement changes: unless it is prevented from doing so, it falls. Because we are so accustomed to this happening, it is easy to forget how mysterious an occurrence it is. An object which was at rest begins to move, and its speed increases. This means that a force must be acting on it all the time it is falling; but nothing, apart from air, is touching the object, and experiments show that objects in a vacuum (in a jar from which the air has been pumped out) fall just as objects in air do.

The force which makes a falling object begin to move and speed up is gravitational force, and its effect is an example of what is known as action-at-a-distance. The idea of action-at-a-distance is useful because it emphasizes that forces, although we cannot say what they are, only what they do, are not imaginary. Force is not just an idea thought up to enable us to explain observations and predict events: forces are as real a part of the world as material things and energy are.

The other example of action-at-a-distance which children will observe and investigate is magnetism. Although they affect only certain kinds of materials (15.3) rather than all objects as gravitation does, magnets also have the property of exerting forces on objects which are not in contact with them. This can easily be shown using a magnet and paper-clip, or ring magnets (Figs 15.1, 15.7).

Fields. When observing the effects of both gravitation and magnetism, the concept of a field is a very useful one. When action-at-a-distance occurs, how large the forces are depends partly on the distance between the objects involved. The smaller the distance between them, if other things remain the same, the larger the forces will be. This can easily be shown with magnets (15.4) and has been demonstrated by many interplanetary flights: once the vehicle is far enough away, the forces tending to pull it back to Earth are undetectable. A field is, simply, the space around an object in which another object experiences a force. In the gravitational field around the Earth, any object experiences a gravitational force which tends to make it fall towards the Earth. The Moon is in the Earth's gravitational field, but is prevented from moving nearer to it by its movement in orbit, just as manufactured satellites are (15.2). The Earth-Moon system is in the Sun's gravitational field, as are all the other planets of the Solar System (18.1). When it is in a gravitational field, any object will experience a force. Magnets also have a field around them, known as a magnetic field, but this affects only magnetic materials (15.3).

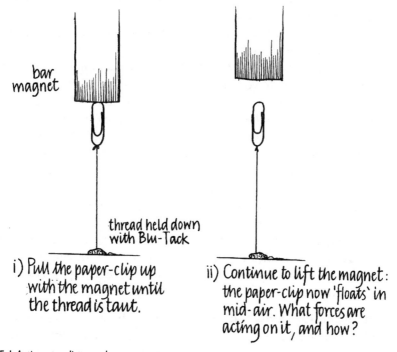

bar
magnet

thread held down
with Blu-Tack

i) Pull the paper-clip up
with the magnet until
the thread is taut.

ii) Continue to lift the magnet:
the paper-clip now 'floats' in
mid-air. What forces are
acting on it, and how?

Figure 15.1 *Action-at-a-distance by a magnet*

Gravity and magnetism: two unexplained phenomena. The goal of science is always understanding: knowledge 'why', as well as knowledge 'that' and knowledge 'how to' (1.1). Teachers, in seeking explanations which their pupils can understand, need to be aware that there are some phenomena which at present are unexplained. Gravity and magnetism are two examples. The forces which cause action-at-a-distance can be measured and related to mass (gravity, 15.2) and the orderly arrangement of atoms (magnetism, 15.3). Very accurate predictions can be made as to how objects in gravitational and magnetic fields will behave; but there is no generally accepted explanation of why they behave as they do. In watching objects fall, or magnets attract and repel each other, we are being confronted with mysteries which human ingenuity has so far failed to resolve and understand.

15.2: Gravity, mass and weight

All objects have gravitational fields, but unless an object is very large, (the Earth, for example), the field is so weak that it has no effect on human activities and can be detected only by using very sensitive measuring methods. An object in a gravitational field experiences a gravitational force which tends to make it move towards the large object creating the field, as a falling ball moves towards the surface of the Earth. This force is the weight of the object.

Children need to experience freely falling and suspended objects in a variety of ways in order to develop two important general observations: the gravitational force acting on any given object is always the same, and it always acts in the same direction. Of the two, direction is the easier to understand. Objects tend to fall vertically, both when they are free and when they are suspended by a string or thread. Objects which are not falling vertically must either have been moving sideways when they began to fall or have another force acting on them sideways and changing their movement (14.6). Examples which children may observe include balls thrown or kicked and the bob of a pendulum pulled out of its vertical fall by the string. The fact that gravitational force always acts vertically downwards is the basis for using plumb-lines to measure verticals and liquid levelling devices to measure horizontals.

The Earth's gravitational field varies very little in intensity over the surface of the planet, and it is always present. This can be shown simply by repeatedly measuring the gravitational force acting on an object (its weight) over a period of some days, using a spring balance or forcemeter. Unless material is added to or removed from the object, its weight remains constant. This observation, so simple that it might appear trivial, is in fact significant in two ways. It not only shows that the gravitational force is constant, but also introduces another concept: the idea of the amount of material in an object, which is known as its mass.

The distinction between mass and weight. This can be stated very simply. Mass is a measure of how much matter is in an object. The unit of mass is the kilogram (kg). Weight is the force which acts on a mass as a result of its being in a gravitational field. The unit of weight, like that of any other force, is the newton (N). At the surface of the Earth, any object of mass 1 kg is pulled down with a force of 9.81 N, so for most purposes the weight of 1 kg is taken to be 10 N. These simple statements, however, do not help much in understanding the two concepts, distinguishing them and using them in scientific explanations of what has been observed.

The confusion between mass and weight arises because, in everyday experience and language, there is no distinction between them. Because we live on the Earth, within its gravitational field, we never experience mass (amount of material) directly, but only through weight: the object is more or less heavy. Because of this, the only simple way to measure the mass of an object is to find its weight, by measuring the gravitational force acting on it and comparing this with another, known, force. Thus, a statement such as 'I weighed out a kilogram of apples' simply means that a quantity of material (mass, measured in kilograms) was measured by finding its weight. In science, however, the distinction between mass and weight is of great importance.

The fact that mass and weight are distinct can be shown by the very simple observation, mentioned earlier, that if an object is suspended from a spring balance, its weight does not change, unless material is removed from it or added to it. Adding or removing material changes the mass of the object, and this causes its weight to change. The amount of material in the object, its mass, is a property of the object itself, whereas weight is simply a measure of the effect which the Earth's gravitational field has on that amount of matter. This observation shows that mass and weight are different, but to understand the difference we have to imagine ourselves to be somewhere other than on the surface of the Earth.

Unless the amount of matter in an object changes, its mass remains constant, no matter where it is. For example, when pieces of rock were brought back from the Moon to the Earth, the amount of material remained the same: their mass did not change as a result of being transported. The weight of an object, on the other hand, will change if it is moved towards or away from the Earth, because weight depends on the intensity of the gravitational field in which the object happens to be at any time. On the surface of the Moon, for example, a kilogram of rock would weigh about 1.6 N, whereas the same rock, brought back to Earth with its mass unchanged, would weigh 9.8 N. The difference comes about because the Moon, being much less massive than the Earth, has a gravitational field which is much less intense. On the surface of a planet more massive than the Earth, a kilogram would weigh much more than its weight on Earth.

Developing concepts of mass and weight. At primary level, the distinction between mass and weight is of direct importance only in a small number of situations, for example when establishing the relationship between displacement and upthrust in a floating object (14.10). It is, however, very helpful to begin establishing mass and weight as distinct concepts by correct use of language. To do this, one need only observe two simple rules.

The first rule is that references to amount of material or its measurement should be made in terms of mass and kilograms or grams, whereas references to the force acting on an object should be made in terms of weight and newtons. For example, a standard 1 kg lump of metal should be called a mass (not a weight), whereas what pushes down on my hand when I hold it is its weight (not its mass), which is 10 N (not 1 kg). The second rule is that the terms relating to mass and weight should never be mixed up or used in place of each other. For example, while I can weigh out (measure by comparing forces) a certain amount of material, such as 1 kg of apples, the apples do not weigh 1 kg: they weigh 10 N.

Real and apparent weightlessness. On Earth, the weight of an object remains the same as long as its mass does not change. But in spite of this simple observation, weight can still be deceptive, appearing to change when in fact it remains the same. Objects may even appear to be weightless: when they are floating, for example. If an object is suspended from a forcemeter and lowered into water, its weight will appear to be reduced as it becomes immersed. This is because, as the object displaces water, the water exerts an upward force on it (upthrust, 14.10). If the upthrust is equal to the weight the object floats and, from the reading on the forcemeter, appears to weigh nothing. This apparent weightlessness is deceptive: the object's weight is a force and this has not changed. All that has happened is that upthrust acting in the opposite direction has balanced the weight.

True weightlessness is quite different from the apparent weightlessness brought about by a balance of forces. The gravitational field around the Earth, and any other large object, varies with distance: the farther away one is, the less intense the field. This means that the weight of an object decreases as its distance away from the Earth increases. At a distance of 15,000 km, for example, 1 kg would weigh only 2 N, one-fifth of its weight on Earth. If an object travels far enough away from the Earth, until no gravitational field can be detected, it will have no weight. This is true weightlessness, which cannot be experienced on Earth.

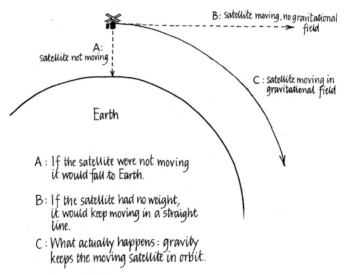

Figure 15.2 *The orbit of a satellite*

Humans in orbit around the Earth in space stations appear to experience true weightlessness and are often said to be living 'in zero-g'. Both statements, however, are false: they are not outside the Earth's gravitational field, and what they experience is another kind of apparent weightlessness, brought about by the way satellites move round the Earth, a condition known as free-fall. Fig. 15.2 helps to explain the movement of a satellite. Because it is in the Earth's gravitational field the satellite has weight, so if it were not moving (A) it would fall towards the Earth. But the satellite is moving, very fast: Skylab travelled at about 28,000 km per hour, or nearly 8,000 ms^{-1} (metres per second). If a satellite were outside the Earth's gravitational field and therefore truly weightless (B), it would keep moving in a straight line. What actually happens (C) is that the satellite is continually falling towards the Earth, but its movement prevents it getting any closer, so both it and the people in it are in free-fall. One effect of free-fall is that the satellite, together with the people and objects in it, appear to be weightless, as do parachutists in free-fall before their parachutes open (Fig. 14.10).

Rate of fall and the swing of a pendulum. Because the Earth's gravitational field is constant, the rate at which any object falls towards it is also constant, unless other forces are acting on it. This means that, unless another force is acting against gravity, all objects fall towards the Earth at the same rate, regardless of their weight. This may seem to contradict everyday experience: feathers and stones, for example, do not fall at the same rate. The difference, however, has nothing to do with gravitational force. It comes about because air resistance (friction, 14.4) tends to slow down light objects with a high surface area, such as feathers, much more than compact objects such as stones. In a chamber with all the air pumped out (in a vacuum), a feather and a stone would fall at the same rate, and this was demonstrated on the Moon during one of the Apollo missions.

Because air resistance slows down the fall of light objects more than heavy ones, even if they are the same size and shape, showing that gravity tends to make them fall at exactly the same rate can be difficult. It can, however, be shown with sufficient accuracy to be convincing by dropping spheres of modelling clay of different weights from the same height. If released at the same time (in itself an interesting technological problem) they will land at almost the same moment.

The behaviour of pendulums is too complex to analyse and explain in detail at primary level, but is connected with the observation that light and heavy objects fall at the same rate, unless air resistance affects them differently. If experiments are made with pendulums using a small arc of swing (not more than 15° on either side of vertical), it will be found that only the length affects the time of swing, not the weight of the bob: the longer the pendulum, the slower its swing. It should, however, be noted that the relationship between time of swing and length is not a simple one. To be exact, time of swing is proportional to the square root of the length, so to double the time of swing the pendulum has to be four times as long.

Because the gravitational field is constant, the time of swing of a pendulum on Earth does not vary unless its length is changed, so pendulums can be used as the basis of time measurement in clocks. In a less intense gravitational field, however, objects fall and pendulums swing more slowly. This means that on the Moon a particular mass would not only weigh less, but would also take longer to fall from a certain height, while a pendulum would swing much more slowly than one of the same length on Earth.

15.3: Magnets and magnetic materials

Two basic properties of magnets, that they attract iron to them and always point in the same direction if free to move, have been known for thousands of years from observations of natural magnets or lodestones, which are a rare variety of iron ore. The magnets used by children today are either metallic, made of special alloys of iron with other metals such as nickel, or ceramic, made of a non-metallic material known as magnadur (15.7). Magnets are made in a wide variety of shapes for different purposes. The most useful for children's investigations are simple bar magnets. Horseshoe magnets are less useful generally, though they do serve to show that magnetism as a property does not depend on shape.

Disc and ring magnets made of black ceramic are very useful for particular demonstrations and investigations (15.4, 15.7). Modern plastic-cased bar-shaped magnets are very robust and in most investigations behave much as simple bar magnets do. It is, however, important to realize that they are not simple, but are made up of a row of ceramic magnets held end to end in a tough case. Consequently, they may give unexpected results when the shape of their magnetic field is observed (see below) and their 'strength' is measured (15.4).

Magnetic materials. When working with magnets it is important to distinguish clearly between magnets and magnetic materials. In doing this, the concept of field (15.1) is very useful. A magnetic material is one which, when placed near a magnet, within its magnetic field, will experience a force tending to pull it closer to the magnet. A commonly used investigation with magnets is to ask children to classify a range of materials into groups, depending on whether they are magnetic (attracted to a magnet) or non-magnetic (no attraction). It will be found that, while all common magnetic materials are metallic, not all metals are magnetic: aluminium and brass, for example, are unaffected by magnets. The only common magnetic materials are iron and its alloys such as steel, but some stainless steels are non-magnetic, and some special materials used to make ceramic magnets (15.7) are non-metallic.

Although magnetic materials experience forces when they are in a magnetic field, they create no magnetic field of their own, unless they are magnetized (see below and 15.6). This means that two objects of magnetic material normally have no tendency to cling together or attract each other.

Magnets are always composed of magnetic material. The distinctive property of a magnet is that it creates a magnetic field around itself, within which magnetic materials and other magnets experience forces. This is an example of action-at-a-distance which children can easily observe for themselves (Figs 15.1, 15.7). The process by which a magnetic material becomes a magnet is called magnetization. This may be achieved either by contact with a magnet (15.6) or electrically (15.8). Once the magnetizing process stops, different materials retain magnetism to different degrees. The magnets which children use retain their magnetism to a very high degree if handled properly and so are known as permanent magnets (15.6). Distinguishing magnets from materials which are magnetic but unmagnetized is discussed in section 15.4.

When a magnetic material is magnetized it does not become more magnetic, but its internal structure becomes more ordered. Within the unmagnetized material are thousands of magnetic zones, known as domains. Each domain acts like a very small magnet, and in an unmagnetized object these are arranged in a random and disordered way. The result is that their magnetic fields cancel each other out and no overall magnetic field results. When the material is fully magnetized, all the atoms in all the domains within it become lined up in the same direction. The result of this orderly arrangement is that their magnetic fields reinforce each other instead of cancelling out, and a single magnetic field is created.

The shape of a magnetic field. This can be shown by placing a piece of thin, stiff card over a magnet and sprinkling a thin layer of finely powdered iron ('iron filings') onto the card. When the card is tapped gently, the particles line up in the magnetic field and show both its shape and the direction in which the magnetic forces are acting. Differently shaped magnets usually have differently shaped fields: comparing a bar magnet, a horseshoe magnet and a ceramic ring magnet standing on its edge will show this clearly (compare Figs 15.3 and 15.6). The way the iron particles cluster also shows how magnetic forces appear to be concentrated in particular places, which are the poles of the magnet (15.4). It can also be observed that the particles nearest the magnet move much less readily when the card is tapped, and line up in a more distinct pattern than those farther away. This shows that the magnetic forces acting on the particles of iron, and so the intensity of the magnetic field, decrease as distance from the magnet increases. Because the particles lose their magnetism as soon as they are removed from the magnetic field, the powdered iron can be re-used. It should be handled with care, as it may be difficult to remove from magnets (use adhesive tape) and may stain clothes by rusting.

Barriers to magnetic fields. Barriers to the field around a permanent magnet can be set up only by magnetic materials. The forces of attraction between a magnet and a magnetic object are entirely unaffected by thin layers of wood, glass, paper, water, plastic and non-magnetic metals, so that (for example) a magnet can be used to remove a steel paper-clip from a cup of water without wetting the hands, by sliding the magnet up the outside of the cup. A thin sheet of iron or steel, on the other hand, does act as a barrier against a magnetic field, though the effectiveness of different kinds of steel may vary. This occurs because the steel or iron itself becomes magnetized (15.6), so the magnetic field is in effect concentrated within it.

15.4: The poles of magnets and their behaviour

The ancient Greeks, early Chinese scientists and Viking navigators all knew that magnets, if free to move, come to rest pointing in a particular direction. An early way of doing this was to place the magnet on wood floating in water, but a more useful way for children's investigations is to suspend a bar magnet from a thread so that it hangs horizontally. If this is done well away from magnetic objects such as steel-framed furniture, the magnet will swing horizontally, twisting and untwisting the thread, until it comes to rest lined up in a north–south direction. The two ends of the magnet, however, do not behave in the same way. If a magnet at rest is turned, so that it is lined up in the same direction as before but with its ends reversed, it will swing until it regains its original position. The significance of this is that when a bar magnet is free to move, one end always points north unless it is deflected by magnetic materials or magnets near it. This end is therefore known as the north-seeking pole of the magnet, or 'north pole' for short. The opposite end is the south-seeking or 'south pole'. Magnets which are free to move line up in this way because the Earth itself is a very large magnet (15.5).

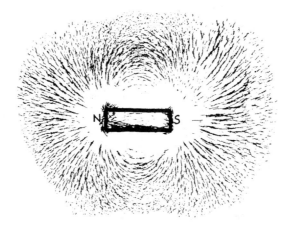

The lines of iron particles show the shape of the field and the direction of magnetic forces in it. These forces act towards the poles of the magnet at either end, but parallel to the sides in the middle.

Figure 15.3 *Observing the field of a simple bar magnet*

When observing the shape of a magnetic field (15.3) or making simple comparisons of the 'strength' of magnets (see below), it will be observed that the magnetic field and the forces of attraction which it produces appear to be concentrated at the poles of the magnet. Steel paper-clips, for example, will not cling to the middle of a bar magnet, though they are strongly attracted to the ends. This gives the impression that the ends of the magnet are much more strongly magnetized than the middle, but this is not so. The whole of the magnet is equally magnetized and all of it contributes to the magnetic field around it. Looking at the shape of the field around a bar magnet (Fig. 15.3), however, shows that in the middle of the magnet, the magnetic forces are acting parallel to the magnet, not towards it. This explains why magnetic materials will not cling to the middle part of the magnet.

If a length of steel wire is magnetized (15.6) and then cut in two, each piece behaves as a separate magnet, showing that the middle of the wire was magnetized just as much as the ends.

Attraction and repulsion. When a material which is magnetic but not itself magnetized is within a magnetic field, it is always attracted to the magnet creating the field. When two magnets are close to each other, however, their behaviour and the forces which affect them depend on their positions. If the north pole of one magnet is brought near to the south pole of another, the two pull towards and attract each other. If the north poles or south poles of two magnets are brought close to each other, exactly the reverse happens: the two magnets experience a pushing force which tends to move them apart. This is known as repulsion. This difference in behaviour gives rise to the simple rule that 'Unlike poles attract; like poles repel'.

Magnetic repulsion provides more convincing evidence for the existence of a magnetic field and of action-at-a-distance (15.1). Ring magnets can show this very clearly (Fig. 15.7), and if one of a pair of bar magnets is suspended horizontally on a thread and allowed to swing until it comes to rest, the other can be used to show action-at-a-distance. By pointing north pole to north pole (or south to south) at a distance of several metres, then moving slowly closer, the suspended magnet experiences a force, is deflected and made to swing away from the other. Depending on the 'strength' of the magnets (see below), deflection may be observed when the magnets are two metres or more apart.

Testing for magnetism. If an object is attracted to a magnet it must be made of, or at least contain, magnetic material, but showing that the object is itself a magnet requires a more critical test: that of magnetic repulsion. One magnet and a piece of magnetic material will never repel each other: they will always be attracted. Only two magnets with like poles opposed will repel. To find out if an unknown object is a magnet, it is necessary to place it near a magnet and observe any movement which results. If at first the two are attracted, reverse the position of the magnet and again observe the movement. Only if the two repel each other is it certain that the object under test is a magnet.

If an object is only weakly magnetized, as for example a needle magnetized by stroking usually is, it may be attracted to a magnet near it rather than being repelled, so that repulsion is difficult to observe. One way to overcome this is to suspend the object from a thread or place it on wood floating in water. It will then be possible to move it with much smaller forces, so any repulsion can be detected when the magnet used for testing is much farther away.

The 'strength' of magnets and measuring it. Both children and adults often refer to magnets as being 'strong' or 'weak'. What is meant is that different magnets create magnetic fields of greater or less intensity, so that magnetic materials experience greater or lesser forces of attraction when near them. The two main factors which affect the 'strength' of a magnet are the material of which it is made and how completely this is magnetized (15.6).

There are two main ways of comparing magnets: by attraction and by repulsion. In general, tests which rely on attraction are simpler but less accurate. The simplest test is to dip the magnets into a large box of steel pins or paper-clips and compare how many each picks up. This can give a very rough comparison of magnetic 'strength', but after a while the steel objects themselves become magnetized. A more controlled version of this test is to hang paper-clips from one pole of each magnet and see how long a chain each will support.

Much more accurate comparisons can be made using repulsion. One magnet is chosen as the standard for all the tests. The magnets to be tested should be placed on as smooth a surface as possible and the standard magnet brought slowly closer to each one, with like poles opposed. When the magnet being tested is moved by repulsion, the distance between the two is recorded. The larger the distance, the 'stronger' the magnet under test. This basic test can be refined in many ways, for example by mounting the magnets on trolleys and pulling the standard magnet closer to the one under test until it and its trolley move. Devising increasingly accurate and sensitive versions of this test can provide not only technological challenges but much insight into forces, friction, lubrication and fair testing. An alternative method is to compare the 'strength' of the magnet with that of the Earth's magnetic field (15.5 and Fig. 15.4).

In a simple metal bar magnet the 'strength' of the two poles is always the same. When testing a modern plastic-cased magnet, the apparent poles may differ in 'strength', because the magnets held in a row inside the case may not be perfectly matched.

15.5: The Earth's magnetism and navigation

The fact that magnets, if free to move, always come to rest pointing in the same direction is evidence that the Earth itself is a magnet. When powdered iron is used to show the shape of the field around a magnet (15.3, Fig. 15.3), the way that the particles line up within the field shows the direction of the magnetic forces acting on them. Just as the lines of particles show the direction of the forces at any point within the field, so a swinging magnet shows the direction of the magnetic forces round the Earth.

There is no generally agreed explanation of why the Earth is a magnet. The core of the planet is probably composed of iron and nickel, both strongly magnetic metals, but it is molten and much too hot to be magnetized. One theory is that material circulating in the Earth's core generates electric currents and, with them, the magnetic field (15.8). Like any magnet, the Earth has two poles. These are near the geographical north and south poles, but their position moves slowly all the time, so that magnetic north and true north are not in the same direction (see below).

Although the Earth is a very large magnet its magnetic field is not an intense one, so we are usually unaware of it. Because magnetic materials do not experience large forces at the surface of the planet, it is necessary to use a magnet which can move freely in order to detect the field at all. Just how 'weak' the Earth's magnetic field is can be judged using a magnet and a fluid-filled compass (or two magnets, one suspended from a thread) as shown in Fig. 15.4. When the magnet is at the critical distance from the compass, its field and that of the Earth will cancel each other out, so that the compass needle will not point in any definite direction. It can then be seen that the Earth's field is equal in intensity to the field at the critical distance from the magnet. This means that although the magnet is very small in comparison with the Earth, the magnetic field near to or in contact with it is much more intense. This demonstration can also be used as an alternative way of measuring the 'strength' of a magnet, since the intensity of the Earth's magnetic field at any place is constant. The 'stronger' the magnet, the farther away from the compass it will be when its field and that of the Earth cancel each other out.

Magnetic compasses and navigation. Magnetic compasses, an example of ancient technology still extensively used today, are simply magnets which are free to move and so to become aligned with the Earth's magnetic field. To make a simple compass

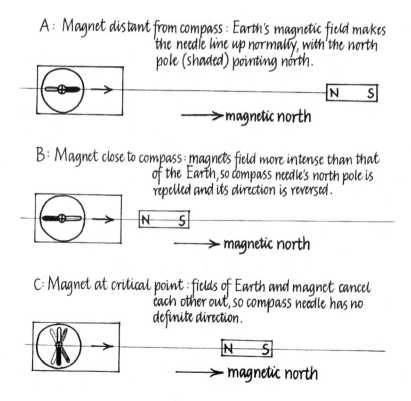

Figure 15.4 *Finding the strength of the Earth's magnetic field*

a magnet can be suspended from a thread, placed on or fixed to wood floating on water, or balanced on a small spike. The most useful compasses for children to use are the modern fluid-filled type used by walkers and orienteers. These have a balanced compass needle whose swing is damped by the fluid around it, so that although it gives a quick reading and is stable in use, it is also sensitive and accurate.

When using magnetic compasses it is important to remember that the compass needle is itself a magnet, so a force of attraction will be set up between it and any magnetic material around it. Steel-framed furniture and buildings, for example, may make it impossible to obtain a consistent north–south bearing in the classroom. If so, compasses can be used for direction-finding only outdoors or in another room.

Because the Earth's magnetic poles are not located at the geographical poles, a magnetic compass does not point to true north. This means that when using a magnetic compass for navigation or locating one's position on a map, it is necessary to make a correction. This is further complicated by the fact that the magnetic north pole moves, so the correction needed varies with place and time. In Britain in 2002, for example, magnetic north lay about 6° west of true north, and this difference is being reduced by about ½° every four years.

15.6: Magnetizing and demagnetizing

A magnetic material is attracted to a magnet because, when it is in a magnetic field, it becomes magnetized. This is called magnetic induction, and can easily be shown by suspending two steel nails from a magnet, having first shown that they are unmagnetized by making sure that they will not repel a compass needle. When suspended from the magnet the nails will not hang vertically, because the poles which are induced at their ends repel each other (Fig. 15.5a), showing that the nails themselves are magnetized. This can be confirmed by bringing another magnet near the nails with like poles opposed, which will cause the nails to be repelled even further (Fig. 15.5b).

Temporary and permanent magnets. When an object in contact with a magnet is magnetized by induction, the magnetic field makes some or all of the magnetic domains in the material line up in the same direction, so that the material develops poles and an overall magnetic field of its own (15.3). How much of this induced magnetism remains when the object is removed from the magnet depends very much on the material of which it is made. Soft iron, such as iron 'filings' or florist's wire, is very strongly magnetized when in contact with a magnet, but when it is removed it loses all its magnetism because its magnetic domains immediately go back to their original disordered state. As a result, soft iron can make only a temporary magnet. Steel, on the other hand, is less strongly magnetized, but when it is removed from the magnet its magnetic domains do not become completely disordered again, so that some of the induced magnetism is retained. As a result it is possible to magnetize steel permanently.

Children can make small permanent magnets from steel wire, for example paperclips straightened out with pliers. Although steel can be slightly magnetized simply by being in contact with a magnet, magnetic induction is much more effective if the steel is stroked with a 'strong' permanent magnet (Fig. 15.5c). It is important when making magnets by stroking to use only one pole of the magnet, always to stroke in the same direction and to move the magnet well away from the steel object when returning it to its starting-point. If the north pole is used for stroking, a north pole will be induced at the start of the stroke and a south pole at the end.

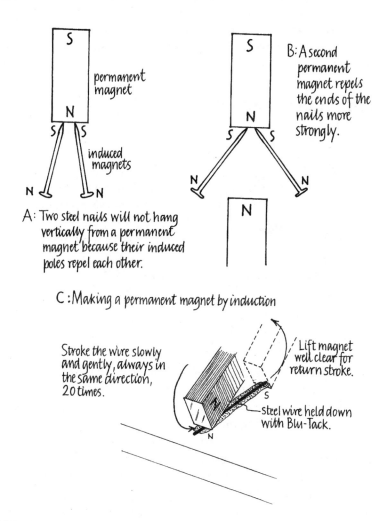

A: Two steel nails will not hang vertically from a permanent magnet because their induced poles repel each other.

B: A second permanent magnet repels the ends of the nails more strongly.

C: Making a permanent magnet by induction

Stroke the wire slowly and gently, always in the same direction, 20 times.

Lift magnet well clear for return stroke.

steel wire held down with Blu-Tack.

Figure 15.5 Induced magnetism

The induced magnetism can be tested by mounting the object as a compass needle and testing it by repulsion (15.4). Because the wire is only weakly magnetized, a good way to test it is to fix it to a disc of cork with Blu-Tac and float it on water.

Demagnetizing. Magnetizing a material involves giving its many small magnetic domains an orderly arrangement (15.3). Any change which tends to break down this order will 'weaken' the magnet and make its magnetic field less intense. A metal magnet will gradually become demagnetized if stored on its own. To prevent this, bar magnets are stored in parallel pairs with pieces of soft iron (keepers) between pairs of unlike poles, and horseshoe magnets are stored with a single keeper. The demagnetizing process is much quicker if metal magnets are subjected to mechanical shocks such as being dropped, so they should be handled with care. These problems do not affect ceramic magnets (15.7), though they also need to be handled carefully, because they are very brittle and can easily be chipped or broken (15.7). A piece of steel can be completely demagnetized by heating it to red heat and then allowing it to cool.

15.7: Non-metallic magnets

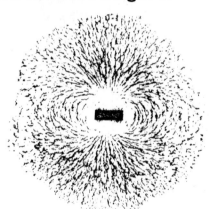

Field of a ring-shaped magnet standing on its edge. Its poles are its faces (contrast Fig.15.3). Cuboid ceramic magnets may be face- or end-polarized.

Figure 15.6 *Field of a ceramic magnet*

Reference has already been made to non-metallic magnets of a manufactured ceramic material known as magnadur. These are black, hard and brittle, and have several advantages. Although very difficult to magnetize, these special materials make 'strong' magnets which are also very permanent, with little tendency to become demagnetized over time, so that they are easy to store. The main disadvantage of ceramic magnets is that the material, though strong and hard, is very brittle, so it can be chipped or broken if dropped. This has largely been overcome in magnets for school use by encasing a row of ceramic magnets in a tough plastic case. These are very useful as a substitute for metal bar magnets in simple investigations, being 'stronger', more robust and long-lasting, but it should be borne in mind that they are not simple bar magnets and may give anomalous results in some investigations (15.3).

Materials similar to those used in ceramic magnets, but in the form of very fine powder, are bonded onto plastic tape and used for audio and video recording. The property which they have of making very permanent magnets is important to this technology, because the recording on the tape is a complex pattern of magnetization, and high-quality playback depends on the material retaining its magnetism to a very high degree.

Ceramic magnets are made in a wide range of shapes and sizes, including discs and rings. Before using any ceramic magnet for an investigation it is necessary to test it to find out how it has been magnetized. Many ceramic magnets are face-polarized: magnetized so that their poles are their flat faces, in contrast to bar magnets whose poles are at their ends. To show how the magnet has been magnetized, stand it on edge and use iron 'filings' on paper to observe the shape of its magnetic field (Fig. 15.6). Ring-shaped ceramic magnets show repulsion (15.4) and action-at-a-distance in a vivid and memorable way, when threaded onto an upright wooden dowel with their like poles opposed (Fig. 15.7). The upper magnet floats with no visible means of support, and will bounce in the air above the lower one if raised a little and then released. It is being supported by magnetic force acting upwards, balancing gravitational force acting downwards.

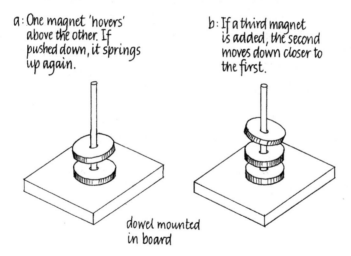

a: One magnet 'hovers' above the other. If pushed down, it springs up again.

b: If a third magnet is added, the second moves down closer to the first.

dowel mounted in board

Figure 15.7 *Repulsion by face-polarized ring magnets*

15.8: Electromagnetism

When an electric current (13.3) is passed through a conductor (13.2), a magnetic field is created around the conductor. The magnetic field can be made much more intense (and therefore easier to detect) if a long piece of wire is wound into a simple coil. This can be done by winding about 60 cm of thin, insulated copper wire around a card or paper tube, about the thickness of a pencil, always winding in the same direction and not allowing one turn to run over another. This coil, still supported by the tube, can then be connected to a 4.5V battery, with a switch to control the current. Two things need to be borne in mind: first, that the resistance of the circuit will be very low, so that when it is switched on the battery will almost be short-circuited (13.11) and will quickly become exhausted. Secondly, the large current in the circuit may cause the coil to become hot. The circuit should therefore be switched on only for a second or two at a time in order to make observations.

If a compass is placed alongside a coil with a current flowing through it, the magnetic field produced by the coil will cause the needle to align itself parallel to the long axis of the coil. If the direction of the current is reversed, the direction of the compass needle will also be reversed.

If magnetic material is placed inside the tube supporting the coil, it will become magnetized by induction (15.6) when current flows in the circuit. This arrangement is a simple electromagnet. Good electromagnets can be made from a bundle of soft iron florist's wire taped together. The iron is strongly magnetized while the current is flowing, but loses its magnetism as soon as the current is switched off. If a steel nail is used instead of soft iron, it will be less strongly magnetized while the current is flowing, but will retain some of its magnetism when the current is switched off. This can be tested by repulsion using a magnetic compass.

Detailed work on electromagnetism is beyond the scope of primary science, but the electromagnetic effect is the basis of the generation of mains electricity and of movement in electric motors. When a conductor (usually a coil) which is part of a circuit is made to move within a magnetic field, kinetic energy is transferred as electrical energy (12.2) and a current flows in the circuit. This is the basis of generating current using dynamos and alternators. The reverse happens when current is passed through a conductor (again, usually a coil) within a magnetic field: the conductor experiences a force which tends to make it move, and electrical energy is transferred as kinetic energy. Exploiting this effect has resulted, among other technologies, in the development of electric motors.

16
Sound

16.1: Sound, waves and vibration

Sound consists of tiny movements in the environment to which the ear responds (3.10). For humans, these movements are usually in air, but sound is also transmitted through water and solids. The movements occur in a pattern which is described as a wave motion. There are many kinds of waves, but those with which children are likely to be most familiar are the visible waves which travel outwards from a source of movement, such as ripples on water when an object is thrown into it. In these waves, the movement which causes the wave we see is at right angles (perpendicular) to the direction in which the wave travels. This can be illustrated by pulses in a rope when one end is moved up and down quickly (Fig. 16.1a). Sound waves also travel outwards from a source, but the movements involved are subtly different.

In sound, the waves themselves are invisible, but the way they move can be illustrated by moving a 'Slinky' spring as shown in Fig. 16.1b and c. As the end of the spring is moved quickly back and forward, a series of pulses pass along it. Within each pulse the coils of the spring are squashed closer together than normal, but between pulses they are stretched further apart. The overall effect is the passage of a wave pattern. As the wave passes, each coil of the spring is moved forwards and then back again, so it ends up in the same position as before and the spring, as a whole, does not move.

Sound waves similarly involve forwards and backwards movements in the air, but they are very rapid and very tiny compared with the much slower waves in the 'Slinky' spring (Fig. 16.1c). As a wave passes, air molecules (8.1) are alternately compressed and moved closer together than normal, then expanded and moved further apart than normal. Because the molecules are moving, they have kinetic energy (12.2). When sound waves enter the ear, some of that kinetic energy is transferred to the eardrum, making it vibrate. This vibration is detected by the ear, which transmits signals to the brain, so the sound is heard.

Sound waves and vibration. Sound waves are generated by objects which themselves are moving rapidly to and fro: the kind of movement usually called vibration.

245

The vibrating object makes the air around it vibrate, generating sound waves which travel outwards through the air. Musical instruments vibrate and produce sound waves in a variety of ways (16.3). If an object is not vibrating it cannot be producing sound waves, but most of the sounds we hear are produced by very small and rapid vibrations, which are difficult or impossible to see. There is therefore a need for children to sense and experience for themselves the connection between vibration and sound. There are many ways in which this can be done. A simple and useful one is to place grains of rice onto the head of a drum and observe their movement when the taut membrane is struck and made to vibrate. Vibration in the voice can be felt by raising the chin, placing the finger-tips lightly on the lower part of the voice-box (larynx) in the throat and singing a single, prolonged note. It is also possible to observe vibration directly in stringed instruments (16.3), especially those with long or thick strings which produce a low note.

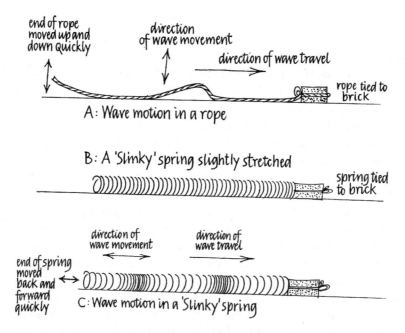

Figure 16.1 *Two kinds of wave motion: in the rope, the vibration is at right angles to the direction of wave travel. In the spring, vibration in the same direction as the direction. Sound waves move like the waves in the spring.*

Transmission of sound. Sound waves travel outwards from the vibrating object which is generating them. We are accustomed to hearing sounds in air, but other materials also transmit sound, many of them much more effectively. Water, for example, transmits sound very well, a property exploited by whales and dolphins which communicate using a complex vocabulary of sounds, and by human technology in echo-sounding (16.2). Many solids, particularly metals, are excellent transmitters of sound, so that a tap on a water-pipe can often be heard by pressing an ear to a connected pipe or tap in any part of a large building.

Sound waves are transmitted by the material through which they travel, so if there is no material around a vibrating object, it cannot generate sound. This is not a situation we normally experience, since we live surrounded by air, but if all the air is pumped from a jar so that it contains a vacuum, a bell suspended inside it can make no sound.

The speed of sound. When sound waves travel outwards from the vibrating object which is generating them, they do so at a definite speed. This means that there is a delay between a sound being generated and its being heard by an observer. When the observer is near the source of the sound, this delay is so small that it is not noticeable. When the distance is greater, the delay may be more easily observed. Light travels so fast (17.1) that for all practical purposes light produced by a source or reflected by an object on Earth reaches an observer at almost the same instant. If an event which generates sound can be seen by an observer some distance away, it is possible to detect the delay between seeing the event and hearing the sound. At a cricket match, for example, the batsman will be seen by spectators to hit the ball before the sound is heard. By measuring the delay between seeing and hearing accurately over a known distance, the speed of sound can be calculated. In air, sound travels at about 340 ms^{-1} (metres per second), or 1 km every three seconds.

Knowing the speed of sound makes it possible to estimate how far away a lightning flash was, by timing the delay between seeing the lightning and hearing the sound it produces (thunder), then dividing by three to give the distance in km. The time taken for sound to travel to an observer also explains why thunder rumbles (11.6). A lightning-stroke may be several km long and is almost an instantaneous event, but its lower end is much nearer an observer on the ground than its upper end. The first sound heard, from the lower end, is usually a loud crack. This is followed by the rumbling thunder as sound waves arrive from more distant parts of the lightning-stroke.

Reflected sound: echoes. When using a 'Slinky' spring to show the way that sound waves move (Fig. 16.1b, c), it will be noticed that when a wave reaches the end of the spring, it bounces off the heavy object to which the spring is anchored and travels back in the reverse direction. Sound waves can be reflected in the same way, and if the distances are great enough the reflected sound will be heard as a distinct echo. The human ear-brain system can hear two sounds as distinct only if they are one-tenth of a second or more apart, so to hear an echo of a sound they make themselves a person has to be at least 20 m away from the surface which is reflecting the sound. The most distinct echoes are made by short, sharp sounds directed at smooth, hard surfaces such as walls and rock-faces, which reflect sound rather than absorbing it (16.4). Some large, dome-shaped buildings, such as the Whispering Gallery in St Paul's Cathedral in London, have multiple echoes.

Echoes can occur in water as well as air. Water transmits sound much faster than air (at about 1,400 ms⁻¹), and also transmits it much more effectively. One technology which exploits this is echo-sounding. Short pulses of sound are produced by a device on the bottom of a ship. These travel to the sea-bed, are reflected back to the ship and detected by a microphone. The delay between sending the signals and receiving the echo depends on the depth of water, which is calculated and registered on a chart by an instrument called a fathometer. This enables the shape and depth of the sea-floor to be charted, and also makes it possible to locate wrecks and shoals of fish.

16.2: Differences between sounds: pitch, loudness and quality

During childhood we learn to distinguish between and recognize a great variety of sounds. Finding out in detail about the differences between the many sounds we hear is a complex branch of science, but children can investigate basic differences and relate them to the concept of sound as waves and the properties of the objects which produce them, such as musical instruments (16.3).

Pitch and frequency. Pitch is the term used by musicians to indicate how high or low a sound is. Under most circumstances, the pitch of the sound which is heard is determined by how rapidly the object producing the sound waves is vibrating. (This may not be true if the source of the sound is moving, see below.) The number of vibrations in one second is the same as the number of sound waves generated, and is referred to as the frequency. The unit of frequency is the hertz (symbol: Hz), 1 Hz being equal to 1 vibration each second. (The idea of frequency is applied to any change which involves oscillation, vibration or wave motion, so it is used to describe such diverse things as the movement of pendulums, radio waves and light, as well as sound.) The higher the frequency of sound waves, the higher the pitch of the sound which is heard.

The normal range of human hearing is between about 20 Hz (a very low sound) to about 20,000 Hz in children, but after childhood most people experience a progressive loss of high-frequency hearing, so that most adults cannot hear sounds above 16,000 Hz. Many animals can hear much higher-pitched sounds than humans. Dogs, for example, can hear sounds up to 35,000 Hz, and can be trained to respond to very high-pitched whistles from a so-called 'silent' dog whistle, which humans cannot hear. Bats make use of very high-pitched sounds, hunting and navigating in near-darkness by using the echoes for location. Many people claim to be able to hear bats squeak, but almost certainly what they hear are the bats' lower-frequency sounds: the high-frequency ones are far beyond the range of the human ear.

Pitch can be investigated using musical instruments (16.3), the most useful being the guitar. The six strings of the guitar are all of the same length (compare the piano), but of different thicknesses, so they produce sounds of different pitches when they are at about the same tension. The thicker strings vibrate at a lower frequency when plucked and so produce lower notes. The pitch of the note produced can be varied in two ways: by changing tension or by changing length. The greater the tension on the string, the higher the pitch of the note it produces. Tension can be changed gradually by turning the tuning pegs, so that strings can be tuned accurately.

If the vibrating part of a string is shortened, the pitch of the note it produces will be higher. On a guitar, this is done by pressing a string down on to the finger-board behind a fret. The principle that 'the shorter the vibrating object, the higher the frequency' applies not only to stringed instruments but also to woodwind and percussion (16.3). The relationship between pitch, length and frequency in a string is quite precise. For example, the fifth string of a guitar (the sixth string is the thickest) is usually tuned to A with a frequency of 110 Hz. If the length of the string is halved by stopping it just behind the twelfth fret, the frequency of its sound is doubled to 220 Hz and the note sounded is again an A, but an octave higher.

The Doppler effect. A phenomenon concerned with the frequency of sound and often remarked on by children is the Doppler effect. If a vehicle with a siren sounding passes close to an observer who is standing still, there is a very marked pattern of change in the pitch of the sounds which are heard. The pitch rises slowly until the vehicle passes, when it suddenly falls. However, the frequency at which the siren is vibrating and the speed of sound do not change. The change in pitch is brought about by the movement of the vehicle in relation to the observer. When the vehicle is approaching, its movement means that more sound waves are reaching the observer every second than would be the case if it were at rest, so the frequency which is heard increases and the pitch rises. When the vehicle passes, the effect is suddenly reversed: because it is now moving away, fewer sound waves are reaching the ear each second, so the pitch of the notes heard is lower. The Doppler effect is also experienced when moving past a stationary sound source, for example when driving past a sounding alarm, but if the observer and the sound source are travelling at the same speed in the same direction, no change of pitch is heard.

Loudness. The loudness of a sound is related to how large a movement of air each sound wave causes. This in turn is related to how widely the object producing the sound waves is vibrating, a property known as amplitude. This relationship can be shown by plucking the bass string of a guitar. If the string is plucked lightly, the amplitude will be small, the vibration will scarcely be visible and the sound produced will be soft. Plucking the string harder, which means distorting it more, results in a much greater amplitude, clearly visible vibrations and a louder sound. Even when a very loud sound is produced the movements are very small, but a larger movement of air causes the ear-drum to vibrate more violently, so the ear is stimulated to a greater degree.

The loudness of sound is measured in decibels (symbol: dB). The decibel is a complex concept, but if the softest sound which can be heard, such as the faint rustling of leaves, is taken as 0 dB, then a whisper is about 30 dB, normal conversation

50–70 dB, a pneumatic drill and a thunderclap 100–110 dB. If sounds over 140 dB reach the ears, pain will be felt and permanent damage to the ears may result. This is perhaps not surprising when it is realized that a sound level of 140 dB represents an input of kinetic energy to the ear 10 million times greater than that of sounds at 0 dB, which can only just be heard. Even at lower levels, prolonged exposure to loud sound may cause permanent hearing loss. Some rock musicians have suffered in this way, and regular medical checks in industry should include hearing tests to monitor possible noise damage.

Quality of sound. Even when considered together, pitch and loudness are insufficient to describe accurately the great variety of sounds we hear, distinguish and recognize every day. There is a difference in the quality or timbre of sound between, say, a piano and a clarinet playing a note at the same pitch, and even more subtle distinctions between the voices of two people saying the same words. These differences in the quality of similar sounds are produced because sound waves, although it is useful to think of them as simple movements such as those we can see in a 'Slinky' spring, may be very complex. Any sound waves from a voice or instrument has a basic frequency and loudness, but superimposed on this are subtle patterns which give the particular sound its individual quality. People with normal hearing are capable of learning to tell the difference between these patterns of sound waves to a very high degree. Analysing patterns of sound requires complex equipment and is not relevant to primary science, but experiencing and learning to distinguish a wide variety of sounds is a very important part of early childhood education, not only in its own right, but also because it is closely linked to oracy, literacy and the confident use of language.

16.3: Musical instruments: a case-study

An effective way to develop the basic concepts needed to understand sound is to work with musical instruments, particularly those which children themselves play or can experience at first hand. In order to understand how an instrument works, we need to know first of all how it makes the air vibrate to produce sounds. With most instruments it is then necessary to find out how the pitch of the sound produced is changed and controlled.

Percussion instruments are those which are struck, either with hands or with beaters of some kind. In all simple percussion instruments, sound is produced by striking an elastic object (7.6). This may be a taut skin or membrane as in a drum, a thin, shaped sheet of metal as in a cymbal, a bar as in a xylophone or a tube as in tubular bells. When the object is struck, the force of the blow changes its shape. Because the material is elastic, it springs back and eventually regains its original shape, but this does not happen at once. After the blow has distorted it the object vibrates, transferring kinetic energy (12.2) to its surroundings as sound waves. The amplitude of the vibrations (16.2) and so the loudness of the sound produced diminish until the object ceases to vibrate and is at rest again.

Looking across the head of a large drum as it is struck will enable the distortion, springing back and subsequent vibration to be seen clearly. In general, the larger the diameter of the drum, the lower the pitch of the sound it produces, but if the tension on the head is increased, the pitch rises. Tuned drums (timpani) have heads whose tension can be changed so that they can be adjusted to produce differently pitched notes. The bars of tuned percussion such as xylophones and metallophones are also elastic, though they appear rigid. When they are struck they vibrate and produce sounds, but the amplitude of their vibrations is so small that they cannot be seen.

Resonance. When a large object such as a drum-head or cymbal vibrates, it produces sound waves directly, by making a large volume of air around it vibrate. Most kinds of musical instruments, however, work in a more complex way. To understand how they produce musical notes, it is necessary to investigate a property known as resonance. A good way to do this is to take a plastic drinks bottle with a standard (narrow) neck, remove the cap and hold the bottle near the top between finger and thumb. Place the lower lip on the rim of the bottle and blow across it until a musical note is produced. Notice that when the note is sounding, the air in the bottle vibrates strongly enough (i.e. with a large enough amplitude) for this to be felt by the lip and fingers. This is an example of resonance.

Resonance occurs when kinetic energy is transferred to a vibrating system (in this case, the bottle and the air in it) at what is known as its natural frequency. The natural frequency of a plastic bottle can usually be heard by tapping the bottom of it with the open palm of the hand. When a stream of air is blown across the rim of the bottle it is broken up and vibrates over a wide range of frequencies. When enough of these vibrations are at the natural frequency, which happens when the air-stream is at a particular speed, a resonance is set up and the air inside the bottle vibrates with a large amplitude. The vibrations can be felt and a loud sound, also at the natural frequency, is produced. The musical instruments whose resonance is most like that of the bottle are woodwind and brass, but the concept of resonance is also needed to explain how stringed instruments make musical sounds.

Woodwind. In woodwind instruments, a stream of air is made to vibrate and produce resonance in a variety of ways. The simplest woodwind instrument to consider is also the one with which children are likely to be most familiar: the recorder. Blowing through the slot in the mouthpiece directs a stream of air at a sharp-edged wedge. This breaks up the air-stream, causing it to vibrate over a wide range of frequencies. Some of these match the natural frequency of the air in the recorder, so resonance is set up, the recorder and the air in it vibrate strongly, and a note is heard. Placing fingers over the holes or removing them changes the length of the air-column in the recorder and so the natural frequency at which resonance occurs, so a note of different pitch is produced. Organ-pipes work in much the same way, except that their natural frequency is fixed and each pipe produces only one note.

Other woodwind instruments work in the same basic way as the recorder, but differ in the way in which the air-stream is made to vibrate and the materials of which they are made. The result is a wide range of timbres or qualities of sound. In playing the flute and piccolo an air-stream is made to vibrate by directing it across a hole, in much the same way that a note was produced in the bottle experiment (see above). In reed woodwinds, the airstream is directed at the very thin edge of a 'reed' made from cane. The clarinet and saxophone have a single reed, fixed to a mouthpiece and controlled by pressure from the lips and teeth. The oboe, cor anglais and bassoon have a double reed, again held and controlled by pressure from the lips.

Both flutes and reed instruments have a very wide range of pitch. To achieve this, the player must not only change the length of the air-column by fingering, but also change the range of frequency at which vibrations are produced in the air-stream. In the flute this is done by varying the speed of the air-stream and in reeds mainly by varying the pressure on the reed.

Brass. In brass instruments the air-stream is made to vibrate by passing it through the lips which are compressed into a conical mouthpiece. The main part of the instrument is a metal tube which widens from the mouthpiece to the bell at the end, and which is coiled to make it easier to play. It has a range of natural frequencies and can be made to resonate at different ones by producing different frequencies at the mouthpiece. This is done by varying the speed of the air-stream and the pressure on the lips. A natural brass instrument such as the bugle is limited to its natural frequencies, so it cannot play all the notes in the scale. Modern brass instruments such as the trumpet, however, incorporate extra air-ways and valves so that complete scales can be played, and the trombone has a sliding tube so that its length can be varied.

Strings. The simplest stringed instrument to consider is again likely to be very familiar: the Spanish or classical guitar. When a taut string is plucked and released, it vibrates because it is elastic. Unlike a drum-head, the string is so small that it makes only a very small volume of air vibrate, so the sound produced by a string alone is so soft as to be almost inaudible, though it will go on vibrating for a long time. To make a note which can be used musically the string has to set up a resonance, and this is done in the hollow body of the instrument. In the guitar, vibrations from the strings are transferred to the body by the bridge, to which the strings are tied. This sets up resonance in the air within the body and the body itself, so a musical note is produced.

The guitar and other stringed instruments have their characteristic shapes because the body and the air within it has to respond and resonate to a wide range of frequencies, so that whichever string is played a musical note of good quality will be produced. The pitch of an open (unfingered) string is fixed, but notes of different pitch are made by fingering the string and so shortening the length which vibrates (16.2).

The main limitation of strings is that if plucked, as in the guitar and harp, or hammered as in the piano, the amplitude of their vibration is quickly reduced as kinetic energy is transferred to the resonating body, so the note fades away. The result is that while short, repeated notes can be played, very long and sustained notes cannot. This limitation has been overcome in the violin family and the double-bass by bowing. The bow is a springy stick carrying a flat band of horsehair which can be tightened. The horsehair has a rough texture and is coated with rosin (powdered pine resin) to give it a high-friction contact with the strings. When the bow is drawn across a string, the bow-hairs grip the string and pull it to one side until it springs free and straightens itself. This happens very rapidly, so the string responds as if it were being plucked many times a second, and a steady vibration is set up. The bow provides a means of transferring kinetic energy to the string continuously, so that with skilful bowing the musical note can be prolonged indefinitely, though short, repeated notes can also be played by separate movements of the bow.

16.4: Noise pollution and soundproofing

Unwanted noise intrudes on the lives and work of many people, including children and teachers in school and at home. At very high levels, sound can cause damage to the ears and loss of hearing (16.2), but even at lower levels, noise in the home or a workplace such as a classroom increases stress and reduces concentration. Unwanted noise intruding into living space, for example from road traffic, aircraft or loud music played by neighbours, can make the most comfortable environment unbearable. Unwanted and intrusive noise should be regarded as a form of pollution which, while it does not physically threaten people's well-being, can seriously diminish their quality of life.

Children in a noisy environment can learn about noise pollution simply by listening to noise around them and comparing noise levels indoors with those outdoors, and with doors and windows open and shut. Tape recorders can be used to make simple comparisons between noise levels at different places and times. Once noise is recognized as a problem, attention can be turned to possible courses of action. Within the environment as a whole, noise prevention is not usually something which individuals can achieve, though children should be made aware of it. Legal limits on vehicle and aircraft noise do already exist, but they limit the severity of the nuisance rather than eliminating it. The same is true of restrictions on traffic and aircraft flights: they transfer the problem but do nothing to solve it. Within buildings, much can be achieved by consideration and co-operation, but often this is not enough: we have to turn from prevention of the nuisance to minimizing it.

Soundproofing. Minimizing the effects of noise pollution usually means using some form of soundproofing. Sound waves have kinetic energy, and are transmitted through air. The basic principle of soundproofing is to ensure, as far as possible, that this kinetic energy is transferred to some object or system before it reaches our ears.

This usually means placing a barrier between the source of the intrusive sound and the people whom it disturbs, which will absorb the sound waves rather than transmitting them. The simplest method of making a noise barrier is to equip workers in a noisy environment with ear-muffs (rather like large headphones) or ear-plugs made from plastic foam material. These are very effective at preventing ear damage from high noise levels, but can make communication difficult and in any case do nothing to solve the problem of noisy working conditions.

The most common effective solution to noise pollution (apart from prevention) is to place a soundproof barrier around the environment which requires protection. Some everyday building materials do this very effectively. For example, a brick wall 250 mm thick will reduce sound levels by about 50 dB, which means that the sound of a car 10 m away would be reduced to the level of someone whispering near the listener. A double layer (cavity) wall with insulating foam in the cavity is even more effective. Unfortunately, windows are much less effective as soundproofing barriers than walls are, since a single glass window reduces noise only by about 15 dB. The effectiveness of the window as a noise barrier is doubled by double-glazing, with two sheets of glass tightly sealed 100 mm apart, and windows of this kind are used in high-speed trains and aircraft as well as in buildings.

Children's own investigations into soundproofing can take two forms. The simpler is to compare the effectiveness of materials as noise preventers, for example by packing a material round a buzzer in a box (with battery and switch outside), and finding out how far away the buzzer can still be heard in a quiet room. Using a variety of materials for the packing will give a rough comparison of their effectiveness as soundproof barriers. The slightly more elaborate version uses a tape-recorder with a detachable microphone, together with an audio system. The microphone is put into a box and packed round with the material under test. The tape-recorder is then switched on while recorded music is played at a certain volume, with the loudspeaker a measured distance from the box. The procedure is repeated for different packing materials but with all other conditions the same. The tape-recordings then give a comparison of the soundproofing qualities of the different packing materials.

17
Light

17.1: Light and vision

Light is the form of radiant energy (12.2) to which our eyes respond. The light we see is just one component in a very wide range or spectrum of radiant energy. Other forms which children are likely to encounter include radio waves in the form of signals for radio and television broadcasts, microwaves used in cooking, infra-red radiation from hot objects which may be felt when it heats the skin, and X-rays used for medical diagnoses. Although visible light is such a small part of the whole range of radiant energy, it is of great importance because response to it is the basis of vision, the sense through which most people gain the greatest amount of information about the world in which they live. This means that the concepts and language used to investigate and communicate about light are important not only in science but in the whole of the primary curriculum.

At primary level, investigations into the behaviour of light are based on an understanding of two of its fundamental properties. The first is that light is a form of energy which travels. This concept underlies an understanding not only of how we see, but also much of what we see, including shadows, reflections and the bending of light (17.2–17.7). The other fundamental property is that light varies not only in amount or intensity, but in kind or quality. The rainbow is a natural demonstration that there is a range of different kinds of light, which we perceive as colours (17.8).

Light as energy which travels. When light is emitted it travels outwards from its source, but we do not experience light as something which moves because its speed is much too great to be perceived. Light travels at 300,000 km, or over seven times the distance round the Earth, each second. Light from the Sun reaches the Earth across 150 million km of space in about eight and a half minutes. The very high speed of light means that, for any practical purpose on Earth, the time taken for it to travel local distances is too small to be detected or measured. As far as our experience tells us, light arrives at the same instant it is emitted. An example of this is the time-lag between seeing a flash of lightning and hearing the thunder which it causes (16.1).

Although we do not experience light as something which moves, the fact that it travels can be established by applying simple logic to everyday experience. Imagine entering a room in darkness and switching on the light. Closing the switch causes current to flow in the circuit and the electric lamp to heat up and emit light. If light did not travel away from its source, it would be impossible to detect whether closing the switch had caused any change. It is only because light travels from objects to our eyes that we can see anything. This may sound so obvious as to be trivial, but seeing is for most people so habitual that an experiment such as switching on a light, where a person causes a change and then observes the result, is needed to make them think about their own experience and what it means. This is important in helping to develop a scientific understanding of light and vision.

Concepts of vision. The generally accepted concept of vision is that light emitted or reflected from objects (12.2) travels to and enters the eye. Light entering the eye is focused by the curved front of the eyeball and the lens behind it, to form an image on the layer of light-sensitive cells (retina) inside the back of the eye. These respond to light falling on them by sending complex patterns of nerve signals to the brain, which uses the incoming information to build up an image of what is seen (3.10).

The modern concept of vision is essentially the same as that held by the School of Democritus in Ancient Greece. At the same period, the School of Pythagoras held an alternative concept which most children and a significant proportion of adults still hold today. This varies in detail, but usually centres around the belief that there is light in the eye and that in order to see an object it is necessary to send out a beam of light from the eye. This is usually coupled with the belief that the light which is sent out then comes back to the eye, so giving information about what is being looked at. Intuitive concepts of vision are important because they are very persistent and, if left unchallenged, make it much more difficult for children (and adults) to investigate and understand how light behaves.

A very useful device for developing a simple scientific concept of vision is the dark-box, which uses the same logic employed earlier to argue that light travels. The dark-box is essentially a model of a darkened room with an electric light inside and spy-holes which can be opened and closed by moving simple shutters (Fig. 17.1). The box can be used both to find out what children's current concepts of vision are, and to develop them beyond the intuitive view. The way the dark-box is used must depend on the concepts and understanding of the children who use it, but it makes two essential observations possible. The first is that nothing can be seen in the dark; the second is that something can be seen in the box only as a result of an action which either causes light to be generated (switching the lamp on) or allows light in from outside (opening a shutter). The logical conclusion is that seeing does not happen as a result of the eye doing something to what lies outside it, but because light from outside comes into the eye.

17.2: Sources, reflectors and transmission of light

All the things we see can be classified into one or other of two groups: those which emit light and those which do not. Light sources (luminous objects) transfer energy in the form of light to their surroundings (12.2), and they can be seen because some of the light they emit travels from them to the eye. Luminous objects use a variety of energy sources. In the Sun, for example, it is nuclear energy; in electric lamps, electrical energy; in a candle-flame, chemical-potential energy and in sparks from steel on a grindstone, kinetic energy. Objects which do not emit light are non-luminous. If a non-luminous object can be seen, this is only because light from a luminous object reaches it and is reflected or scattered from it into the eye. Any non-luminous object which can be seen is therefore a reflector of light, and the overwhelming majority of objects which we see are reflectors of this kind.

The difference between light sources and light reflectors can be seen very clearly by contrasting the visible properties of the Sun and Moon (18.1), but more conveniently by using a dark-box (Fig. 17.1). When switched on, the electric lamp in the box is luminous: it emits light, some of which travels directly to the eye, so it can be seen. In contrast, a non-luminous object placed in the box emits no light and cannot be seen until light is made to fall on it, by switching on the lamp or removing a shutter to allow light in from outside. It can be seen only when light from the lamp or outside the box is reflected from it into the eye.

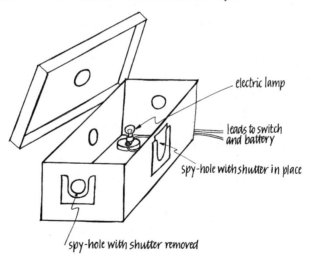

The inside of the box and lid should be painted matt black.

Figure 17.1 Dark-box

Transmission of light. Unlike sound waves (16.1), light needs no material medium in order to travel away from its source. For example, light from the Sun reaches the Earth across 150 million km of space, which is almost entirely empty of material.

Another way of saying this is that light can be transmitted through a vacuum. Light can also be transmitted through some materials.

When light travels from a light source or a reflecting object to the eye, it has to travel through air, and often through other objects as well, for example glass windows. Materials can be classified into three groups, according to the way in which light passes or fails to pass through them. Materials which allow no light to pass through are opaque: light falling on them is either absorbed (17.5) or reflected (17.7). Materials through which distant objects can be seen clearly are transparent. Those through which some light can pass, but through which distant objects cannot be seen clearly, are translucent.

These three concepts are useful for simple descriptions and everyday communication, but in practice there are no sharp divisions between them, so they cannot be employed where a precise description of properties is needed. For example, it may be difficult to determine whether a material is opaque or not. Thin black polythene sheet may appear opaque in ordinary light conditions, but in intense light, such as that from an overhead projector, it can be seen that it does allow some light through. Similarly, the idea of transparency may not be as simple to children as it seems to adults, because they often take 'transparent' to mean 'colourless', and so may not regard coloured plastic and glass bottles as transparent, although they are.

Transparency, translucency and scattering of light. When light travels through transparent materials, it does so with a minimum of interference. As a result, we see a sharp image of what lies on the far side of the material, as when looking through thin plain glass, plastic or air. The image may be distorted by refraction (17.6) but is still sharp. The transparent material may be coloured, but this means only that it absorbs part of the light passing through it (17.8), and it does not interfere noticeably with the remainder. In contrast, translucent materials such as tracing paper or foggy air allow light to pass through them but scatter some or all of it in many different directions. The effect of slight scattering is that sharp images are lost and what we see appears fuzzy, with distant objects or light sources being affected most. A greater degree of scattering means that distant objects cannot be seen at all, as when looking through tracing paper or walking in very dense fog.

Some translucent materials children use can cause confusion. When looking through a tracing sheet, for example, distant objects cannot be seen at all, whereas images on paper in contact with the tracing sheet can be seen clearly. This does not mean that the tracing sheet is transparent. It is translucent, but when it is in contact with the paper, scattering of light is greatly reduced and a more or less clear image can be seen through it.

17.3: The direction in which light travels

The concept that light is a form of energy which travels away from its source is basic to any understanding of its behaviour. In order to understand and predict the behaviour of light, however, this basic idea has to be developed a little further to include the direction in which light travels. Light beams passing through air can often be seen from the side because some light is scattered from suspended dust or smoke particles. As a result, it is often possible to see that beams of light travel in straight lines. Examples include sunbeams through gaps in cloud, car headlights in fog, theatre lights and the beam from a slide projector in a darkened room. Such simple observations are examples of the principle that light travels in straight lines unless it is prevented from doing so.

To demonstrate that light travels in straight lines requires careful observation and some simple logic, but can be done on a small scale using the principle of sighting-poles. Two thin, straight canes or dowels are placed on marks on the floor at either end of a large room. By sighting as near floor level as possible, a third cane is placed about halfway between and exactly in line with the first two, and its position marked. A thin string is then stretched taut between the two end marks, showing the shortest path and therefore a straight line between them. The third mark will, if the sighting and marking were accurate, lie on the same straight line. Since the sighting was done using light travelling from the distant cane to the near one and the observer's eye, the line of sight and therefore the direction of the light must itself have been a straight line.

Although the principle that light travels in straight lines is important as a sort of baseline for thinking about how light behaves, the most interesting observations and investigations are made when it is prevented from moving in this way. Apart from scattering (17.2), this can happen in three main ways which children can investigate, depending on the properties of the material upon which the light falls or through which it passes. First, some or all of the light may be absorbed by the material, and transferred as other forms of energy (17.5). Secondly, the light may be bent from its straight line path by passing through different transparent materials, such as air and water, a change known as refraction (17.6). Thirdly, the light may be reflected from surfaces on which it falls and travel away in other directions (17.7).

17.4: Shadows

The principle that light travels in straight lines also makes it possible to explain the formation and properties of shadows. A shadow is simply part of a surface on which less light falls than on the areas around it, because light travelling towards it has been obstructed, and either absorbed or reflected. An area in shadow appears darker than the area around it because less light is reaching it, so less light is reflected from it into the eye of the observer. When investigating shadows, four properties may be observed and considered: size, shape, depth or intensity and how sharp or diffuse the edges are. As so often happens in science, the simplest case of shadow formation is the most artificial, and most of the examples encountered in everyday experience are more complex.

Shadow formation using a point source of light. The most easily understood case of shadow formation occurs when light is emitted from a very small or point source. The most convenient point source for primary science is a torch lamp in a holder and without a reflector, though it must be used in a well-darkened room to be effective. Light from the lamp filament travels out in all directions. If an opaque object such as a shape cut from card is placed between the lamp and a screen or wall, it will cast a shadow with the same shape as itself and with very sharp edges. If either the lamp or the object is moved, the size of the shadow will change, but its sharpness will not. Fig. 17.2 shows how this can be explained in terms of light rays travelling in straight lines. By using diagrams drawn accurately to scale, it is possible to predict the size of shadow an object will cast when it is at various distances from the lamp and screen.

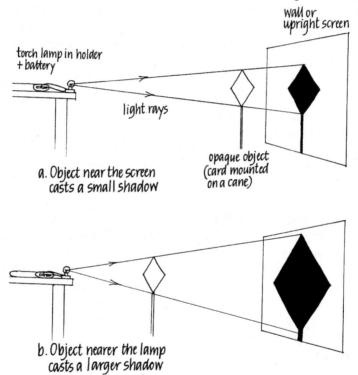

Figure 17.2 *Shadows from a point source of light: because light travels in straight lines, moving the object (or the lamp) causes the size of its shadow to change, but the edges of the shadow remain sharp.*

Shadow formation using an extended source of light. Most light sources are much larger than point sources such as torch lamps. They are known as extended light sources, and shadows of a different kind are produced when their light is obstructed. An ordinary 60W pearl electric lamp is a good extended light source for investigations. This should be used in a holder screwed to a baseboard, without a shade or reflector and taking care that children do not touch the lamp, which will become hot in use.

    When light from an extended source falls on an opaque object very near a screen or wall, a fairly sharp shadow is cast (Fig. 17.3a). As the object is moved away from the screen, the shadow increases in size but also becomes blurred at its edges, so that there is full shadow in the centre, surrounded by a less dark, partly shadowed zone (Fig. 17.3b). Because light travels out in straight lines from all parts of the lamp, the paths of light rays from different parts cross each other. As Fig. 17.3a shows, when the object is very near the screen, light rays which cross at its edges have such a short distance to travel before they meet the illuminated surface that the partly shadowed zone is narrow and the shadow appears fairly sharp. When the object is moved away from the screen (Fig. 17.3b), the crossing rays have further to travel behind it, so the partly shadowed zone becomes wider and the shadow appears very fuzzy and indistinct in outline.

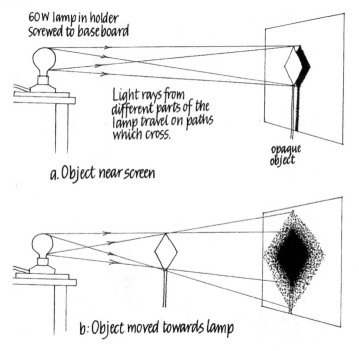

Figure 17.3 *Shadows from an extended source of light: when the object is near the screen there is little room for light rays to cross before they reach the screen, so the shadow is fairly sharp. When the object is further away the shadow is larger. There is much more room for the crossing rays to move apart so the shadow is fuzzy. The full shadow is surrounded by a zone of part shadow.*

Shadows in sunlight. Shadows cast in sunlight present a different combination of properties. The Sun is a very large object, so that although it is very distant it acts as an extended source of light, not as a point source. This can be seen by holding an object close to a sunlit wall to cast a sharp shadow, then observing the changes in the shadow as the object is moved further away (Fig. 17.4). The shadow becomes blurred as a zone of part shadow forms at its edges, but the size of the full shadow in the middle does not change (contrast Fig. 17.4 with Fig. 17.3).

The Sun is so far away that rays of light from any part of it are travelling on almost parallel paths when they reach the Earth. But the Sun is also a very large object, so rays of light reaching Earth from its edge (as we see it) are not travelling in exactly the same direction as those from its centre. The result is that the Sun is an extended light source, so that moving an object away from a sunlit surface allows light rays moving in different directions to form a diffuse zone of part shadow, while the full shadow remains the same size (Fig. 17.4b). Eclipses of the sun are very large-scale examples of shadows in sunlight which involve both full and part shadow (18.3).

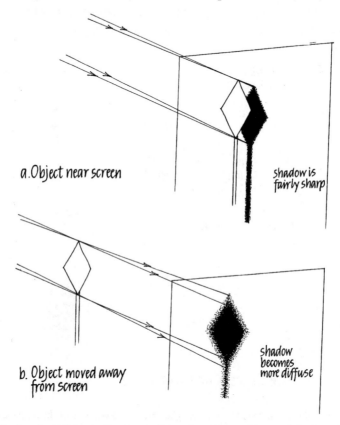

a. Object near screen   shadow is fairly sharp

b. Object moved away from screen   shadow becomes more diffuse

Figure 17.4 *Shadows in sunlight: the Sun is very distant but also very large, so light from different parts of it reach the Earth at slightly different angles. This means that the Sun is an extended light source, not a point source. As the object is moved away from the screen, the size of the full shadow does not change, but the part shadow caused by crossing light rays makes a diffuse zone round it.*

Shadows in classrooms, which children will see very frequently, may appear complex because they are blurred and indistinct, but usually are not difficult to understand. There are two main kinds, depending on whether light is coming through windows or from artificial lighting. When sunlight is obscured by cloud, the cloud becomes in effect a very large extended light source. The window allows light into the room from many different directions, some of which will be reflected from the walls and ceiling. This means that any point in the room is being illuminated from many different directions at once. The result is that an opaque object has to be very near a surface to cast any full shadow. Even at the end of a room farthest from the window, shadows will be diffuse, and the nearer the observer moves to the window, the more indistinct they will become.

Well-designed artificial lighting has exactly the same effect, even though most of the light comes from above rather than from the side. Ideally, overhead lighting should allow no shadows at all, so that light conditions remain the same over the whole room and however children are working. This is impossible in practice, but well-positioned fluorescent tube lights, coupled with reflection from the ceiling and walls, should ensure that light reaches the working area from many different directions, so that under normal working conditions all shadows are very diffuse.

Shadows, time and the seasons. Because light travels in straight lines, changes in the position of the Earth's surface in relation to the Sun can be followed on a sun-lit day by means of shadows. The simplest way of doing this is to fix a straight rod upright on a level surface and mark the end of its shadow throughout the day, together with the time of each record. A particularly useful method is to drill an exactly vertical hole near the middle of one side of a 50 x 50 cm square of block-board, and glue into it a dowel about 30 cm long, shaped to a point at its tip. Permanent records of shadows can then be made on paper attached to the board.

As the Earth rotates (18.2), both the direction and the length of the shadow change, providing an opportunity to develop the concept that the direction of sunlight is constant, and that it is the Earth which is moving, not the Sun. The relative lengths of shadows and the pattern they form throughout the day varies with the seasons, though the shadow is always longest in the morning and evening and shortest about mid-day. The other constant factor is that the shortest shadow on any day always points due north.

At any particular time of year, plotting the pattern of shadow at fixed intervals during the day will produce a simple solar clock, which can be used for a few days afterwards to tell the time if the weather is sunny and the board's position has not been changed. Over longer periods, however, it will begin to show an error, because the earth's orbit round the Sun (18.2) is not quite circular and solar time runs alternately faster and slower than standard time. For the same reason, making any kind of solar clock or sundial which will be accurate throughout the year is a complex undertaking. A simple sundial, even when accurately made and set up, shows correct standard time on four days of the year only: 16 April, 14 June, 1 September and 24 December. On any other day, corrections have to be made according to a graph known as the Equation of Time.

17.5: Absorption of light

Any light falling on a material which is neither transmitted through it (17.2) nor reflected from it (17.7), is absorbed by it. If a material could absorb all the light falling on it, it would reflect no light at all and so would be perfectly matt black, whereas one which absorbs very little light is white, and shades of grey are in between. If a material absorbs more of some colours than others, the light it reflects will appear coloured (17.8).

Light is a form of radiant energy, so when a material absorbs light, energy is transferred to it. In most materials all the radiant energy is transferred as thermal energy (12.2), so the material is heated and its temperature rises (12.3). In some materials, however, some of the light energy absorbed is transferred as other forms of energy. The two examples of this which children will encounter are solar panels and plants. Solar panels transfer about 10 per cent of the radiant energy falling on them as electrical energy. They are already in widespread use on a very small scale in so-called 'solar' watches and calculators, on a larger scale in satellites and space-stations, and increasingly as a renewable energy source (12.4).

Solar panels may in the future be an important source of energy, but far more important on a worldwide scale is the absorption of light by plants, in the process of photosynthesis by which they make their own food materials (4.4). In this process, some of the light energy absorbed is transferred as chemical-potential energy (12.2) in substances such as sugars. Plants neither absorb nor use all the light falling on them. Most plants are green because they absorb red and blue light for photosynthesis and reflect the green light (17.8). Almost all life on Earth depends on photosynthesis and therefore on light energy from the Sun, because it is the only large-scale way in which energy can be transferred to the biosphere and food-chains (5.7). Fossil fuels such as coal and oil, formed by incomplete decay of plants and animals in the past, are also indirect products of light absorption by photosynthesis.

17.6: Refraction

If a material is colourless and transparent, as air and water are, it might be thought that it would transmit light without changing it in any way. Many everyday observations, however, show that this is not so. Examples include the shimmer in the air above a road or car on a hot day, and the distortion and appearance of movement seen when looking down through moving water. These are the results of the bending of light by refraction.

The colourless and transparent materials with which children are most familiar are air, water, glass and plastics such as 'Perspex'. When light travels from one transparent material to another, for example from water into air, its speed changes. The speed of light is usually quoted as being 300,000 kms^{-1} (kilometres per second), but this is its greatest speed, which occurs only when light is passing through a vacuum such as outer space. When passing through transparent materials light travels more slowly, and different materials slow it to differing degrees. Of those mentioned, glass and 'Perspex' slow light down most, water slows it down rather less and air very little.

When the speed of light is changed by passing from one transparent material to a different one, the light is said to be refracted. The usual result of refraction is that the light is bent out of its straight-line path. This bending of light gives rise to many effects which not only make it possible to observe refraction, but which also are of great importance and interest both scientifically and in everyday life. The only situation in which refraction does not result in bending is when light strikes the boundary between two transparent materials at a right angle.

Basic observations. As in the formation of shadows (17.4), the simplest and most easily understood examples of refraction are the most artificial: real-life examples are usually more complex. Basic observations can most easily be made using a cuboidal block of glass or 'Perspex' whose sides have been accurately ground flat and polished. A good if less convenient substitute is a cuboidal box of thin, transparent plastic partly filled with water, in which the water acts as the main refracting material. Refraction can be observed simply by holding the block or box horizontally at eye level and looking through two parallel faces at vertical edges such as the sides of a window or door. The part of the edge seen through the refracting material appears to be out of place. Such displacement or distortion occurs in all the examples of refraction children are likely to investigate, so it is important to understand it.

When we learn to see, usually in very early childhood, we learn to interpret what is seen in terms of light travelling in straight lines. As long as the light reaching the eyes is travelling in straight lines we are not aware of any distortion: things appear to have the shapes and to be in the places where memory or other evidence (such as touch) tells us they really are. If the light reaching the eyes has been prevented from travelling in straight lines, however, there is likely to be a mismatch between what we see and the world as we know it to be: the image is displaced or distorted. We know the edge of a window or door is an upright straight line, but when seen through a glass block or water-filled box, part of it appears out of line because the light from it is reaching the eye from a slightly different direction. The only situation in which this does not occur is when refraction does not result in bending of light, for example when looking through parallel faces of the refracting material exactly at right angles to the line of sight.

The refraction and bending of light can be seen directly, by using a torch or a special ray-box to direct a narrow beam of light through a glass block or water-filled box standing on paper. The bending of the beam can be seen clearly and it should be noticed that the direction of bending as the beam enters the material is reversed as it leaves. If special lighting is not available, refraction can be observed by drawing, which in any case has the advantages that it produces a permanent record and allows refraction to be studied in more detail.

Place a transparent block or water-filled box on paper and draw round it, then draw a straight line to the rectangle at about 60° (Fig. 17.5). Now look through the transparent material in the opposite direction, so that the line can be seen. Place a ruler so that it appears to be aligned exactly with the first line, draw along its edge and then remove the block or box. The ruler will show that the two lines are not in fact in the same straight line, although they are parallel, i.e. in the same direction. The path of light through the material can be plotted (Fig. 17.5). This shows that light travelling through the glass, plastic or water has been bent out of its straight-line path by refraction when entering the material and bent through an equal angle in the opposite direction when leaving it. This last observation is important because it shows that light is refracted not only when passing from air to glass or water, but also when passing in the opposite direction.

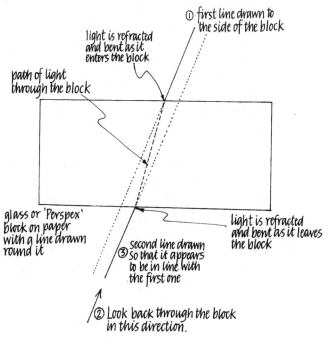

Figure 17.5 *Plotting refraction through a block of glass or 'Perspex'*

Refraction when light passes from water into air. The different kinds of distortion observed when looking into water are caused by refraction as light passes from water into air. They are of two main kinds, depending on whether the surface of the water is still or moving.

If the water is still, two main effects may be observed: displacement or distortion of shape, and a false impression of depth. A variety of distortions and displacements may be observed, especially if tanks or boxes of transparent plastic are available. The most familiar distortion is probably the 'bent stick' illusion: the apparent bending of a straight stick when placed obliquely in water. Notice, however, that when the stick is placed vertically it does not appear bent, though it will appear to be short-ened (see below). This illusion can be explained by remembering that the brain interprets what is seen as if light always travelled in straight lines, so the stick is seen in a position where, in reality, it is not (Fig. 17.6a).

An important example of the same effect is the false impression of the depth of water

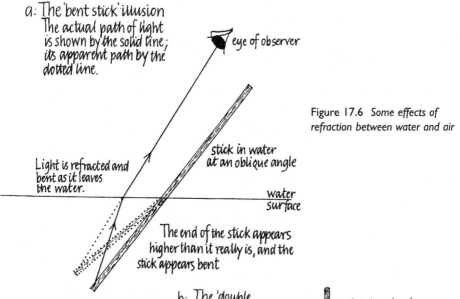

a: The 'bent stick' illusion
The actual path of light
is shown by the solid line;
its apparent path by the
dotted line.

eye of observer

Figure 17.6 *Some effects of refraction between water and air*

stick in water
at an oblique angle

Light is refracted and
bent as it leaves
the water.

water
surface

The end of the stick appears
higher than it really is, and the
stick appears bent

when looking down into it. This can be shown by placing a ruler upright in water and looking at it from an oblique angle. The ruler does not appear bent, but does seem to be much shorter than it really is, with the centimetre markings under the water appearing much closer together than those above it. The same effect can be seen by looking at the vertical side of a swimming-pool lined with square tiles. This illusion has important implications for water safety. Young children especially may happily jump or step into water much deeper than their own height, because it appears much shallower than it really is.

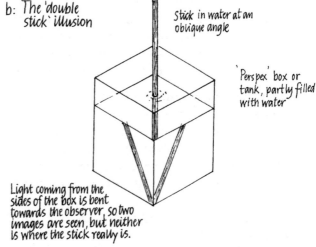

b: The 'double
stick' illusion

Stick in water at an
oblique angle

'Perspex' box or
tank, partly filled
with water

Light coming from the
sides of the box is bent
towards the observer, so two
images are seen, but neither
is where the stick really is.

Both illusions occur because the observer interprets what is seen
as if light reaching the eye were travelling in straight lines.

The use of water-filled transparent boxes makes it possible to experiment with many more illusions. A more complex example is the 'double stick' illusion shown by the sketch in Fig. 17.6b. The shape of the water-filled box means that light reflected from the stick and bent as it leaves the box reaches the eye of the observer from two directions at once. The result is that two images of the stick are seen, though neither is where the stick is in reality. The eye-brain system is 'seeing' something which the observer knows is not true; an experience which some people find mildly disturbing.

If the surface of the water is not still, what is seen when looking down through it will not only be distorted, but also appear to move. To understand why this illusion of movement occurs, imagine a stationary object under water, from which light is reaching the eye. As light passes from the water to the air above, it is refracted and bent, but because the surface is not flat and is continuously moving, the direction from which the light reaches the eye is continuously changing. As a result, the brain interprets what is seen not as a stationary object, but as a moving one. At the same time, refraction at the curved surface of the water will also cause the object to appear distorted. Again, these illusions can be seen very clearly when looking into a swimming-pool lined with square tiles.

Refraction when light passes from air to water. Light passing from air to water is refracted and bent. If the surface of the water is not still, the light passing into it will be bent in different directions. In sunlight, or where bright beams of light are projected downwards, the result is a shifting pattern of light and dark at the bottom of the water as light is bent towards some areas and away from others. This can be shown in reverse, as it were, by placing a clear plastic tray or tank onto an overhead projector and putting a thin layer of water into it. When ripples or bubbles are made on the water, the pattern of disturbance on the surface is reproduced as a pattern of light and dark projected onto the screen or wall. This is a simple version of the ripple-tank, extensively used in secondary science to investigate the properties of waves.

Refraction through lenses. Lenses are pieces of glass or transparent plastic, with curved surfaces specially shaped to refract light in particular ways. Most investigations involving lenses are beyond the scope of primary science, but some simple experiments and observations are relevant and useful. Lenses have one or both faces curved. The most familiar kind of lens has both surfaces curved outwards and is known as a biconvex lens. This is the form of the simple magnifying glass, and large hand-magnifiers, with lenses about 10 cm in diameter, are good for children to play with and observe.

A convex lens can be used to project an image of a distant object onto a surface. On sunny days, vivid images of windows and the scene outside can be projected on to paper or a white wall. The image has three important properties: it is smaller than the real object, it is in full colour (children are often surprised by this), and it is upside down. It is also noticeable that a sharp image is formed only when the lens is at exactly the right distance from the screen or wall, and parallel to it. If the lens is tilted the image is distorted, and if the lens is moved forward or back, the image becomes blurred and out of focus.

The lens forms an image in this way because its shape causes light passing through it to be bent inwards by refraction, and focused. The image is fully focused and sharp at the point where all the light rays reaching the lens from the same part of the object are brought together again (Fig. 17.7a). A camera forms an image on film in exactly the same way. This can be shown with a disused camera by putting tracing paper in place of the film, opening the shutter and pointing the camera, with its back open, towards a brightly lit scene.

A convex lens can also be used in bright sunlight as a burning-glass. The ease with which fires can be started in dry, sunny weather may make it inadvisable to introduce this topic, but if children play with lenses anyway, ignorance of the possible consequences may be more dangerous than understanding. When a lens focuses light by bending it inwards, it concentrates the light falling on it into an area much smaller than itself, which is brightly lit as a result. As well as visible light, the lens also focuses infra-red radiation. This cannot be seen, but causes any object on which it falls to be heated. When a lens is used to focus light from the Sun it produces a small, very bright image. Radiant energy, including infra-red, is transferred very rapidly as thermal energy (12.2) to the surface on which the light is focused, causing intense heating and temperatures high enough not only to burn skin, but also to set paper or dry plant material on fire.

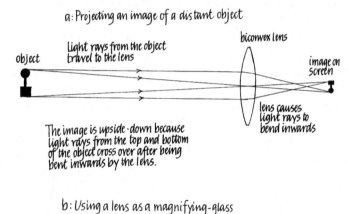

a: Projecting an image of a distant object

object

Light rays from the object travel to the lens

biconvex lens

image on screen

lens causes light rays to bend inwards

The image is upside-down because light rays from the top and bottom of the object cross over after being bent inwards by the lens.

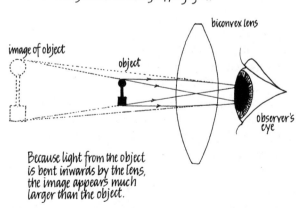

b: Using a lens as a magnifying-glass

biconvex lens

image of object

object

observer's eye

Because light from the object is bent inwards by the lens, the image appears much larger than the object.

Figure 17.7 *Experimenting with convex lenses*

The other main use children will make of convex lenses is as magnifying glasses. When used in this way, both the object and the eye of the observer are close to the lens (Fig. 17.7b). Light from the object, which is much too close to be seen clearly by the unaided eye, is bent inwards by the lens so that the eye can focus it into a clear image (see below). Because the brain interprets what is seen as if the light were reaching the eye in straight lines, the object is seen as being much larger than it really is. The light rays from the top and bottom of the object do not cross, so the image is the right way up.

Refraction in the eye. In order to see clearly, the eye has to focus a sharp image on the light-sensitive layer inside the back of the eyeball (3.10, Fig. 3.4). To do this, light has to be refracted and bent inwards as it is in a camera, but the eye and the camera work in rather different ways. The eye has a flexible lens in it, whose shape can be changed to bring about fine adjustments of focus, but unlike the camera lens it does not bring about all, or even most, of the bending of light needed to form an image. This is achieved by the clear, curved front of the eyeball. If the eyeball is slightly the wrong shape, the eye may form only a blurred or distorted image of near or distant objects. These defects are corrected by wearing spectacles or contact lenses, which bend light passing through them and so enable the eyes to focus light properly.

Children with both long and short sight may ask questions about, and enjoy experimenting with, the effects of looking through a very small hole such as a pin-hole in a piece of card held very close to the eye. In bright light, and without glasses or contact lenses, they will be able to see much sharper images than they usually can unaided. This happens because the hole in the card is making the eye work like a pin-hole camera, which can produce a sharp image without a lens. It can do this because the narrow beam of light passing through the pin-hole strikes the centre of the eyeball at right angles and travels straight to the retina with little or no bending by refraction. Because the cornea and lens affect the light very little, focusing problems are avoided. Only a little light enters the eye so the image is less bright than usual, but it is quite sharp regardless of whether the observer is long- or short-sighted.

Refraction through prisms. Prisms, like lenses, are specially shaped to refract (and sometimes reflect) light in particular ways. The most useful prisms for children to use are triangular ones with their faces at 60° to each other, made of glass or transparent plastic. These are expensive, however, and children can make quite effective prisms for themselves using water in a corner or end of a transparent plastic box. Held in different ways, these can show both of the main refraction effects of prisms (Fig. 17.8a, b). Another possibility is to obtain 90°–45°–45° prisms by dismantling disused prismatic binoculars.

Children can investigate two main effects of prisms: the displacement of images and the rainbow effect, properly known as the dispersion of light. When looking through two sides of a prism, objects will not be seen in their real positions and there may be distortion of the image as well (Fig. 17.8b). This is another example of the illusions caused by the bending of light and discussed above.

Dispersion of light, leading to the rainbow effect, is most easily seen when looking through two sides of a prism towards a window or light source. Objects seen through the prism, as well as appearing displaced, appear to have fringes of rainbow colours round them. This is caused by the separation of white light into bands of differently coloured light by refraction and bending. This effect can easily be observed, but to see clearly how it comes about, a ray-box and a glass prism are needed, as discussed in connection with colour (17.8).

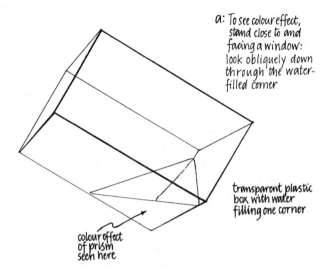

a: To see colour effect, stand close to and facing a window: look obliquely down through the water-filled corner

transparent plastic box with water filling one corner

colour effect of prism seen here

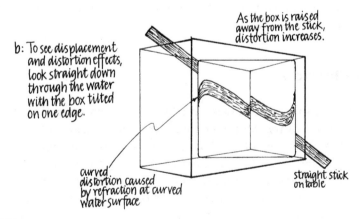

b: To see displacement and distortion effects, look straight down through the water with the box tilted on one edge.

As the box is raised away from the stick, distortion increases.

curved distortion caused by refraction at curved water surface

straight stick on table

Figure 17.8 *Making water prisms*

Refraction in air: distortions and mirages. Because air slows down light very little, there is usually no obvious refraction as light passes through it. When there is little or no wind, and especially in very hot or very cold conditions, layers or pockets of air may form, which are either much hotter or much colder than the air above or below them. If light passes at a shallow angle through layers of air at different temperatures it will be refracted and bent. The commonest example of this is the magnification and distortion of the Sun's image as it sets on a clear, calm evening. At such a time, light from the Sun travels at a shallow angle through layers of air near the Earth's surface, as these are cooling down. This causes refraction and bending of the light, so that the image of the Sun is not only magnified but often distorted as well. (The colour effect of the sunset is discussed in section 17.8.) The other common example of atmospheric refraction in temperate climates is heat shimmer, usually seen as a wavering distortion above hot surfaces such as car roofs or tarmac roads on hot, sunny days. A similar effect may be seen in the hot plume of exhaust gases from a jet aircraft taking off, or even from a large lorry, especially on a still, cold day. It is caused by refraction as light passes through the layer or plume of heated air. The shimmering effect is caused by turbulence as the hot air mixes with the cooler air around it.

Mirages are much less common in temperate climates. In a heat mirage, light from the sky is bent upwards towards the eye of the observer as it passes through a layer of heated air near the ground, so that an illusion is produced, for example of shimmering water on the surface of the land. Sometimes vehicles can be seen apparently reflected in a mirror-like surface of a very hot tarmac road, but this is another form of heat mirage, caused by refraction. Mirages of a different kind occur when layers of cold air form, often above very cold water, or ice in polar regions. Cold mirages bend light downwards, sometimes for long distances around the curvature of the Earth, so that it is possible to see objects which are below the observer's horizon and so normally invisible. Outside the very cold regions of the world such mirages are rare, but occasionally mountains or islands hundreds of kilometres away can be seen. There is, for example, reason to believe that Greenland had been seen from Iceland in cold mirages before Viking explorers set out on the very difficult voyage between the two islands.

17.7: Reflection

Objects which do not themselves emit light (non-luminous objects) can be seen only because some of the light which reaches them is reflected from them into the eye. Reflection always involves changing the direction of light, but the way in which this happens, and so the appearance of objects and materials, depends on the properties of their reflecting surfaces. Under the microscope it can be seen that matt (non-shiny) surfaces are quite rough, even though they may appear smooth to the unaided eye. When light falls on a matt or rough surface, some of it is absorbed (17.5) and some reflected, but the roughness means that as the light is reflected it is also scattered in many different directions. As a result the surface appears dull rather than shiny, and no 'picture' or image can be seen in it. This kind of reflection is known as diffuse or non-specular (not mirror-like) reflection.

If the surface is very smooth, as in the case of water, glass or polished metal, there is very little scattering of light, so the surface appears shiny and images can be seen in it. This kind of reflection is known as regular or specular (mirror-like) reflection. The difference between diffuse and regular reflection can easily be shown by holding a mirror and a piece of white card upright on a sheet of white paper, and directing a narrow beam of light at each in turn. When the beam falls on the mirror it is reflected with very little scattering, still as a narrow beam. When the beam is directed at the card, however, scattering causes the reflected light to spread out widely and become diffuse.

Mirrors. Most of the investigations on reflection which children are likely to carry out involve regular reflection and the use of mirrors. Glass mirrors are made of a sheet of glass with a very thin layer of metal deposited on one side, which is protected by an opaque layer of paint or plastic material. Flexible mirrors are made of very thin metal foil between two layers of tough, transparent plastic. In both cases, the main reflecting surface is the metal foil: the glass or plastic is simply a transparent layer which supports and protects it. Glass mirrors reflect very well with little distortion, but usually shatter if dropped and, unless ground smooth, their edges may cut the hands. These problems can largely be overcome by fixing a layer of thin, self-adhesive plastic to the back of the mirror and over its edges. Flexible mirrors are usually good when new, but are very easily scratched and rendered useless by careless handling and cleaning. They are, however, very safe and useful for experiments on distorted images. It is often necessary to hold a mirror upright on a surface. This can be done either with a bulldog clip or, more safely, with a pair of wooden blocks, each with a slot into which the mirror fits.

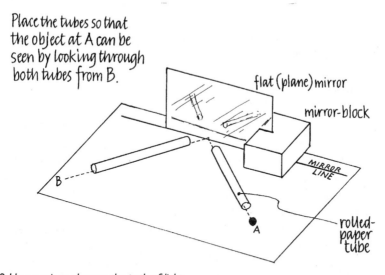

Figure 17.9 *How a mirror changes the path of light*

Reflection in mirrors: angles. When light falls on a mirror it is reflected in a very predictable way: the angle at which the light strikes the mirror and the angle at which it is reflected are the same. This can be shown most easily by directing a narrow beam of light from a masked flashlight or a special ray-box onto a flat (plane) mirror, held upright on paper. However the mirror or light are moved, the two angles are always the same. This can also be shown by plotting and drawing, which gives a permanent record. The same effect can be shown without special equipment by sighting through narrow tubes made of rolled paper (Fig. 17.9). The mirror is held upright on a baseline using a wooden block with a slot in it, or a bulldog clip. The observer moves the tubes so that the object at A can be seen by looking from B, through both tubes and the mirror. The angles between the tubes and the mirror baseline will always be the same.

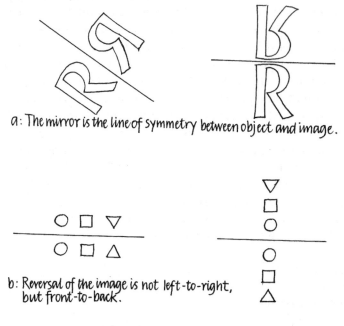

a: The mirror is the line of symmetry between object and image.

b: Reversal of the image is not left-to-right, but front-to-back.

Figure 17.10 *Mirror Images*

Because light travels in straight lines unless it is prevented from doing so, it is normally impossible to see round corners. Dentists use a mirror to overcome this problem when examining or working on parts of the mouth which cannot be seen directly, for example the teeth in the upper jaw. Mirrors can also be used to see what is behind, for example when driving, though many mirrors used in cars and lorries are not flat but curved, to give a wider field of view (see below). Devising various ways of seeing round obstacles provides useful opportunities for children to extend their understanding of reflection and the properties of mirrors. Possible examples range from simply seeing round corners using one mirror, to mazes which use three or four. All such experiments can serve to establish the principle that the angle at which light reaches a mirror is equal to the angle at which it is reflected. A mirror periscope is essentially a two-mirror maze used upright instead of on a flat surface.

The same property can also be investigated by observing images of a small object placed between two upright mirrors, with their edges touching, at differing angles to one another. When the mirrors are at right angles, two images can be seen. As the angle between the reflecting surfaces is reduced, the number of images increases because light is reflected back and forth between the mirrors before reaching the eye. When the mirrors are at 60° to each other, five images can be seen, together with the real object, and the field of view is divided into six equal sectors; an effect used in the kaleidoscope.

Reflection in mirrors: images. When we look into a mirror, what we see is so familiar that it may seem to need no explanation, but mirror images are far from easy to understand. The first concept needed to understand them is that of line symmetry. An object and its image are always symmetrical (Fig. 17.10a), with the mirror as the line of symmetry. What this means, however, is that the reversal characteristic of mirror images is not parallel to the mirror but at right angles to it. The image is not reversed left-to-right, as it is often said to be, but front-to-back (Fig. 17.10b). This can be shown and reinforced in many ways; a good example being to write in front of a mirror. When writing, the hand moves left to right, and so does its image in the mirror. The fact that it looks like someone writing with the opposite hand is irrelevant to this part of the investigation. Another way is to place a mirror parallel with the needle of a magnetic compass. In the mirror image, the north pole of the needle still points north, so left and right have not been reversed, though front and back (east and west) have.

These observations explain a property of mirrors which often puzzles children (and adults): that when a mirror is held vertically, the image appears to be reversed left-to-right, but is not upside-down. The answer is that the image is neither reversed left-to-right nor up-to-down, but back-to-front. To say that mirror images show left–right reversal is a misleading convention of language, which has grown up because we are deeply aware of the distinction between left and right in ourselves. What mirrors in fact do is show us an image of an impossible world; of what would be seen if we could look in the opposite direction at a world in which everything had been reversed left-to-right. To show this, write a word such as LIGHT in large letters on a sheet of transparent acetate (OHP) film. Hold it up in front of a mirror so that the letters look the right way round to you, then look in the mirror.

Curved mirrors. Flat (plane) mirrors form images which are reversed from front to back, but which otherwise are not distorted. Curved mirrors, on the other hand, form images in which the size, shape and orientation of the image may be quite different from reality. If flexible plastic mirrors are available, children can experiment with them and draw the distorted faces they see. These mirrors can show not only that a very small amount of curvature affects the image, but also the different effects of bulging (convex) and hollow (concave) reflecting surfaces. The images formed by different kinds of curved mirror are too complex to analyse in detail at primary level, but children may encounter two applications of curved mirrors which they can observe.

The first is a shaving mirror, which is concave. When an object is very near a concave mirror, as the face of the user is when shaving, the image of it is upright and magnified, which makes it easier to shave thoroughly without cutting oneself. It is, however, noticeable that the image of a distant object in the same mirror is upside-down and reduced. In contrast to this, a convex mirror forms an image of distant objects which is upright, reduced and also somewhat distorted. A convex mirror has the disadvantage that it makes objects seem much further away than they really are, but the great advantage of giving a wide field of view. As a result, convex mirrors are useful where a person needs to scan over a wide angle and round a corner or behind them. Many drivers prefer a convex mirror to a plane one, and large circular convex mirrors are often placed opposite concealed entrances to help drivers enter and leave safely. They are also used in buses to allow the driver to scan the whole of the inside of the vehicle without moving.

17.8: Colour

When investigating shadows, the absorption of light or its refraction and reflection (17.4–17.7), we are concerned with the amount of light, with the direction in which it is travelling, with how this can be changed and what the consequences are. When investigating colour, we are concerned with the quality of light. White light is not one kind of light, but a band of radiant energy whose different parts have slightly different properties. Normally we do not see this, and become aware of it only when the white light is separated into narrower bands which we perceive as colours.

Dispersion and the spectrum. One way in which white light can be separated into bands of coloured light is by an effect known as dispersion. When any light is split up in this way, the range of coloured light produced is known as a spectrum. Children are likely to observe the formation of a spectrum from white light by dispersion in two ways: by using prisms and by seeing a rainbow.

The simplest way to observe dispersion is to look through two faces of a 60° prism made of glass or plastic, though water prisms can also be used (Fig. 17.8). If a 60° prism is used, look through any two faces. If a 90°–45°–45° prism is used, look through two of the faces at 45° to each other. Particularly when facing a window or light source, objects viewed through the prism will appear to have coloured fringes: red to yellow on one side and blue to violet on the other. The green light in the middle of the spectrum may be difficult to see in this way, but the full spectrum can be seen by cutting a narrow (2 mm) slot in a piece of card and looking through the prism at bright daylight coming through it. The spectrum produced by dispersion of white light always has the same colours in the same order: red, orange, yellow, blue and violet. The spectrum is in fact a band of light whose properties change continuously in passing from one side to the other: it is the human eye-brain system which perceives it as being made up of distinct zones of colour.

Dispersion of white light is easily observed, but to show how it comes about requires a good 60° prism, a darkened room and a ray-box which can produce an intense, narrow beam of light. If the beam is directed through the prism as shown in Fig. 17.11, a spectrum is projected onto the screen. Looking at the prism from above, it can be seen that the light is bent by refraction (17.6) both when it enters the prism and when it leaves. The spectrum is formed because different bands of light become separated as each is bent through a slightly different angle, the red light being bent least and the violet most.

Dispersion of white light also occurs naturally when a rainbow is formed, the transparent material causing refraction being the water of falling raindrops. A rainbow will be seen only when the observer is standing between the Sun and rain falling in sunlight some distance away, facing towards the rain and away from the Sun. Raindrops are approximately spherical as they fall. Light entering the top half of a raindrop is refracted downwards, then reflected off the inside surface of the drop, back towards the observer, and finally refracted again as it leaves the drop. As in the prism, the different components of white light are refracted and bent through slightly different angles, resulting in dispersion and the formation of the spectrum. The reflection inside the raindrops directs light back to the eye of the observer. Because red light is bent less than violet, the red band of the rainbow is always on the outer side of the curve and the violet on the inner side. Sometimes a fainter, secondary rainbow is seen on the outside of the main one, and this has its colours in the reverse order.

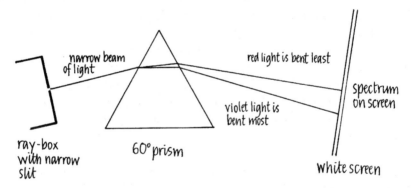

Figure 17. 11 *Dispersion of light using a prism: a spectrum is produced because light we see as having different colours is bent through different angles as a result of refraction. This results in the spectrum which we see as bands of rainbow colours*

Colours created by reflection and interference. Apart from prisms and rainbows, children are likely to encounter many natural and manufactured examples of objects which appear coloured because they create a spectrum in a different way. Examples include oil films on water, bubbles of soap or detergent solution, iridescent feathers of birds, hologram pictures and CD discs. All these objects appear coloured when viewed from certain angles, because light is reflected from their surfaces in a complex way. In an oil film or soap bubble, for example, light is reflected from both the inner and outer surfaces of the liquid film, which are only about a thousandth of a millimetre apart. The two beams of reflected light interact with each other (this is called interference) and bands of coloured light are produced as a result. The shifting pattern of colours on an oil film or bubble is caused by movements and slight changes in the thickness of the reflecting layer. Holograms, CD discs and iridescent feathers also produce colours by interference, but as a result of very fine, regular patterns on their reflecting surfaces.

Colour by absorption: coloured objects. Most of the colour we see in everyday life is not produced by dispersion or interference. Objects and materials which appear to have a colour of their own, such as leaves, bricks, cars, people, clothes and paints, interact with light in a different way. When light falls on a coloured object such as a green leaf, some is absorbed (17.5) and some is reflected by diffuse reflection (17.7), but the leaf does not absorb light from all parts of the spectrum equally. The leaf uses red and blue light as the energy source for photosynthesis (4.4), so the red and blue parts of the spectrum are strongly absorbed and very little of them is reflected. Green and yellow light are not used in photosynthesis and so are reflected, giving the leaf its green appearance.

The same principle is true of all coloured objects, regardless of whether they are opaque, translucent or transparent. The colours which we see are made up of the light which they do not absorb and which as a result is reflected if the object is opaque, or transmitted through if it is transparent. A red object, for example, will absorb violet, blue and green very strongly, together with some of the yellow, so that red is the colour most strongly reflected or transmitted.

Objects which absorb light from all parts of the spectrum more or less equally have no colour. If the object reflects a high proportion of the light falling on it and absorbs only a little, it appears white. If it absorbs a high proportion and reflects very little it will appear black, while materials with intermediate levels of absorption and reflection are seen as shades of grey.

Colour mixing: paints and dyes. Substances used to impart colour to other materials are of two main kinds. Pigments are insoluble solids, finely ground and made into solid sticks (pastels, pencil crayons), or carried in a medium, which may itself be solid (wax crayons) or liquid (paint). Dyes are soluble and used in solution in the form of fabric dyes and coloured inks. As far as the principles of colour mixing are concerned, pigment-based and dye-based materials are very similar.

When working with pigments and dyes, it is found that there are three colours which cannot be made by mixing other colours together. These are the so-called primary colours: red, blue and yellow. When they are mixed, other colours are produced, but this process is far from simple and occurs only because dyes and pigments themselves reflect or transmit a mixture of colours, not a single pure colour. For example, a yellow paint absorbs violet, blue and red, and reflects yellow very strongly, but also reflects quite a lot of orange and green. A blue paint absorbs red, orange and yellow and reflects blue very strongly, but also reflects quite a lot of green and violet. The only colour which neither absorbs strongly and which both reflect is green, so the result of adding blue paint to yellow is green (Fig. 17.12).

In a similar way, red can be mixed with yellow to give orange, and blue with red to give purple. Green, purple and orange are known as secondary colours. Because mixing pigments and dyes produces different colours by absorbing and removing some colours from white light falling on the material, it is known as colour mixing by subtraction.

Colour mixing by subtraction can be investigated by mixing paints, but mixing transparent dyes or inks, such as those used in felt- and fibre-tipped pens, may show more clearly how it works. The mixing of these dyes can be carried out directly by applying a layer of ink, allowing it to dry, then adding a second colour layer on top. Each layer acts as a colour filter, removing light from the white light falling on it. Because of this, colour mixing by subtraction usually gives increasingly dark-toned colours as more layers are added.

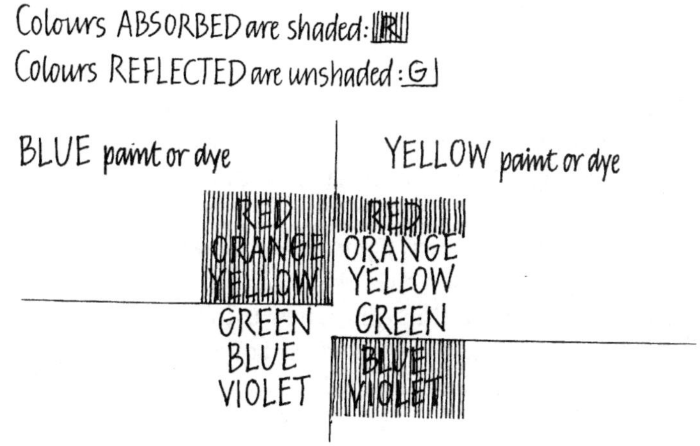

Figure 17.12 *Colour mixing by subtraction: green is the only colour reflected by both blue and yellow, so a mixture of blue and yellow appears green*

Colour mixing: coloured lights. Transparent colour filters are coloured for exactly the same reason that a dye is: they absorb some parts of the spectrum and transmit others. When white light is directed through a colour filter, the light transmitted is the coloured light we see and the remainder is absorbed by the filter. Mixing beams of coloured light, however, produces quite different results from mixing dyes or pigments.

To show mixing of coloured lights convincingly by projection, it is necessary to use a special ray-box, which produces much brighter light than flashlights or torches, together with mirrors and high-quality colour filters. The ray-box can produce three beams of light at once, and these can be overlapped on a screen in any combination by using the mirrors. The three primary coloured lights, which cannot be made by mixing other colours, are red, blue and green (not yellow). Blue and green together give a blue-green called cyan. Red and blue together give a purple-pink known as magenta. The surprise usually comes when red and green are mixed: together they produce yellow. When all three colours are directed on to the same part of the screen they produce white light, if the colour filters are well-balanced.

Mixing coloured light can also be investigated in a slightly different way using a colour TV monitor and a large magnifying glass. Ideally, the TV monitor should be controlled by a computer using an art programme, so that areas of different colours can be put on screen and examined at leisure. The screen of a colour TV has very fine vertical lines which can be made to emit light of the three primary colours: red, blue and green. From a normal viewing distance these are much too small to be distinguished, so if more than one set of lines is emitting light, the lights blend and are seen as a single colour. When using the TV to study colour mixing, a colour is put on screen and then examined with the magnifying glass to see what combination of primary colours has been switched on in order to produce it. The three primaries are each produced by one set of lines, the three secondaries (cyan, magenta and yellow) by two, and if all three sets of lines are emitting light, the screen appears white.

Safety note: This method of studying colour mixing requires children to examine a TV screen closely, but only for very short periods of time. This does not present a hazard, but they should not be allowed to look at the screen closely without a magnifying glass, or for longer than is necessary, as it may cause headaches.

In both methods of mixing coloured lights, it is noticeable that the tone of the mixed (secondary) colours is lighter than that of the primaries which produce them, while white, produced by adding the three primaries, is the lightest of all. This is because light is being added as the colours are mixed, and more light is being reflected or emitted from the screen, so the process is called colour mixing by addition.

Coloured lights and coloured objects. The colour which an object appears to be depends on the colour of the light which is reflected from it into the eye. If the light falling on an object is white, the colour of the object will be seen clearly, unless the light is very dim. If an object is lit with coloured light or viewed through a colour filter, however, its colour may appear to change. There are many ways to investigate this. A good one is to make a set of removable lids to fit on a dark-box (Fig. 17.1), each with a panel of transparent colour filter in it. Objects placed in the box can then be viewed in the differently coloured lights and their appearances compared.

Another method is to place differently coloured objects or draw coloured patterns on white paper, and observe them through coloured filters. For example, if a red object on white paper is observed through a red filter, it and the paper appear the same colour, and writing or drawing in red may become invisible. In contrast to this, a green object seen through a red filter usually appears black, because very little of the light reflected from it is transmitted through the filter. Such observations show that using colour filters in this way involves colour subtraction. Once the concept of colour subtraction is understood, children should be able to interpret their observations in a reasoned way and make accurate predictions.

Colours of the sky and sunset. Two things which are part of our everyday lives and so familiar that they are rarely questioned are the colours of the sky and the sunset yet both are remarkable phenomena brought about by the interaction between sunlight and the atmosphere. Light travels in straight lines unless prevented from doing so (17.3). Why then, when the Sun shines on our planet from a particular direction, do we receive light from the whole of the sky? And why is it blue?

To astronauts, the sky appears black: the only light they see is from the Sun and stars, or reflected from the Earth and Moon. Since we see the sky as blue, light must be coming from the atmosphere into our eyes. This happens because very small dust particles and water-droplets suspended in the air intercept some of the sunlight passing through the atmosphere and scatter it in many directions. Some of this light is scattered downwards towards the Earth's surface and this is the light we see. The sky appears blue because the atmosphere scatters blue light more effectively than red, so more of the blue light is deflected downwards. A model of light-scattering by the atmosphere can be made by putting one or two drops of milk into a glass of water. The particles suspended in the milk are small enough to scatter blue light, so when lit from the side, the mixture has a bluish tint.

At midday, the colour of the Sun is yellow-white, but as it sets this changes gradually to orange-yellow and often to a deep red-orange. This change of colour towards red as the Sun sets has exactly the same cause as the blue of the sky: the scattering of blue light by the atmosphere. To understand this, we need to remember that while the sky only scatters light, the Sun is a source of light. At sunset, light from the Sun strikes the atmosphere at a very shallow angle. This means that the light has to travel through the air for a much greater distance to reach the Earth's surface than at midday. The air tends to scatter blue light more than red, so at sunset more of the blue light is scattered and more of the red light gets through the air to the observer. The same effect can be seen in the milk-water mixture, by looking directly through the liquid at a light source. The light reaching the eye will appear much redder than normal because more of the blue light is being scattered.

18

The Earth in Space

18.1: The Solar System

The planet we live on, which we call the Earth, is one of nine planets which are in orbit round a star, which we know as the Sun. The Sun, its planets, their moons and other bodies such as comets make up the Solar System. The Sun is an unremarkable star: observations suggest that even in our own star cluster (galaxy), which we see across the night sky as the Milky Way, there are thousands of millions of stars very like it. On the scale of the galaxy, therefore, the Sun is small and ordinary, but in comparison with the planets it is huge and dominant: its mass is more than 750 times greater than that of all the planets added together. To put it another way: the Sun contains over 99.8 per cent of all the material in the Solar System.

The Sun is the only large light source (luminous object, 17.2) in the Solar System. In the innermost part of the Sun, at temperatures of around 15 million degrees Celsius, nuclear fusion occurs (12.4), in which matter is transformed into very large amounts of nuclear energy (12.2) by fusing pairs of hydrogen atoms to form atoms of helium. This is basically the same process which occurs in hydrogen bombs, and results in the transfer of very large amounts of energy to the surface of the Sun and, partly in the form of radiant energy (12.2), to the space around it. The radiant energy transferred from the Sun to the space around it includes light which we can see (17.1), which is the major energy source for the Earth. Unlike the Sun, the planets and their satellites are non-luminous. With the very minor exceptions of volcanoes on Earth, they emit no light of their own and are visible only because they reflect (17.7) sunlight falling on them.

Planets in orbit. The planets are in orbit round the Sun. To understand how they remain in orbit, it is useful to make a simple model by attaching a soft ball to a length of thread or thin string and swinging it in a circle around one's head. The ball is then moving much as an object in orbit does, but if the string breaks or is released, it flies out of its circular path and falls to the ground. This shows that for an object to stay in orbit, there must be a force acting inwards on it, preventing it from flying off in a straight line. In the model, this force is exerted by the inward pull of the thread, but in the Solar System the force keeping the planets in orbit is gravitational. The Sun is so massive that its gravitational field (15.2) can keep planets from flying off into space even when they are thousands of millions of kilometres away from it.

If the Solar System could be viewed by an observer completely outside it, it would be seen that the planets move in orbit in a very particular way. With one exception (Pluto) all the planets move as if they were on a huge flat disc with the Sun at its centre. The orbits of most of the planets have only a slight tilt to this imaginary disc, and it was because of this, and the particular positions of the planets, that the Voyager spacecraft could make close encounters with Jupiter, Saturn, Uranus and Neptune between 1979 and 1989. Astronomers call this imaginary disc around the Sun the plane of the ecliptic, and the way the Earth spins in relation to it causes the seasons we experience every year (18.4). An observer outside the Solar System would also notice that all the planets move in their orbits in the same direction: anticlockwise when viewed from above the North Pole of the Earth.

Modelling the Solar System. It is very difficult to gain an idea of the scale of the Solar System, not only because the sizes of the Sun and planets are so different, but also because the distances between the planets are very large in comparison with their diameters. Because of this, tables showing the actual dimensions of planets and their distances from the Sun (Table 18.1) may be of limited use in helping children gain any concept of the scale of the Solar System. What may be more helpful is to make a model of the Sun and at least the inner planets on a human scale. To do this, we have to scale down the Solar System enormously. A convenient model

Table 18.1 *Some basic information on the planets of the Solar System*

Name	Diameter (km)	Mass (Earth = 1)	Distance from Sun (millions of km)	Time taken to circle Sun	Number of moons
Mercury	4,878	0.06	60	88 days	0
Venus	12,104	0.82	108	225 days	0
Earth	12,756	1.00	150	365.25 days	1
Mars	6,794	0.11	228	687 days	2
Jupiter	142,800	318	778	11.9 years	16+
Saturn	120,000	95	1,430	29.5 years	22+
Uranus	50,800	14.5	2,870	84 years	15+
Neptune	49,100	17.2	4,500	165 years	8
Pluto	2,280	0.002	5,900	248 years	1

Table 18.2 *Modelling the Solar System (scale: 1 to 5,000 million); at this scale the Sun is 28 cm in diameter and can be represented by a beach-ball*

Planet	Scaled-down diameter (mm)	Suggested model	Scaled-down distance from Sun (m)
Mercury	1.	poppy seed	12
Venus	2.4	peppercorn	22
Earth	2.5	peppercorn	30
Mars	1.3	mustard seed	45
Jupiter	28.5	(clay ball)	156
Saturn	24.	(clay ball)	285
Uranus	10.3	small glass marble	574
Neptune	10.	small glass marble	900
Pluto	0.5	poppy seed	1,180

can be made 5,000 million times smaller than reality (i.e. all dimensions divided by 5×10^9). At this scale the sun can be represented by a beach-ball 28 cm in diameter. The scaled-down sizes of the planets and their distances from the Sun are given in Table 18.2, which also suggests some suitable objects to use for models of the smaller planets, Jupiter and Saturn being represented by balls of modelling clay made to size. Actually measuring out the distances on a playing-field and seeing the sizes of the planets to the same scale (at least, those from Mercury to Mars or Jupiter) will help to show how small the planets are in relation to the Solar System as a whole, and how large the distances between them are in comparison to the Earth, which seems enormous to us.

18.2: The Earth in orbit

The Earth's orbit round the Sun is almost circular, with the Sun at the centre of the circle. The orbit is actually an ellipse (an oval shape), but it is so nearly circular that the difference would be difficult to detect if both were drawn out on paper. The Earth moves round this orbit at a very high speed: about 107,000 km each hour, or nearly 30 kms^{-1}, but we are usually quite unaware of this, because we and the Moon (18.3) are carried along with the Earth, anchored to it by gravitational forces, and have no object near enough to act as a point of reference by which to judge our speed through space.

Years and days. The Earth completes one journey in its orbit round the Sun every year, and this is how our year is defined. However, as it travels in orbit, the Earth also spins. To an observer in space, the Earth would appear to be spinning slowly around an imaginary axis whose outer ends are at the North and South Poles. The observer would also notice that this axis of spin is tilted to the Earth's orbit round the Sun (the plane of the ecliptic, 18.1): this is important in understanding the seasons (18.4). As the Earth spins, different parts of its surface are turned towards the Sun. We call the time taken for one complete spin a day, although over most of the Earth this also includes the dark time we call night.

Night and day can easily be modelled using a terrestrial globe, preferably one mounted at the correct angle of spin, with the beam from an overhead projector to represent the Sun. It is important when using this model to ensure that the light source is level with the middle of the globe. At any time, it is day over the half of the Earth which is illuminated by the Sun, and night over the half in shadow. As the Earth spins, in an anticlockwise direction when viewed from above the North Pole, different parts of the Earth are carried into the path of light from the Sun, while others are carried into the Earth's own shadow and the darkness of night. For purposes of telling the time, the day is divided into 24 hours, but unlike years and days, the hour is an artificial time unit which has been in use since the fourteenth century, when mechanical clocks came into use.

Leap years and the calendar. Because they arise from the movement of the Earth in orbit and its spin, years and days are natural units of time, but there is no simple relationship between them, and a year is not made up of an exact number of days. One year is 365 days, 5 hours, 48 minutes and 46 seconds. The result is that in order to have a usable dating system or calendar, we need a system which allows for the 'extra' length of each year over and above the 365 days. The calendar in general use today is the Gregorian Calendar, introduced by Pope Gregory XIII in 1582, though not adopted in England until 1752. This is itself a refinement of the Julian Calendar introduced by Julius Caesar in 45 BC. The Julian Calendar uses the rough correction which we know as the leap year: one day (29 February) is added to the calendar every fourth year, when the number of the year can be divided by four (e.g. 1992, 1996). This slightly over-corrects the error, so the Gregorian Calendar introduced a second correction: a leap year does not occur in a centurial year (e.g. 1800, 1900) unless it is still divisible by four when two zeros have been removed (e.g. 2000, 2400).

The apparent motion of the Sun. Unless an observer on Earth makes very accurate measurements of the stars, there is nothing to show that the planet is in orbit round the Sun. The effects of the Earth's spin, however, are visible at any time of the day or night, whenever the sky is clear. The most obvious effect of the Earth's spin is the apparent movement of the Sun across the sky during the day and the resulting changes in length and direction of shadows, which are discussed in section 17.4. Careful observation of stars over a period of some hours shows that they too appear to move (18.5).

In relation to the rest of the Solar System, the Sun is a fixed, central point. It appears to move across the sky because the spinning Earth carries an observer round with it, exactly as a roundabout or carousel carries a rider. The angle from which a rider sees fixed objects distant from the carousel is constantly changing, but the angle from which the moving carousel is viewed remains the same. The result is often the illusion that the world is moving round the carousel, which seems to remain still. During a sunny day we experience the same illusion, but in a much stronger form, because the Sun seems to move in relation to all the fixed objects which we use as landmarks to orient ourselves within the world around us. Our experience is that if something changes position when we ourselves have not, it has moved, and the only exceptions to this we ever see are the Sun and, if we observe them carefully, the stars.

Showing that the apparent movement of the Sun is an illusion may take a long time, but models can be helpful. One good one is again to use a terrestrial globe lit by a horizontal beam of light from an overhead projector. The first thing to determine is which way the Earth spins. The Sun appears to move from east to west, so the Earth must be moving in the opposite direction, i.e. anticlockwise when viewed from above the North Pole. Position the globe so that the children's home country is on the boundary between light and shadow. Turn the globe a little in the correct direction. Has the place moved into light or into shadow? If into light, it was at the point of sunrise; if into shadow, at the point of sunset. Now ask the children to imagine that they are tiny people on the globe. Where would the light seem to come from, and how far above the horizon would the Sun appear to be? At sunrise and sunset, light strikes the Earth at a shallow angle: the Sun is low in the sky. As a particular place on the globe is turned from a sunrise position to a mid-day position, the angle at which light strikes that part of the Earth becomes steeper: the Sun would appear higher in the sky, and this of course is exactly what is observed in reality. In addition, the Sun appears due south at noon to an observer in the Northern Hemisphere, but due north to one in the Southern Hemisphere. On a large globe lit in this way, observations can also be made with very small shadow-sticks (short pieces of thin wire attached with masking tape), which mimic the variation in length and direction of shadows formed in sunlight using full-size shadow-sticks (17.4).

18.3: The Earth and the Moon

All the planets of the Solar System except Mercury and Venus have one or more satellites or moons in orbit around them (Table 18.1). The Earth has one satellite, which we simply call the Moon, and which is unusual in that it is very large in relation to its planet, having a diameter (3,476 km) nearly a quarter that of the Earth. The moon is held in orbit round the Earth by the Earth's gravitational field (15.2), much as the Earth and Moon together are held in orbit round the Sun. Although the Moon is large for a satellite its mass is much less than that of the Earth, so its gravitational field is much less intense: 1 kg on the Moon weighs only 1.6 N, whereas on Earth it weighs 9.8 N (15.2). One result is that the Moon has retained no atmosphere and is completely lifeless.

The average distance between the Earth and the Moon is 384,000 km, so the Moon is far closer to us than either the Sun or the nearest planet, Venus. The Moon is by far the smallest of all the objects we can see in the night sky without a telescope, but because it is so close to us it is, when it can be seen, by far the most prominent. Its nearness also means that the Moon has other effects on the Earth which children may observe: eclipses and tides (see below).

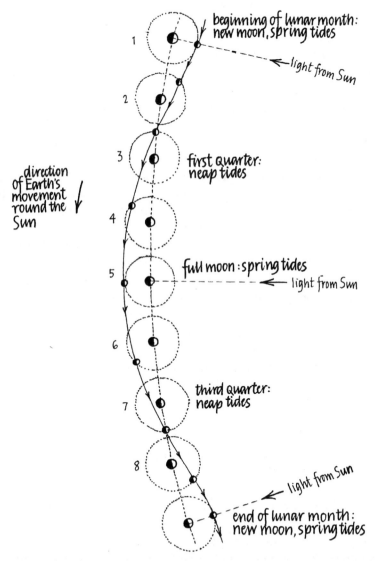

Figure 18.1 *The Moon's orbit and its path through space: the position of the Moon is shown at eight points during the lunar month. These correspond to the phases of the Moon shown in Figure 18.2. The path of the Moon through space is shown by the solid arrowed line*

The Moon in orbit. The Moon moves in orbit round the Earth once in about 28 days, a period known as a lunar month. It travels in the same direction as the Earth itself orbits the Sun: anticlockwise when viewed from above the Earth's North Pole. During each lunar month the Moon's appearance undergoes a series of progressive changes known as the phases of the Moon (see below). The Moon also spins on its axis, but it takes exactly the same time to spin once as to move once round in its orbit, so it always has the same face towards the Earth. A simple model can help to show this. Place a large ball on a table to represent the Earth. Put a mark on a small ball, which is to represent the Moon, and move it round the large one, always keeping the mark on the 'Moon' facing the 'Earth'. In travelling once round the 'Earth' the 'Moon' will also have rotated once on its axis. When using this model, care is needed to avoid suggesting that the Moon moves through space in a circular path. The Moon's orbit round the Earth is almost circular but, as Fig. 18.1 shows, its path through space is quite different because the Earth itself is in orbit round the Sun.

Phases of the Moon. During a lunar month the Moon's appearance, if it is visible, changes in a regular and predictable way. The beginning and end of the lunar month are taken to be the short period when the side of the Moon facing the Earth is wholly in shadow. Even during this period the Moon may be faintly visible if the sky is very clear, because light reflected from the Earth travels to the Moon and some of it is reflected back again as 'earthlight'.

As the Moon moves in its orbit round the Earth, the angles between the Moon, the Earth and the Sun are continually changing (Fig. 18.2). As a result, the proportions of the Moon's face in light and shadow change throughout the lunar month. This can be modelled by acting out Fig. 18.2, using a ball painted half black and half white as the 'Moon', with a window to represent the Sun. One child, acting as the Moon, carries the ball in a circle around observers who represent the Earth, but so that the white half of the ball is always directly facing the window. When the 'Moon' is nearest the window, the observers will see only the black half of the ball: this represents the new moon phase. As the 'Moon' moves round them, the observers turning to look at it will see more and more of the white face of the ball, until the 'Moon' is at its farthest from the window, when only the white half of the ball will be seen: this represents the full moon phase. Here again it may be relevant to remind children that although the Moon's orbit is nearly circular, its path through space is not (see Fig. 18.1).

Eclipses and tides. Three complex kinds of event, two rare and one which occurs every day, are the result of the Moon moving in orbit round the Earth. These are eclipses of the Moon, eclipses of the Sun, and tides in the seas. A comprehensive understanding of any of these events is far beyond the scope of primary science, but for children who observe them, simple explanations, though incomplete, are useful and interesting.

Eclipses of the Moon (lunar eclipses) occur only at full moon, on the rare occasions when the Earth moves into line between the Sun and the Moon. Because light travels in straight lines, this causes the Earth's shadow to fall on the Moon, darkening it. If only part of the Moon's face is darkened the eclipse is said to be partial, whereas if the whole face is in shadow the eclipse is total. Total eclipses of the Moon can last for several hours, unlike total eclipses of the Sun (see below). When an eclipse of the Moon occurs, it can be seen from any part of the Earth from which the Moon itself is visible, but because the Moon's orbit is tilted in relation to that of the Earth, the exact lining-up of the Earth, Moon and Sun which causes it is a rare event.

Eclipses of the Sun are actually commoner than those of the Moon, but because each one can be seen only from a fairly small part of the Earth, they are very rare

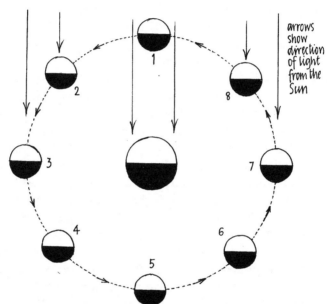

a: How the Moon and Earth would appear to an observer in space (not to scale).

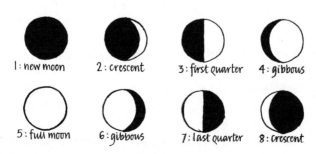

b: How the Moon appears from Earth.

Figure 18.2 *Phases of the Moon*

events in any one place. They occur only at new moon, when the Moon moves between the Sun and the Earth. Seen from the Earth, the Moon is just large enough to obscure the Sun completely and make a total eclipse for a few minutes. When this happens, a bright halo of light (the corona) can be seen around the dark disc of the Moon. When a total eclipse is seen in one part of the Earth, observers a few hundred kilometres to the north or south will see only a partial eclipse, in which the Moon does not obscure the Sun completely. For example, an eclipse in 1954 was seen as total in Sweden but only partial in Britain. The last total eclipse of the Sun visible in Northern Europe was on 11 August 1999 and the next one visible in the U.K. is not until 2090, though a partial eclipse will be visible from north-west Scotland on 20 March 2015.

Tides are the twice-daily rise and fall of the sea, which can be observed on the seashore and in harbours. Tides are caused by the changing balance between a complex set of three forces acting on the water of the Earth's oceans: the gravity of the Moon and Sun, together with an outward force caused by the way in which the Moon and Earth move around each other. The cause is complex, but the result can be described fairly simply. The forces combine to make the water in the oceans bulge out slightly, both on the side of the Earth nearest the Moon and on the opposite side. These bulges in the water are only a few metres high, and therefore very slight in comparison with the size of the Earth, but they are like two very broad, shallow waves which seem to travel round the shorelines of the world as the Earth spins, causing the water level to rise and fall. What actually happens is that the tidal bulges stay in more or less the same place during a 24-hour period while the Earth spins underneath them, so most shorelines have two high tides a day as they are carried past the bulges, and two low tides as they are carried past the slight troughs between them.

There is a longer-term pattern of tides over and above the twice-daily rise and fall, which is linked to the phases of the Moon (Fig. 18.1). At full moon and new moon, when the Moon, Earth and Sun are almost in line with each other, the range of the tides is wide: they rise higher and fall lower than the average. These are called spring tides. At the first and third quarters, when the Moon and Sun are at right angles in relation to the Earth, the range of tides is narrow, so their rise and fall are smaller than average. These are called neap tides.

18.4: The movement of the Earth and the seasons

The earth moves round the Sun in an orbit which is like the edge of a huge, imaginary and almost circular disc (the plane of the ecliptic, 18.1). This imaginary disc is also the direction in which light travels to the Earth from the Sun. As it moves in orbit, the Earth spins once a day on an imaginary axis through the North and South Poles. The Earth's axis is not at right angles to its orbit: it is tilted by almost 23½°, which is why terrestrial globes are usually mounted on a tilted stand. This means that the spin of the Earth is tilted in relation to the light reaching it from the Sun.

This in turn causes changes in the length of day and night during the year, as well as very important effects on climate, especially in the temperate and polar regions, which we call the seasons.

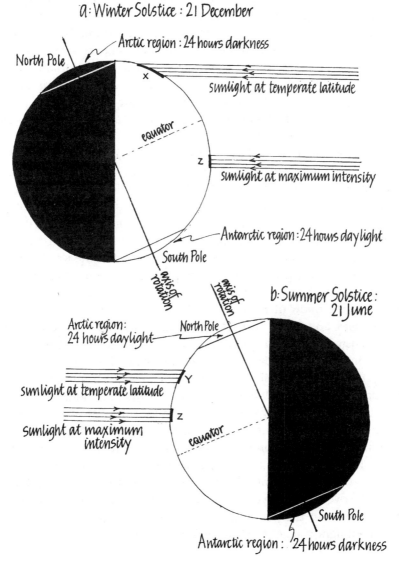

Figure 18.3 *The tilt of the Earth and the seasons*

Even though it is moving in its orbit round the Sun, the direction in which the Earth spins does not change. This is shown by the way in which the North Pole always points towards the Pole Star whatever the season of the year (18.5). Because the direction of the Earth's spin does not change, there is a time in the year when the North Pole is as far away from the Sun as possible, as shown in Fig. 18.3a. This always happens on 21 December, the Winter Solstice, which in the Northern Hemisphere is the shortest day of the year, whereas in the Southern Hemisphere it is the longest. Fig. 18.3a compares sunlight falling at maximum intensity with that falling at a north temperate latitude, about that of southern Europe or the northern USA. It shows that the angle between the sunlight and the Earth's surface is shallow at the temperate latitude: the Sun is low in the sky, even at midday. This means that, to put it very simply, the same amount of light is spread over a much larger area (X) in the temperate zone than it is in the tropics (Z). The result is that the intensity of light (i.e. the amount of radiant energy reaching each square metre of the Earth's surface each second) is much lower in the temperate zone, so the rate of energy transfer and heating by the Sun is low. A low rate of energy transfer and short days result in cold weather: it is winter.

When the North Pole is tilted as far as possible towards the Sun, which happens on 21 June, the Summer Solstice, it is the longest day in the Northern Hemisphere and the shortest day in the Southern (Fig. 18.3b). At midday, sunlight reaches north temperate latitudes at a much steeper angle than in winter, so that the same amount falls on a much smaller area (Y). As a result, sunlight is much more intense, so energy transfer and heating occur at a much faster rate than at the Winter Solstice. Long days and a high rate of energy transfer result in the weather being much hotter: it is summer in the Northern Hemisphere. All these changes occur in the reverse way in the Southern Hemisphere, where the summer solstice is on 21 December and the midwinter solstice on 21 June.

These changes, and others such as equinoxes which occur in between them, can be modelled using a terrestrial globe and an overhead projector. This can show very clearly the changes in both day-length and the angle of sunlight at midday during the year. It also makes it possible to see why polar regions have 24 hours of daylight around midsummer and of darkness around midwinter. In addition, it can help to overcome the very commonly held but quite mistaken belief that temperate regions are hotter in summer because they are tilted towards the Sun and are therefore nearer to it, rather as a person moves nearer to a fire to keep warm. As the model outlined in Table 18.2 shows, the distance between the Sun and the Earth is so huge in relation to the size of the planet that the tilt cannot make any significant difference to it. The overall pattern of our seasons is caused, not by our moving nearer to or farther away from the Sun, but by changes in the length of daylight and the angle at which light reaches the surface of the Earth.

Midsummer and midwinter. Although the overall pattern of the seasons in temperate parts of the earth is determined by changes in energy input from the Sun, there are variations which are not. In Britain, for example, the summer solstice is popularly known as 'Midsummer Day' and the winter solstice as 'Midwinter Day'. This can be confusing for children because neither solstice coincides, in most years, with the hottest and coldest weather. Midsummer Day is only about one-third through the season thought of as 'summer' in Western Europe. The popular naming of the solstices is arbitrary, a historical accident, but the question remains as to why in Britain the extremes of temperature lag significantly behind the periods of maximum and minimum input of solar energy.

This delay between energy input and climatic response occurs because the sea and, less significantly, the land surface, act as thermal energy reservoirs, rather like gigantic 'night storage' heaters. Sea temperatures of North-West Europe continue to rise well beyond the summer solstice so that our warmest weather usually occurs in July and August, when the sea temperature and solar input are both high. The annual cycle of temperature change is, however, further complicated by warm water from the North Atlantic Drift. This not only causes the seas around Britain and Ireland to be much warmer overall than they would otherwise be, giving these islands a very mild climate in relation to their latitude, but also makes them warm up more quickly than they cool down. The result is that the time-lag between the Winter Solstice and the coldest weather (typically eight to ten weeks) is much longer than that between the Summer Solstice and the hottest weather (typically four to six weeks).

18.5: Stars

The Sun is our local star; one of billions in the huge star-cluster or galaxy we call the Milky Way, and which can be seen as a faintly luminous band across the night sky. Even without a telescope it is possible to identify many bright stars and major star groups or constellations. Observing the night sky just above the horizon gives confirmation of the spin of the Earth in much the same way that observing the Sun by day does: the stars appear to move across the sky, from east to west if the observer is facing south. Even more interesting are the stars around Polaris or the Pole Star, which always appears in the same direction (due north) and at the same angle above the horizon (the latitude of the observer). The North Pole of the Earth points almost directly towards this star whatever the season of the year, so that it alone of all the stars in the sky never seems to move. The stars around it appear to move, but unlike those just above the horizon their apparent path is not across the sky but in a circle whose centre is the Pole Star. This can be shown (though not easily by children) by pointing a camera on a tripod at the Pole Star on a clear, moonless night and leaving the shutter open for several hours. The curved tracks of the stars on the resulting photograph are a record of the spin of the Earth.

All stars are luminous objects (17.2) and most, like the Sun, give out light and other forms of radiant energy as a result of the nuclear fusion inside them (12.2). This is the same kind of reaction which results in the explosion of hydrogen bombs, but stars like the Sun do not explode because they are so massive: they are held together by their intense gravitational fields. Most stars are very large, many much bigger than the Sun, but they are so far away that they appear very small. The star nearest to the Solar System is so far away that light from it (travelling at 300,000 km each second) takes 4½ years to reach us, and most stars are very much more distant than that.

Stars and planets. Stars are so far away, and the distances between them are so great, that to us they seem to have fixed positions in relation to each other. Their positions are in fact changing, but from Earth the changes appear so gradual that they cannot be detected without very accurate measurements.

Groups of stars in the sky (constellations) have suggested mythological beings or animals to peoples all over the world, who have given them names. From one such set of names we have inherited our Signs of the Zodiac. Because the stars do not seem to change their positions in relation to one another, they were known to many ancient astronomers as fixed stars, to distinguish them from other bright objects in the sky, which appear to move quite quickly against the background of unchanging constellations. These were known as the wandering stars, which today we know are not stars at all, but planets. Venus, Jupiter and Mars can all be seen from Earth without a telescope and often appear larger and brighter than stars because, although they are very much smaller than any star and only reflect light from the Sun, they are also very much nearer to us.

The twinkling of stars. Without a very large telescope, stars appear as no more than tiny points of light. Their apparent size from Earth is so small that they show a familiar but interesting property: they twinkle. A twinkling star not only seems to vary in brightness but may also seem to move about slightly. One clue to the cause of twinkling is that stars directly overhead on a clear, warm night often seem to twinkle less than those near the horizon or in very cold or windy conditions. Twinkling is, in fact, an effect of the Earth's atmosphere, so when seen from a space station or the Moon, the stars shine steadily. Light from the stars has to travel through the atmosphere to reach us, but the atmosphere is never still. Movement and temperature differences in the air cause very small amounts of refraction and bending of the light passing through it (17.6). Normally we are unaware of this, but from the Earth the stars appear so small that even a tiny amount of refraction makes them look as if they were moving slightly and varying in brightness. The same effect can sometimes be seen when looking at distant street lamps on a windy night. In contrast to the stars, the planets do not twinkle, and this is usually the easiest way to distinguish between a planet and a bright star. The reason is simply that the planets are near enough to us to appear larger than the stars, so that they shine steadily while the much greater but much more distant stars appear to dance.

References

Note: the numbers in brackets at the end of each entry show the chapter(s) for which the source was used for reference, or to which it is relevant as further reading. The entry (all) indicates that the source was used throughout this book.

Abrams, Bernard and Moore, Patrick (1989) *Astronomy*, Stanley Thornes, Cheltenham (18).

Archer, David (1991) *What's Your Reaction? Background Reading for Primary Science*, Royal Society of Chemistry, London (8–10).

Barry, Roger G. and Chorley, Richard J. (2003) *Atmosphere, Weather and Climate* (8th edn), Routledge, New York (11).

Beckett, B.S. (1986) *Biology: A Modern Introduction* (GCSE edn), Oxford University Press, Oxford (2–5).

Blackledge, J., Carter, Derek and Milbourn, J. J. (1971) *Using Materials* (Nuffield Secondary Science), Longman, London (7, 9, 10).

Blamey, Marjorie, Fitter, Richard and Fitter, Alastair (2003) *Wild Flowers of Britain and Ireland*, A & C Black, Edinburgh (5).

Breithaupt, Jim (2000) *New Understanding Physics for Advanced Level*, Nelson Thornes, Cheltenham (6, 7, 8, 12–17).

Chinery, Michael (1977) *Natural History of the Garden*, Collins, London (5).

Clegg, C.J. and D.G. Mackean (2000) *Advanced Biology: Principles and Applications*, John Murray, London (2–5).

Cobb, Vicki (1974) *Science Experiments You Can Eat*, Penguin Educational, Harmondsworth (9).

Drive Publications (eds) (1980) *AA Book of British Birds* (2nd edn), Drive Publications, London (5).

Drive Publications (eds.) (1988) *AA Book of the British Countryside* (revised edn), Drive Publications, London (5).

Duncan, Tom (1995) *GCSE Physics* (3rd edn), John Murray, London (12–17).

Greenler, Robert (1980) *Rainbows, Halos and Glories*, Cambridge University Press, Cambridge (17, 18).

Hann, Judith (1992) *The Family Scientist*, Bloomsbury Books, London (12, 16, 17).

Harlen, Wynne (1993) *Teaching and Learning Primary Science* (2nd edn), Paul Chapman Publishing, London (1).

Harlen, Wynne, Elstgeest, Jos and Jelly, Sheila (2001) *Primary Science: Taking the Plunge* (2nd edn), Heinemann, Portsmouth, NH (1).

Harrison, R.D. and Ellis, Hendrina (eds) (1984) *Nuffield Advanced Science Book of Data* (revised edn), Longman, Harlow (12–17).

McDuell, Bob (ed.) (2000) *Teaching Secondary Chemistry* (ASE Handbook), John Murray, London (6, 8, 9).

Monger, Grace (ed.) (1974) *Nuffield Biology*, 4 vols (revised edn), Longman, London (3–5).

Moore, Patrick (ed.) (1987) *The Astronomy Encyclopaedia*, Mitchell Beazley, London (18).

Musk, Leslie F. (1988) *Weather Systems*, Cambridge University Press, Cambridge, (11).

Pople, Stephen (1987) *Explaining Physics* (2nd edn), Oxford University Press, Oxford, (12–17).

Radford, Don (1973a) *Change* (Schools' Council Science 5/13 Project), Macdonald Educational, London (9, 12).

Radford, Don (1973b) *Metals: Background Information* (Schools' Council Science 5/13 Project), Longman, London (9, 10).

Reiss, Michael (ed.) (1999) *Teaching Secondary Biology* (ASE Handbook), John Murray, London (2–5).

Richards, Roy (1972) *Time* (Schools' Council Science 5/13 Project), Macdonald Educational, London (18).

Sang, David (ed.) (2000) *Teaching Secondary Physics* (ASE Handbook), John Murray, London (12–18).

Scott, Michael (1994) *Ecology*, Oxford University Press, Oxford (5).

Toole, Glenn and Toole, Susan (1999) *New Understanding Biology for Advanced Level*, Nelson Thornes, Cheltenham (2–5).

Walker, P.M.B. (ed.) (1995) *Larousse Dictionary of Science and Technology*, Larousse, New York (all).

Wellington, J. (ed.) (1989) *Skills and Processes in Science Education*, Routledge, London (1).

Wood, Alexander (1975) *The Physics of Music* (7th edn), Chapman and Hall, London (16).

Zelanski, Paul and Fisher, Mary Ann (1999) *Colour* (3rd edn), Herbert Press, London (17).

Index